2019

Social Panorama
of Latin America

UNITED NATIONS

ECLAC

FOR SUSTAINABLE
DEVELOPMENT WITH EQUALITY

Alicia Bárcena
Executive Secretary

Mario Cimoli
Deputy Executive Secretary

Raúl García-Buchaca
Deputy Executive Secretary
for Management and Programme Analysis

Laís Abramo
Chief, Social Development Division

Rolando Ocampo
Chief, Statistics Division

Paulo Saad
Chief, Latin American and Caribbean Demographic Centre (CELADE)-
Population Division of ECLAC

Mario Castillo
Officer in Charge, Division for Gender Affairs

Ricardo Pérez
Chief, Publications and Web Services Division

Social Panorama of Latin America is a publication prepared annually by the Social Development Division and the Statistics Division of the Economic Commission for Latin America and the Caribbean (ECLAC), headed by Laís Abramo and Rolando Ocampo, respectively, with the collaboration of the Latin American and Caribbean Demographic Centre (CELADE)-Population Division of ECLAC, headed by Paulo Saad, and the Division for Gender Affairs of ECLAC, under the supervision of Mario Castillo.

The preparation of the 2019 edition was coordinated by Laís Abramo, who also worked on the drafting together with Alberto Arenas de Mesa, Catarina Camarinhas, Miguel del Castillo Negrete, Ernesto Espíndola, Álvaro Fuentes, Carlos Maldonado Valera, Xavier Mancero, Jorge Martínez Pizarro, Marta Rangel, Rodrigo Martínez, Iskuhi Mkrtchyan, Iliana Vaca Trigo and Pablo Villatoro. Ernesto Espíndola, Álvaro Fuentes, Carlos Howes, Carlos Kroll, Felipe López, Rocío Miranda and Felipe Molina worked on the statistical processing. Valuable contributions and comments relating to different sections of the document were received from Simone Cecchini, Jorge Dehays, Andrés Gutiérrez, Javiera Muñoz, Lucía Scuro, José Suárez and María Elena Valenzuela.

United Nations publication

ISBN: 978-92-1-122030-8 (print)

ISBN: 978-92-1-047954-7 (pdf)

ISBN: 978-92-1-358267-1 (ePub)

Sales No: E.19.II.G.6

LC/PUB.2019/22-P/Rev.1

Distribution: G

Explanatory notes:
- Three dots (...) indicate that data are not available or are not separately reported.
- A dash (-) indicates that the amount is nil or negligible.
- A full stop (.) is used to indicate decimals.
- The word "dollars" refers to United States dollars, unless otherwise specified.
- A slash (/) between years (e.g. 2013/2014) indicates a 12-month period falling between the two years.
- Individual figures and percentages in tables may not always add up to the corresponding total because of rounding.

This publication should be cited as: Economic Commission for Latin America and the Caribbean (ECLAC), *Social Panorama of Latin America, 2019* (LC/PUB.2019/22-P/Rev.1), Santiago, 2019.

CONTENTS

Introduction.. 11

Chapter I
Persistent inequality in societies facing great uncertainties.................................... 37
    Introduction 39
    A. Recent trends in household income inequality... 39
    B. Income inequality re-evaluated: estimates based on combined data sources 44
        1. Limitations of data sources and new methodologies to estimate inequality......... 46
    C. Social classes at the centre of the social inequality matrix 50
        1. Trends in socioeconomic stratification in Latin America 51
        2. The importance of education and employment in socioeconomic status............ 59
        3. Intersecting inequalities 69
        4. The risk of falling into poverty owing to loss of labour income 72
        5. Conclusions and research agenda 77
    Bibliography... 78
    Annex I.A1 82

Chapter II
Poverty in latin america: one of the critical obstacles to sustainable development 89
    Introduction 91
    A. Income poverty trends... 92
        1. Poverty and extreme poverty at the regional level and by subgroups of countries......... 92
        2. Poverty and extreme poverty by country 94
        3. Poverty and extreme poverty by population subgroups 100
    B. Factors related to the recent poverty variations 107
        1. Level and distribution of household income.. 107
        2. Trends in the income sources of lower-income households 111
        3. Possibility of achieving the Sustainable Development Goal of no poverty 115
    Bibliography... 117
    Annex II.A1 118

Chapter III
Social spending: recent trends and financing needs for achieving Sustainable Development Goal 1 121
    Introduction 123
    A. Social public spending in 2000–2018.. 124
        1. Recent evolution of social spending in the region 126
        2. Per capita social spending... 129
        3. Social spending by function in the region 130
        4. The distribution of functional social spending in the countries...................... 132
        5. Public social spending in broader institutional coverage than central government:
            selected countries 137
    B. Estimated resources needed to close the poverty and extreme poverty income gap
        in Latin America by 2030 139
        1. Household resources needed to bridge poverty income gaps 139
        2. Comparing resource requirements, social public spending, tax revenues, and levels of tax
            evasion and avoidance.. 142
        3. Estimates of the costs of achieving the Goal on poverty over a 10-year period
            through income transfers... 144
    C. Conclusions... 147
    Bibliography 148
    Annex III.A1 149

Chapter IV
Migration in the region and its main dimensions 151
    Introduction 153
    A. Changes and continuities in migration 154
        1. Patterns and trends.. 154
        2. Declining extraregional emigration: a short-term trend? 161
        3. The growing trend of intraregional migration 164
        4. Recent Venezuelan migration: imperative cooperation needs................................ 167
    B. Migration and its problems in the subregions 167
        1. Central America and Mexico 167
        2. The Caribbean 173
        3. South America 177
    Bibliography.. 182

Chapter V
Migration and social and labour inclusion for equality... 187
    A. The complex relationship between migration, poverty and international remittance flows...... 189
        1. Poverty and immigration: unequal relationships from one country to the next 189
        2. International remittance flows and their impact on poverty in the countries
            of Latin America.. 191
    B. Migration and social and labour inclusion 200
        1. Differences in the social and labour inclusion of the local population and of recent
            and long-term migrants.. 200
    C. Racism, discrimination and migration 207
    D. The institutional framework for migrants in the region 212
        1. The international and national juridical/normative dimension of migration-related issues 212
        2. The institutional and organizational dimension of migration and human trafficking issues.......... 222
    E. Migration cycle and challenges for inclusion and social protection: some priority policy areas........ 229
        1. Social protection instruments in the migration cycle... 229
        2. Areas of priority attention to protect migrants and foster their social and labour inclusion 230
        3. Institutional challenges in relation to migrants and social protection 234
    F. Concluding remarks... 236
    Bibliography.. 238
    Annex V.A1 241

ECLAC recent publications.. 249

Tables

Table 1   Latin America (13 countries): poverty rate with and without remittances, total population
               and remittance-receiving households, national totals, around 2017............................. 33

Table I.1   Latin America (18 countries): threshold values of per capita income strata and changes
               in distribution of strata between 2002 and 2017 57

Table I.A1.1   Latin America (18 countries): indicators of individual income distribution, 2001-2018 82

Table I.A1.2   Latin America (18 countries): households by strata of per capita income, around 2002,
               2008 and 2017.. 84

Table I.A1.3   Latin America (18 countries): population by stratum based on per capita income,
               around 2002, 2008 and 2017 85

Table I.A1.4   Latin America (17 countries): annual income and share of per capita income of different
               strata, around 2017.. 87

Table I.A1.5   Latin America (18 countries): simulation of changes in status owing to the elimination
               of labour income of the main breadwinner, that of additional recipients
               and all labour income, around 2017 88

Table II.1   Latin America (15 countries): classification of countries by poverty and extreme
               poverty rates, 2018.. 95

Table II.2	Latin America (15 countries): classification of countries by poverty and extreme poverty rates, 2014	95
Table II.3	Latin America (15 countries): poverty and extreme poverty rates according to estimates by ECLAC and official national figures, 2015–2018	96
Table II.4	Latin America (8 countries): incidence of poverty and by ethnicity and area of residence, 2018	107
Table II.5	Latin America (15 countries): annual variation in labour income, in income per recipient and in the number of recipients, lower-income households, 2014–2018	114
Table II.A1.1	Latin America (18 countries): poverty and extreme poverty indicators, 2000–2018	118
Table II.A1.2	Latin America (15 countries): non-contributory transfer programmes analysed in chapter II	120
Table III.1	Latin America (16 countries): amount needed to bridge gaps and as a percentage of central government social expenditure, around 2017	143
Table III.A1.1	Latin America and the Caribbean (24 countries): central government social spending by function, 2018	149
Table III.A1.2	Latin America (9 countries): social expenditure by institutional coverage, by function, 2018	150
Table IV.1	Latin America and the Caribbean: immigrants and emigrants relative to the total population, by country of residence and birth, 2019	156
Table IV.2	Bolivarian Republic of Venezuela: estimations of population living abroad, 1990–2019	165
Table IV.3	North Central American countries: indicators of absolute migration, 2017	168
Table V.1	Latin America (9 countries): poor persons, by country and migrant status, most recent year available (specific estimate, lower and upper limits of the confidence interval)	190
Table V.2	Latin America (9 countries): estimated marginal effort of migrant status on poverty	190
Table V.3	Latin America (18 countries): workers' remittances and employees' earnings received, 1990–2018	192
Table V.4	The Caribbean (16 countries): workers' remittances and employees' earnings received, 1990–2018	195
Table V.5	Latin America (13 countries): households receiving income from remittances, by per capita income quintiles, around 2017	198
Table V.6	Latin America (13 countries): share of remittances in income, by quintiles of per capita income, around 2017	199
Table V.7	Latin America (13 countries): poverty rate with and without remittances, for the total population and for households receiving remittances, national totals, around 2017	199
Table V.8	Latin America (6 countries): unemployment rate of the local population and recent and long-term migrants, by sex, around 2015	203
Table V.9	Latin America and the Caribbean (15 countries): specific rights of migrants identified in migration laws, by country	217
Table V.10	Latin America (14 countries): instruments on human trafficking and migrant smuggling and their ranking in the legal hierarchy, by country	222
Table V.A1.1	Quality indicators of the probit regression model adjusted to explain the poverty situation based on a set of determinants, 2014–2017	241
Table V.A1.2	Latin America and the Caribbean (31 countries): main instruments regulating migration, by country, August 2019	242
Table V.A1.3	Latin America and the Caribbean (9 countries): main instruments regulating emigration, by country, August 2019	244
Table V.A1.4	Latin America and the Caribbean (32 countries): structure and oversight of agencies responsible for migrants, August 2019	245
Table V.A1.5	Latin America and the Caribbean (16 countries): ministerial portfolios that include the intersectoral coordination bodies responsible for matters relating to victims of trafficking in persons, August 2019	246
Table V.A1.6	Latin America and the Caribbean (17 countries): ministerial portfolios that include the intersectoral coordination mechanisms for protecting and assisting migrants, August 2019	247

Figures

Figure 1   Latin America and the Caribbean and other countries: productivity and the Gini index, 2014 15
Figure 2   Latin America (18 countries): poverty and extreme poverty rates and persons living
              in poverty and extreme poverty, 2002–2019 17
Figure 3   Latin America (18 countries): poverty and extreme poverty rates by area of residence
              and various sociodemographic features 19
Figure 4   Latin America (15 countries): annual variation in total per capita income among
              lower-income households, by source of income, 2014–2018 20
Figure 5   Latin America (15 countries): Gini inequality index, 2002–2018 21
Figure 6   Latin America (4 countries): share of the richest 1% in total income and wealth,
              latest year with data available 23
Figure 7   Latin America (5 countries): richest 1% of the population's share of total income,
              2000–2015 24
Figure 8   Latin America (18 countries): population size and trends by per capita income strata,
              2002, 2008 and 2017 27
Figure 9   Latin America (18 countries): persons aged 25 years or over not in education or employment,
              without complete secondary education, by per capita income stratum, around 2017 29
Figure 10   Latin America (18 countries): pension system contribution or affiliation among the active
              population aged 15 years or over, persons aged 65 years or over receiving pensions,
              and average monthly pensions by per capita income stratum, around 2017 30
Figure I.1   Latin America (15 countries): Gini inequality index, 2002–2018 40
Figure I.2   Latin America (15 countries): Gini, Theil and Atkinson indices, 2014–2018 41
Figure I.3   Latin America (15 countries): relative income growth by decile, 2014–2018 42
Figure I.4   Latin America (15 countries): absolute income growth by decile, 2014–2018 43
Figure I.5   Latin America (5 countries): richest 1% of the population's share of total income,
              2000–2015 44
Figure I.6   Latin America (6 countries): Gini index for the total population, for adults aged 20 years and
              older (percentiles 1 to 99) and for adults aged 20 years and older, adjusted, 2000–2017 45
Figure I.7   Latin America (18 countries): population size and trends by per capita income strata,
              around 2002, 2008 and 2017 55
Figure I.8   Latin America (18 countries): population by per capita income strata, around 2017 57
Figure I.9   Latin America (17 countries): share and volume of annual income by strata of per capita
              income, around 2002, 2008 and 2017 59
Figure I.10   Latin America (18 countries): composition of household income by source and average
              per capita income, by socioeconomic stratum, around 2017 60
Figure I.11   Latin America (18 countries): level of education attained by population aged 25 and over,
              by strata of per capita income, around 2002, 2008 and 2017 62
Figure I.12   Latin America (18 countries): average schooling by type of entry into the labour market
              and socioeconomic status, around 2017 63
Figure I.13   Latin America (17 countries): type of labour market participation of employed persons
              aged 15 and over, by socioeconomic strata, around 2017 65
Figure I.14   Latin America (16 countries): average monthly labour income of the primary wage earner
              and other wage earners, by type of employment and per capita income strata, around 2017 67
Figure I.15   Latin America (18 countries): average household size, average number of wage earners
              per household and percentage of single-parent and single-person households,
              by per capita income strata, around 2017 68
Figure I.16   Latin America (18 countries): relationship between socioeconomic strata and age group,
              geographic location, ethnicity, race, and wages earned by gender, around 2017 70
Figure I.17   Latin America (18 countries): probability of persons remaining in the same stratum and risk
              of falling into poverty or extreme poverty owing to loss of labour income, around 2017 74
Figure I.18   Latin America (18 countries): pension system contribution or affiliation among the active
              population aged 15 years and older, persons aged 65 years and older receiving pensions,
              and average monthly pensions by stratum based on per capita income, around 2017 76

Figure II.1   Latin America (18 countries): poverty and extreme poverty rates and persons living in poverty and extreme poverty, 2002–2019 93

Figure II.2   Latin America (17 countries): poverty and extreme poverty rates by country and subregion, 2008–2018 94

Figure II.3   Latin America (15 countries): poverty rate, relative and absolute annualized variations, 2008–2014 and 2014–2018 98

Figure II.4   Latin America (15 countries): extreme poverty rate, relative and absolute annualized variations, 2008–2014 and 2014–2018 99

Figure II.5   Latin America (18 countries): incidence of poverty and extreme poverty by area of residence, 2014–2018 101

Figure II.6   Latin America (18 countries): incidence of poverty and extreme poverty by age group, 2014–2018 102

Figure II.7   Latin America (18 countries): incidence of poverty and extreme poverty by gender, 2014–2018 103

Figure II.8   Latin America (18 countries): incidence of poverty and extreme poverty by employment status, 2014–2018 104

Figure II.9   Latin America (5 countries): incidence of poverty by ethnicity and race, 2014 and 2018 105

Figure II.10   Latin America (8 countries): incidence of poverty and extreme poverty by ethnicity, 2014–2018 106

Figure II.11   Latin America (15 countries): annual variation in poverty rate and relative contribution of growth and distribution effects, 2008–2014, 2014–2018 and 2008–2018 110

Figure II.12   Latin America (15 countries): annual variation in total per capita income among lower-income households, by source of income, 2014–2018 112

Figure II.13   Latin America (14 countries): contribution of wages and income from self-employment to total income variation among lower-income households, 2014–2018 113

Figure II.14   Latin America (14 countries): contribution of pensions, non-contributory transfers and other transfers to total income variation among poor and vulnerable households, 2014–2018 114

Figure II.15   Latin America (18 countries): projected regional poverty rate in 2030 with different scenarios of per capita GDP growth and changes in income distribution 116

Figure II.16   Latin America (18 countries): projected regional extreme poverty rate in 2030 with different scenarios of per capita GDP growth and changes in income distribution 117

Figure III.1   Latin America (17 countries): central government social spending, 2000–2018 126

Figure III.2   The Caribbean (5 countries): central government social spending, 2008–2018 127

Figure III.3   Latin America and the Caribbean (22 countries): central government social spending by country and subregion, 2018 128

Figure III.4   Latin America and the Caribbean (22 countries): per capita central government social spending by subregion, 2018 129

Figure III.5   Latin America and the Caribbean (22 countries): central government social spending by function, 2000–2018 130

Figure III.6   Latin America and the Caribbean (23 countries): distribution of central government social spending by function, 2018 133

Figure III.7   Latin America (16 countries): average annual gaps per person for extreme poverty, poverty and 1.8 poverty lines, by country, 2017 140

Figure III.8   Latin America (16 countries): total resource increase needed in the population income to end extreme poverty and poverty, by country, 2017 141

Figure III.9   Latin America (16 countries): percentage of general government tax revenues that would need to be allocated to bridging gaps, around 2017 143

Figure III.10   Latin America (16 countries): increase in resource transfers needed to close poverty and extreme poverty gaps in 10 years, 2020–2030 146

Figure IV.1   Latin America and the Caribbean: immigrant population by place of origin, 1970–2019 157

Figure IV.2   Latin America and the Caribbean: share of immigrants and emigrants in national populations by subregion, around 2010 and 2019 160

Figure IV.3   The Caribbean (26 countries): share of immigrants and emigrants in national populations, 2019 161

Figure IV.4   Latin America and the Caribbean: principal emigrant destinations, 2019.................................. 162

Figure IV.5   Latin America and the Caribbean: principal emigrant destinations, excluding Mexicans
in the United States, 2019.. 162

Figure IV.6   Latin America and the Caribbean: distribution of emigrants in other continents
and subregions of the world, by subregion of origin, 2019.. 164

Figure IV.7   Latin America and the Caribbean: distribution of migrants in traditional destination
countries elsewhere in the world, by subregion of origin, 2019.. 164

Figure IV.8   Bolivarian Republic of Venezuela: annual growth of emigration, 1990–2020.......................... 166

Figure IV.9   United States: immigrants from Mexico and Central America living in the country,
January 1995–July 2017.. 166

Figure IV.10   Northern Central American countries: reasons for migrating declared by migrants
sent back by the United States authorities, 2016 171

Figure IV.11   Mexico, the United States and northern Central American countries: minimum
and average monthly wages, 2017–2019 172

Figure V.1   South America (9 countries): workers' remittances and employees' earnings, incoming
and outgoing, 1990–2017 193

Figure V.2   Mexico and Central America (5 countries): workers' remittances and employees' earnings,
incoming and outgoing, 1990–2017 194

Figure V.3   The Caribbean (15 countries): workers' remittances and employees' earnings, incoming
and outgoing, 1990–2017 196

Figure V.4   Latin America (7 countries): female presence in the local population and among long-term
and recent migrants, people aged 15 years and over, around 2015... 201

Figure V.5   Latin America (7 countries): age structure, local population and recent and long-term
migrants, both sexes, around 2015.. 201

Figure V.6   Latin America (7 countries): educational achievement (complete cycles) of the local
population and recent and long-term migrants, population aged 18 and over,
both sexes, around 2015.. 202

Figure V.7   Latin America (7 countries): proportion of the employed population working
in low-productivity sectors, around 2015 204

Figure V.8   Latin America (5 countries): proportion employed in construction, men aged 15 and over,
around 2015 204

Figure V.9   Latin America (5 countries): proportion employed in paid domestic work, women aged 15
and over, around 2015 205

Figure V.10   Latin America (6 countries): overqualification in migrant and local populations,
employed persons over 14 years of age, by sex, around 2015 205

Figure V.11   Latin America (7 countries): social and labour inclusion indicators, local population
and recent and long-term migrants, around 2015... 206

Figure V.12   Latin America and the Caribbean (33 countries): signature and ratification of or accession
to covenants, conventions and treaties on the economic, social and cultural rights
of migrants.. 213

Figure V.13   Latin America and the Caribbean (31 countries): year of promulgation of countries' principal
migration laws 215

Figure V.14   Latin America and the Caribbean (28 countries): year of the enactment of the main national
laws on human trafficking 221

Figure V.15   Latin America and the Caribbean (32 countries): lead official government agency responsible
for coordinating public action for migrants 225

Figure V.16   Latin America and the Caribbean (17 countries): year of founding of the main intersectoral
coordinating offices for migrant protection and policies, 1900–2020... 226

Figure V.17   Latin America and the Caribbean (16 countries): year of founding of the main intersectoral
coordinating offices for trafficking victim protection and assistance.. 228

Figure V.18   Latin America and the Caribbean (26 countries): lead official government agency
responsible for coordinating services for trafficking victims, 2000–2020.................................... 228

Boxes

Box I.1　Measurement of inequality using multiple data sources: Mexico 48

Box I.2　Methodology for estimating socioeconomic strata 53

Box II.1　Income poverty measurement employed by the Economic Commission for Latin America
and the Caribbean (ECLAC) 91

Box II.2　Effect of changes in distribution and levels of household income on poverty 108

Box III.1　Statistical information on public social spending 125

Box III.2　Method for estimating the resources needed to end poverty 145

Box IV.1　The importance of achieving the objectives of the Global Compact for Safe,
Orderly and Regular Migration 2018 155

Box IV.2　Possibilities and shortcomings of household surveys for estimating migration 157

Box IV.3　Latin American female domestic employees in the United States 163

Box IV.4　Central America: unaccompanied migrant children and adolescents 170

Box IV.5　Haiti and the impact of disasters on mobility 176

Box V.1　Racialization of migrants 210

Box V.2　Indigenous peoples and migration 211

Box V.3　International Labour Organization conventions on migrant workers 214

Box V.4　Gender mainstreaming in institutional and regulatory frameworks for the protection
of the rights of women migrants: evidence from the repository of regulations
on international migration of the Gender Equality Observatory
for Latin America and the Caribbean of ECLAC 220

Box V.5　The 2013 Montevideo Consensus: international migration and protection
of the human rights of all migrants 224

Box V.6　Building an institutional framework for the City of São Paulo's municipal policy
for the immigrant population 227

Diagram

Diagram 1　Risks, vulnerabilities and needs of migrants at the different stages of the migration cycle 32

Introduction

A. The centrality of equality for sustainable and inclusive development

B. Setbacks regarding poverty and extreme poverty

C. Slow reduction in income inequality

D. Income inequality and the richest 1%

E. Middle-income strata: expansion, exclusion and vulnerability

F. Migration: challenges for inclusion and social protection

G. New social compacts for equality

Bibliography

A. The centrality of equality for sustainable and inclusive development

The struggle against inequality, poverty eradication and the quest for fairer, more inclusive societies with higher levels of well-being are at the heart of the 2030 Agenda for Sustainable Development. In Latin America and the Caribbean, the challenges associated with these objectives are structural, multifaceted and persistent. However, the current global and regional situation appears to be a more adverse context in which to address them, at least when compared to the first decade and a half of this century. Not only has social progress of various kinds slowed or levelled off in a weak economic environment, but there are strong signs that in some respects it has gone into reverse.

The structural shortcomings of the region have become more evident after five years of slow growth, and among the demands of large groups in society, particularly the new generations, is that they be corrected. These demands include the rejection of a persistent culture of privilege in its many dimensions, particularly those associated with the concentration of wealth, segmented access to high-quality public and cultural services and failure to recognize the dignity of individuals and communities. This is what many actors mean when they demand an end to abuses.

These causes are compounded by the problems associated with the effects of disasters and climate change, the demographic, epidemiological and nutritional transitions, the intensification of migratory movements and uncertainties related to the technological revolution, which will create new needs, risks and priorities. In addition, the world is witnessing a period of global geopolitical change, great social discontent and growing polarization, accompanied in many cases by a process of delegitimization of politics and a growing rejection of traditional forms of organization and expression of interests. In some cases, this has precipitated far-reaching political changes and challenges to consensuses of various kinds built up in recent decades, some of which have represented advances in the rights and inclusion agenda, while others have contributed to the reproduction of inequalities, exclusions and different forms of vulnerability.

This edition of *Social Panorama of Latin America* offers the customary analysis of trends in income inequality, poverty and social spending in Latin America, and includes an analysis of migration, which has moved up the region's political and social agenda. Apart from this, three major themes stand out. First, the book shows that the income of the richest 1% of the population has continued to climb and that estimates of inequality arrived at by combining the share of the richest 1% as ascertained from tax records with data from household surveys are substantially higher than those based on household surveys alone. Improving the measurement of inequality is crucial as a support for public policies to combat it in the region. Second, the book presents an analysis of the evolution and expansion of middle-income strata, a phenomenon closely associated with the downward trend in poverty and extreme poverty that prevailed in the region between 2000 and 2014, which resulted in improved living conditions and an increase in the social expectations and demands of a large proportion of people, but did not go far enough to meet them to the extent hoped for or to remove a number of vulnerabilities. The information presented confirms that middle-income strata continue to face different vulnerabilities (low levels of education, poor integration into the labour market, the low coverage and inadequacy of pension system provision). All of this calls for a broader vision and progress towards comprehensive and universal social protection systems. Third, a decisive commitment to equality requires a new social compact to consolidate agreements between different actors, conferring legitimacy and solidity on transformative policies and structural reforms. A social compact for equality is one focused on redistributing income and other assets, recognizing diverse identities and autonomies and overcoming structural heterogeneity. Among other elements, this requires a fiscal covenant to enhance distributive equity and the sustainability of social protection.

1. Equality as the strategic objective of sustainable development

Since its creation more than a quarter of a century ago, *Social Panorama of Latin America* has been analysing poverty and inequality as structural problems associated with the predominant development models in the countries of the region, with their various forms and characteristics. For the past decade, moreover, the Economic Commission for Latin America and the Caribbean (ECLAC) has posited the centrality of equality as the guiding principle and strategic objective of development and as an inescapable ethical imperative (ECLAC, 2010).

The notion of equality developed by ECLAC refers not only to equality of means (income, productive and financial assets and ownership), but also of capacities, autonomies and reciprocal recognition and, fundamentally, equality of rights. What is sought is not only equality of opportunity and treatment, but also equality of outcomes.

Inequality is a historical and structural characteristic of Latin American and Caribbean societies, and has been maintained and reproduced even in periods of economic growth and prosperity. It is an obstacle to the eradication of poverty, to sustainable development and to the safeguarding of people's rights. It is rooted in a highly heterogeneous and undiversified production system and in a culture of privilege, which has been a historical hallmark of Latin American societies. This system is characterized by a complex structure in which inequalities of socioeconomic origin intersect with gender, territorial, ethnic, racial and generational inequalities (ECLAC, 2016c).

The path towards equality requires a change of development model, understood as a progressive structural change, with an environmental big push. This means diversifying the production mix, i.e. overcoming the dependence on natural resources that still characterizes most of the countries of Latin America and the Caribbean and increasing value added. It will also entail transformation of the production structure, incorporating new technologies and increasing their use, with a sustainable increase in productivity.

Democratic societies are built on the notion of equality and participation, whereby everyone has the right and opportunity to play a role and take responsibility in decision-making. Equal rights are thus fundamental to the exercise of citizenship and the basis for a cohesive society that shares goals and values, with reciprocal recognition and a sense of belonging, and they are therefore crucial for democratic governance. Conversely, inequality is a direct source of conflict and a risk to democratic coexistence and the sustainability of development. Accordingly, all members of society, in both the public and private sectors, have a responsibility to promote equality.

This path towards equality requires the State to restore and strengthen its role in regulation, oversight, distribution, orientation of investments and production of goods and services to foster growth and guarantee rights. Policy is the fundamental instrument on the path to equality, and what is required is the design and implementation of public policies based on a rights approach and the construction of a new relationship between the State, the market and society, with the expansion of spaces for political and social participation and the construction of pacts and consensuses for equality, and with strengthened institutions and democratic governance (ECLAC, 2010, 2012 and 2014). The international community has recognized the importance of equality by including it among the core principles of the 2030 Agenda and its Sustainable Development Goals.

2.   Inequality is inefficient

In addition to its intrinsic value from a normative perspective, equality also has the role of fostering sustainable development by contributing to innovation, increased productivity and environmental sustainability. Equality is not only a result of the economic system, but also an explanatory variable for its long-term efficiency. Economies that are now at the forefront of sustainable development, —development that appropriately conjoins the social, economic and environmental dimensions— are found to combine equality, economic growth, productivity and democracy to a large degree (ECLAC, 2018b).

In other words, reducing inequality is not only an imperative for social development and the safeguarding of people's rights; it is also a precondition for sustainable economic growth. Figure 1 shows that there is an inverse correlation between productivity and inequality, as measured by the Gini coefficient, in several countries, including those of Latin America; in other words, the higher income inequality is, the lower productivity will be, which calls into question the very common assumption in economic theory that inequality is necessary to stimulate higher productivity and thence economic growth. The chart shows the opposite, namely, that inequality hinders productivity growth and economic growth and is therefore inefficient.

Figure 1
Latin America and the Caribbean and other countries: productivity and the Gini index, 2014
(Purchasing power parity (PPP) dollars and percentages)

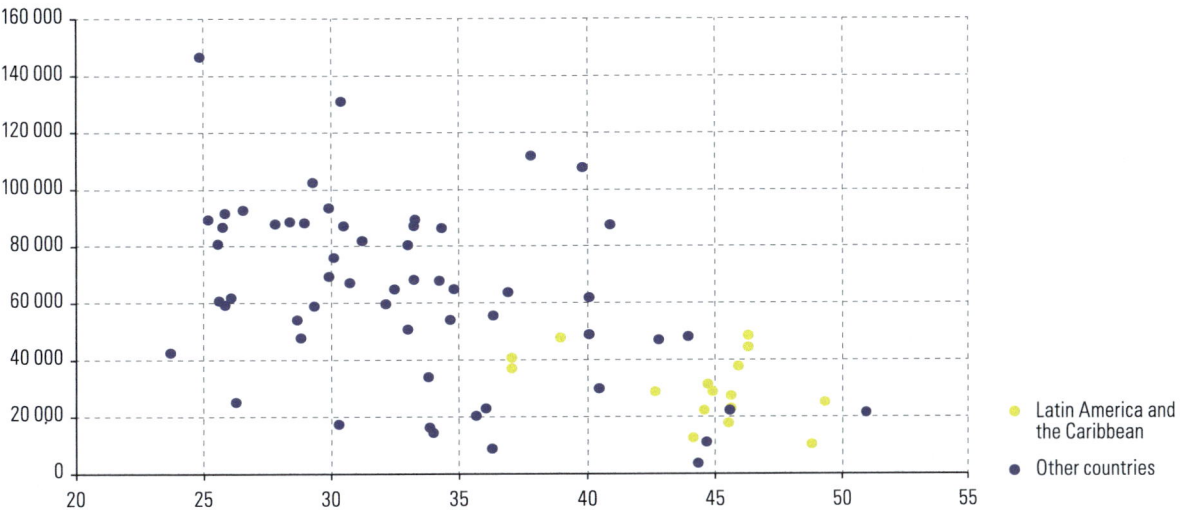

Source: Economic Commission for Latin America and the Caribbean (ECLAC), on the basis of University of Groningen, Penn World Table [online database] https://www.rug.nl/ggdc/productivity/pwt/, and Harvard University, Standardized World Income Inequality Database (SWIID) [online database] https://dataverse. harvard.edu/dataset.xhtml?persistentId=hdl:1902.1/11992.
Note: The Gini index is expressed in percentage terms. Productivity is expressed in output per employee in PPP dollars at constant 2011 prices.

Equality, on the other hand, is efficient, first and foremost because it generates more inclusive institutions, which in turn increases opportunities for making better use of the creative and productive capacities of a country's entire population, and strengthens markets by increasing domestic demand thanks to the expansion of the purchasing power of vast sectors of the population. Equal access to capabilities and opportunities is especially important in view of the technological revolution, which requires more and better education and technical training at critical stages of the life cycle, coordination and cooperation between actors to absorb new technologies and build new economic and production sectors, and a universal and inclusive social protection system capable of ensuring a degree of well-being for all during the process of change. Equality also strengthens democracies, which provide the most public goods and positive externalities of the kind required for technological change, economic and political stability and care for the environment. In the global economy, equality helps to expand aggregate demand by incorporating sectors of the population that were previously excluded even from the consumption of essential goods, thus avoiding the risk of recession (ECLAC, 2018b).

B.   Setbacks regarding poverty and extreme poverty

The eradication of poverty and extreme poverty and the reduction of inequality in all its dimensions continue to be central challenges for the countries of Latin America and one of the cruxes of the difficulties facing the region in its quest for sustainable development. Despite significant progress between the beginning of the last decade and the middle of this one, there have been setbacks since 2015, particularly the increase in the average regional rate of extreme poverty. This is a matter of great concern and a strong warning sign, especially in a regional context of low economic growth, growing challenges linked to the increasingly frequent disasters and the climate emergency, increasing and more complex migration and profound demographic transformations (population ageing and the feminization of that ageing) and labour market changes, caused both by the current wave of technological revolution and by the relocation and reconfiguration of production chains and processes of change in labour regulation that have had the effect of greatly increasing informal and insecure employment in some countries. In this situation, eradicating poverty and substantially and significantly reducing inequality must be at the centre of the debate and of the countries' efforts. It is imperative to develop and strengthen public policies for social protection and the labour market, including measures for social and occupational inclusion and redistributive income policies. To that end, it is essential to protect and safeguard social spending, strengthen social and labour institutions and pay special attention to the causes that make poverty, inequality and exclusion much more severe among children, adolescents and young people, women, indigenous people and Afrodescendants.

Poverty and extreme poverty were reduced considerably in the region between 2002 and 2014, as were various indicators of social inequality. This process was associated not only with a more favourable economic environment, but also with a political context in which the eradication of poverty and the reduction of social inequality, as well as the objective of broadening social inclusion and extending social protection, were given unprecedented prominence on the public agendas of many Latin American countries and, to a certain extent, the region as a whole. The rights agenda has been expanded, State action and social institutions have been strengthened, investment in social areas has been expanded and redistributive policies have been implemented in the social sphere and the labour market. Countries have increasingly moved beyond the conception of social policy that marked the 1980s and 1990s (a reductionist focus on extreme poverty, as opposed to universal public policies) and restored the objectives of social policy universalization, as opposed to the privatization trends that characterized previous decades, especially in the areas of social protection, and particularly education, health and pensions (ECLAC, 2016b and 2017b).

The end of the commodity export boom and the consequent economic slowdown changed the trend from 2015 onward, a process that was intensified by the reduction in fiscal space and adjustment policies which affected the coverage and continuity of anti-poverty and social and labour inclusion policies (Abramo, Cecchini and Morales, 2019). In this new context, labour indicators deteriorated: unemployment rose and the tendency towards greater formalization of employment was curbed.

This has been reflected in trends in poverty and extreme poverty rates. The regional average poverty rate fell significantly between 2002 and 2014, from 45.4% to 27.8%, with 66 million people emerging from poverty. At the same time, the extreme poverty rate decreased from 12.2% to 7.8%. However, from 2015 onward the levels of poverty and especially extreme poverty increased. In 2018, about 30.1% of the regional population was below the poverty line, while 10.7% was below the extreme poverty line. This meant that about 185 million people were living in poverty, 66 million of them in extreme poverty. Although the rising poverty trend eased between 2017 and 2018, total poverty in 2018 was 2.3 percentage points higher than in 2014, an increase of about 21 million people, of whom 20 million were living in extreme poverty (see figure 2).

Figure 2

Latin America (18 countries): poverty and extreme poverty rates and persons living in poverty and extreme poverty, 2002–2019[a]

(Percentages and millions of persons)

A. Percentages

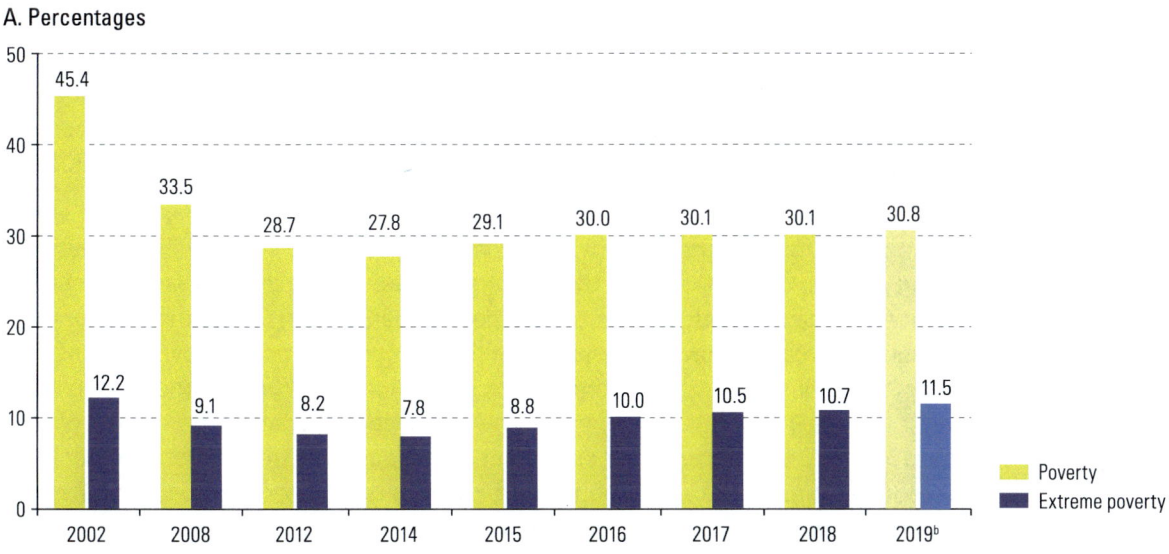

B. Millions of persons

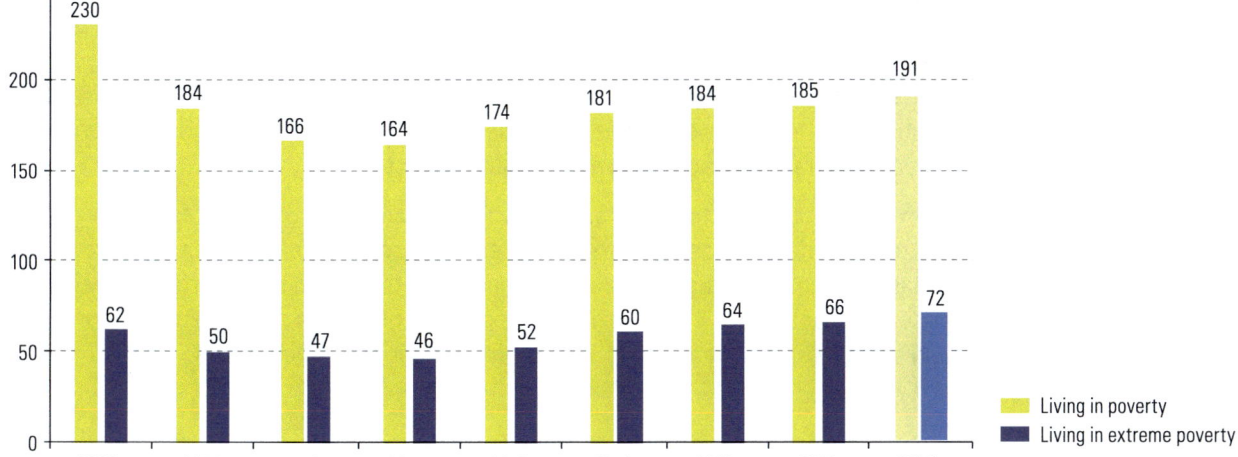

Source: Economic Commission for Latin America and the Caribbean (ECLAC), on the basis of Household Survey Data Bank (BADEHOG).

[a] Weighted averages for the following countries: Argentina, Bolivarian Republic of Venezuela, Brazil, Chile, Colombia, Costa Rica, Dominican Republic, Ecuador, El Salvador, Guatemala, Honduras, Mexico, Nicaragua, Panama, Paraguay, Peru, Plurinational State of Bolivia and Uruguay.

[b] The data for 2019 are projections.

Poverty at the regional level is an aggregate of dynamics that vary greatly from country to country. The increase in the overall regional rate between 2015 and 2018 is mainly explained by the rise in poverty in the Bolivarian Republic of Venezuela and Brazil, while in the rest of the countries the trend was for poverty to decline, albeit at a slower pace than between 2008 and 2014. The percentage of poor people in South America (excluding the countries mentioned) fell between 2014 and 2017 before rising slightly in 2018 as a result of the increase in Argentina that year. In turn, poverty in the group comprising Central America and Mexico fell from 45% in 2014 to 42% in 2018.

Regional aggregates for poverty and extreme poverty are projected to increase to 30.8% and 11.5%, respectively, in 2019. If these estimates are borne out, there will be 27 million more poor people than in 2014; worse still, 26 million of them will be extremely poor.

Poverty does not affect the different subgroups of the Latin American population alike. For example, ECLAC (2019a), going by data from around 2017, indicated that the regional aggregates for the incidence of poverty and extreme poverty were higher among persons living in rural areas, children and adolescents, women, indigenous persons and Afrodescendants, among other groups. These inequalities were observed and analysed by ECLAC in previous studies (ECLAC, 2014, 2016c, 2017b and 2018b).

These inequalities, which are clear manifestations of social inequality and the effects of the culture of privilege and abuse, remained unchanged in 2018. The incidence of poverty was over 40% among those living in rural areas, children and adolescents aged 0–14, unemployed persons and indigenous persons. In four of the five countries in Latin America that have information on the incidence of poverty by racial or ethnic status from household surveys, the poverty rate among the Afrodescendent population was 2.8 times that of non-indigenous, non-Afrodescendent people in Uruguay, while in Brazil and Peru the ratio was 2.2 and 2 times, respectively.[1] In contrast, poverty levels were lower among the urban population, older persons, wage earners and persons who were neither indigenous nor Afrodescendent (see figure 3).

Changes in the incidence of income poverty over time are linked to changes in average household income and in the distribution of income among households. The significant gains in reducing both poverty and improving income distribution are linked to two main factors: income growth in the lower-resource deciles thanks to increases in labour income, which makes up 72% of all household income (ECLAC, 2019a), and public transfers under social protection systems, with expanded and diversified entitlements. In some countries, especially in Central America and the Caribbean, migrant remittances also have an important impact.

In all the countries that substantially reduced poverty (by 5% or more) between 2014 and 2018, and in almost all the countries with moderate declines in poverty, the increase in labour income was the main reason for the rise in the income of low-income households (see figure 4). In Brazil, where poverty grew, the drop in labour income was main driver of the contraction in income for low-income households.

---

[1]   Panama is the only country where the poverty and extreme poverty rates (as measured by household surveys) are lower for Afrodescendants than for persons who are neither indigenous nor Afrodescendent.

Figure 3
Latin America (18 countries): poverty and extreme poverty rates by area of residence
and various sociodemographic features[a]
(Percentages)

A. By area of residence, sex, age group, ethnicity and activity status, 2018

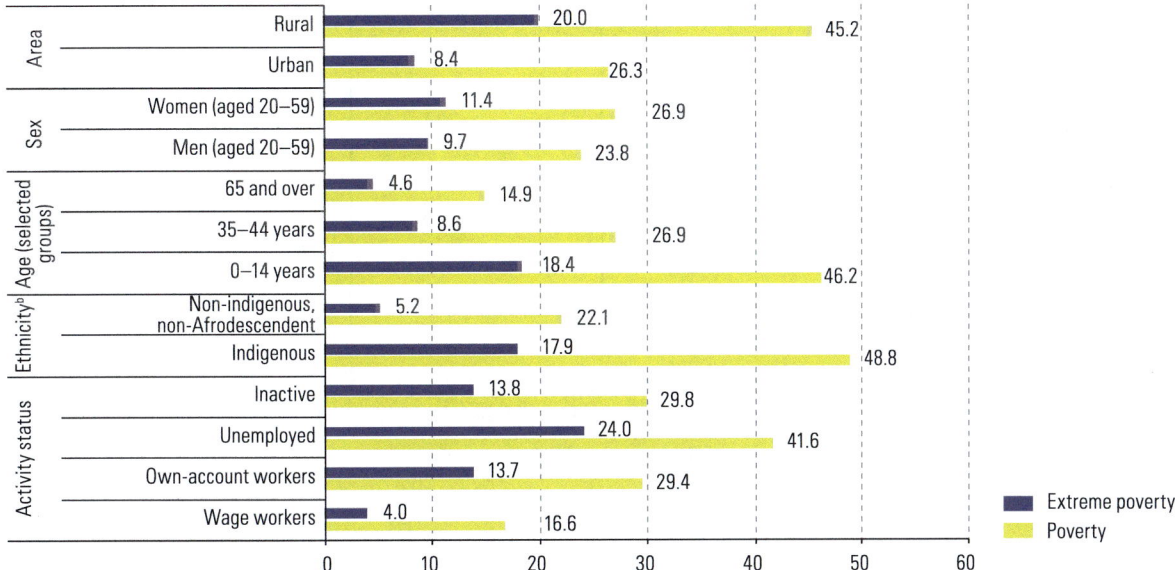

B. Selected countries: poverty rate by race or ethnicity, 2014 and 2018

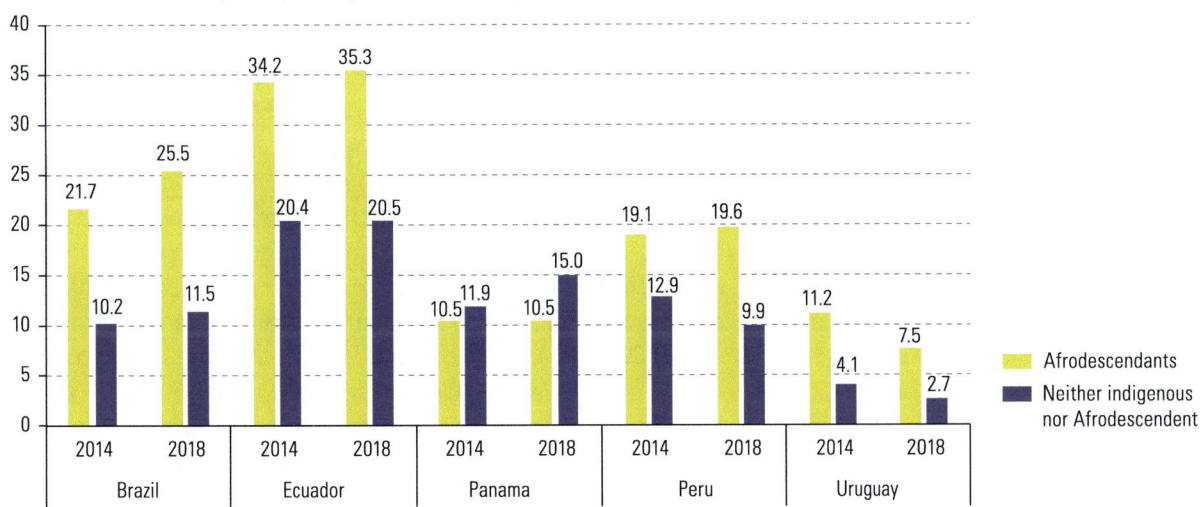

Source: Economic Commission for Latin America and the Caribbean (ECLAC), on the basis of Household Survey Data Bank (BADEHOG).
[a] The countries included are: Argentina, Bolivarian Republic of Venezuela, Brazil, Chile, Colombia, Costa Rica, Dominican Republic, Ecuador, El Salvador, Guatemala, Honduras, Mexico, Nicaragua, Panama, Paraguay, Peru, Plurinational State of Bolivia and Uruguay.
[b] Weighted average for the following countries: Brazil, Chile, Ecuador, Guatemala, México, Panama, Peru, Plurinational State of Bolivia and Uruguay.

Figure 4
Latin America (15 countries): annual variation in total per capita income among lower-income households, by source of income, 2014–2018[a]
(Annualized figures in percentages)

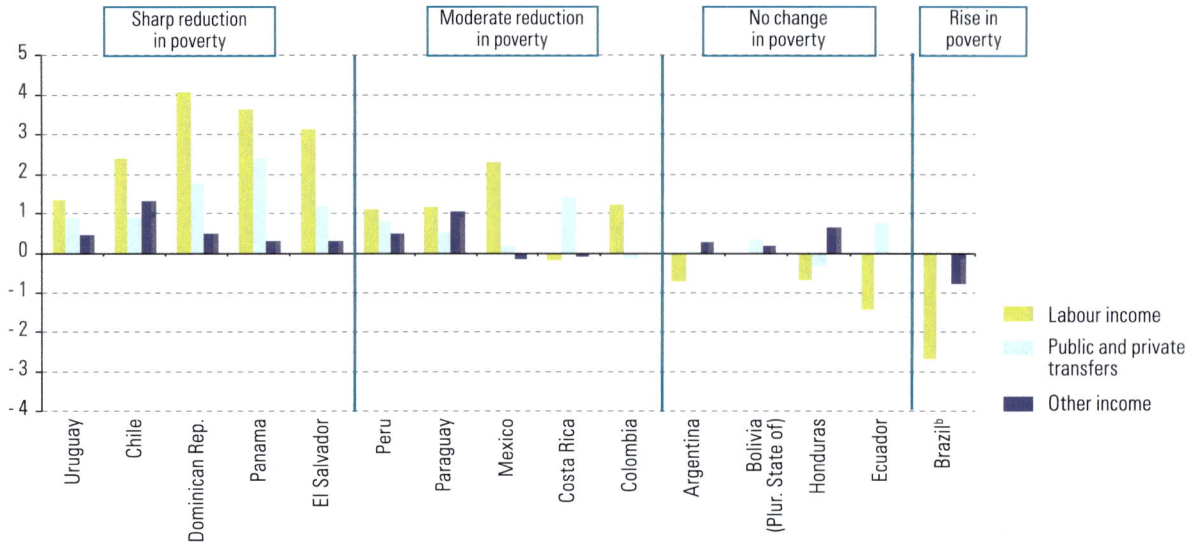

Source: Economic Commission for Latin America and the Caribbean (ECLAC), on the basis of Household Survey Data Bank (BADEHOG).
[a] Countries ranked by magnitude of reduction in poverty. Data refer to the subperiod 2014–2018, except in the case of Chile (2013–2017).
[b] In Brazil, the "other income" category includes public and private transfers. Differences in the continuous national household survey (PNAD Continua) with respect to the national household survey (PNAD) used before 2016 prevent a more detailed comparison of income sources.

Income from public and private transfers also had an impact, but to a lesser degree than labour income.[2] In 7 of the 10 countries with marked or moderate reductions in poverty, income from public or private transfers was the second-ranked income stream in terms of contributions to the increase in income for low-income households. In Costa Rica in particular, transfers were the topmost driver of the rise in incomes of such households. In Costa Rica, Panama and Paraguay, the rise in transfer income was the result of growth in social protection income (especially conditional cash transfer programmes for poverty reduction and non-contributory transfers); meanwhile, in two of the five countries, (Dominican Republic and El Salvador), the higher transfer income was due entirely to growth in remittances. Conversely, contributory retirement and pension payments made no contribution to income transfer gains in the great majority of the countries, which could be accounted for by the low level of affiliation to contributory pension systems among low-income households.

In summary, the best outcomes in terms of reductions in poverty were recorded in countries that experienced increases in public and private transfers in addition to rises in labour income. Redistribution has been fundamental in poverty reduction, complementing economic growth in boom periods and staving off rises in poverty and distributive deteriorations in most of the countries at times of slower economic growth. Between 2014 and 2018, in 7 of the 13 countries in the region where poverty fell, there was a marked distribution effect.

---

[2]   Income from public and private transfers is broken down into pensions and retirement pensions, non-contributory transfers and other transfers, including remittances.

C. Slow reduction in income inequality

Latin America has the unfortunate distinction of being the most unequal region in the world. Income inequality is one of the most obvious facets of that inequality, representing an obstacle to development and to the guarantee of rights and well-being, as well as standing in the way of innovation, productivity gains and economic growth (ECLAC, 2017a and 2018b). The region's inequality is also a stubborn trait, having persisted even through periods of economic growth. Although income inequality eased significantly between 2002 and 2014, this trend lost momentum from 2015 onward. The factors driving this dynamic are similar to those that underlie trends in poverty and extreme poverty.

Income inequality, measured by the Gini index (average of 15 countries in Latin America) fell from 0.538 in 2002 to 0.477 in 2014, 0.469 in 2017 and 0.465 in 2018.[3] Thus, this indicator declined by 13.6% in 16 years, or 0.9% per year on average. The pace of this decrease slowed over the period: the average between 2014 and 2018 was 0.6% per year, compared with 1.0% per year between 2002 and 2014 (see figure 5). However, these averages mask very uneven patterns from one country to another, in relation both to inequality and to the intensity and direction of the changes in these different periods. Argentina, El Salvador and Uruguay recorded the lowest levels, below 0.400, while Brazil and Colombia recorded levels higher than 0.520.

Figure 5
Latin America (15 countries): Gini inequality index, 2002–2018[a]

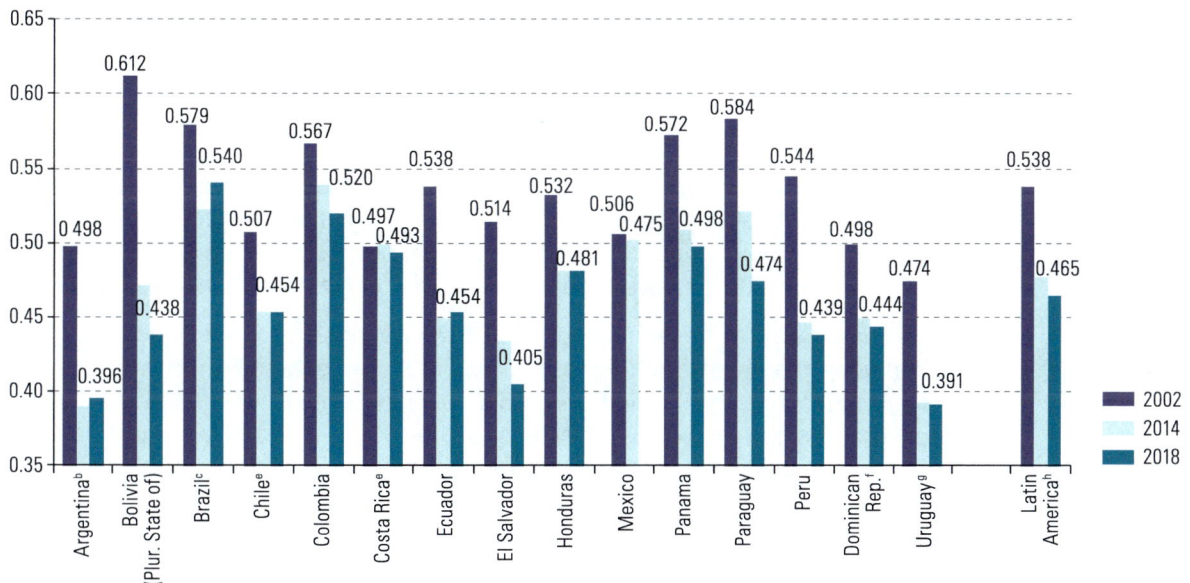

Source: Economic Commission for Latin America and the Caribbean (ECLAC), on the basis of Household Survey Data Bank (BADEHOG).
[a] The Gini index was calculated on the basis of income equal to zero.
[b] Urban total.
[c] The figures for 2002 and 2014 were adjusted for the difference between the National Household Sample Survey (PNAD) and the Continuous National Household Sample Survey (PNAD Continua) of 2014, to make them comparable with 2018 figures.
[d] Figures for 2002, 2014 and 2018 refer to 2003, 2015 and 2017, respectively.
[e] Figures from 2010 onward are not comparable with those of previous years.
[f] Figures for 2018 are not strictly comparable with those of 2002 and 2014.
[g] Figures for 2002 refer to urban areas.
[h] Simple average based on the data available for the nearest year for each of the 15 countries.

---

[3]   The average for each year is constructed on the basis of information from the closest year available for each of the 15 countries, although this does not necessarily maintain comparability over the whole period analysed.

Between 2014 and 2018,[4] four countries reduced their levels of inequality based on the Gini index: El Salvador, Paraguay and the Plurinational State of Bolivia recorded cumulative declines of 7% or more, while Colombia posted a decrease of 2%. Brazil was the only country to record an increase of more than 3% in the Gini index.[5]

Income inequality is usually analysed and quantified in terms of averages. For inequality to decline, the income of the poorest households must grow at a faster rate than that of the wealthiest. This trend is reflected in all the countries that recorded a decrease in income inequality between 2014 and 2018. In some cases, such as the Dominican Republic and Panama, the faster growth at the low end of the distribution scale was accompanied by considerable increases in income throughout the entire scale. In other countries, including Colombia, Paraguay and the Plurinational State of Bolivia, household surveys show a decline in income in the wealthiest households in real terms, while the purchasing power of the poorest households increased. Meanwhile, in Argentina, Brazil, Ecuador and Honduras, where income inequality increased over the period, the income of the poorest households fell in real terms, while that of the wealthiest households grew or posted smaller decreases.

As with poverty and extreme poverty, rising income at the lower end of the distribution was linked to improvements in the labour market (until 2014, these included falling unemployment, a rising proportion of wage work, increasing labour formalization and, in some countries, gains in minimum wages and stronger collective bargaining) and the expansion of social protection systems.

Income inequality can also be analysed in absolute terms, in which case achieving a decline in inequality is more demanding than in the relative analysis, as the incomes of the poorest households must grow by a larger amount than those of the wealthiest. Thus, a decline in relative inequality does not guarantee a reduction in absolute inequality.[6]

Between 2014 and 2018,[7] the gap between the first and tenth income deciles increased in 10 countries in absolute terms, even though several of these countries recorded declines in inequality indices. For example, in Chile and Panama, where inequality indices decreased in relative terms, the income of households in the first decile posted annual growth of 0.03 times the poverty line in both countries, compared with annual growth of 0.36 and 0.59 times the poverty line, respectively, for households in the tenth decile.[8]

The data from the household surveys of five countries[9] show a narrowing of the gap between the lowest and highest deciles in absolute terms. In these countries, although the income of the first decile did not grow significantly (barely 0.01 times the poverty line per year) or even decreased, the tenth decile lost income in absolute terms, of up to 0.33 times the poverty line per year.[10]

---

4   Data between 2014 and 2018 for Brazil and the Dominican Republic are not totally comparable. Figures for Brazil up to 2014 are adjusted for the difference between the continuous national household survey (PNAD Continua) and the traditional national household survey (PNAD).

5   The use of complementary inequality indicators, such as the Theil index and the Atkinson index (with two inequality aversion parameters, 1.0 and 1.5), strengthens the evidence of a decline in inequality in the region, on average. Between 2014 and 2018, the three aforementioned indices decreased by 1.3%, 0.9% and 1.0% per year, respectively, while the Gini index fell by 0.6% per year.

6   As underscored by ECLAC (2014), although the indicators traditionally used to quantify inequality favour the relative approach, both this method and the absolute approach are suitable and theoretically correct, and the use of one or the other is a value judgement.

7   Argentina, Brazil, Chile, Costa Rica, Dominican Republic, Ecuador, El Salvador, Panama, Peru and Uruguay.

8   To analyse changes in absolute inequality, income must be expressed in comparable units, eliminating the impact of inflation (comparison over time) and of monetary units (comparison of different countries). Expressing household income in multiples of the poverty line of each country is one way of fulfilling both requirements.

9   Colombia, Honduras, Mexico, Paraguay and Plurinational State of Bolivia.

10 These results may be at least partly influenced by the difficulties of household surveys in reflecting the income of the richest households consistently, as will be analysed below.

D. Income inequality and the richest 1%

The traditional method of estimating inequality on the basis of household survey data does not adequately reflect the phenomenon in its entirety or convey the income gaps between the sectors with the most resources and the rest of society.

In previous editions of the *Social Panorama of Latin America*, ECLAC improved measurement methods and expanded its analysis of inequalities in the distribution of income and wealth. Moving beyond inequalities in current income between households and individuals, the analysis focused on the functional distribution of income and inequalities in the distribution of physical and financial assets. One of the most salient findings was that the concentration of ownership of physical and financial assets is higher, more acute and more persistent than the concentration of current income (ECLAC, 2019a). As figure 6 shows, tax registers and financial surveys provide information on the share of income and wealth of the wealthiest population, which is much higher than when estimated with the usual instruments.

Figure 6
Latin America (4 countries): share of the richest 1% in total income and wealth, latest year with data available[a] [b]

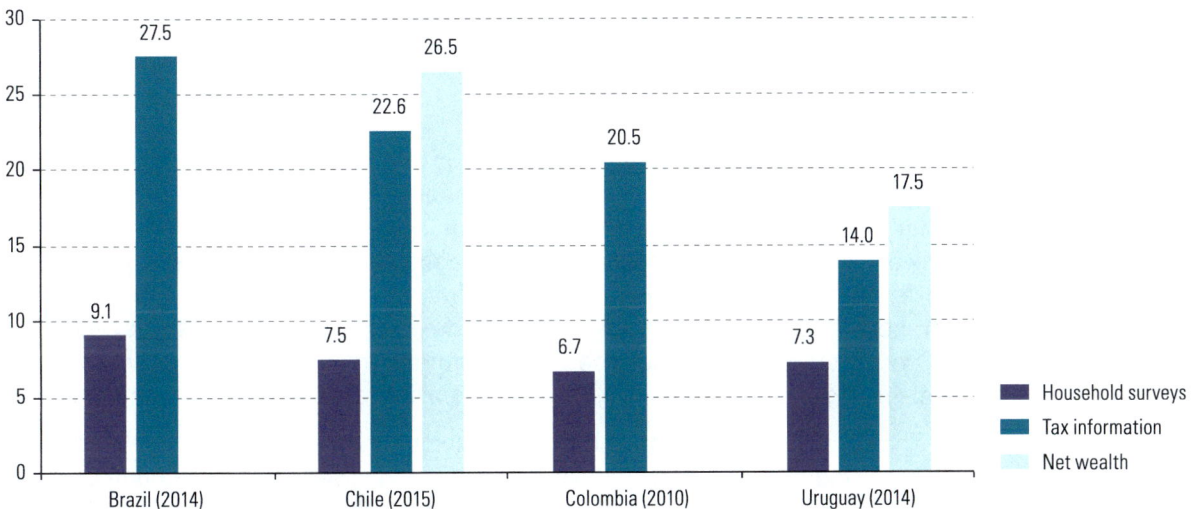

Source: Economic Commission for Latin America and the Caribbean (ECLAC), on the basis of data from World Inequality Lab.
[a] Refers to share in net national income, before tax, including retirement income but excluding cash transfers or other transfers.
[b] The data on net wealth (assets minus liabilities) refer to 2017 in the case of Chile, and the period 2013/2014 in the case of Uruguay.

This edition of *Social Panorama* takes the analysis of this issue further, based on the results of recent studies that estimate the share of the highest-income percentile in net national income,[11] complementing information from household surveys with distributional data derived from tax records. The analysis conducted for five Latin American countries shows that levels of inequality calculated using this methodology[12] are considerably higher than those reported on the basis of household surveys. The percentage of income received by the highest-income percentile varies widely from one country to the next, from a minimum of around 13% for Argentina in 2001 to a maximum of 29% for Brazil in 2011. Although the series are not long enough, all the countries except Uruguay reflect a slight upward trend, with some fluctuations (see figure 7).

---

[11]   Corresponds to the share of net national income, before taxes, including retirement income but excluding cash transfers of any other kind.
[12]   The analysis is based on research conducted for Argentina (Jiménez and Rossignolo, 2019), Brazil (Morgan, 2017), Chile (Atria and others, 2018), Colombia (Alvaredo and Londoño Vélez, 2013) and Uruguay (Burdín, Esponda and Vigorito, 2014).

Figure 7
Latin America (5 countries): richest 1% of the population's share of total income, 2000–2015[a]
(Percentages)

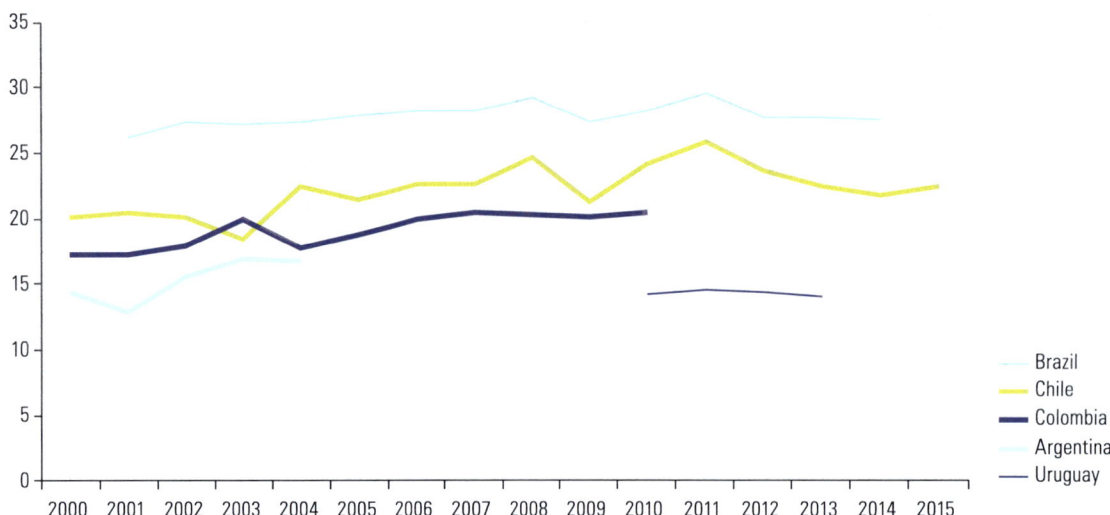

Source: Economic Commission for Latin America and the Caribbean (ECLAC), on the basis of data from World Inequality Lab.
[a] Refers to the share of net national income, before tax, including retirement income but excluding other types of cash transfer.

The Gini index calculated by combining information on the highest income percentile's share of total income and household survey data shows considerably higher values than those produced based on household surveys alone.[13] The Gini index adjusted to take into account persons aged 20 and older stands at around 0.60 in Brazil and Colombia, 0.58 in Chile, 0.55 in Argentina[14] and 0.45 in Uruguay. The average difference between the adjusted index and the household survey estimate is 3 percentage points in Colombia, 4 percentage points in Uruguay, 7 percentage points in Argentina, 8 percentage points in Brazil and 10 percentage points in Chile.

The combined use of tax and household survey data moderates —but does not reverse— the downward trend in inequality seen in several of these countries when only household surveys are considered. The biggest differences are evident in the case of Chile, for which surveys indicate a decline of 0.06 in the Gini index from 2000–2015, compared with a decrease of 0.01 when a combination of data sources is used.

In order to produce more comprehensive income distribution measurements, progress is required on two fronts. First, in evaluating the accuracy of estimates corresponding to the different sources of income deriving from household income accounts within national accounts, as they are the general reference on total amounts of income received by households. Second, in encouraging tax data disclosure, along with the production of better records to be used together with household surveys and national accounts.

---

[13] The methodological details are set out in chapter I.
[14] A more recent estimate of the Gini index for Argentina (Jiménez and Rossignolo, 2019) shows a higher value, 0.58 on average for 2004–2015. The difference stems mainly from the fact that this study considers income before tax and contributions in the Permanent Household Survey.

E. Middle-income strata: expansion, exclusion and vulnerability

Following the substantial reduction in poverty and income inequality achieved in the region, it is increasingly thought that most Latin American countries are on trend to become middle-class countries (or societies). However, that view is dominated by an over-hasty definition of middle class as the automatic result of exceeding the monetary poverty threshold defined for each country.

This edition of *Social Panorama* contributes to this discussion through an analysis of the middle-income strata. It is important to examine what has happened to the region's social structure after some 15 years in which vast swathes of the Latin American population (with all the problems, limitations and weaknesses of the process discussed in previous sections) have (i) risen out of extreme poverty and income poverty; and (ii) secured rights and improved well-being in other areas of social development (such as health, education, social protection, access to drinking water, sanitation and electricity). What position, then, do these groups occupy in the social structure? Do they in fact form a new "middle class", or rather segments that are socially very vulnerable? To what extent is there a process of upward social mobility, and how extensive, robust or risky is it? How are these sectors identified and how do they (or could they) relate to the culture of privilege or the culture of equality, to democracy and to the need to build and consolidate consensuses and new social compacts capable of underpinning the progressive structural change needed to construct fairer, more egalitarian and more cohesive societies?

There is currently little knowledge or statistics on Latin American middle classes, their professions, income and education profiles, cultural and sociopolitical leanings and other characteristics, this despite recurring mention thereto. The "middle class" seems to have become a kind of grey area of Latin America's social structure, frequently referred to without there being any greater clarity or accuracy in the identification of its particular defining features (Sémbler, 2006).

ECLAC has addressed the issue of social stratification on various occasions, but the significant transformations that have occurred in Latin American societies have rendered this an increasingly complex and multi-faceted task, both in terms of the composition of strata and the dynamics and analysis thereof (see, for example, Marinho and Quiroz, 2018). Added to this, comparative research and the analysis of changes in social structures at the regional level are significantly hindered by the relative lack of comparability between different sources of information, the absence of issues that are relevant today (for example self-identification, spending and borrowing, material and symbolic consumption, and social mobility) or their inclusion in instruments that cannot be easily incorporated, and issues such as population ageing, which make it difficult to apply occupational criteria to all households.[15]

The analysis presented in this edition of *Social Panorama* is based on four fundamental considerations. First, conceptually and operationally, it is more appropriate to advance the discussion on the middle classes (plural) rather than the middle class (singular), because, from a sociological perspective, these segments of the population reflect a variety of situations and processes, and show significant differences in terms of income and many other socioeconomic variables.

---

[15] The instruments used (multipurpose household surveys) do not usually collect information on pensioners' occupational history or last occupation (and wages), which means that additional criteria must be used to rank those households in the social structure. While such information is collected in longitudinal surveys on social protection, they are conducted in but a few countries.

Second, the criteria that may be used to define the middle classes and their boundaries with other social classes or strata need to be identified —essentially, a necessary exercise of updating the theory of social stratification in Latin America and the Caribbean. In this regard, although the discussion on social stratification and in particular on social classes involves many dimensions (occupation, education, income and expenditure, material and symbolic consumption, social networks, identities, among others), this edition of *Social Panorama* addresses changes in the socioeconomic structure in terms of the size of the various strata, as defined by different per capita income thresholds.[16] Therefore, the concept used is that of middle-income strata and the analysis is confined to the characterization of those strata and their evolution between 2002 and 2017.

Third, the analysis does not concur with the notion that accession to the "middle class" is an automatic result of exceeding the monetary poverty threshold defined by each country. It is essential to recognize that a segment of the Latin American population, despite having passed the monetary poverty threshold, is highly vulnerable and at risk of returning to poverty as a result of unemployment or precarious working conditions, spikes in inflation, natural disasters or catastrophic social, personal and family events. It is therefore important to identify a sector of the population in the non-poor low-income strata lying between those classified as poor and the middle-income strata. This stratum is made up of those whose per capita household income is between 1 and 1.8 times the poverty line. In 2017, this was the case for one in four people in Latin America (25.8% of the total population, or 157 million people in absolute terms).

Fourth, this study analyses stratification by income in relation to other axes of the social inequality matrix (territorial inequalities, age, gender, and ethnicity and race), with a particular focus on the changes in middle-income strata.

The results of this analysis show that the middle-income strata expanded as a proportion of the total population, from 26.9% in 2002 to 41.1% in 2017.[17] At the same time, the share of the low-income strata (the sum of those living in poverty and extreme poverty and the low-income population vulnerable to poverty) shrank from 70.9% to 55.9%. The size of the population in the high-income strata (individuals whose per capita income exceeds 10 poverty lines) also increased slightly, from 2.2% to 3.0% (see figure 8).

Despite these improvements, the social structure (from the point of view of per capita income) is still highly pyramidal. Data for 2017 show that persons living in poverty (including in situations of extreme poverty), still account for the largest share of the population (30.1%), followed by the low-income non-poor strata (25.8%). Together, those two groups account for more than half the population. With the lower-middle income strata (1.8 to 3 times the per capita poverty line) representing 20.9% of the population, this means that 76.8% of the total population of Latin America belong to lower- or lower-middle strata.

---

[16]   Unlike other recent studies, for example OECD (2019), which defines thresholds relative to income, the analysis below uses absolute and time-bound thresholds expressed in multiples of each country's poverty lines (see box I.2 for a more detailed description). This criterion was considered more appropriate for the region given its high levels of inequality and the traditional method of using absolute measures for poverty (on the basis of defined baskets of basic needs valued at market prices in each country).

[17]   The middle-income strata comprise individuals whose per capita household income is between 1.8 and 10 times the poverty line. It is made up of three substrata: the lower-middle stratum (between 1.8 and 3 times the poverty line), the intermediate-middle stratum (over 3 to 6 times the poverty line), and upper-middle stratum (over 6 to 10 times the poverty line).

Figure 8

Latin America (18 countries[a]): population size and trends by per capita income strata, 2002, 2008 and 2017
(Percentages and millions of persons)

A. Population size and trends, by per capita income strata
(percentages)

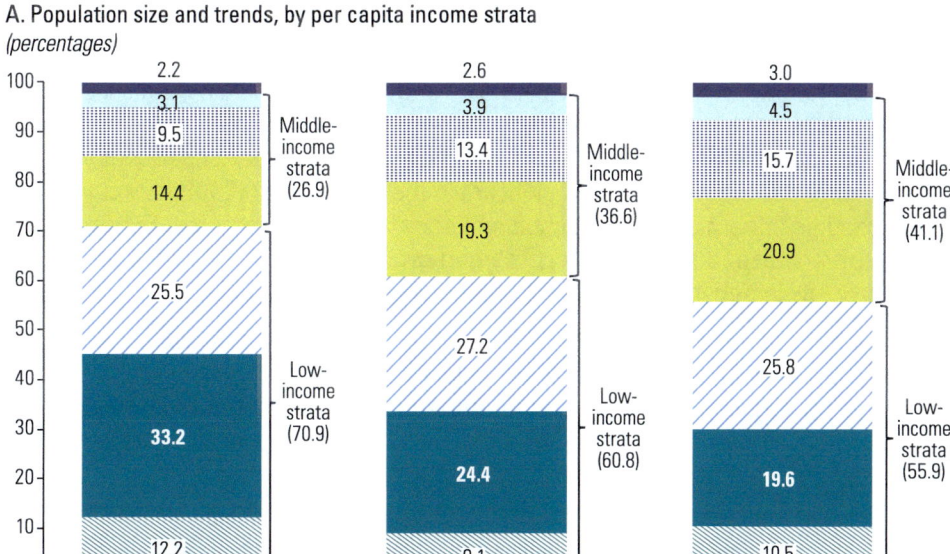

B. Changes in per capita income strata
(millions of persons)

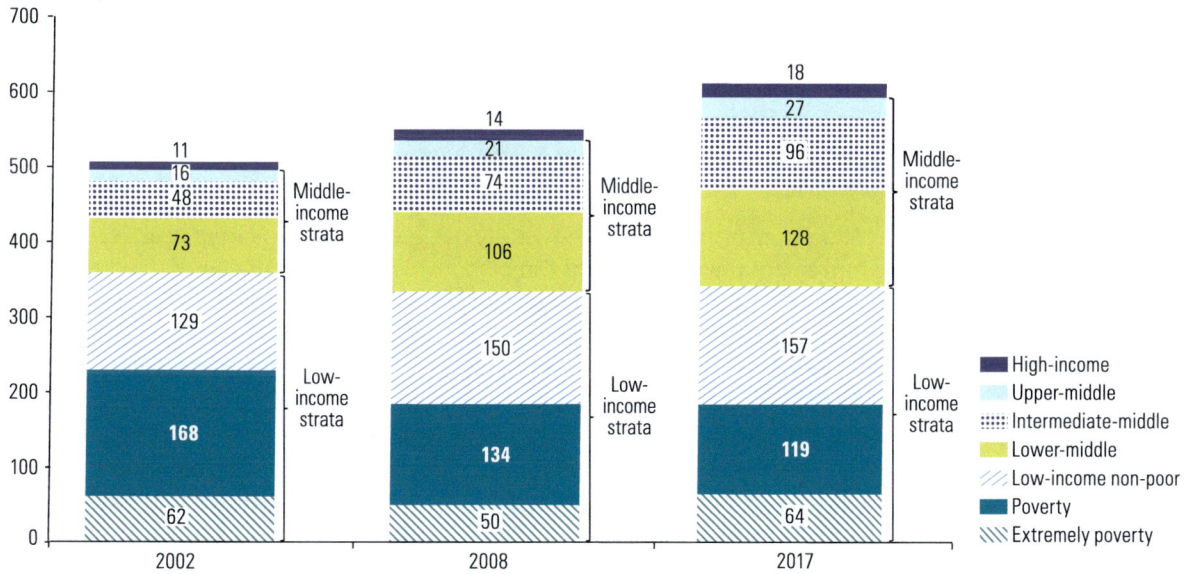

Source: Economic Commission for Latin America and the Caribbean (ECLAC), on the basis of Household Survey Data Bank (BADEHOG) and World Population Prospects 2019 [online database] https://population.un.org/wpp/.

Note: Figures adjusted for population projections of World Population Prospects, 2019 revision, and estimated poverty trends in countries for which figures are not available for the years indicated.

[a] The countries included are: Argentina, the Bolivarian Republic of Venezuela, Brazil, Chile, Colombia, Costa Rica, the Dominican Republic, Ecuador, El Salvador, Guatemala, Honduras, Mexico, Nicaragua, Panama, Paraguay, Peru, the Plurinational State of Bolivia and Uruguay.

There has been significant decrease in and reconfiguration of the low-income strata and growth in the middle-income strata. The share of the low-income strata as a percentage of the total fell by 15 percentage points (from 359 million to 341 million people). This figure is the result of a significant drop (by 49 million) in the number of persons in the poor stratum, and a slight increase in the number of persons in the extremely poor stratum (2 million), and an increase in number of persons in the vulnerable stratum (28 million).[18] At the same time, the share of the middle-income sectors increased by 14.1 percentage points (from 136 million to 250 million people, with higher growth in the lower-middle stratum), while the proportion corresponding to the upper stratum grew by only 0.8 percentage points.

The intermediate-middle stratum grew most rapidly —by almost 65% over the period— followed by the upper-middle stratum (45.9%) and the lower-middle stratum (45.8%); however, the poor stratum contracted by 40.9% and the extremely poor stratum by 13.6%. Also, increases in per capita income in the region, with the consequent "upward mobility" across strata, were more significant in the period 2002–2008, coinciding with the commodities boom and the expansion of social and labour policies. Subsequently, the pace of increase in per capita income and growth in the middle sectors slowed, and poverty levels began to rise again in some countries from 2015.

The significant increase in the size of middle-income strata has also increased the purchasing power of large sectors of the population, which is also associated with wider use of banking services by these sectors of the population. In consumerist societies, the acquisition of new goods and services that not only improve living standards and quality of life but are also, in some cases, positional in nature (symbols of status or economic success), a level of monetary comfort and access to credit —and the consequent disincentive to savings— can sometimes encourage consumption that is unsustainable in the long term, culminating in over-indebtedness and subsequent loss of the acquired goods.

In the early 2000s, the middle-income strata accounted for 49.4 % of the income of all households, with an annual economic capacity of US$ 550 billion (at constant 2018 prices); that share increased to 55.3 % in 2008 and 57.7 % in 2017, representing US$ 820 billion and over US$ 1.1 trillion respectively. In terms of the increase in overall income, yearly growth in the consumption capacities of the low-income strata was just 1.2% (a cumulative 19% between 2002 and 2018), compared with 5.1% for the middle-income strata (a cumulative 111%), and 4.5% for the high-income strata (a cumulative 93%).[19]

A question thus arises of the sustainability of middle-class consumption in the medium and long terms, not only because of the high levels of indebtedness of middle-income families (which means that a significant portion of their income is spent on debt repayment) but also because of the weakness of social protection systems to act as safety nets in the event of individual or collective income shocks. Families in the middle-income strata are still vulnerable to adverse economic circumstances or other negative situations that pose risks to their well-being and can severely compromise their disposable income, in a context in which, despite the significant expansion of social protection systems in the region, large gaps remain in coverage, quality and sufficiency (ECLAC, 2019b). The poor and lower-middle strata make up 46.7% of the population, with a high risk of falling into poverty or severe destabilization of well-being as a result of unemployment or precarious working conditions, catastrophic illness, accidents or natural disasters.

The middle-income strata also have vulnerabilities to various factors other than poverty. For example, in 2017, 52% of those aged 25 or over in the middle-income strata had not completed secondary education, considered the minimum level of schooling for breaking the cycle of intergenerational poverty transmission and accessing decent work. In the lower-middle-income strata, this proportion was as high as 62% (see figure 9).

[18] Despite this variation in absolute numbers, the share of the vulnerable stratum in the total population has remained constant over the period analysed.
[19] The annual growth rates in the total income of the middle-income and high-income strata were higher between 2002 and 2008 (6.9% and 4.7% respectively).

Figure 9
Latin America (18 countries): persons aged 25 years or over not in education or employment, without complete secondary education, by per capita income stratum, around 2017
(Percentages)

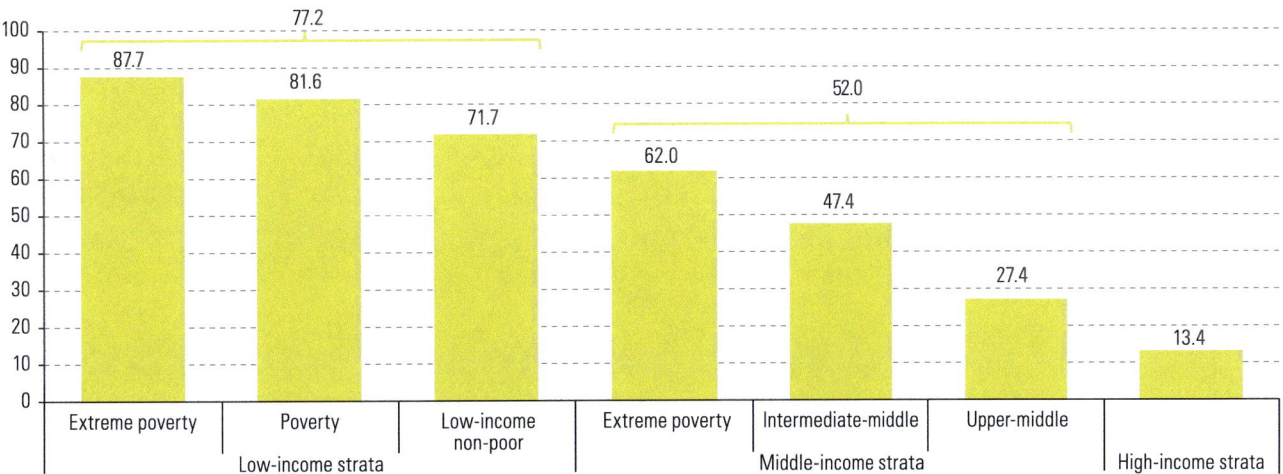

Source: Economic Commission for Latin America and the Caribbean (ECLAC), on the basis of Household Survey Data Bank (BADEHOG).

Indicators of pension system coverage and adequacy in the region show that, despite the growth documented in previous editions of *Social Panorama* (ECLAC, 2018a and 2019a), inequalities and underprotection remain highly prevalent: in 2017, only 47.5% of the economically active population aged 15 or over in the lower-middle income strata were affiliated or paying into a pension system; that rate rose to 60.1% in the intermediate-middle strata and just 69.8% in the upper-middle strata. Accordingly, even in this last category, almost one in three economic active people were not affiliated or paying into a pension system. On average, 31.8% of the population in the low-income and lower-middle-income strata (which make up 76.8% of the total), are covered (affiliated or contributing) by the pension system, which confirms both the concentration of social unprotection in the poor or extremely poor strata, and the magnitude of the sustainability challenges (with adequate coverage, benefit sufficiency and financial sustainability) facing pension systems in the region (Arenas de Mesa, 2019) (see figure 10A). What is more, even in a context of low levels of access to pension systems, there are remarkably large differences between workers (and unemployed) in the non-poor low-income stratum (32.8%) compared to those who are poor (16.6%) or extremely poor (4%), and between workers in the lower-middle strata (47.5%) and upper-middle strata (69.8%).

The relationship between access to contributory social protection and socioeconomic stratification also suggests a link between job formality and sufficiency of labour income. The considerable lack of social protection and low labour income affecting much of the economically active population at the bottom and in the middle of the socioeconomic pyramid in Latin America has direct consequences for well-being in the long term: less than one third (31.7%) of persons aged 65 years and older in the low-income strata benefited from pension coverage, which was equivalent to US$ 234 per month, on average (at 2018 prices). Although this coverage rises to 67.2% in the lower-middle-income strata, the average amount of these pensions was US$ 295 per month (at 2018 prices), representing 43% of the average amount received by retirees in the upper-middle strata. Retirees in high-income strata received, on average, pensions that were twice the amount received by those in upper-middle-income strata and six times more than those in the low-income strata (see figure 10B). Thus, almost 80% of the population aged 65 and over in Latin America received monthly pensions of less than US$ 295.

Figure 10

Latin America (18 countries): pension system contribution or affiliation among the active population aged 15 years or over, persons aged 65 years or over receiving pensions, and average monthly pensions by per capita income stratum, around 2017
(Percentages)

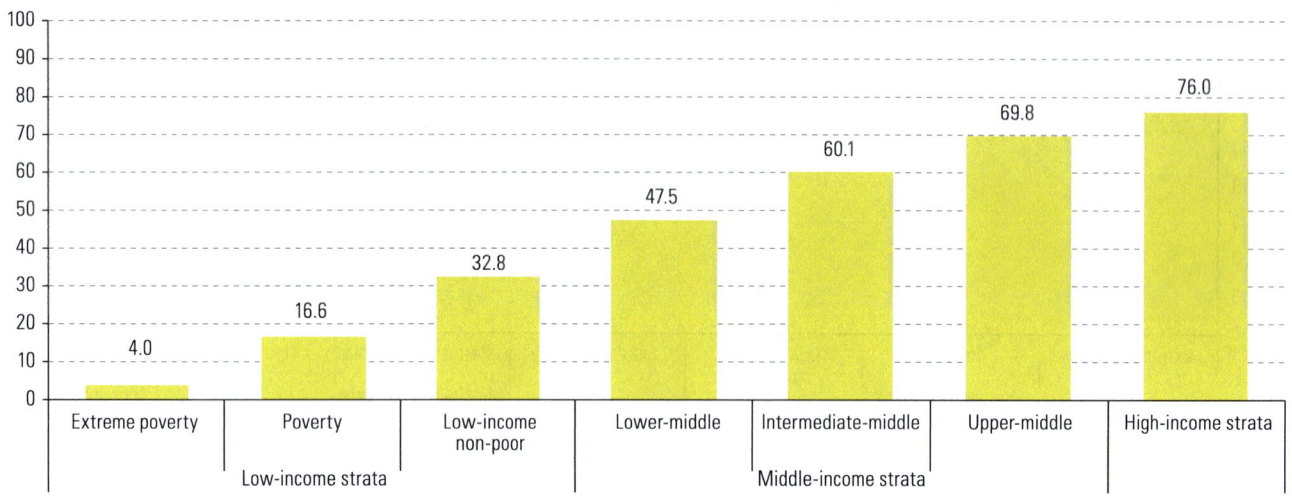

A. Pension system contribution or affiliation[a] among the economically active population aged 15 years or over[b]

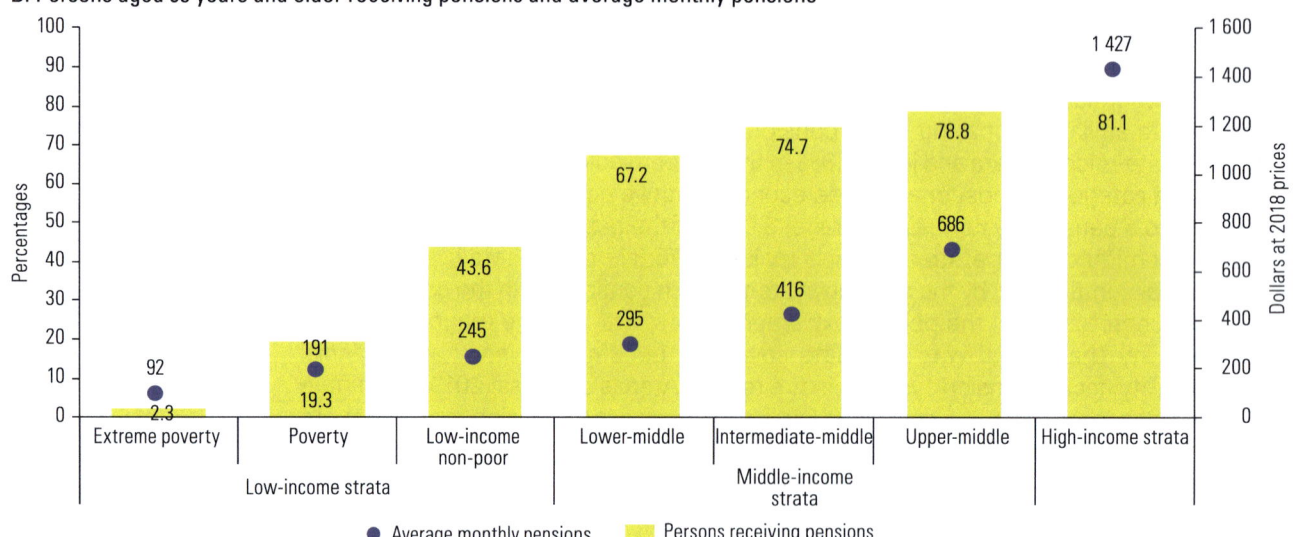

B. Persons aged 65 years and older receiving pensions and average monthly pensions[c][d]

● Average monthly pensions   ▮ Persons receiving pensions

Source: Economic Commission for Latin America and the Caribbean (ECLAC), Household Survey Data Bank (BADEHOG).

[a] The indicator of access refers to affiliation with pension systems in the Dominican Republic, Ecuador, Panama and the Plurinational State of Bolivia.
[b] Includes the unemployed.
[c] Does not include Nicaragua. Refers to contributory pensions except where it is impossible to fully distinguish between contributory and non-contributory pensions (Chile and Costa Rica).
[d] The Bolivarian Republic of Venezuela is not included owing to a lack of data for currency conversion.

In short, given the adverse impacts of weak economic growth, the myriad signs of profound changes in the labour market caused by automation and the ever more visible consequences of the climate crisis, developing economies need to design public policy responses and progress towards building welfare States that can provide broad guarantees of access to social services essential for development, such as education and health, from a perspective of rights and addressing existing differences and inequalities. This must include universal, comprehensive social protection systems to help protect purchasing power and access to quality public services (pensions, health, education, transport, housing, basic infrastructure) for the Latin American population —including the middle-income strata— and the provision of adequate tools for adapting to present and future work, economic and environmental scenarios.

F. Migration: challenges for inclusion and social protection

International migration has gained increasing prominence on the region's political and social agenda. Migration is high on the agenda today not only because of its effect on international police and on cultural and economic exchanges between countries of origin and destination, but because of the humanitarian, social and economic challenges it brings.

Migration —which is increasingly forced in several corridors of the region— will remain a core trend within and between our societies, owing to persistently disparate levels of development, enjoyment of rights, well-being, economic and political stability, the state of processes of demographic change in different locations, greater relative ease of movement and communication across borders and, more generally, a multitude of motivations and driving factors. Although in the medium to long term, migration flows generally contribute positively to the economy, increase diversity and enrich culture, in the near term they pose numerous policy challenges at the local, national and regional levels.

The migrant population of Latin America and the Caribbean is estimated at 40.5 million, representing about 15% of the world's migrant population of nearly 272 million (United Nations, 2019). The three most salient patterns of international migration in Latin America and the Caribbean since the second half of the twentieth century have been outward migration from the region, historical overseas immigration and intraregional exchanges. A fourth pattern is return to the countries of origin, either planned or forced (Martínez Pizarro, Cano and Soffia, 2014).

In the first case, extraregional outmigration, especially from Mexico to the United States, has recently been showing an unstable trend, with signs of a slowdown, unlike emigration from Central America. Immigration from other regions has also declined in importance. Exchanges within the region are the flows that have intensified the most: a large part of immigration flows today come from other countries within the region. In addition, the number of countries of origin has increased, and new destinations have emerged in the region. Negative net migration —that is, the predominance of emigration over immigration— continues to be a defining feature of the region's exchanges with the rest of the world, with current estimates reporting six emigrants for every two immigrants. It is essential to adopt an approach that takes into account the different vulnerabilities of migrants at the various stages of the migration cycle (see diagram 1), and that is based on awareness of gender, rights and the life cycle.

Migration is the product of serious problems of poverty, inequality, deficits of decent work, racism, various forms of violence and economic, political and environmental crises. Migration can also be a new vector of inequality, especially when it intersects with other axes of the social inequality matrix, such as inequalities relating to gender, territory, age, ethnicity and race. Migrants often face different forms of discrimination and xenophobia on the basis of their national origin, or their ethnicity or race, particularly in the case of Afrodescendent or indigenous migrants. In this regard, migration challenges and can elicit reactions from the culture of privilege.

Diagram 1
Risks, vulnerabilities and needs of migrants at the different stages of the migration cycle

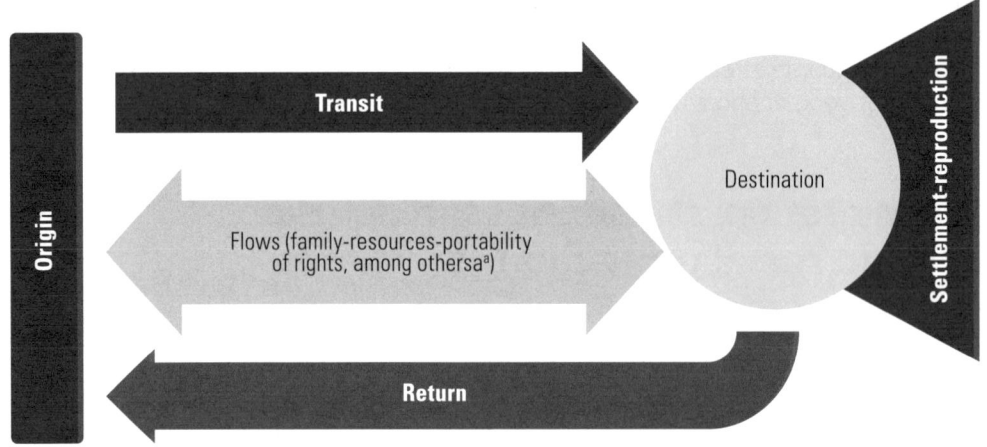

Transnationality

Source: C. Maldonado Valera, J. Martínez Pizarro and R. Martínez, "Protección social y migración: una mirada desde las vulnerabilidades a lo largo del ciclo de la migración y de la vida de las personas", Project Documents (LC/TS.2018/62), Santiago, Economic Commission for Latin America and the Caribbean (ECLAC), 2018.
[a] Transnational migration-related flows naturally also bring ideas, practices, skills, social capital and cultural norms (for example, see [online] https://comparativemigrationstudies.springeropen.com/articles/10.1186/s40878-016-0032-0).

Although the relationship between poverty and migration is an uneven one (migrants are not necessarily poor in the countries for which data are available), remittances place a key role in alleviating poverty for numerous families in several of the region's countries, particularly in Central America and the Caribbean. For example, without remittances, poverty rates among the total population would be between 1.5% and 2.4% higher in the Dominican Republic, El Salvador, Guatemala and Honduras (see table 1). Among households that receive remittances, the poverty rate would be between 12.4% and 27.6% higher in eight countries (Dominican Republic, Ecuador, El Salvador, Guatemala, Honduras, Mexico, Plurinational State of Bolivia and Uruguay). What is more, in some cases, remittances are significant as a percentage of GDP or exports and import, particularly in Central America and some Caribbean countries.

Migration poses a major challenge of inclusion and social protection, and there are gaps in access to basic services, decent work and social protection in destination countries, as well as multiple unmet needs in countries of origin or return. In turn, addressing migration-related issues in transit scenarios has particular challenges of its own.

The response requires a national institutional framework with mechanisms for social and labour inclusion (especially access to social protection and decent work) and international cooperation (regional and subregional) to guarantee the rights and well-being of migrants —particularly the most vulnerable— during transit and return, if these journeys are not made by choice but by force. Advances should begin by adapting national regulatory frameworks to international standards and implementing such standards effectively, as well as achieving effective intersectoral coordination at the central level, resulting in national and systemic strategies for social and labour inclusion of migrants and the protection of their rights, affording due importance to the mainstreaming of a gender perspective.

Table 1
Latin America (13 countries): poverty rate with and without remittances, total population and remittance-receiving households, national totals, around 2017
(Percentages)

	Poverty rate, total adult population			Poverty rate, population in households receiving remittances		
	Total	Without remittances	Difference	Total	Without remittances	Difference
Bolivia (Plurinational State of) (2017)	35.1	35.9	0.8	27.3	39.9	12.5
Chile (2017)	10.7	10.8	0.1	15.5	24.8	9.4
Colombia (2017)	29.8	30.0	0.2	21.1	31.2	10.1
Costa Rica (2017)	15.1	15.2	0.1	8.8	19.6	10.8
Dominican Republic (2017)	25.0	27.2	2.2	33.3	60.8	27.6
Ecuador (2017)	23.6	24.1	0.5	12.7	29.9	17.2
El Salvador (2017)	37.8	39.9	2.1	41.5	54.1	12.6
Guatemala (2014)	50.5	52.0	1.5	39.5	57.2	17.7
Honduras (2016)	53.1	55.5	2.4	39.5	53.3	13.8
Mexico (2016)	43.7	44.4	0.7	46.2	61.7	15.5
Paraguay (2017)	21.5	22.1	0.6	26.1	33.5	7.4
Peru (2017)	18.9	18.9	0.1	4.1	8.2	4.1
Uruguay (2017)	2.7	2.7	0.1	3.3	15.7	12.4

Source: Economic Commission for Latin America and the Caribbean (ECLAC), Household Survey Data Bank (BADEHOG).

With regard to the effective incorporation of a gender perspective, progress has been made, as reflected by the repository of regulations on international migration of the Gender Equality Observatory for Latin America and the Caribbean of ECLAC, which contains 95 laws from 21 countries in Latin America and the Caribbean. Of this total, 31 legal instruments (including constitutions) refer centrally to migration, its regulation and the protection of migrant populations; 19 refer to matters relating to prevention of trafficking and smuggling of persons, punishment of such acts and assistance for victims; 45 refer to miscellaneous related issues. Also, given the role played by civil society organizations in the very different migration scenarios, the space for collaboration and complementarity between authorities and civil society must be defined, without this resulting in policies that fail to fulfil national and international commitments in relation to migrants.

Lastly, one area where more work is needed in the medium term is the portability of contributory social protection rights. As migration flows have become more complex and a person's working life is likely to include fluctuations between episodes of formality and informality, possibly in two or more countries, it is crucial to build access channels and guarantee pension entitlements.

G. New social compacts for equality

Poverty and inequality remain structural phenomena in the region, and are taking worrying directions. A sustained effort must be made to reduce and eradicate them, in keeping with the 2030 Agenda for Sustainable Development and with regional instruments, such as the regional agenda for inclusive social development. Given that these efforts now have to be pursued in a less auspicious economic scenario than in previous periods, priority must be given to expediting responses and anticipating the emergence of new trends that may bring fundamental risks to the well-being of individuals and households and pose new obstacles to inclusive social development in the region.

The expansion of middle-income strata groups is an important step forward for a significant proportion of the population in the region; however, the gaps and uncertainties these groups experience in access to essential mechanisms for social well-being —such as increasing levels of education and social protection— are worrying from a rights perspective, and in terms of sustainable development, democracy and social cohesion. Migrations, with all their multiple dimensions, contributions, expressions and vulnerabilities, place new demands and requirements on States, which must be met amid global and regional tensions surrounding economies, multilateralism and the capacity to process cultural diversity.

At the beginning of the last decade, ECLAC underscored the need to promote a social and fiscal compact in the region in order to move towards a new a new State-market-society equation with an approach based on equality and sustainable development (ECLAC, 2010 and 2014, Hopenhayn and others, 2014). It was argued that a firm commit to equality urgently needed a social compact to crystallize agreements among different stakeholders in order to confer legitimacy and solidity on transformative policies and structural reforms. A social compact is viewed as an instrument that affords political viability to efforts to instil a new development pattern capable of ensuring progressive degrees of equality with sustainability, on the basis of proposals formulated and implemented in a participatory and democratic manner. A social compact for equality was defined as an agreement aimed at redistributing income and other assets, and at correcting structural heterogeneity. Among other elements, it required a fiscal covenant to improve distributive equity, and consensus-building to consolidate national political agreements, accepting the existence of conflicting interests and the fundamental mediating role of the political system (ECLAC, 2010, p. 245). The social compact therefore "involves discussions and agreements on long-term coexistence projects, sacrifice of immediate interests for the sake of the common good and the development dynamic, and a general commitment to a better society and better-quality political action" (ECLAC, 2010, p. 266).

To move towards equal and sustainable development, ECLAC also identified several key policy areas in which broad social accords are required. In the fiscal sphere, to provide States with the resources required to advance policies on the strategic goals of equality, sustainability and structural change. In the social and labour sphere, to strengthen the redistributive capacity of the State and reduce gaps in relation to gender, productivity, quality employment and appropriation between capital and labour. Likewise, a compact for greater social well-being is imperative, giving public policy the right tools to improve the quality of public services —such as transport, education, health and environmental services— and widen access to them, thereby increasing the population's sense of belonging and reducing well-being gaps. Other areas involved in the compact are investment and industrial policy, environmental sustainability and governance of natural resources (ECLAC, 2014).

This call to action is all the more relevant today given the complex challenges Latin American countries are facing at the current juncture. The levels of inequality now being seen are not only socially unjust, they are also highly inefficient in economic terms and acutely constrain democratic governance (ECLAC, 2018b). They also have the potential to increasingly obstruct coexistence in society. The need for social compacts is increasingly urgent, in view of States' limited capacity to process the diverse and complex demands and needs of different populations, including migrants, indigenous persons and Afrodescendants, or to address persistent territorial and gender inequalities, resulting from the current social organization of care, based on an unfair gender division of paid and unpaid work. Social compacts must encompass all these elements, by opening discussions and addressing issues that have been pushed back or even disregarded by major political and economic shareholders, despite mounting demands for change.

In order to move towards full social and labour inclusion and towards sustainable development, the deep inequalities between the people of the region in the exercise of economic, social and cultural rights must be addressed once and for all. The perspective offered by the social inequality matrix can contribute considerably to such analysis and to identifying gaps to address and close. Progress in this direction would enable the consolidation of the broad consensuses needed to underpin major transformations and contribute to the construction and expansion of welfare States. It is necessary, then, to lay the foundations for rights-based welfare States (ECLAC, 2018b) that look beyond the subsidiarity rationale, strengthen social cohesion, and decommodify welfare access and delink it from the family nucleus, fostering redistribution policies (ECLAC, 2010) and providing citizens with access to universal and comprehensive social protection systems and to essential social and public goods, such as quality health and education, care, housing, transport and basic services. This will require a social policy geared towards universalism that is sensitive to difference, a firm commitment to social investment, proactive engagement of the State and the eradication of the culture of privilege.

Bibliography

Abramo, L., S. Cecchini and B. Morales (2019), *Social programmes, poverty eradication and labour inclusion: lessons from Latin America and the Caribbean*, ECLAC Books, No. 155 (LC/PUB.2019/5-P), Santiago, Economic Commission for Latin America and the Caribbean (ECLAC).

Alvaredo, F. and J. Londoño Vélez (2013), "High incomes and personal taxation in a developing economy: Colombia 1993–2010", *CEQ Working Paper*, No. 12, New Orleans, Commitment to Equity (CEQ).

Arenas de Mesa, A. (2019), *Los sistemas de pensiones en la encrucijada: desafíos para la sostenibilidad en América Latina*, ECLAC Books, No. 159 (LC/PUB.2019/19-P), Santiago, Economic Commission for Latin America and the Caribbean (ECLAC).

Atria, J. and others (2018), "Top incomes in Chile: a historical perspective of income inequality (1964–2015)", *WID.world Working Paper series*, No. 2018/11, World Inequality Lab.

Bárcena, A. and A. Prado (2016), *El imperativo de la igualdad: por un desarrollo sostenible en América Latina y el Caribe*, Buenos Aires, Economic Commission for Latin America and the Caribbean (ECLAC)/Siglo XXI.

Burdin, G., F. Esponda and A. Vigorito (2014), "Desigualdad y sectores de altos ingresos en Uruguay: un análisis en base a registros tributarios y encuestas de hogares para el periodo 2009–2011", *Documentos de Trabajo series*, No. 06/2014, Montevideo, Institute of Economics, University of the Republic.

Campos, R., E. Chávez and G. Esquivel (2014), "Los ingresos altos, la tributación óptima y la recaudación posible", *Finanzas Públicas*, vol. 6, No. 18.

Cortés, F. and D. Vargas (2017), "La evolución de la desigualdad en México: viejos y nuevos resultados", *Revista de Economía Mexicana. Anuario UNAM*, No. 2.

Del Castillo Negrete, M. (2015), "La magnitud de la desigualdad en el ingreso y la riqueza en México: una propuesta de cálculo", *Studies and Perspectives series-ECLAC Subregional Headquarters in Mexico*, No. 167 (LC/L.4108; LC/MEX/L.1199), Mexico City, Economic Commission for Latin America and the Caribbean (ECLAC).

ECLAC (Economic Commission for Latin America and the Caribbean) (2019a), *Social Panorama of Latin America, 2018* (LC/PUB.2019/3-P), Santiago.

___(2019b), *Fiscal Panorama of Latin America and the Caribbean, 2019* (LC/PUB.2019/8-P), Santiago.

___(2019c), *Critical obstacles to inclusive social development in Latin America and the Caribbean: background for a regional agenda* (LC/CDS.3/3), Santiago.

___(2019d), *Proposed regional agenda for inclusive social development* (LC/CDS.3/4), Santiago.

___(2018a), *Social Panorama of Latin America, 2017* (LC/PUB.2018/1-P), Santiago.

___(2018b), *The Inefficiency of Inequality* (LC/SES.37/3-P), Santiago.

___(2018c), *Towards a regional agenda for inclusive social development: bases and initial proposal*, (LC/MDS.2/2), Santiago.

___(2017a), *Social Panorama of Latin America, 2016* (LC/PUB.2017/12-P), Santiago.

___(2017b), *Linkages between the social and production spheres: gaps, pillars and challenges* (LC/CDS.2/3), Santiago.

___(2017c), "Situación de las personas afrodescendientes en América Latina y desafíos de políticas para la garantía de sus derechos", *Project Documents* (LC/TS.2017/121), Santiago.

___(2016a), *Social Panorama of Latin America, 2015* (LC/G.2691-P), Santiago.

___(2016b), *Inclusive social development: the next generation of policies for overcoming poverty and reducing inequality in Latin America and the Caribbean* (LC. L/4056/Rev.1), Santiago.

___(2016c), *The social inequality matrix in Latin America* (LC/G.2690(MDS.1/2)), Santiago.

___(2016d), *Horizons 2030: Equality at the Centre of Sustainable Development* (LC/G.2660/Rev.1), Santiago.

___(2014), *Compacts for Equality: Towards a Sustainable Future* (LC/G.2586(SES.35/3)), Santiago.

___(2012), *Structural Change for Equality: An Integrated Approach to Development* (LC/G.2524 (SES.34/3)), Santiago, July.

___(2010), *Time for Equality: Closing Gaps, Opening Trails* (LC/G.2432(SES.33/3)), Santiago.

Hopenhayn, M. and others (eds.) (2014) "Pactos sociales para una protección social más inclusiva: experiencias, obstáculos y posibilidades en América Latina y Europa", *Seminars and Conferences series*, No. 76 (LC/L.3820), Santiago, Economic Commission for Latin America and the Caribbean (ECLAC).

Jiménez, J. P. and D. Rossignolo (2019), *Concentración del ingreso y desigualdad en América Latina: el caso argentino*, Buenos Aires, Centro de Estudios para el Cambio Estructural (CECE).

Jorda, V. and M. Niño-Zarazúa (2016), "Global inequality: how large is the effect of top incomes?", *WIDER Working Paper*, No. 2016/94, World Institute for Development Economics Research (UNU-WIDER).

Maldonado Valera, C., J. Martínez Pizarro and R. Martínez (2018), "Protección social y migración: una mirada desde las vulnerabilidades a lo largo del ciclo de la migración y de la vida de las personas", *Project Documents* (LC/TS.2018/62), Santiago, Economic Commission for Latin America and the Caribbean (ECLAC).

Martínez Pizarro, J., V. Cano and M. Soffia (2014), "Tendencias y patrones de la migración latinoamericana y caribeña hacia 2010 y desafíos para una agenda regional", *Population and Development series*, No. 109 (LC/L.3914), Santiago, Economic Commission for Latin America and the Caribbean (ECLAC).

Martínez Pizarro, J., L. Reboiras and M. Soffia (2009), "Los derechos concedidos: crisis económica mundial y migración internacional", *Population and Development series*, No. 89 (LC/L.3164-P), Santiago, Economic Commission for Latin America and the Caribbean (ECLAC).

Morgan, M. (2017), "Falling inequality beneath extreme and persistent concentration: new evidence for Brazil combining national accounts, surveys and fiscal data, 2001–2015", *WID. world Working Paper*, No. 2017/12.

OECD (Organization for Economic Cooperation and Development) (2019), *Under Pressure: The Squeezed Middle Class*, Paris, OECD Publishing.

Santaella, J., G. Leyva and A. Bustos (2017), "¿Quién se lleva los frutos del éxito en México?: una discusión sobre la verdadera distribución del ingreso", *Nexos*, 28 August [online] https://www.nexos.com.mx/?p=33425.

Sémbler, C. (2006), "Estratificación social y clases sociales: una revisión analítica de los sectores medios", *Social Policy series*, No. 125 (LC/L.2637-P), Santiago, Economic Commission for Latin America and the Caribbean (ECLAC).

United Nations (2019), "International migrant stock 2019", Department of Economic and Social Affairs, Population Division [online] https://www.un.org/en/development/desa/population/migration/data/estimates2/estimates19.asp.

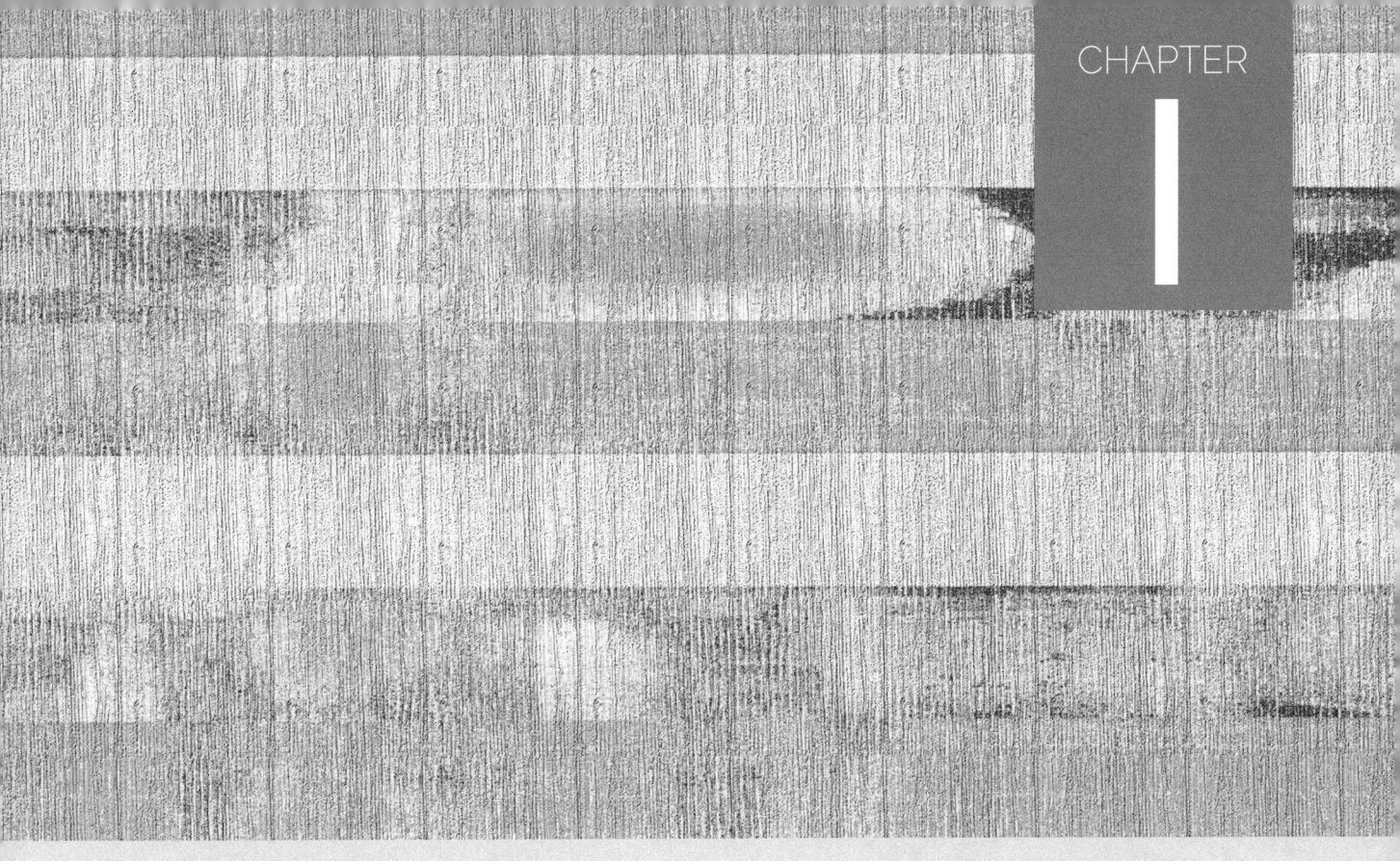

Persistent inequality in societies facing great uncertainties

Introduction

A. Recent trends in household income inequality

B. Income inequality re-evaluated: estimates based on combined
   data sources

C. Social classes at the centre of the social inequality matrix

Bibliography

Annex I.A1

Introduction

Various publications of the Economic Commission for Latin America and the Caribbean (ECLAC) place equality at the centre of development, because it provides policies with a foundation in rights and because it is a condition for moving towards a development model focused on the closure of structural gaps and convergence towards greater productivity and economic and environmental sustainability. Against this backdrop, inequality is inefficient and constitutes an obstacle to sustainable development (ECLAC, 2018).

Social inequality in Latin America is the result of a complex matrix of determinants, and is rooted in the structural heterogeneity of production systems and the culture of privilege. Social stratum or class is one of the structural axes of the social inequality matrix, along with gender, age (life cycle), ethnicity, race and territory, among other factors. The socioeconomic status of an individual, family or group (including intra- or inter-generational changes) is shaped by the other structural axes of this matrix, and is at once a reflection and explanation of many of the dimensions in which inequality is expressed: employment and work, access to productive resources and income, education, health, basic services, housing, information and communications technologies, food security, social protection, opportunities to live a life free from violence, technology, participation and agency, among other elements (ECLAC, 2016b and 2018).

This chapter of *Social Panorama of Latin America* presents the latest information on income inequality among people and households in the region. It also shows that the traditional method for estimating inequality, based on data gathered from household surveys, is insufficient. Household survey data combined with tax data and national accounts provide more comprehensive measurements of inequality. This chapter also includes a section on the social inequality matrix, using income to define and analyse socioeconomic stratification in the region in the present day, with a focus on middle-income strata.

A. Recent trends in household income inequality

The income inequality revealed in household surveys has continued to trend downwards but is declining more slowly than over the previous decade. Between 2014 and 2018, the Gini index of per capita income fell in six countries. However, in some countries the decline in this indicator did not prevent the widening of the gap, in absolute terms, between the groups at the lowest and highest ends of the distribution scale.

Historically, Latin America has been characterized by high levels of inequality and several countries in the region reflect some of the highest levels of income inequality in the world.

According to the most recent household survey data available, the Gini index averages 0.465[1] for Latin America as a whole. Argentina, El Salvador and Uruguay recorded the lowest levels, below 0.400, while Brazil and Colombia recorded levels higher than 0.520.

Various editions of *Social Panorama of Latin America* have pointed out that current inequality levels are lower than in the early 2000 decade (ECLAC, 2019), and this is still the case according to the most recent data.

---

[1]   Average for 15 countries on the basis of information from household surveys conducted in 2018, except in the case of Chile, for which data refer to 2017.

The simple average of the Gini indices of 15 countries in the region fell from 0.538 in 2002 to 0.477 in 2014, 0.469 in 2017 and 0.465 in 2018.[2] Thus, this indicator declined by 13.6% in 16 years, or 0.9% per year. This decrease reflects a slowdown: the average between 2014 and 2018 was 0.6% per year, compared with 1.0% per year between 2002 and 2014 (see figure I.1).

Figure I.1
Latin America (15 countries): Gini inequality index, 2002–2018[a]

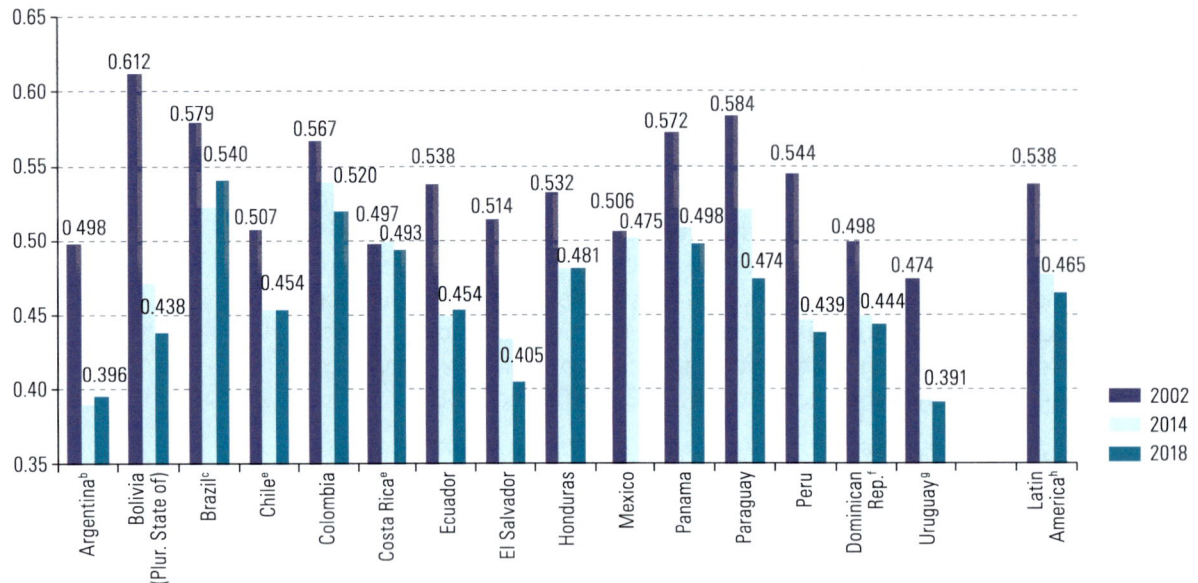

Source: Economic Commission for Latin America and the Caribbean (ECLAC), on the basis of Household Survey Data Bank (BADEHOG).
[a] The Gini index was calculated on the basis of income equal to zero.
[b] Urban total.
[c] The figures for 2002 and 2014 were adjusted for the difference between the National Household Sample Survey (PNAD) and the Continuous National Household Sample Survey (PNAD Continua) of 2014, to make them comparable with 2018 figures.
[d] Figures for 2002, 2014 and 2018 refer to 2003, 2015 and 2017, respectively.
[e] Figures from 2010 onward are not comparable with those of previous years.
[f] Figures for 2018 are not strictly comparable with those of 2002 and 2014.
[g] Figures for 2002 refer to urban areas.
[h] Simple average based on the data available for the nearest year for each of the 15 countries.

Between 2014 and 2018,[3] four countries reduced their levels of inequality based on the Gini index. El Salvador, Paraguay and the Plurinational State of Bolivia recorded cumulative declines of 7% or more, while Chile posted a decrease of 2%. Brazil was the only country to record an increase of more than 3% in the Gini index.

The use of complementary inequality indicators, such as the Theil index and the Atkinson index (with two inequality aversion parameters, 1.0 and 1.5), strengthens the evidence of a decline in inequality in the region, on average. Between 2014 and 2018, the three aforementioned indices decreased by 1.3%, 0.9% and 1.0% per year, respectively, while the Gini index fell by 0.6% per year. Moreover, these complementary indices show some situations that the Gini index does not. In particular, they include two additional countries that recorded a deterioration in income distribution: Argentina and Honduras (see figure I.2 and table I.A.1 in the annex).

---

[2]   The annual average is based on the data available for the nearest year for each of the 15 countries, even though figures are not necessarily comparable for the entire period analysed.

[3]   Data between 2014 and 2018 for Brazil and the Dominican Republic are not totally comparable. Figures for Brazil up to 2014 are adjusted for the difference between the PNAD Continua and PNAD.

Figure I.2
Latin America (15 countries): Gini, Theil and Atkinson indices, 2014–2018[a]

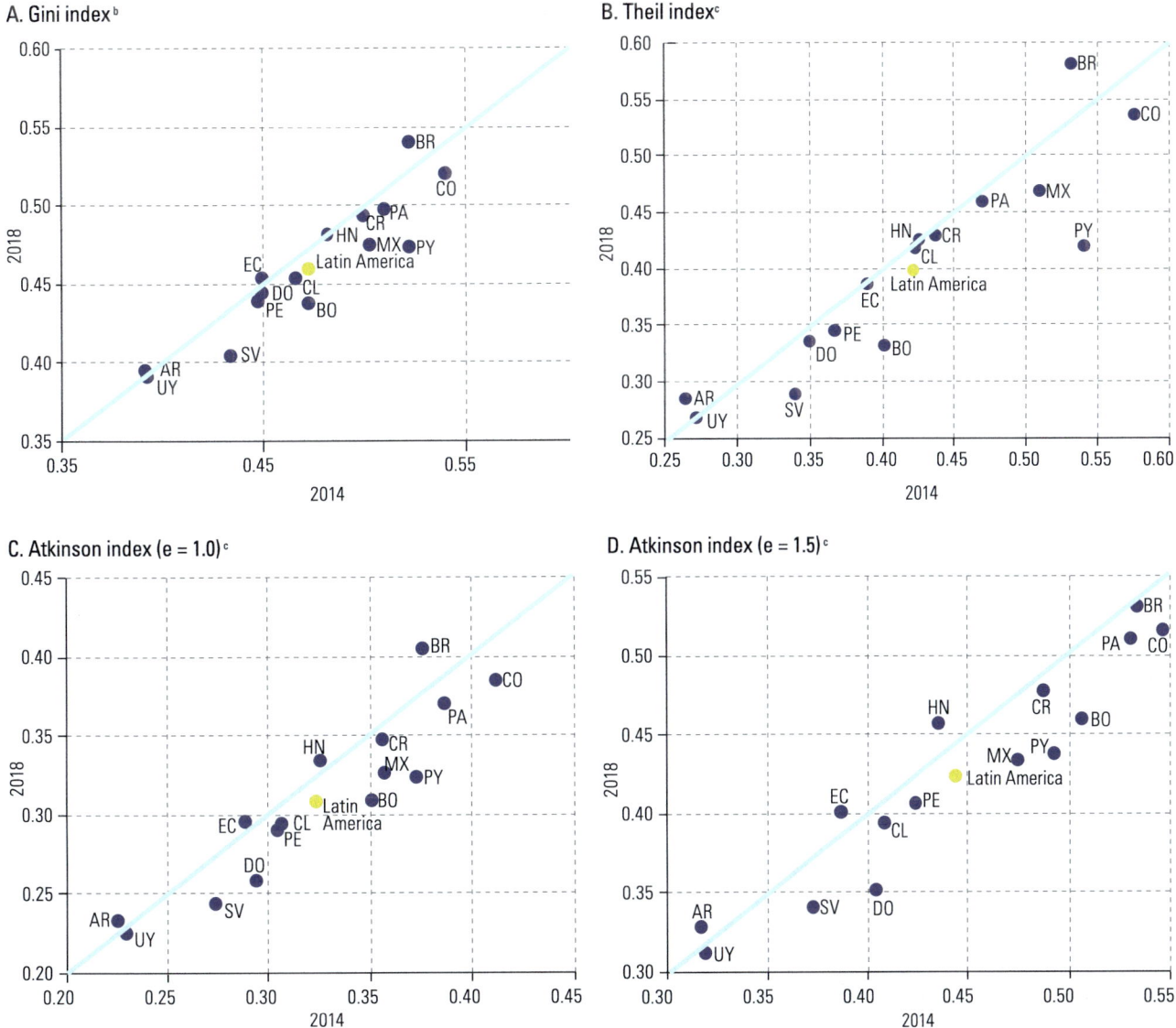

Source: Economic Commission for Latin America and the Caribbean (ECLAC), on the basis of Household Survey Data Bank (BADEHOG).
[a] Average based on the data available for the nearest year for 15 countries. The solid line shows the same value in both axes. In the case of Brazil, the figures for 2014 were adjusted for the difference between the National Household Sample Survey (PNAD) and the Continuous National Household Sample Survey (PNAD Continua) of that year, to make them comparable with 2018 figures.
[b] The Gini index was calculated on the basis of income equal to zero.
[c] The calculation of the Theil and Atkinson indices did not include income equal to zero or the three higher-income observations.

Income inequality is usually analysed and quantified in terms of averages. In this case, for inequality to decline the income of the poorest households must grow at a faster rate than that of the wealthiest. This trend is reflected in all the countries that recorded a decrease in income inequality between 2014 and 2018. In some cases, such as Chile, the Dominican Republic and Panama, the faster growth at the low end of the distribution scale was accompanied by considerable increases in income throughout the entire scale. In other countries, including Colombia, Paraguay and the Plurinational State of Bolivia, household surveys show a decline in income in the wealthiest households in real terms, while the purchasing power of the poorest households increased (see figure I.3A).

Meanwhile, in Argentina, Brazil, Ecuador and Honduras, where income inequality increased over the period, the incomes of the poorest households fell in real terms, while that of the wealthiest households grew or posted smaller decreases (see figure I.3B).

Figure I.3
Latin America (15 countries): relative income growth by decile, 2014–2018
(Percentages)

A. Countries with the highest relative growth in the first income decile

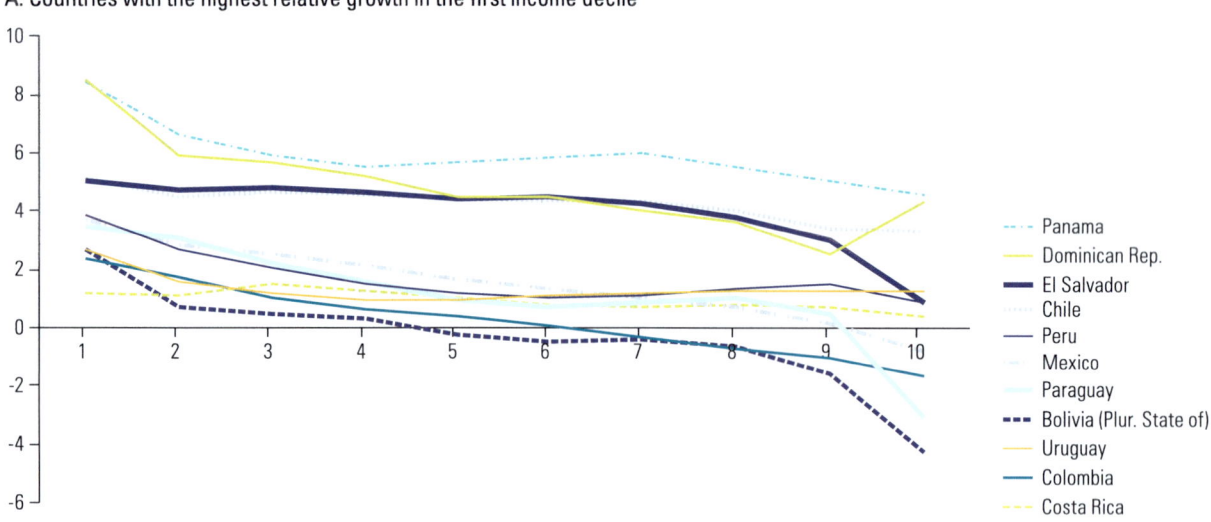

B. Countries with the lowest relative growth in the first income decile

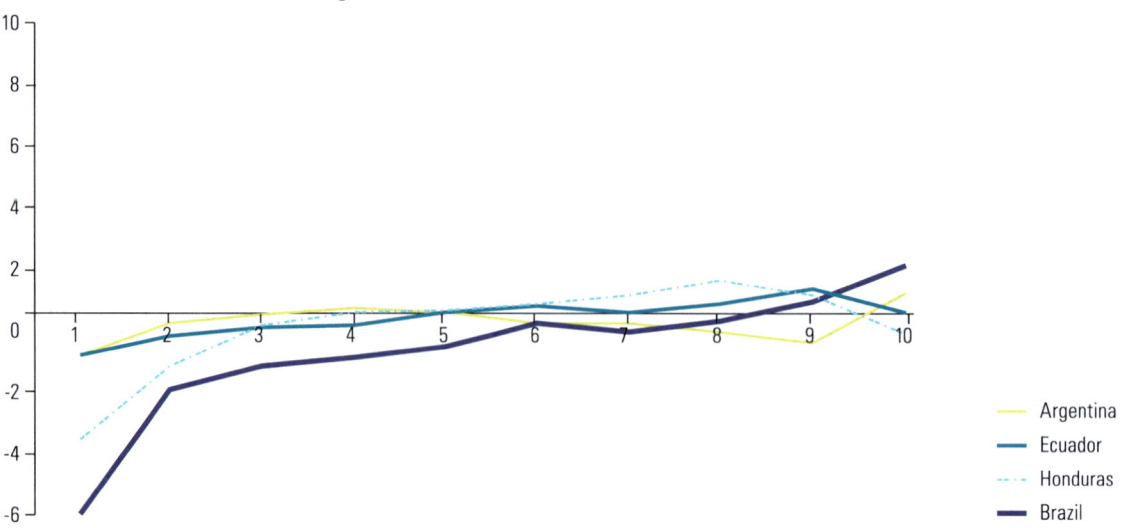

Source: Economic Commission for Latin America and the Caribbean (ECLAC), on the basis of Household Survey Data Bank (BADEHOG).

Inequality can also be analysed in absolute terms. In this case, for inequality to decline the requirement is stricter than that of the analysis in relative terms: the incomes of the poorest households must grow more than those of the wealthiest. Thus, a decline in relative inequality does not guarantee a reduction in absolute inequality.[4]

Between 2014 and 2018, the gap between the first and tenth income deciles increased in 10 countries in absolute terms, even though several of these countries recorded declines

---

[4]   As underscored by ECLAC (2014), although the indicators traditionally used to quantify inequality favour the relative approach, both this method and the absolute approach are suitable and theoretically correct, and the use of one or the other is a value judgement.

in inequality indices (see figure I.4A). For example, in Chile and Panama, where inequality indices decreased in relative terms, the income of households in the first decile posted annual growth of 0.03 times the poverty line in both countries, compared with annual growth of 0.36 and 0.59 times the poverty line, respectively, for households in the tenth decile.[5]

The data from the household surveys of five countries show a narrowing of the gap between the lowest and highest deciles in absolute terms (see figure I.4B). In these countries, although the income of the first decile did not grow significantly (barely 0.01 times the poverty line per year) or even decreased, the tenth decile lost income in absolute terms, to the tune of up to 0.33 times the poverty line per year. These results may have been influenced, at least in part, by the fact that it is difficult for household surveys to consistently reflect the incomes of the wealthiest households, which will be examined in the next section.

Figure I.4
Latin America (15 countries): absolute income growth by decile, 2014–2018
(Multiples of the poverty line)

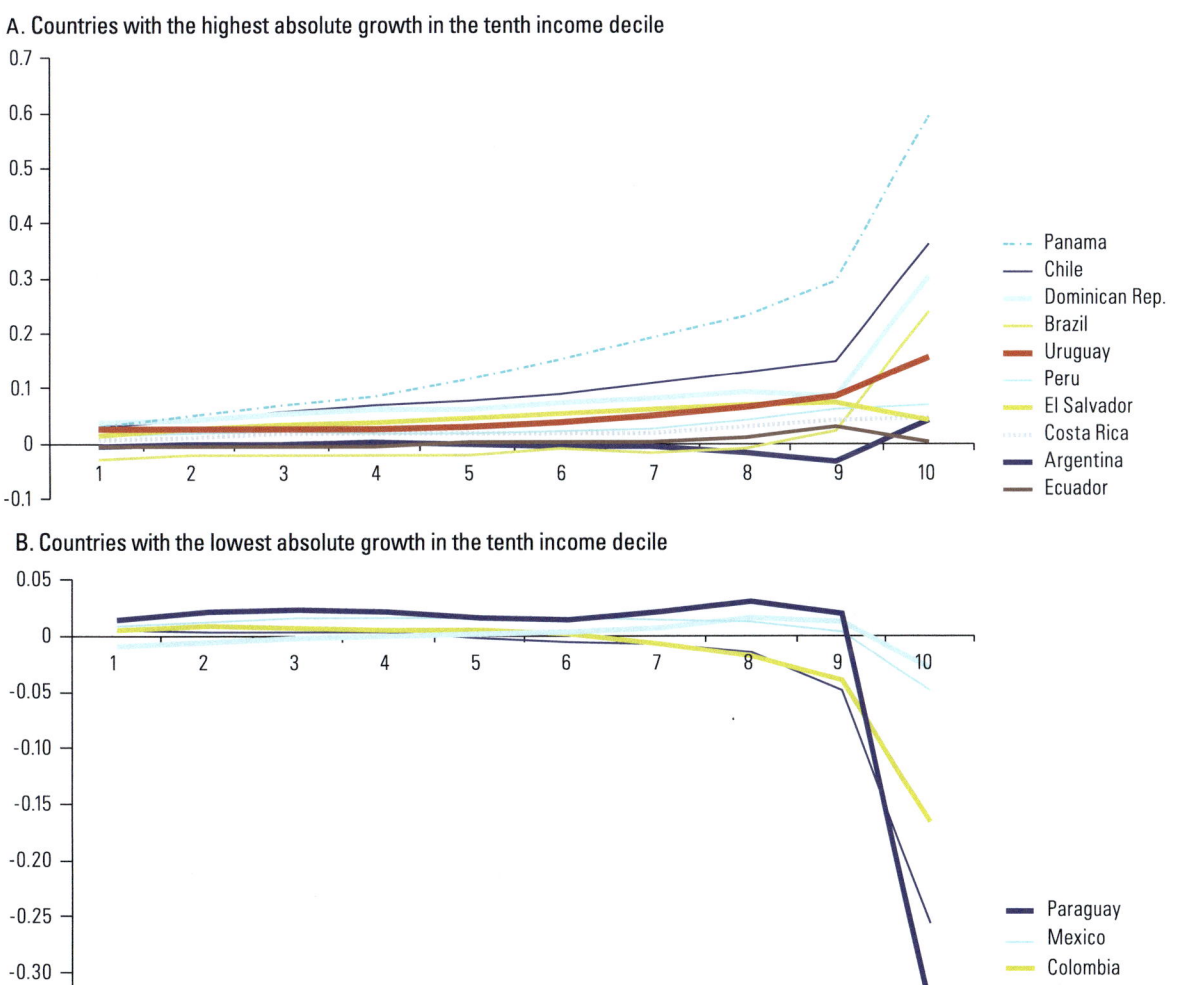

A. Countries with the highest absolute growth in the tenth income decile

Legend: Panama, Chile, Dominican Rep., Brazil, Uruguay, Peru, El Salvador, Costa Rica, Argentina, Ecuador

B. Countries with the lowest absolute growth in the tenth income decile

Legend: Paraguay, Mexico, Colombia, Bolivia (Plur. State of), Honduras

Source: Economic Commission for Latin America and the Caribbean (ECLAC), on the basis of Household Survey Data Bank (BADEHOG).

---

[5]   To analyse changes in absolute inequality, income must be expressed in comparable units, eliminating the impact of inflation (comparison over time) and of monetary units (comparison of different countries). Expressing household income in multiples of the poverty line of each country is one way of fulfilling both requirements.

B. Income inequality re-evaluated: estimates based on combined data sources

Household surveys are not enough to quantify income inequality levels and trends. The combination of data gathered from these surveys with tax data and national accounts facilitates more comprehensive measurements of inequality levels, which are much higher than those based solely on surveys.

The traditional method of estimating inequality on the basis of household survey data does not adequately reflect the phenomenon in its entirety or convey the income gaps between the sectors with the most resources and the rest of society. Therefore, in recent years various studies have been carried out in Latin American countries to estimate the highest income percentile's share of total income by complementing household survey data with distributive data from tax records.

Figure I.5 shows the highest income percentile's share of net national income,[6] based on studies on Argentina (Alvaredo, 2007), Brazil (Morgan, 2017), Chile (Atria and others, 2018), Colombia (Alvaredo and Londoño Vélez, 2013) and Uruguay (Burdin, Esponda and Vigorito, 2014). These percentages vary widely from one country to the next, from a minimum of around 13% for Argentina in 2001 to a maximum of 29% for Brazil in 2011. Although the series are not long enough, all the countries except Uruguay reflect a slight upward trend, with some fluctuations.

Figure I.5

Latin America (5 countries): richest 1% of the population's share of total income, 2000–2015[a]

(Percentages)

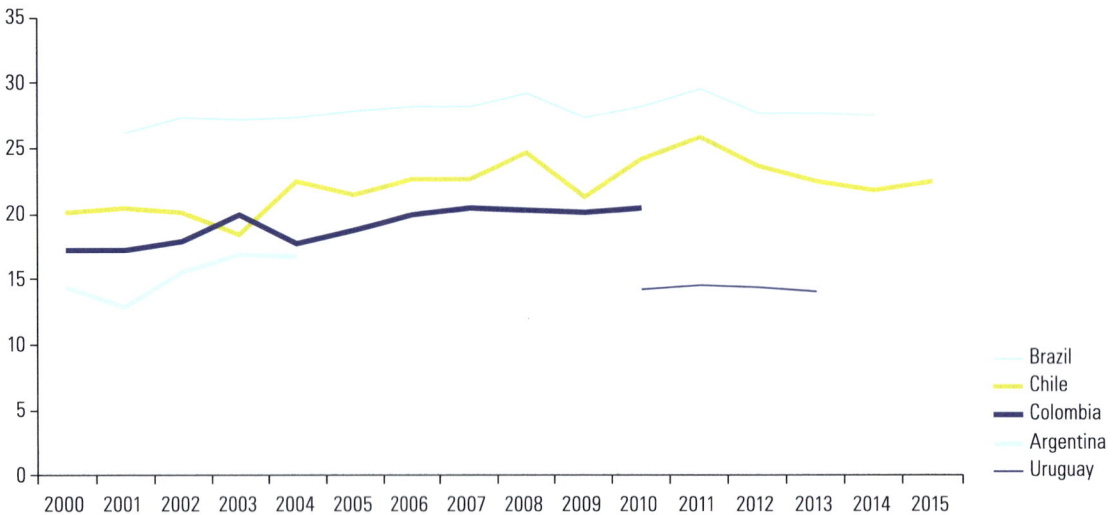

Source: Economic Commission for Latin America and the Caribbean (ECLAC), on the basis of F. Alvaredo, "The rich in Argentina over the twentieth century: from the conservative republic to the Peronist experience and beyond 1932–2004", *Working Paper*, No. 2007-02, Paris, Paris School of Economics, 2007; M. Morgan, "Falling inequality beneath extreme and persistent concentration: new evidence for Brazil combining national accounts, surveys and fiscal data, 2001-2015", *WID.world Working Paper*, No. 2017/12, 2017; J. Atria and others, "Top incomes in Chile: a historical perspective of income inequality (1964-2015)", *WID.world Working Paper*, No. 2018/11, World Inequality Lab, 2018; F. Alvaredo and J. Londoño Vélez, "High incomes and personal taxation in a developing economy: Colombia 1993-2010", *CEQ Working Paper*, No. 12, New Orleans, Commitment to Equity (CEQ), 2013; G. Burdin, F. Esponda and A. Vigorito, "Desigualdad y sectores de altos ingresos en Uruguay: un análisis en base a registros tributarios y encuestas de hogares para el periodo 2009-2011", *Documentos de Trabajo series*, No. 06/2014, Montevideo, Institute of Economics, University of the Republic, 2014.
[a] Refers to the share of net national income, before tax, including retirement income but excluding other types of cash transfer.

---

[6] Refers to the share of net national income, before tax, including retirement income but excluding other types of cash transfer.

The Gini index, calculated by combining information on the highest income percentile's share of total income (see figure I.5) and household survey data, reflects considerably higher values than those produced by household surveys alone.[7] The Gini index adjusted to take into account persons aged 20 and older stands at around 0.60 in Brazil and Colombia, 0.58 in Chile, 0.55 in Argentina[8] and 0.45 in Uruguay (see figure I.6). The average difference between the adjusted index and the household survey estimate is 3 percentage points in Colombia, 4 percentage points in Uruguay, 7 percentage points in Argentina, 8 percentage points in Brazil and 10 percentage points in Chile.

The combined use of tax and household survey data moderates —but does not reverse— the downward trend in inequality seen in several of these countries when only household surveys are considered. The biggest differences are evident in the case of Chile, for which surveys indicate a decline of 0.06 in the Gini index from 2000–2015, compared with a decrease of 0.01 when a combination of data sources is used.

Figure I.6
Latin America (6 countries): Gini index for the total population, for adults aged 20 years and older (percentiles 1 to 99) and for adults aged 20 years and older, adjusted, 2000–2017

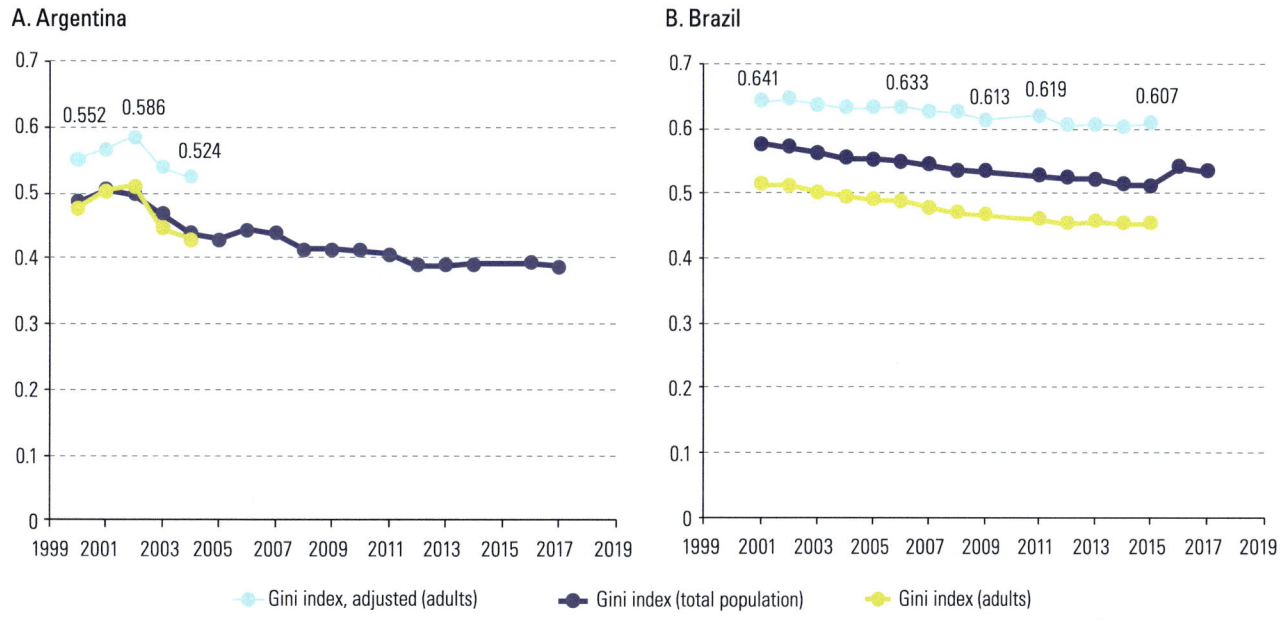

A. Argentina

B. Brazil

Gini index, adjusted (adults)   Gini index (total population)   Gini index (adults)

---

7   According to Atkinson and Piketty (2011), the Gini index (G) can be adjusted (G*) to include information on the share of total income of an extremely small group which nonetheless accumulates a large share (S*), with the following equation: $G^* = S^* + (1 - S^*) G$.

    This adjustment is applied by calculating the Gini index for adults aged 20 years and older for percentiles 1 to 99 and by considering the estimated share of the highest income percentile. Income derives from wages, assets, pension system transfers and imputed rent, and excludes other transfers and income. There are differences in the methodologies used to determine income in the surveys of the different countries. Income before tax is used in Brazil, while income after tax is used in the other countries. This approach was used by Atkinson, Piketty and Saez in 2011 to estimate the Gini index for the United States, on the basis of data from Burkhauser, Feng and Jenkins (2009).

8   A more recent estimate of the Gini index for Argentina (Jiménez and Rossignolo, 2019) shows a higher value, 0.58 on average for 2004–2015. The difference stems mainly from the fact that this study considers income before tax and contributions in the Permanent Household Survey.

Figure I.6 (concluded)

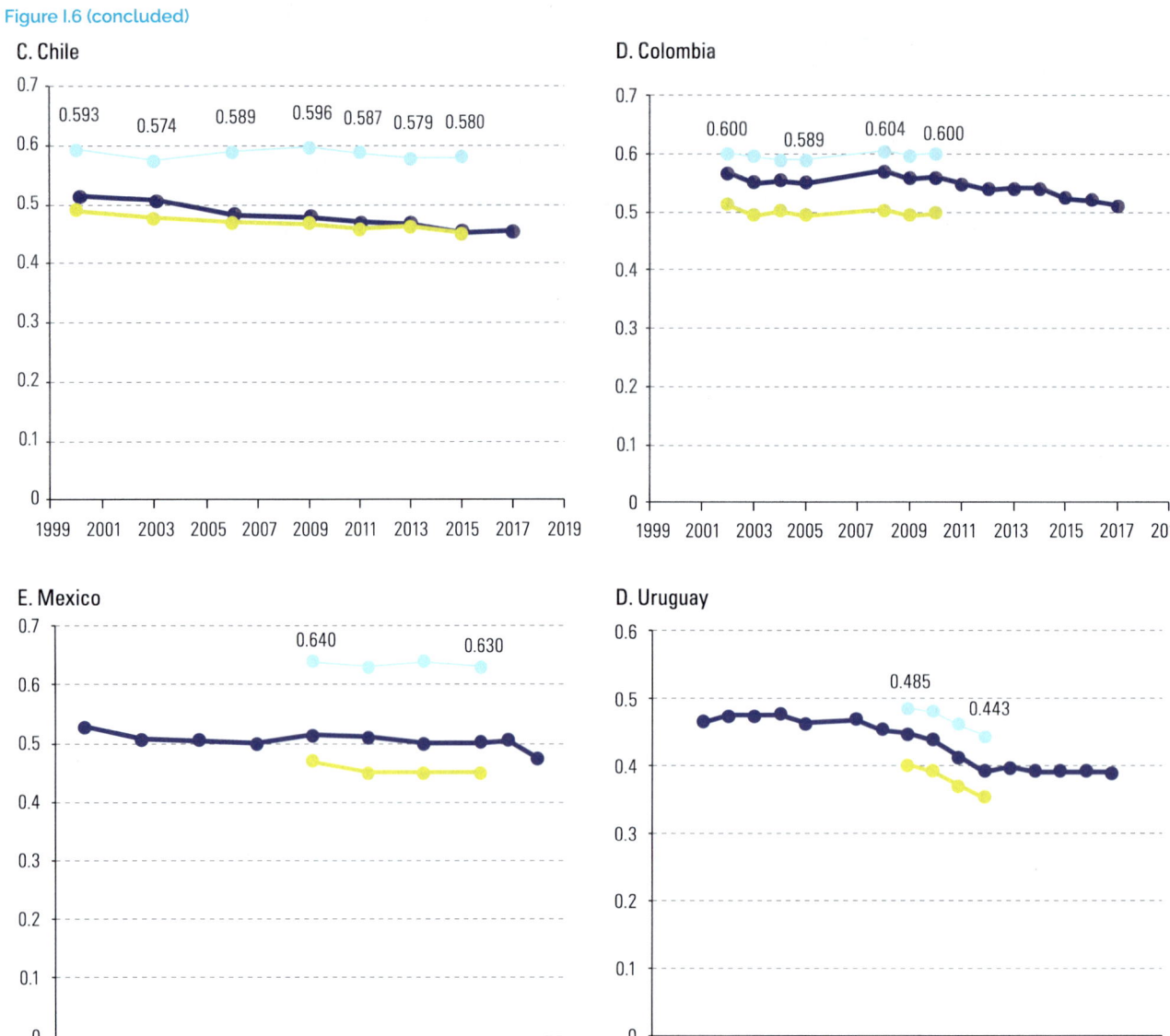

C. Chile

D. Colombia

E. Mexico

D. Uruguay

Gini index, adjusted (adults)   Gini index (total population)   Gini index (adults)

Source: Economic Commission for Latin America and the Caribbean (ECLAC), on the basis of Household Survey Data Bank (BADEHOG); World Inequality Lab, and J. Santaella, Leyva and A. Bustos, "¿Quién se lleva los frutos del éxito en México?: una discusión sobre la verdadera distribución del ingreso", Nexos, 28 August 2017 [online] https://www.nexos.com.mx/?p=33425.

1.   Limitations of data sources and new methodologies to estimate inequality

The problems linked to obtaining complete and comparable inequality estimates from household surveys have been acknowledged for decades now. As regards the measurement of inequality, the relative absence of respondents from the wealthiest income groups is particularly relevant, given the low probability of them being included in the sample, their greater tendency to not complete the survey and their refusal to disclose full information on their different sources of income.

Until 2015, the methodology used by ECLAC aimed to reduce the income underestimation bias and to improve the international and intertemporal comparability of poverty and inequality estimates based on Altimir (1979 and 1987). This involved drawing a comparison between incomes obtained from surveys and household accounts within national accounts (per capita and based on compatible definitions of the different components), then calculating an "adjustment factor" by which values corresponding to each source of income were multiplied (wages and salaries, income of independent workers, property income, retirement income and pensions, and imputed rent) (Altimir, 1987; Feres and León, 1992). This factor remained constant throughout the distribution scale, except for property income, in which case the income gap was attributed to the wealthiest income quintile, resulting in a higher estimate of inequality.

This methodology is based on various assumptions which, given the evidence examined, are not fully justified (ECLAC, 2018). For example, the data from the household income and expenditure account of the System of National Accounts is assumed to provide suitable estimates of the total amounts of each source of household income and therefore, any difference between these figures and those obtained from surveys stem from errors in survey measurement. Although national accounts are based on a solid conceptual framework and reconciliation processes that aim to guarantee consistency, in practice, household account estimation often lacks the basic statistics required, which limits the capacity to produce correct estimates. Thus, on a number of occasions the trends conveyed by surveys have been considered more reliable than those obtained from household accounts for the adjustment process (ECLAC, 2018). Moreover, less than half of the countries in Latin America regularly prepare household accounts.

A second disadvantage of this methodology is the lack of information about the distribution of income reported in household accounts but not measured in surveys. The fact that the failure to adequately capture information is more evident at the top of the distribution scale derives from both underreporting of income received and the lack of high-income respondents in the survey sample (truncation). Various authors have proposed mechanisms to deduce the distribution of high incomes based on different assumptions. These assumptions, including the degree to which the failure to adequately capture information stems from underreporting or truncation, directly affect inequality estimates, so results are not conclusive (Cortés and Vargas, 2017). Box I.1 shows the sensitivity of results to assumptions, using various studies on Mexico as a reference.

In this context, the use of tax administration data provides an opportunity to better understand how income is distributed at the top of the distribution scale. This information helps to better identify the nature and level of missing data relating to high incomes in household surveys, and to reduce the sensitivity of results to assumptions about distribution parameters. However, tax records also present limitations.[9]

Therefore, in order to produce more comprehensive income distribution measurements, the two aforementioned issues must be addressed. First, the preparation of household income accounts must be analysed in detail, to evaluate the accuracy of estimates corresponding to the different sources of income and to

---

[9] Generally, incomes lower than the minimum taxable amount and the recipients of this income are not included, unlike in surveys and national accounts. Income from informal activities is not included either. This data source is also subject to possible underestimation bias, given the very clear incentives for tax avoidance and evasion. Other possible disadvantages derive from the fact that the definitions of income and units of analysis may not coincide with those used in distributive analyses, for example in cases where units apply to only part of the period.

better understand the discrepancies between the figures recorded in these accounts and those obtained from household surveys. Second, tax data disclosure should be encouraged, along with the production of better records to be used together with household surveys and national accounts.[10]

Advances in these areas will facilitate the creation of distributional national accounts, which will help to determine the distribution of net national income among households based on the combined use of the three types of data source: national accounts, surveys and administrative records. This instrument allows the study of growth and inequality together, based on microdata consistent with internationally comparable macroeconomic statistics (Alvaredo and others, 2017) and the intensive use of statistical information from different sources.[11]

To sum up, the emergence of new methodological guidance has led to a re-evaluation of the extent of inequality in the region. The combination of different data sources has revealed higher levels of inequality than those estimated solely on the basis of surveys. More evidence will be collected in the next few years, and this will improve the characterization of a phenomenon which ECLAC has underscored persistently for more than a decade (ECLAC, 2010).

Box I.1
Measurement of inequality using multiple data sources: Mexico

Mexico is one of the countries in which income inequality has been the subject of most studies that draw upon data sources other than household surveys. These works came about because of the recognition of the growing gap between the income estimates deriving from household surveys and those from national accounts. Indeed, Cortés and Vargas (2017) show that this gap grew from 38% in 2006 to 66.5% in 2014. Meanwhile, Fesseau, Wolff and Mattonetti (2013) calculated that the gap recorded in 2010, of around 70%, was the largest seen among countries of the Organization for Economic Cooperation and Development (OECD).

Various studies have focused on adjusting the income measured in surveys, taking into account the possible lack of responses, underreporting of income and truncation (relative absence of wealthiest respondents in the sample). Estimations address the problem from different angles, ranging from the examination of information from surveys exclusively, to the adjustment of income amounts or distribution recorded in surveys based on external information from national accounts or rich lists such as those produced by Forbes.

All these studies agree that income inequality in Mexico considerably exceeds the figures recorded by the National Household Income and Expenditure Survey (ENIGH), albeit they differ in the actual levels found. On the basis of the studies considered in figure 1, in 2014, the adjusted Gini index included values ranging from less than 0.54 to more than 0.75 (as a reference, the index based on the survey is 0.50). This indicates the extreme sensitivity of inequality levels based on the methodology used.

Additionally, trends in the series analysed differ, both in terms of variations on a biennial basis and over the entire period between 2008 and 2014. Of the five series with data between 2008 and 2012, inequality grew in two series during the period, decreased in two others and remained unchanged in one. Moreover, the direction of change does not coincide across all the estimates in any of the possible two-yearly variations.

---

[10]   Some methodological innovations in this area include the generalized Pareto interpolation method (Blanchet, Fournier and Piketty, 2017), which produces a complete distribution with a variable Pareto coefficient based on aggregate tax data and rescaling and calibration methods applied to aggregate tax data to generate an income distribution based on microdata (Blanchet, Flores and Morgan, 2018).

[11]   As regards Latin American countries, an estimation of distributional national accounts is available for Brazil (Morgan, 2017).

Box I.1 (concluded)

In short, although all the studies show that income inequality is underestimated when only survey estimates are taken into account, there is still no consensus on how to correct this downward bias. The wide range of methodologies used spans from adjustments for the absence of responses and high incomes exclusively, on the basis of data from surveys alone, to adjustments for different functions of probability distribution to estimate distribution tails, to the calculation of more or less sophisticated adjustment factors by income stream, using information not included in the survey. As seen in the data from the studies carried out in Mexico, the final result depends heavily on the methodology used.

Mexico: Gini index according to different estimation methodologies, 2008–2014

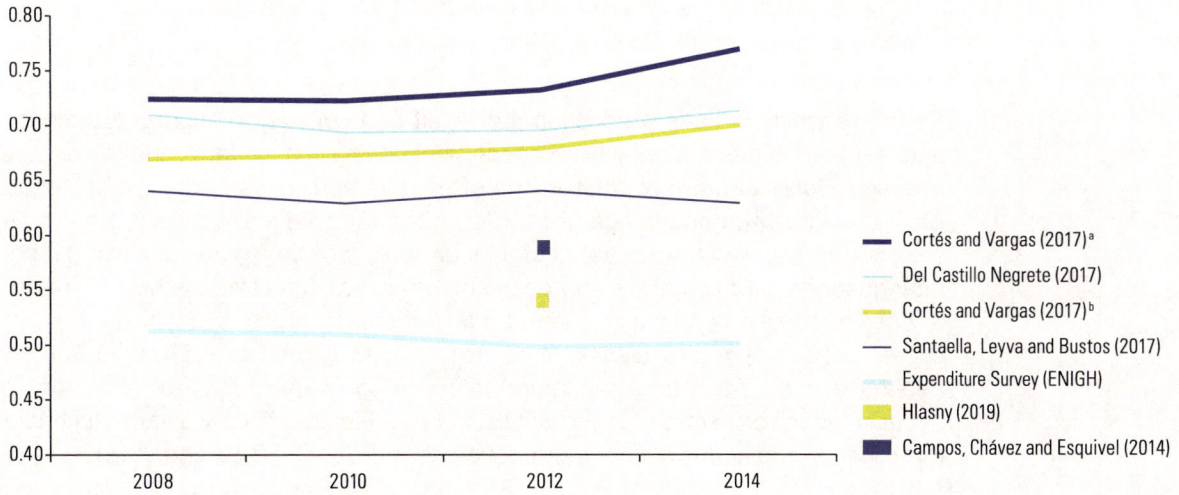

Source: Economic Commission for Latin America and the Caribbean (ECLAC), on the basis of Household Survey Data Bank (BADEHOG); R. Campos, E. Chávez and G. Esquivel, "Los ingresos altos, la tributación óptima y la recaudación posible", *Finanzas Públicas*, vol. 6, No. 18, 2014; F. Cortés and D. Vargas, "La evolución de la desigualdad en México: viejos y nuevos resultados", *Revista de Economía Mexicana. Anuario UNAM*, No. 2, 2017; M. del Castillo Negrete, "La magnitud de la desigualdad en el ingreso y la riqueza en México: una propuesta de cálculo", *Studies and Perspectives series-ECLAC Subregional Headquarters in Mexico*, No. 167 (LC/L.4108; LC/MEX/L.1199), Mexico City, Economic Commission for Latin America and the Caribbean (ECLAC), 2015; M. del Castillo Negrete, "Thomas Piketty para México", *Estudios*, No. 110, vol. XII, 2014; M. Fesseau, F. Wolff and M. Mattonetti, "A cross-country comparison of household income, consumption and wealth between micro sources and national accounts aggregates", *Statistics Working Papers*, No. 2013/03, Paris, OECD/Publishing, 2013; and J. Santaella, G. Leyva and A. Bustos, "¿Quién se lleva los frutos del éxito en México?: una discusión sobre la verdadera distribución del ingreso", *Nexos*, 28 August 2017 [online] https://www.nexos.com.mx/?p=33425.

[a] Estimates based on the assumption of underreporting proportional to income from the fifth to the tenth deciles only, and of the following distribution of the difference between surveys and national accounts: 50% owing to underreporting and 50% owing to truncation.

[b] Estimates based on the assumption of underreporting proportional to the square of income, and of the following distribution of the difference between surveys and national accounts: 50% owing to underreporting and 50% owing to truncation.

Source: Economic Commission for Latin America and the Caribbean (ECLAC), on the basis of Household Survey Data Bank (BADEHOG); R. Campos, E. Chávez and G. Esquivel, "Los ingresos altos, la tributación óptima y la recaudación posible", *Finanzas Públicas*, vol. 6, No. 18, 2014; F. Cortés and D. Vargas, "La evolución de la desigualdad en México: viejos y nuevos resultados", *Revista de Economía Mexicana. Anuario UNAM*, No. 2, 2017; M. del Castillo Negrete, "La magnitud de la desigualdad en el ingreso y la riqueza en México: una propuesta de cálculo", *Studies and Perspectives series-ECLAC Subregional Headquarters in Mexico*, No. 167 (LC/L.4108; LC/MEX/L.1199), Mexico City, Economic Commission for Latin America and the Caribbean (ECLAC), 2015; M. del Castillo Negrete, "Thomas Piketty para México", *Estudios*, No. 110, vol. XII, 2014; M. Fesseau, F. Wolff and M. Mattonetti, "A cross-country comparison of household income, consumption and wealth between micro sources and national accounts aggregates", *Statistics Working Papers*, No. 2013/03, Paris, OECD/Publishing, 2013; and J. Santaella, G. Leyva and A. Bustos, "¿Quién se lleva los frutos del éxito en México?: una discusión sobre la verdadera distribución del ingreso", *Nexos*, 28 August 2017 [online] https://www.nexos.com.mx/?p=33425.

C. Social classes at the centre of the social inequality matrix

Social class, analysed on the basis of income strata in this edition of the *Social Panorama of Latin America*, is a central axis of the social inequality matrix in the region. Between 2002 and 2017, the proportion of the overall population in the low-income strata shrunk significantly, from 70.9% to 55.9%, while the proportion in the middle-income strata grew from 26.9% to 41.1%. Within this category, the lower-middle-income stratum accounted for more than 50% of the population compared with only 11% for the upper-middle-income stratum. In 2017, the consumption capacity of all middle-income strata —expressed in constant dollars at 2018 prices— amounted to US$ 1.16 trillion.

Social inequality in Latin America is the result of a complex matrix of determinants, and is rooted in the structural heterogeneity of production systems and the culture of privilege. Social stratum or class is one of the structural axes of the social inequality matrix, along with gender, age (life cycle), ethnicity, race and territory, among other factors. The socioeconomic status of an individual, family or group (including intra- or inter-generational changes) is shaped by the other structural axes of this matrix, and is at once a reflection and explanation of many of the dimensions in which inequality is expressed: employment and work, access to productive resources and income, education, health, basic services, housing, information and communications technologies, food security, social protection, opportunities to live a life free from violence, technology, participation and agency, among other elements (ECLAC, 2016b and 2018).

Sociological reflection on social structure emerged in Latin America in the mid-twentieth century in response to development issues in the countries of the region, with a view to modernizing socioeconomic structures in order to overcome the economic underdevelopment and inequality inherent in traditional agrarian societies. Within this framework, State-led import substitution industrialization was the cornerstone of the modernization project of the day. The prevailing approach aimed, first, to identify the social groups that could play an important role in driving modernization —which is the social foundation of development— and, second, to understand the main transformations seen in traditional social categories and in those born out of the changes the region was experiencing, such as urbanization, industrialization and the expansion of education. The analysis of middle-income sectors was critical to understanding the dynamics and tensions that marked the Latin American development project. This is because the middle classes not only played an essential role in the formation of the social partnerships (for example, State-citizen alliances) promoted under developmental policies in the region but were also one of the main social groups to benefit from and be transformed in terms of make-up and orientation by the changes arising from such policies (see Medina Echavarría, 1967; Germani, 1968; De Ipola and Torrado, 1976; Costa Pinto, 1981; Filgueira and Geneletti, 1981; Filgueira, 2001).

The crisis in the developmentalist model and the structural adjustment programmes promoted in the region during the 1980s and part of the 1990s caused a significant thematic shift in analytical and research concerns, signalled in part by the decline of studies on stratification, social classes and social mobility. Specifically, most studies shifted their focus to identifying social exclusion and poverty, as well as the new forms of work and labour market participation resulting from structural adjustments; there was less interest in attempting a systematic analysis of patterns in the structure of and distinctions between groups and classes in different societies, with a notable absence of regional or comparative studies.

It is, therefore, hardly surprising that there is a dearth of knowledge or statistics on Latin American middle classes, their professions, income and education profiles, cultural and sociopolitical leanings and other characteristics, this despite the recurring mention of the middle classes in the media and the middle-class aspirations of a significant proportion of the Latin American population. The "middle class" seems to have become a kind of grey area of Latin America's social structure, frequently mentioned without there being any greater clarity or accuracy in the identification of its particular constitutive features (Sémbler, 2006).

ECLAC has addressed the issue of social stratification on various occasions, but the significant transformations that have occurred in Latin American societies have rendered this an increasingly complex and multi-faceted task, both in terms of the composition of strata and the dynamics and analysis thereof (see, for example, Marinho and Quiroz, 2018). Added to this, comparative research and the analysis of changes in social structures at the regional level are significantly hindered by the relative lack of comparability between different sources of information, the absence of issues that are relevant today (for example self-identification, spending and borrowing, material and symbolic consumption, and social mobility) or their inclusion in instruments that cannot be easily incorporated, and issues such as population ageing, which makes it difficult to apply occupational criteria to all households.[12]

In the light of the available information and the need for comparison, there has been a growing tendency in international discussions to use income as the main, if not only, criterion for social stratification, despite the consensus that it is insufficient.

The present section of this edition of the *Social Panorama of Latin America* focuses on this structural axis of the social inequality matrix by using income to define and analyse the current socioeconomic stratification in the region —with particular interest in the changes in middle-income strata— and how this relates to the other axes of the matrix.

1. Trends in socioeconomic stratification in Latin America

A strong and prosperous middle class is essential to a successful economy and cohesive society. The middle class is responsible for a significant share of consumption and investment in education, health and housing and plays a key role in supporting social protection systems through fiscal contributions. A recent Organization for Economic Cooperation and Development (OECD) study found that in the last few decades, there has been little growth and even stagnation in the number of middle-income households in some OECD countries. This has fuelled perceptions that the current socioeconomic system is unfair and that the middle class has not benefited from economic growth in a manner commensurate with its contributions (OECD, 2019).[13]

Since the 1970s, economic development processes in many countries in Latin America have, for the most part, been shaped by neoliberalism, based on extractive models and heavily dependent on natural resources. Other features of such models include the reduced role of the State; privatization of public services such as education, health and social security; labour markets that have high levels of informality and are structurally incapable of absorbing the entire workforce and generating quality employment; and social protection systems that provide low coverage and very limited benefits. The beginning of the twenty-first century, however, marked a significant

---

[12]   The instruments used (multipurpose household surveys) do not usually collect information on pensioners' occupational history or last occupation (and wages), which means that additional criteria must be used to rank those households in the social structure. While such information is collected in longitudinal surveys on social protection, they are conducted in but a few countries.

[13]   See OECD (2019). In this study, middle-income classes are defined relative to equivalised household disposable income and comprise households with income between 75% and 200% of the national median income (see box I.2).

change in this situation. A more favourable economic context, characterized by the commodities boom and expanding fiscal space, and a political context in which a number of regional governments placed greater focus on reducing poverty and inequality and on social inclusion, led to more comprehensive State action and substantial paradigm shifts. There has been an increase in social spending and programmes to combat poverty and extreme poverty, while public services, mainly in education and health have proliferated; in addition, social protection systems have been strengthened and the topic of universal coverage has once again come to the forefront of the public agenda in a number of countries. There have also been improvements in labour markets: unemployment and informality rates have fallen and real incomes have risen. This is clearly a result of a relatively more promising economic scenario, but it is also attributable to active labour market policies, including increases in the minimum wage, the strengthening of labour inspection and collective bargaining processes, and policies and programmes to promote formal sector employment, including legislative and tax simplification measures aimed at microenterprises and own-account workers (ECLAC, 2016b, 2016c, 2017, 2018 and 2019). All these elements have led to a relative decline in levels of inequality[14] and a significant reduction in poverty (from 45.4% in 2002 to 27.8% in 2014, with 65 million people lifted out of poverty) and also to an overall improvement in the well-being of large swathes of the population and great progress in social and labour inclusion (ECLAC, 2019). However, there have been standstills and even reversals in some of these trends since 2015, as discussed in previous editions of the *Social Panorama* (see chapter II).

The question therefore arises as to what transformations Latin American social structure has undergone and whether said changes mirror those that occurred in developed countries. Notwithstanding the fact that the debate on social stratification and in particular on social classes is multidimensional (involving employment, education, income and expenditure, material and symbolic consumption, and social capital, among others), this edition of the *Social Panorama* will address changes in the socioeconomic structure in terms of the size of the various strata defined for different thresholds of per capita income, as well as their consumption capacity, their main sociodemographic characteristics and the associated risks.[15]

Taking into account the above-mentioned methodological differences (see box I.2), significant growth can be observed in the middle-income strata in Latin America (see figure I.7A). In a region marked by high levels of poverty, there has been a significant contraction of low-income strata[16] (from 70.9% to 55.9% between 2002 and 2017), and a considerable increase in middle-income strata[17] (from 26.9% to 41.1%). This has been the result of poverty reduction efforts combined with higher household per capita income related both to improvements in social protection systems and public transfers to low-income households, and to higher wages and greater female participation in the labour force, with the consequent increase in the number of wage earners within households. There has also been a slight increase in the high-income strata (individuals in households whose per capita income is above 10 poverty lines).[18]

---

[14] As discussed in the first section of this chapter, income inequality, as measured by the Gini coefficient in household survey data from 17 Latin American countries, fell from 0.54 to 0.46 between 2002 and 2018. There have also been significant declines in other social inequality indicators. However, partial results from the analysis of other sources (such as tax records) appear to point to increases in the levels of wealth concentrated among the richest 1% of the population (see section B of this chapter).

[15] Unlike the aforementioned OECD study, which defines thresholds relative to income, the analysis below uses absolute and time-bound thresholds expressed in multiples of each country's poverty lines (see box I.2 for a more detailed description). This criterion was considered more appropriate for the region given its high levels of inequality and the traditional method of using absolute measures for poverty (on the basis of defined baskets of basic needs valued at market prices in each country).

[16] The low-income strata correspond to persons living in households with per capita income below 1.8 poverty lines, and comprise three subgroups: households in extreme poverty, households in poverty and households highly vulnerable to poverty (with income between 1 and 1.8 poverty lines).

[17] Income between 1.8 and 10 poverty lines.

[18] To simplify the presentation of information, although households were initially used as units of analysis, the statistics shown hereinafter correspond to individuals, unless otherwise indicated. The distribution of households by per capita income strata can be found in table I.A1.1 in annex.

Box I.2
Methodology for estimating socioeconomic strata

International and regional studies on social stratification have approached the topic using various types of income-based measurement. This strategy is largely a reflection of the challenges involved in working with measurement instruments from different countries, which makes it difficult to generate comparable classifications that include a standard set of conventional factors for defining social classes, particularly with regard to occupational categories and branches of activity, and which occasionally lack sufficient information to develop these typologies. However, the fact that income is a relatively simple representation of levels of individual and family well-being makes it easier to examine the distribution of national income and subsequently determine strata based on income, using various factors to establish the lower and upper thresholds that delimit the groups.

In general, there are three approaches to stratification based on per capita income, and these have sometimes been combined. Most of them aim first to identify the middle sector(s), which automatically makes it easier to define the low-income and high-income strata. Typical strategies include:

- Measurement of the position in income distribution, which usually involves the selection of quintiles or deciles that make up the middle stratum, although specific quantiles may be chosen (for example, percentile 95). Examples of the use of these methods to define the middle-income class can be found in Easterly (2001), where quintiles 2–4 are used, and Solimano (2008), who groups deciles 3–9. In a comparison over time and based on this definition, the middle-income strata can get richer or poorer but not increase or decrease, and purchasing powers are not comparable, nor are countries.

- Definition of thresholds relative to the median of equivalised income, similar to the methodologies on which the measurement of relative poverty is based. Examples of the upper and lower bounds of the middle strata can be found in several studies: in Blackburn and Bloom (1985), within 60% and 225% of the national median income [author: please confirm]; in Thurow (1987) and in Birdsall, Graham and Pettinato (2000), within 75% and 125% of the median; in Davies and Huston (1992), Castellani and Parent (2011), OECD (2010) and Castellani, Parent and Zentero (2014), within 50% and 150% of the median, and OECD (2019), within 75% and 200% of the median. On the basis of this methodology, the middle strata can get richer or poorer, grow or shrink (with smoothed effects), but purchasing power —particularly for individuals close to strata thresholds— is not comparable.

- Definition of absolute (and time-bound) thresholds. Examples include studies by Ravallion (2010), which defines the middle class as households with an income of between US$ 2 and US$ 13 dollars per day at 2015 purchasing power parity (PPP); Banerjee and Duflo (2008), which defines it as households whose daily per capita expenditures valued at purchasing power parity are between $2 and $10; Kharas and Gertz (2010) and Cárdenas, Kharas and Henao (2011), which define it as households with daily expenditures between $10 and $100 per person in purchasing power parity terms; and Birdsall (2010), in which the middle class is identified in a hybrid methodology as people living in households with income per capita between $10 and the 95th percentile. López Calva and Ortiz-Juárez (2011), Birdsall (2012), Ferreira and others (2013) and López Calva and Ortiz-Juárez (2014) define the middle class as households living on between $10 and $50 per day in PPP. Analyses based on this methodology provide an indication over time of the likelihood of the middle class becoming wealthier or poorer, growing or shrinking, and purchasing power is comparable. While it is possible for households and individuals to move to a higher or lower stratum as a result of cyclical events such as unemployment, it is unlikely that there will be an "impoverished middle class" in literal terms.

The method used in the current edition of the *Social Panorama* is absolute thresholds, expressed in multiples of poverty lines. This made it possible to identify the low-income strata, which comprise three substrata defined on the basis of normative thresholds: extremely poor (people living in extreme poverty, with a per capita income below the extreme poverty lines developed by ECLAC); poor (people living in poverty with per capita income below the poverty lines); and low-income non-poor (with per capita income below 1.8 times the poverty line). Three middle-income strata were also identified, defined by the empirical boundaries that take into consideration the risks of falling into poverty (see figure I.17), the distribution of these strata by country and discontinuities in a combined index of possession of basic goods and services. The lower-middle stratum was defined as having an upper threshold of 3 times the poverty line, the intermediate-middle having an upper threshold of 6 times the poverty line, and the upper-middle having an upper threshold of 10 times the poverty line. Values above 10 times the poverty line make up the high-per-capita-income strata.

Box I.2 (concluded)

Table I.1 briefly summarizes the distribution and trends of the low-, middle- and high-income segments and the substrata that comprise them; the lower and upper thresholds for each stratum, expressed in multiples of the poverty line; and the equivalence (weighted average of 17 countries) in constant dollars at 2018 prices. It must be borne in mind that poverty lines differ between urban and rural areas within each country.

The figure below presents a comparative overview of different methodologies for defining the middle class: the ECLAC methodology (for broad strata); the use of thresholds of between 75% and 200% of the relative to national equivalised median income per capita (household income divided by the square root of household size), applied in OECD (2019); and the absolute thresholds used in various World Bank documents, first published in 2011, equivalent to US$ 10 and US$ 50 per capita per day at PPP.

Latin America (18 countries): application of various methodologies for defining middle-income strata thresholds, around 2002, 2008 and 2017[a]
(Percentages)

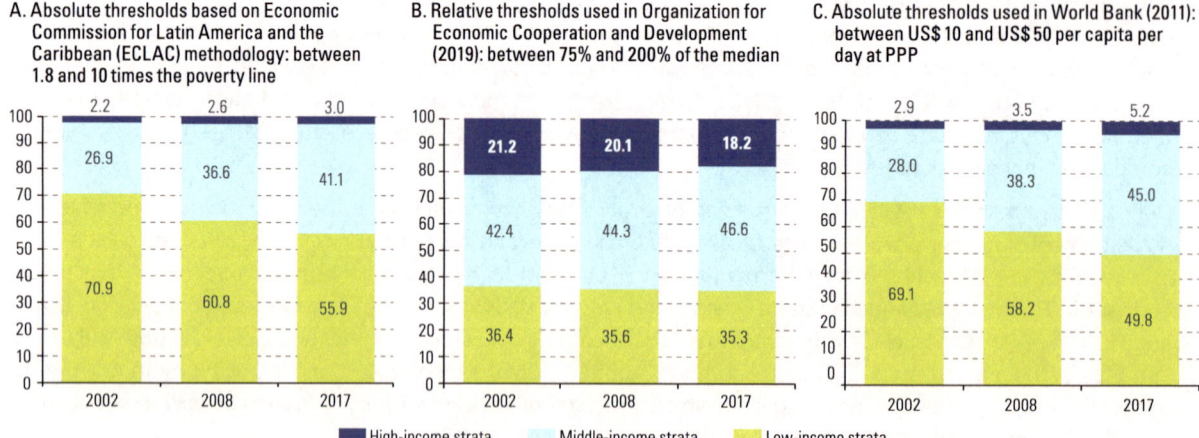

A. Absolute thresholds based on Economic Commission for Latin America and the Caribbean (ECLAC) methodology: between 1.8 and 10 times the poverty line

B. Relative thresholds used in Organization for Economic Cooperation and Development (2019): between 75% and 200% of the median

C. Absolute thresholds used in World Bank (2011): between US$ 10 and US$ 50 per capita per day at PPP

■ High-income strata   ■ Middle-income strata   ■ Low-income strata

Source: Economic Commission for Latin America and the Caribbean (ECLAC), on the basis of Household Survey Data Bank (BADEHOG).

[a] The countries included are: Argentina, Bolivarian Republic of Venezuela, Brazil, Chile, Colombia, Costa Rica, the Dominican Republic, Ecuador, El Salvador, Guatemala, Honduras, Mexico, Nicaragua, Panama, Paraguay, Peru, Plurinational State of Bolivia and Uruguay.

Source: Economic Commission for Latin America and the Caribbean (ECLAC), on the basis of W. Easterly, "The middle class consensus and economic development", *Journal of Economic Growth*, vol. 6, No. 4, 2001; A. Solimano, "The middle class and the development process", *Macroeconomics of Development series*, No. 65 (LC/L.2892-P), Santiago, Economic Commission for Latin America and the Caribbean (ECLAC), 2008; M. Blackburn and D. Bloom, "What is happening to the middle class?", *American Demographics*, vol. 7, No. 1, 1985; L. Thurow, "A surge in inequality", *Scientific American*, vol. 256, Nº 5, 1987; N. Birdsall, C. Graham and S. Pettinato, "Stuck in the tunnel: is globalization muddling the middle class?", *Working Paper*, No. 14, Washington, D.C., Center on Social and Economic Dynamics, The Brookings Institution, 2000; J. C. Davies and J. H. Huston, "The shrinking middle-income class: a multivariate analysis", *Eastern Economic Journal*, vol. 18, No. 3; 1992; F. Castellani and G. Parent, "Being 'middle class' in Latin America" *OECD Development Centre Working Paper*, No. 305, Paris, OECD Publishing, 2011; M. Ravallion, "The developing world's bulging (but vulnerable) 'middle class'", *World Development*, vol. 38, No. 4, 2010; A. Banerjee and E. Duflo, "What is middle class about the middle class around the world?", *Journal of Economic Perspectives*, vol. 22, No. 2, 2008; H. Kharas and G. Gertz, "The new global middle class: a cross-over from West to East", Washington, D.C., The Brookings Institution, 2010 [online] https://www.brookings.edu/research/the-new-global-middle-class-a-cross-over-from-west-to-east/; M. Cárdenas, H. Kharas y C. Henao, *Latin America's global middle class*, Washington, D.C., The Brookings Institution, 2011; N. Birdsall, "The (indispensable) middle class in developing countries; or, the rich and the rest, not the poor and the rest", *Working Paper*, No. 207, Washington, D.C., Center for Global Development, 2010; F. Castellani, G. Parent and J. Zentero, "The Latin American middle class: fragile after all?", *IDB Working Paper Series*, No. 557, Washington, D.C., Inter-American Development Bank (IDB), 2014; L. F. López Calva and E. Ortiz-Juárez, "A vulnerability approach to the definition of the middle class", *Policy Research Working Paper*, No. 5902, Washington, D.C., World Bank, 2011; López Calva, L. F. and E. Ortiz-Juárez, "A vulnerability approach to the definition of the middle class", *Journal of Economic Inequality*, vol. 12, No. 1, 2014; Organization for Economic Cooperation and Development Económicos (OECD), *Under Pressure: The Squeezed Middle Class*, Paris, OECD Publishing, 2019; OECD, *Latin American Economic Outlook 2011: How middle-class is Latin America?*, Paris, OECD Publishing, 2010.

Figure I.7
Latin America (18 countries[a]): population size and trends by per capita income strata, around 2002, 2008 and 2017

A. Population size and trends, by per capita income strata
(percentages)

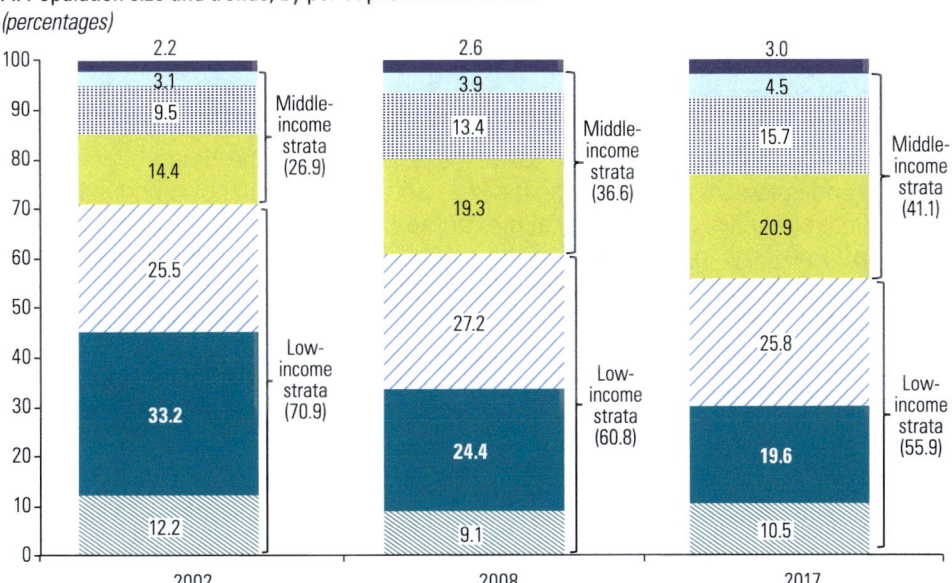

B. Changes in per capita income strata
(millions of persons)

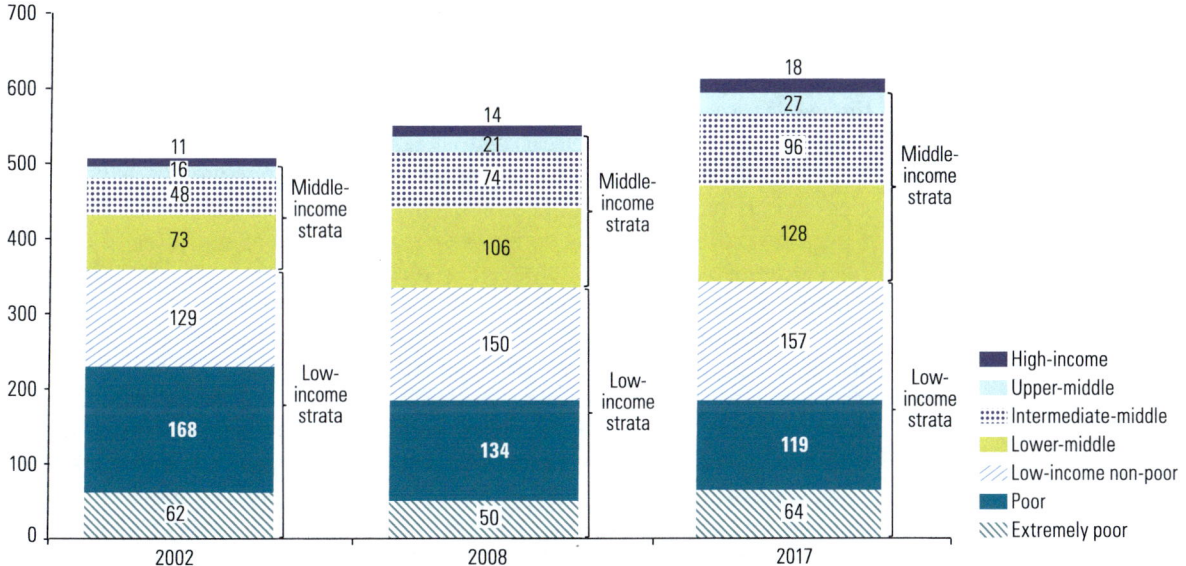

Source: Economic Commission for Latin America and the Caribbean (ECLAC), on the basis of Household Survey Data Bank (BADEHOG).
Note: Figures adjusted for population projections of World Population Prospects, 2019 revision, and estimated poverty trends in countries for which figures are not available for the years indicated.
[a] The countries included are: Argentina, the Bolivarian Republic of Venezuela, Brazil, Chile, Colombia, Costa Rica, the Dominican Republic, Ecuador, El Salvador, Guatemala, Honduras, Mexico, Nicaragua, Panama, Paraguay, Peru, the Plurinational State of Bolivia and Uruguay.

Despite improvements, the social structure —considered from the perspective of per capita income— remains resolutely pyramidal. Taking into account all persons living in poverty in 2017 (including in situations of extreme poverty), the data show that this lower stratum subgroup still accounts for the largest share of the population (30.1%), followed by the low-income non-poor group (25.8%). Together, those two groups account for more than half the population. With the lower-middle income strata (1.8 to 3 times the per capita poverty line) representing 20.9% of the population, this means that 76.8% of the total population of Latin America belong to lower- or lower-middle strata. The intermediate-middle stratum (more than 3 times and up to 6 times the poverty line) accounts for 15.7% of the population while the upper-middle-income stratum (more than 6 times and up to 10 times the poverty line) accounts for only 4.5%; individuals in the high-income strata represent 3.0% of the total population.

(a) Upward mobility?

While it is impossible to speak strictly of "social mobility" without using panel-type or similar instruments to monitor households and individuals and study their intra- and intergenerational movements up or down the social ladder, the data show that the regional trend is towards a modest shift out of poverty for households and individuals in the lowest strata (living in poverty and extreme poverty) but that they remain highly vulnerable to poverty. In turn, those in the highly vulnerable to poverty stratum move up to and swell the ranks of the lower-middle-income stratum. This raises the question of whether the stratum of non-poor individuals is a transitional one, given that it tends to remain proportionately stable as poverty declines and the middle sectors grow. In terms of population size, the upper-middle and high-income strata appear to have more barriers to entry,[19] as their growth involves a much smaller proportion of the population. Between 2002 and 2017, the upper and upper-middle strata combined (6 times the per capita poverty line or higher) rose from 5.2% to 7.5% of the overall population, a total of 46 million people. As will be seen below, inclusion in these strata tends to be related more to the high labour income of a household's primary wage earner (defined as the employed person with the highest earnings in the household), rather than greater participation in the labour force among household members or a significant share of income from other sources (such as public transfers, property income, or corporate profits). In addition, high labour income levels are not determined by the level of education attained.

However, the significant decrease in and reconfiguration of the low-income strata between 2002 and 2017 was accompanied by growth in the middle-income strata. The share of the low-income strata as a percentage of the total fell by 15 percentage points (from 359 million to 341 million people, as seen in figure I.7B). This figure is the result of a significant drop (by 49 million) in the number of persons in the poor stratum, although the number of persons in the extremely poor stratum increased by 2 million, and an increase in number of persons in the low-income non-poor stratum (28 million). At the same time, the share of the middle-income sectors increased by 14.1 percentage points (from 136 million to 250 million people, mainly as a result of growth in the lower-middle stratum), while the proportion corresponding to the upper stratum grew by only 0.8 percentage points in the same period (see table I.1). An analysis of these changes by percentage rate of variation shows that the intermediate-middle stratum grew most rapidly —by almost 65% over the period— followed by the upper-middle stratum (45.9%) and the lower-middle stratum (45.8%); however, the poor stratum contracted by 40.9% and the extremely poor stratum by 13.6%. Also noteworthy is the fact that increases in per capita income in the region, with the consequent "upward mobility" across strata, were more significant in the period 2002–2008, coinciding with the boom in commodity demand and the expansion of social and labour policies. Subsequently, the pace of increase in per capita income and growth in the middle sectors slowed, and poverty levels began to rise again in some countries from 2015 (see chapter II of this publication and ECLAC, 2019).

These trends have not been homogenous in all the countries of the region, however. Apart from the fact that strata sizes may differ significantly, there are exceptions in which the decline in the low-income strata and the growth of the middle-income strata have not been substantial. For example, around 2017, only in Brazil, Chile, Costa Rica, Panama, Paraguay, Peru and Uruguay (urban areas) did less than half the population belong to low-income strata (see figure I.8). In El Salvador, Guatemala, Honduras, Mexico and Nicaragua, more than 70% of the population live in households with per capita income

---

[19]　Because analysis is based exclusively on income, it is impossible here to assess the lower probability of moving up to higher income strata in terms of social permeability/ impermeability or social closures, which are included in more traditional studies of social classes and social mobility (see Reygadas, 2008).

below 1.8 times the poverty line, which ECLAC considers to be the minimum value for reducing the risk of sliding into poverty as a result of economic shocks such as job losses. Furthermore, between 2002 and 2017, there were no significant changes —or very slight improvements— in El Salvador, Guatemala, Honduras, Mexico and the Dominican Republic. The situation worsened in El Salvador and the Dominican Republic in 2008, resulting in a return to pre-2002 socioeconomic conditions for the population. However, the other countries had recorded an improvement, albeit moderate, between 2002 and 2008, meaning that the current situation is a step backwards in terms of individual and household economic conditions (see annex tables I.A1.2 and I.AI.3).

Table I.1
Latin America (18 countries): threshold values of per capita income strata and changes in distribution of strata between 2002 and 2017[a]
(Poverty lines, constant dollars at 2018 prices, percentages and percentage points)

Strata	Threshold values for per capita income		Percentage distribution			Cumulative percentage point variation			Cumulative percentage rate of variation		
	Multiples of poverty line (PL)	In constant dollars at 2018 prices[b]	2002	2008	2017	2002–2008	2008–2017	2002–2017	2002–2008	2008–2017	2002–2017
High-income	**> 10 PL**	**> 1 095.8**	**2.2**	**2.6**	**3.0**	**0.4**	**0.4**	**0.8**	**19.5**	**15.9**	**38.5**
Total middle	**1.8–10 PL**	**197.2–1 095.8**	**26.9**	**36.6**	**41.1**	**9.7**	**4.4**	**14.1**	**36.1**	**12.1**	**52.5**
Upper-middle	>6 – 10 PL	>657.5–1 095.8	3.1	3.9	4.5	0.8	0.6	1.4	27.2	14.7	45.9
Intermediate-middle	>3 – 6 PL	>328.7–657.5	9.5	13.4	15.7	3.9	2.3	6.2	41.1	16.8	64.9
Lower-middle	1.8 – 3 PL	197.2–328.7	14.4	19.3	20.9	5.0	1.6	6.6	34.6	8.3	45.8
Total low-income	**0 – <1.8 PL**	**0 – < 197.2**	**70.9**	**60.8**	**55.9**	**-10.1**	**-4.9**	**-15.0**	**-14.3**	**-8.0**	**-21.1**
Low-income non-poor	1 – <1.8 PL	109.6 – <197.2	25.5	27.2	25.8	1.7	-1.4	0.3	6.6	-5.3	1.0
Non-extreme poverty	1 EPL – <1 PL	51.2 – <109.6	33.2	24.4	19.6	-8.8	-4.8	-13.6	-26.4	-19.7	-40.9
Extreme poverty	<1 EPL	<51.2	12.2	9.1	10.5	-3.1	1.4	-1.7	-25.1	15.4	-13.6

Source: Economic Commission for Latin America and the Caribbean (ECLAC), on the basis of Household Survey Data Bank (BADEHOG).
Note: PL: poverty line; EPL: extreme poverty line.
[a] The countries included are: Argentina, Bolivarian Republic of Venezuela, Brazil, Chile, Colombia, Costa Rica, the Dominican Republic, Ecuador, El Salvador, Guatemala, Honduras, Mexico, Nicaragua, Panama, Paraguay, Peru, Plurinational State of Bolivia and Uruguay.
[b] Weighted averages. The values do not include the Bolivarian Republic of Venezuela owing to the lack of updated information on variations in the consumer price index and the exchange rate.

Figure I.8
Latin America (18 countries): population by per capita income strata, around 2017[a]
(Percentages)

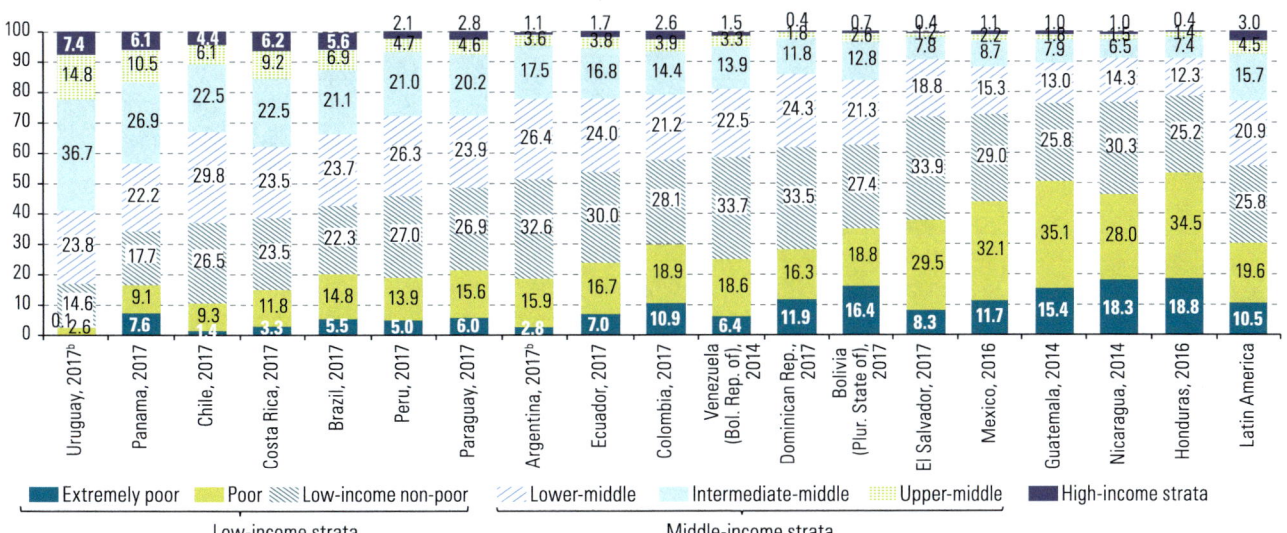

Source: Economic Commission for Latin America and the Caribbean (ECLAC), on the basis of Household Survey Data Bank (BADEHOG).
[a] Countries are ranked by the distribution of middle strata in the population, from highest to lowest.
[b] Urban areas.

(b) Increased consumption capacity

One of the prevailing views in global and regional economic discourse is that the middle class is a driver of the economy, an argument that has been sometimes used to strengthen social protection systems for the middle class, and on other occasions, to avoid measures that could affect middle-class consumption capacity. From an economic perspective, middle strata —and, to a lesser extent, lower-income strata— are consumers whose demand patterns tend to focus primarily on products that are produced and/or sold in the national market (for example, non-tradables such as housing), which is a key behavioural pattern when there is a need to boost a country's economy through consumption. The increased consumption capacities that emerging middle sectors acquire can open access to public and private services such as education and health, among others, as well as reproduce and improve their intergenerational socioeconomic position and resilience to adverse economic conditions. However, if this capacity is not real, or deteriorates over time, it can generate feelings of frustration and disrupt existing electoral trends in the region's democracies.

In Latin America, the significant increase in the size of middle-income strata has also led to higher average per capita income for large sectors of the population and, therefore, greater consumption capacities. The existence of middle-income strata comprising individuals with relatively stable income fosters the use of banking services by these sectors of the population. In consumerist societies, the acquisition of new goods and services that not only improve living standards and quality of life but are also, in some cases, positional in nature (symbols of status or economic success), a level monetary comfort and access to credit —and the consequent disincentive to savings— can sometimes encourage consumption that is unsustainable in the long term. Such consumption is often the result of poor financial education or loss of income sources, culminating in over-indebtedness and subsequent loss of the acquired goods.

Household surveys for 17 countries in the region show that in the early 2000s, the middle-income strata accounted for 49.4 % of the income of all households, with an annual economic capacity of US$ 550 billion (at constant 2018 prices); that share increased to 55.3 % in 2008 and 57.7 % in 2017, representing US$ 820 billion and over US$ 1.1 trillion respectively (see figure I.9). In 2017, the lower-middle stratum accounted for 51 % of the middle class, with an absolute consumption capacity of US$ 375 billion annually, which is equivalent to slightly more than 32 % of the total volume of resources of all middle-income strata. The intermediate-middle stratum accounted for 38.2 % of the middle class, with a consumption capacity of 44 %, equal to US$ 511 billion annually, while the upper-middle stratum, which only made up 11 % of middle-income groups, concentrated a consumption capacity of 23.6 % (close to US$ 274 billion).[20]

In terms of growth in the total volume of income, while the consumption capacities of the lower strata only expanded at an annual rate of 1.2 % (19 % cumulative growth between 2002 and 2018),[21] the middle strata grew at an annual clip of 5.1 % (111 % cumulative growth), and the high-income strata at an annual rate of 4.5 % (93 % cumulative growth). Importantly, the annual growth rates in income of the middle-income and high-income strata had picked up between 2002 and 2008 (6.9 % and 4.7 % respectively). A breakdown by country for 2017 is given in annex I.A1.4.

---

[20] Figures come from household surveys and may therefore differ from estimates in systems of national accounts (see table I.C4 for country figures).

[21] There is a high correlation between low income growth in the lower strata and the graduation of a significant proportion of households from these strata to the middle sectors. Since this is not a longitudinal study with panel samples, figures for income growth per stratum must be taken with caution: they illustrate potential consumption capacities and not necessarily the extent of the improvement of living conditions within strata.

Figure I.9
Latin America (17 countries): share and volume of annual income by strata of per capita income, around 2002, 2008 and 2017[a]
(Percentages and billions of constant dollars at 2018 prices)

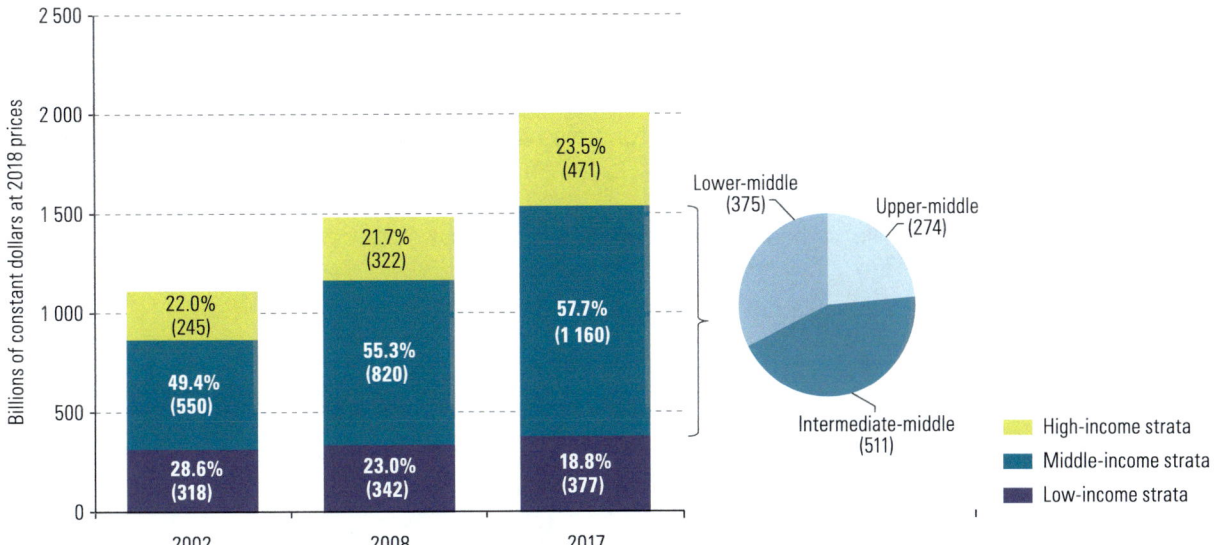

Source: Economic Commission for Latin America and the Caribbean (ECLAC), on the basis of Household Survey Data Bank (BADEHOG).
[a] The countries included are: Argentina, Brazil, Chile, Colombia, Costa Rica, the Dominican Republic, Ecuador, El Salvador, Guatemala, Honduras, Mexico, Nicaragua, Panama, Paraguay, Peru, the Plurinational State of Bolivia and Uruguay. The Bolivarian Republic of Venezuela is not included owing to a lack of data for currency conversion.

The question of the sustainability of the middle-class consumption in the medium and long term thus arises, not only because of the high levels of indebtedness of middle-income families (which means that a significant portion of their income is spent on debt repayment) but also because of the weakness of social protection systems. Families in the middle-income strata thus remain vulnerable to a marked deterioration in quality of life that may result from adverse economic conditions or other negative situations. The low-income non-poor and lower-middle strata still make up more than 46% of the population, with a high risk of falling into poverty as a result of unemployment or precarious working conditions, catastrophic illness, accidents or natural disasters. Therefore, the negative impact on developing economies of low economic growth, the myriad signs of profound changes in the labour market caused by automation and the ever more visible consequences of the climate crisis have made it necessary to design public policy responses and social protection systems that help to safeguard the purchasing power of the Latin American population and provide sufficient tools for adapting to future labour, economic and environmental scenarios.

2. The importance of education and employment in socioeconomic status

The rung which the vast majority of Latin American households occupy on the socioeconomic ladder is determined by the participation of one or more family members in the labour market. Although households may have multiple sources of income, labour income is central: in all the strata included in this study it accounts for a constant share of total income (between 64% and 68%), with the exception of extremely poor households, where labour income represents just under half (47%) of total income. Among households living in extreme poverty, the lower weight of labour income is associated with its low levels and the greater relative importance of income from public and private transfers and remittances from abroad (together equivalent to almost a third of the total). This is also true for households in poverty (16% of the total). In the low-income non-poor stratum, transfers represent a smaller proportion and pensions are beginning to play a greater role in addition to labour income. In middle- and high-income households, the share of pensions in total income increases (17% of the total) while that of transfers and other non-autonomous sources of income decreases. Capital income (such as profit sharing and property income) accounts for a significant share only in upper-middle-strata and upper-sector households (see figure I.10). However, labour and pension income account for the lion's share of income in the vast majority of households, especially among the middle and upper classes, which attests to the importance of employment and the quality thereof in the socioeconomic position of households and the individuals who belong to them.

Figure I.10

Latin America (18 countries): composition of household income by source and average per capita income, by socioeconomic stratum, around 2017[a][b]

A. Composition of income
(percentages)

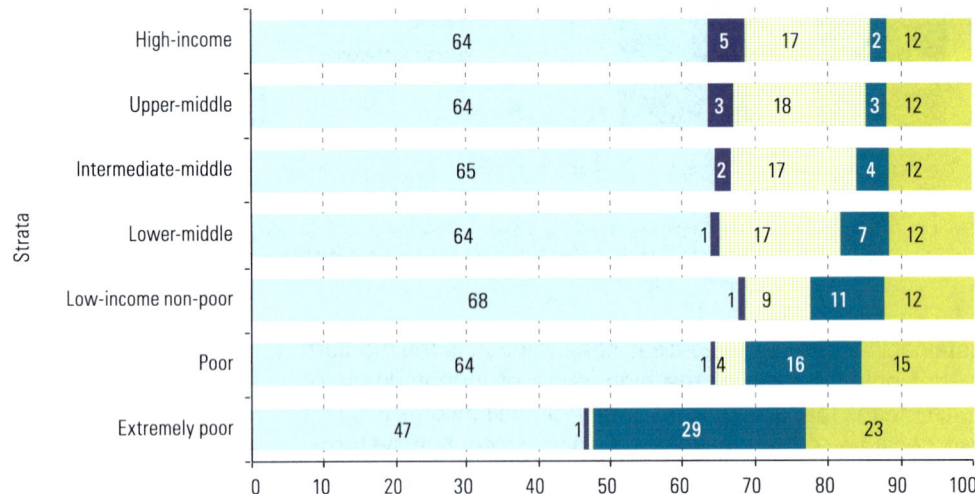

B. Average per capita income by source
(constant dollars at 2018 prices)

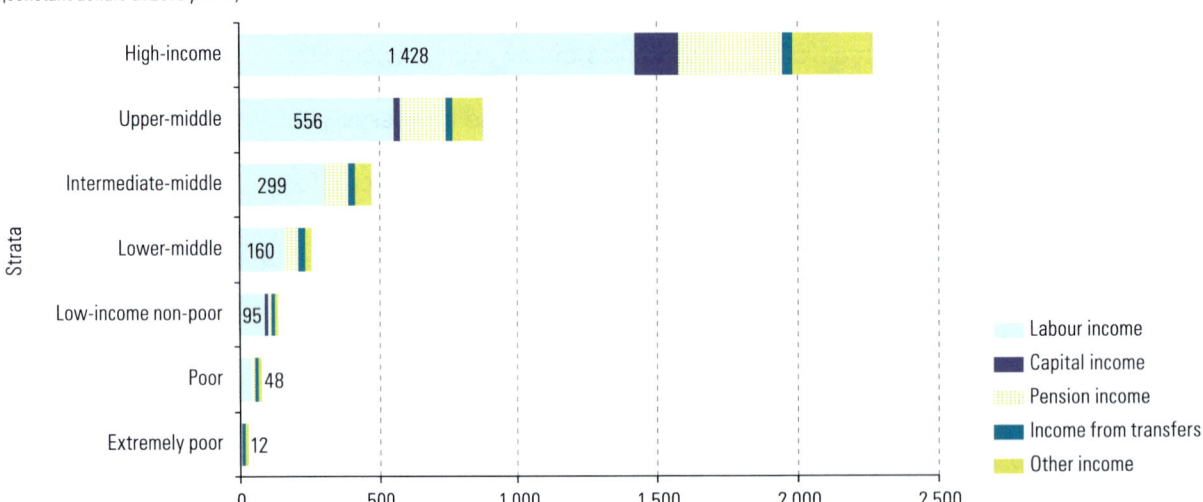

Source: Economic Commission for Latin America and the Caribbean (ECLAC), on the basis of Household Survey Data Bank (BADEHOG).

[a] The countries included are: Argentina, Bolivarian Republic of Venezuela, Brazil, Chile, Colombia, Costa Rica, the Dominican Republic, Ecuador, El Salvador, Guatemala, Honduras, Mexico, Nicaragua, Panama, Paraguay, Peru, Plurinational State of Bolivia and Uruguay. Data for the Bolivarian Republic of Venezuela is not included in figure B owing to a lack of data for currency conversion.

[b] Figures may differ from those published in previous versions of the *Social Panorama of Latin America* due to recent changes in poverty measurement methods. Previous versions included, among other things, the adjustment of labour incomes and pensions to aggregates estimated from systems of national accounts. Labour incomes include wages, income earned from self-employment and other labour income; capital income refers to monthly withdrawals or distribution of profits and property income; pension income refers to payments from contributory and non-contributory pensions (where it is impossible to fully distinguish between the two) and retirement benefits; income from transfers refers to public and private transfers (such as remittances from abroad); and other income includes income that does not fall into any of the other categories and imputed rent received by homeowners.

Undoubtedly, the characteristics of labour market participation are determined by the economic cycle, the functioning of the labour market (extent of informality and labour regulation, and the level of the minimum wage and its coverage, among other factors), level of education, associated with the demand for certain types of qualifications, and factors such as gender, ethnic and racial origin and territorial characteristics (of local economies), networks of contacts and cultural capital. These factors are addressed in section 3 of this chapter.

(a) Education as a necessary, but insufficient, condition of improving entry to the labour market

A more educated workforce should bring with it a greater share of knowledge-related jobs in the economy, although this also depends on the characteristics of the production system and the consequent demand for skilled labour. In a labour market that calls for specialization, a higher education level has a positive impact on the probability of obtaining a job entailing more complex tasks and requiring a high level of qualification, and a negative impact on the probability of being unemployed or of having access only to jobs involving manual and non-manual routine or low-skilled tasks. Education provides an even greater advantage for workers who have gone on to tertiary level compared with those who have completed secondary education, the latter being basic requirement for any chance of escaping poverty in the region (ECLAC/OIJ, 2004).

Of the factors usually included in wage level analyses, the level of education is the most important determinant of labour income in most countries (without disregarding the influence of factors such as occupational segmentation and discrimination based on gender, race and ethnicity and territory). However, the strength of this correlation also differs significantly across countries and sectors of the economy. There are also significant differences in the wages earned by workers with more experience and technical knowledge. How much labour markets reward education and experience is determined by the relative conditions of supply and demand (Carlson, 2001).

As previous editions of the *Social Panorama* have shown, Latin America has made significant progress in education in recent years, with increases in coverage and completion rates and a reduction in school dropout rates and the educational lag. Primary education is now virtually universal, and there is widespread access to secondary education. However, many challenges remain in the area of secondary school completion. Around 2016, only 59.5% of young people between 20 and 24 years of age had completed secondary school, and substantial socioeconomic inequalities in this respect remained: while 83.5% of young people belonging to the fifth income quintile had completed secondary school, the figure was only 35.4% among young people from the first quintile. In addition, access to both technical-vocational and university education continues to be insufficient and stratified; the quality of education, especially in compulsory schooling, is also insufficient (ECLAC, 2019).

Analysis of educational attainment by income strata reveals that there have been significant but insufficient reductions in the difficulty of access and dropout rates in primary and secondary education, especially in the lower strata. According to 2017 data, one third of the population aged 25 and over belonging to the lower-income sector did not complete primary education, which clearly represents a significant drop from the 45% observed for 2002 (see figure I.11). However, when the percentage of that population that did not complete secondary education is added, it becomes evident that close to 75% of this population group have low levels of educational attainment; this is compounded by the fact that only 8.5% of individuals in this age group have undertaken post-secondary studies. By contrast, by the early 2000s, the percentage of individuals in the upper-income brackets who had completed post-secondary education was as high as 65 %, reaching around 70 % by 2017; over the same period, the share of individuals who had completed university education increased by 6 percentage points (from 40.4 % to 46.2 %). However, a significant percentage of this segment (18%) has not completed secondary education, although this is much lower than in other strata.

Figure I.11
Latin America (18 countries): level of education attained by population aged 25 and over, by strata of per capita income, around 2002, 2008 and 2017[a]
(Percentages)

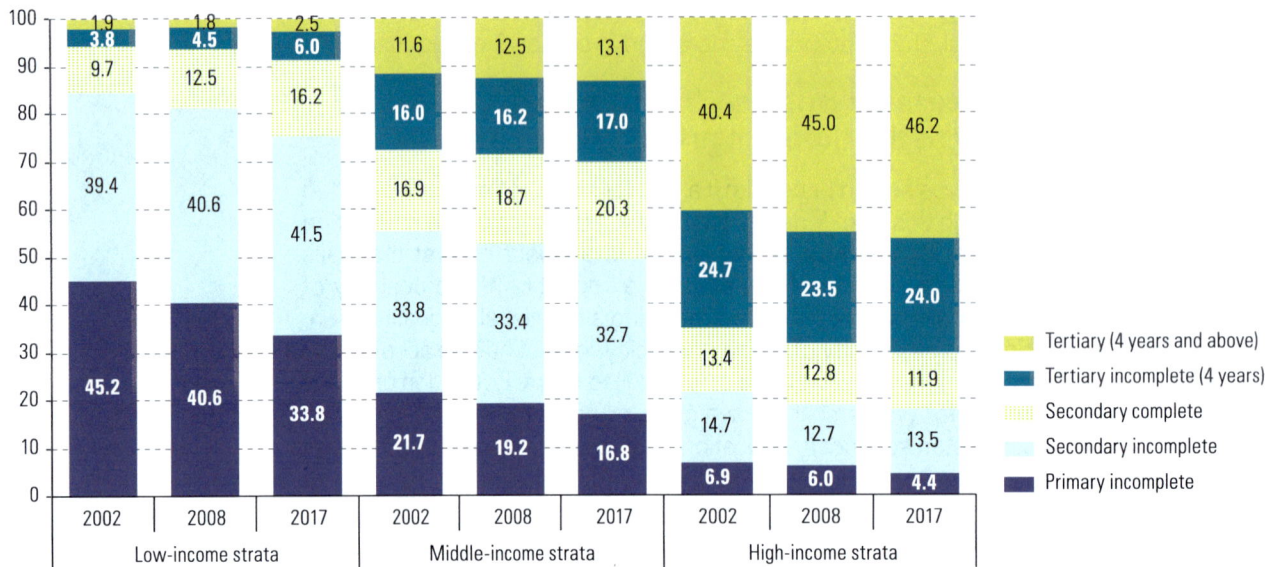

Source: Economic Commission for Latin America and the Caribbean (ECLAC), on the basis of Household Survey Data Bank (BADEHOG).
[a] The countries included are: Argentina, Bolivarian Republic of Venezuela, Brazil, Chile, Colombia, Costa Rica, the Dominican Republic, Ecuador, El Salvador, Guatemala, Honduras, Mexico, Nicaragua, Panama, Paraguay, Peru, Plurinational State of Bolivia and Uruguay.

Figure I.11 shows that progress has been slower in relative terms in the middle class, and concentrated mainly in primary and secondary education: the proportion of individuals with post-secondary education rose from 27.6% in 2002 to 30.1% in 2017, while the share of those with incomplete primary and secondary education [based on figure] fell from 55.5% to 49.5%, which is still very high. This is owed, to a certain extent, to the fact that the rise in income occurred mainly in the lower strata of the middle class (lower-middle and intermediate-middle strata), which saw the inclusion of a group people with lower levels of education, but with higher incomes than in the early 2000s.

Although education is a relatively good predictor of wages, it is less so for overall labour income, since the dynamics of wages for other categories of work, such as employers or own-account workers, rely much more heavily on economic growth. Likewise, while more schooling helps workers to enter the labour market in higher quality jobs, there are significant variations in the level of education within the same type of entry (combination of occupational group, occupational category and company size). Thus, the average number of years of schooling among individuals describing themselves as employers (of microenterprises or larger enterprises) varies considerably, as does that of employees in small, medium and large enterprises. Surprisingly, there are fewer dispersions in the number of years of study of own-account workers, although educational levels are clearly higher among own-account workers describing themselves as professionals. Along with the latter, public sector employees have the highest average level of education, with relatively small differentials between strata. Lastly, domestic workers have the lowest average level of education and the smallest differentials, regardless of the socioeconomic stratum to which their families belong (see figure I.12).

The above offers some —albeit inconclusive— evidence that education operates not so much as a differentiating factor between occupational categories (employees, own-account workers and employers), but rather within each occupational category to explain differences in labour income, as will be seen below.

Figure I.12
Latin America (18 countries): average schooling by type of entry into the labour market and socioeconomic status, around 2017[a]
(Number of years)

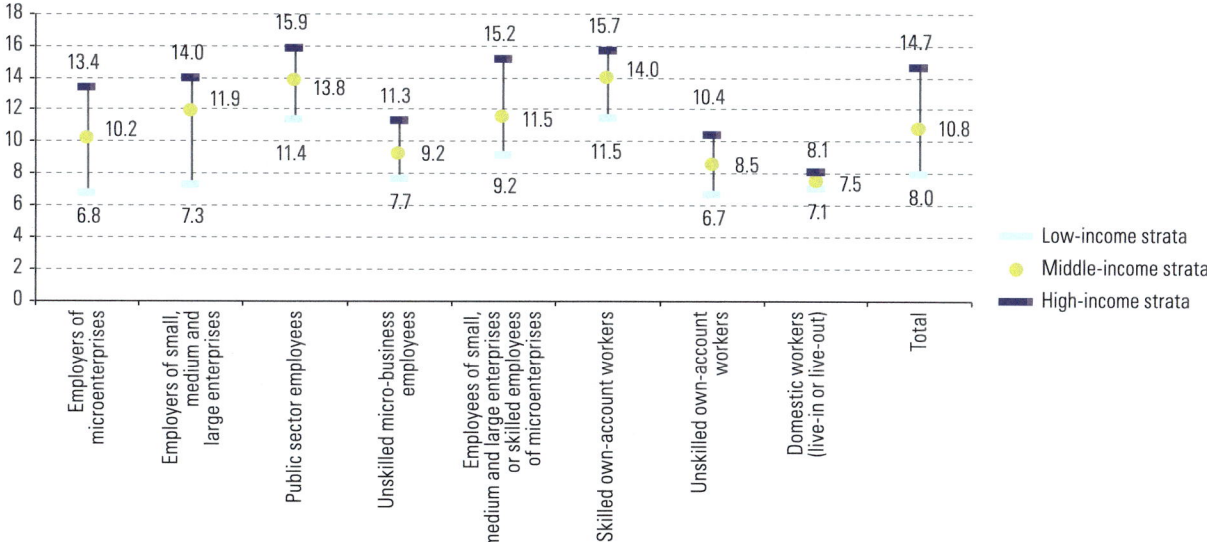

Source: Economic Commission for Latin America and the Caribbean (ECLAC), on the basis of Household Survey Data Bank (BADEHOG).
[a] The countries included are: Argentina, Bolivarian Republic of Venezuela, Brazil, Chile, Colombia, Costa Rica, the Dominican Republic, Ecuador, El Salvador, Guatemala, Honduras, Mexico, Nicaragua, Panama, Paraguay, Peru, Plurinational State of Bolivia and Uruguay.

(b) The importance of employment in socioeconomic status

The boundaries between occupational groups have been blurred as a result of the many changes in the labour market (decline in the agricultural population, the introduction of new technologies and automation, new organization of production units and chains, the increase in women's labour market participation and the expansion of the service sector, among others). In the traditional approaches to social stratification, manual labour was considered to correspond to the lowest-income class; however, some types of manual labour have raised qualification requirements and workers can actually climb the social ladder, for example, when they have a higher level of education. Naturally, trends are mixed depending on the size of the production unit,[22] and this is especially evident among employers (Marinho and Quiroz, 2018).

At the same time, more traditional studies on social stratification focused primarily on occupation, examining the employment status of the head of household; this classification was then extended to include the other members of the household based on the concept of the breadwinner. The changes mentioned above, in particular the increase in women's participation in the labour market, together with population ageing, have complicated this analysis. This is because of the presence of several income earners in the household, as well as the presence of pensioners, who are either heads of household or parents of the head of household, in a significant proportion of households. These changes can be seen in the decreasing prevalence of the head of household as the principal recipient of labour income in the household: according to information from 17 countries, in 2017 the primary wage earners were heads of household in 65.5% of cases, spouses in 14.6% of cases, sons or daughters of the head of household in 15% of cases, and other relatives or non-relatives of the head of household in just under 5%. The employment category of all employed persons is thus

---

[22] Unfortunately, in conducting a comparative analysis based on household surveys, the only way to establish a classification by the size of the enterprise or production unit in to which workers belong is to distinguish between employees of enterprises with five or fewer workers and those employed in larger production units (this is the only distinction common to all instruments).

analysed below (see figure I.13), but the occupational situation of the main breadwinner and that of other income earners is highlighted if significant differences are observed.

- The most common type of employment among employed persons in the low-income strata is self-employment or unskilled own-account work (36.2% of employed persons in these strata). However, employees of small, medium and large enterprises or skilled employees of microenterprises (33.6%) tend to be the main wage earners in these strata.

- Although there are employers in all strata, the highest proportion is observed in the high-income strata (where they account for 15.9% of the employed and 18.4% of breadwinners). In the low-income and middle strata, slightly less than 4% of employed persons are microenterprise employers.

- In the low-income and middle strata, around 50% of employed heads of household are private sector wage earners, and in the high-income strata this percentage drops to 38%. There is a greater concentration of unskilled micro-business employees in the low-income strata: from 18.5%, this figure falls to 9.8% in the middle sectors and 1.5% in the high-income strata. The trend is similar among the principal wage earners, but at lower levels (except in the low-income strata), and is systematically more pronounced among the other wage earners.

- Public employees make up a proportionally higher share of employed persons in the high-income strata (almost 26%); this percentage drops to 14.5% in the middle strata and only 5.6% in the low-income strata. They account for an even higher share among primary wage earners (approximately 29%, 17% and 7%, respectively).

- In the high-income strata, just over 10% of employed persons are skilled own-account workers (this proportion is even higher among employed persons who are not the primary wage earners). These percentages are much lower in the middle and low-income strata.

- Conversely, paid domestic work is concentrated mainly in the low-income sectors (where it accounts for 5.9% of employed persons —primarily women— and 8.5% of other household wage earners). These percentages are also relatively significant in the middle strata (3.9% and 5.7% respectively).

The above illustrates that when socioeconomic stratification in Latin America is analysed on the basis of income, it becomes evident that types of employment are not exclusive to specific strata, but rather some of them are more prevalent in different strata depending on the income they generate and they determine a household's position on the socioeconomic ladder. Thus, a specific type of employment —employer, employee or own-account worker, employee in micro-business or larger production unit, skilled or unskilled— is not the sole determining factor of socioeconomic status.

Nevertheless, it is true that certain types of employment tend to be more typical of certain strata: unskilled own-account and private sector employees (regardless of enterprise size) in the low-income strata (in that order); unskilled private sector employees in small, medium and large enterprises, skilled employees in microenterprises, and unskilled own-account and public-sector employees in the middle-income strata; and private sector employees in small, medium or large enterprises, skilled micro-business employees, public servants and skilled own-account workers in the high-income strata.

Figure I.13

Latin America (17 countries): type of labour market participation of employed persons aged 15 and over, by socioeconomic strata, around 2017[a]

(Percentages of the employed population of each stratum)

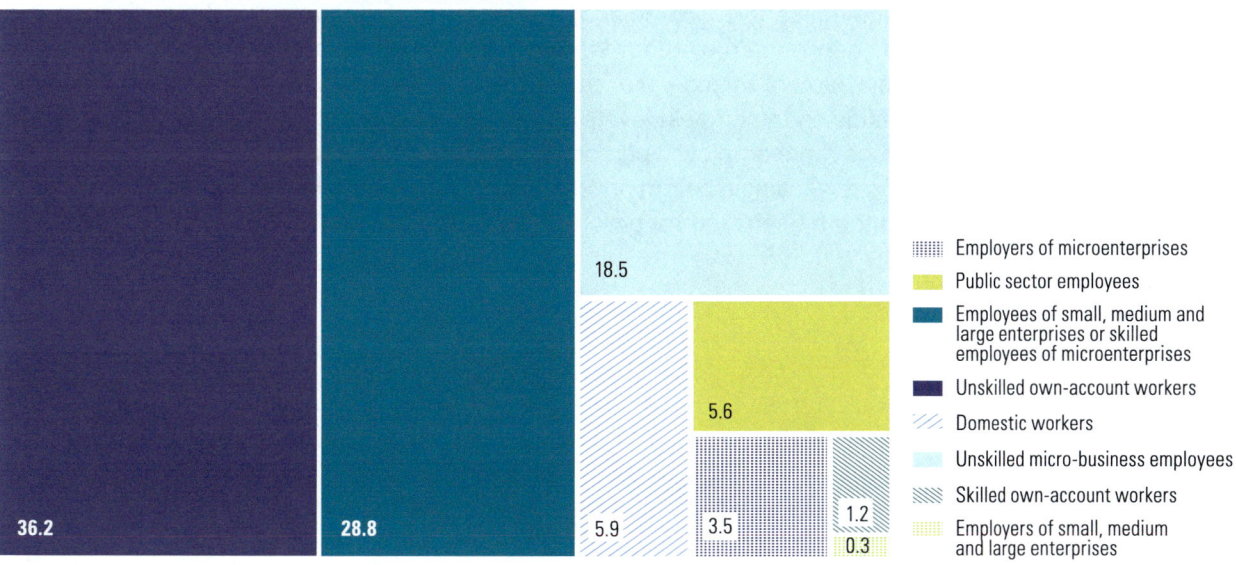

Source: Economic Commission for Latin America and the Caribbean (ECLAC), on the basis of Household Survey Data Bank (BADEHOG).

[a] The countries included are: Argentina, the Bolivarian Republic of Venezuela, Brazil, Chile, Colombia, Costa Rica, the Dominican Republic, Ecuador, El Salvador, Guatemala, Honduras, Mexico, Panama, Paraguay, Peru, the Plurinational State of Bolivia and Uruguay. Data for Nicaragua are not included because the categories of labour market participation cannot be reproduced.

(c) Labour income and the number of workers in households

For a given type of employment, there is a wide dispersion in terms of the financial remuneration received, both between and within strata. This explains the relatively low differentiation that exists between types of employment by stratum, since stratification is also determined by other factors such as family structure, the number of employed persons in the household, the number and type of dependents, and access to additional sources of income.

One way of illustrating the differences in labour income within socioeconomic strata is to compare the income received by the primary wage earner with that of any other wage earners in the household. Figure I.14 illustrates this counterpoint: even when comparison does not apply within a household, it is clear that, regardless of the socioeconomic stratum and the type of employment, the average labour income of the primary wage earner is systematically much higher than the average labour income of any additional wage earners.[23] Differences that are relatively recurrent depending on the type of employment, and which are more marked among primary wage earners, can also be observed: on average in Latin America, employers in small, medium or large enterprises have the highest monthly labour income (except in the low-income strata); by comparison, skilled own-account workers earn 46% of the wages earned by employers; public sector employees earn 44%; micro-entrepreneurs earn 33%; unskilled private sector employees (or skilled micro-business employees) earn less than 30%; and workers in other types of employment (unskilled micro-business employees, unskilled own-account workers and domestic workers) earn less than 16%. The differentials are substantially smaller in the low-income strata. However, within households and or the same type of employment, there is a trend towards a narrowing of the gap between primary wage earners and other earners (in favour of the latter) in the middle strata.

As mentioned above, the effect of the income of each employed person on the per capita household income and, therefore, on the position on the socioeconomic ladder is determined by other factors, some of which are presented in figure I.15. The main factors include the size, structure and composition of the household: households on the highest levels of the socioeconomic ladder are smaller and have on average more employed persons (see figure I.15A); the higher the socioeconomic level, the fewer single-parent households (primarily female-headed households) there are and the higher the proportion of single-person households (see figure I.15B).

---

[23]   By definition, this applies to households with two or more wage earners, and the comparison would be redundant if all individuals in households with two or more wage earners had the same type of employment. However, for the purposes of this study, the comparison between primary wage earners and other wage earners by type of employment and income strata applies to categories of employed persons and not households.

Figure I.14
Latin America (16 countries): average monthly labour income of the primary wage earner and other wage earners, by type of employment and per capita income strata, around 2017[a][b]
(Constant dollars at 2018 prices)

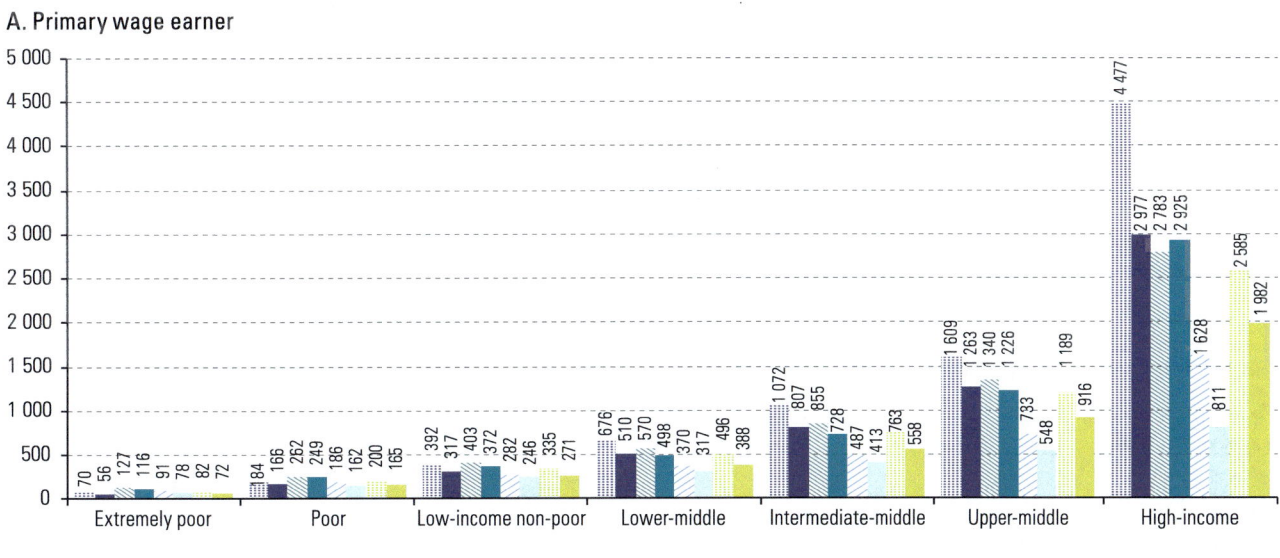

A. Primary wage earner

B. Other wage earners

Legend:
- Employers of small, medium and large enterprises
- Employers of microenterprises
- Public sector employees
- Employees of small, medium and large enterprises or skilled employees of microenterprises
- Unskilled micro-business employees
- Domestic workers
- Skilled own-account workers
- Unskilled own-account workers

Source: Economic Commission for Latin America and the Caribbean (ECLAC), on the basis of Household Survey Data Bank (BADEHOG).

[a] The countries included are: Argentina, Brazil, Chile, Colombia, Costa Rica, the Dominican Republic, Ecuador, El Salvador, Guatemala, Honduras, Mexico, Panama, Paraguay, Peru, the Plurinational State of Bolivia and Uruguay. Data for Nicaragua are not included because the categories of labour market participation cannot be reproduced; data for the Bolivarian Republic of Venezuela are not included owing to the lack of information needed for currency conversion.

[b] The types of employment are ordered by major occupational categories (employers, employees and own-account workers) and then in descending order according to the average labour income of the household's primary wage earner. Figure A shows the average labour income of the employed person earning the highest wage in the household, and figure B shows the average income of each additional wage earner. It should be noted that a significant proportion of households have only one wage earner.

These characteristics point to a gradual drop in dependency ratios (expressed as number of employed persons in the household: total number of household members). In the low-income strata, households in extreme poverty have an average ratio that is lower than 1:4; this ratio approaches 1:3 in households in poverty and increases to just over 2:5 in low-income non-poor households. In the middle segment, the lower-middle stratum registers a dependency ratio of 1:2, which rises to 3:5 in the intermediate-middle stratum and slightly higher in the upper-middle stratum. In the high-income strata, the ratio between employed persons and the total number of household members is 2:3. Furthermore, it should be borne in mind that more than 30% of these households are single-person and less than 15% of them are single-parent. However, these are not the ones with the highest average number of wage earners —it is precisely in middle class households that, on average, the most household members are mobilized to participate in the labour market.

Figure I.15
Latin America (18 countries): average household size, average number of wage earners per household and percentage of single-parent and single-person households, by per capita income strata, around 2017[a]

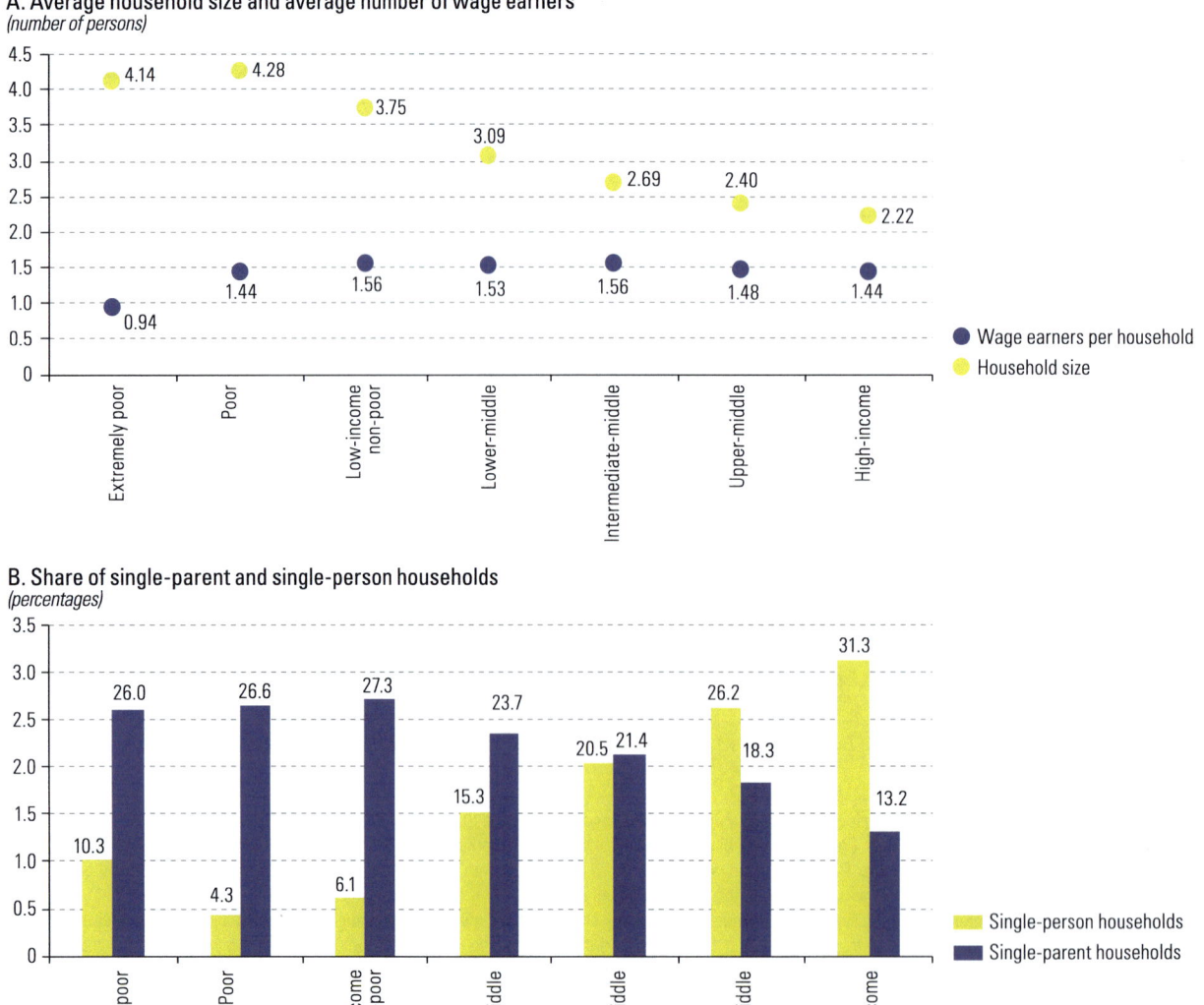

A. Average household size and average number of wage earners
(number of persons)

B. Share of single-parent and single-person households
(percentages)

Source: Economic Commission for Latin America and the Caribbean (ECLAC), on the basis of Household Survey Data Bank (BADEHOG).
[a] The countries included are: Argentina, Bolivarian Republic of Venezuela, Brazil, Chile, Colombia, Costa Rica, the Dominican Republic, Ecuador, El Salvador, Guatemala, Honduras, Mexico, Nicaragua, Panama, Paraguay, Peru, Plurinational State of Bolivia and Uruguay.

To sum up, assuming that the type of occupation and associated labour income are the same, a household with more wage earners, and that is smaller in size and has fewer dependent members (in this case, members who are not in employment) is more likely to be located in higher socioeconomic strata than those that do not have those characteristics.

3. Intersecting inequalities

Latin America's social inequality matrix is heavily conditioned by its production systems, which are characterized in turn by great structural heterogeneity and a culture of privilege. For ECLAC, the multiple causes and characteristics of social inequality and the mechanisms that perpetuate it can be conceived as a "social inequality matrix", consisting of various factors that structure inequality and its multiple expressions.

The first and most basic determinant of inequality is social class (or, simply, socioeconomic stratum). Nonetheless, gender, racial, ethnic and territorial inequalities and those connected to the different stages of the life cycle are also axes of this matrix and crucial determinants of the size and reproduction of the gaps identified in some of the main areas of social development and the exercise of rights, such as income levels and access to production resources, education, health care, decent work, social protection and opportunities for participation, among others (ECLAC, 2016b).

The axes structuring the social inequality matrix intersect, reinforcing and linking up with one another throughout the life cycle and giving rise to a multiplicity of inequality or discrimination factors that operate simultaneously or cumulatively over time. The confluence of multiple types of inequality characterizes the "hard cores" of poverty, vulnerability and social exclusion, entrenching and reproducing them (ECLAC, 2016b). It also facilitates the reproduction of other socioeconomic positions and makes upward mobility more difficult, especially into higher social classes. Social class crystallizes the link between these factors and all the inequalities they produce.

This section seeks to illustrate with empirical evidence the intersection between the different structural axes of social inequality, each of which acts as a differentiating factor, if not a discriminating factor, beyond the capacities and potentialities of each individual. The intertwining of these axes therefore reinforces and multiplies inequality throughout individual and family history, allowing it to be perpetuated from one generation to the next.

Naturally, the simplification of class structure and relationships on the basis of income does not fully reflect the crystallization of inequalities and differences, which shape this phenomenon. By contrast, stratification on the basis of income shows how these factors are related, particularly the other structural axes of inequality.

Figure I.16 shows the relationship between socioeconomic strata and each of the main structural axes of social inequality in Latin America: inequalities on the basis of gender, ethnicity, race, geographic location and life cycle. The life cycle is represented by the age structures within the different strata. The shapes of the population pyramids are very different: the low-income strata reflect a structure similar to that of a population in full demographic transition, in which young people account for the largest share of the population, but with a narrowing of the base (smaller proportion of children); the middle-income strata reflect a relatively old demographic structure, in spite of the predominance of the relatively young population of working age; meanwhile, the structure corresponding to the high-income strata is more stable and fairly old, although there are also unusual trends such as the predominance of the population aged 25–39 years and 50–64 years, and more women, which may all be associated with the greater prevalence of single-person households (see figure I.16A).

Figure I.16
Latin America (18 countries): relationship between socioeconomic strata and age group, geographic location, ethnicity, race, and wages earned by gender, around 2017[a]

A. Age structure, in five-year periods
(percentages)

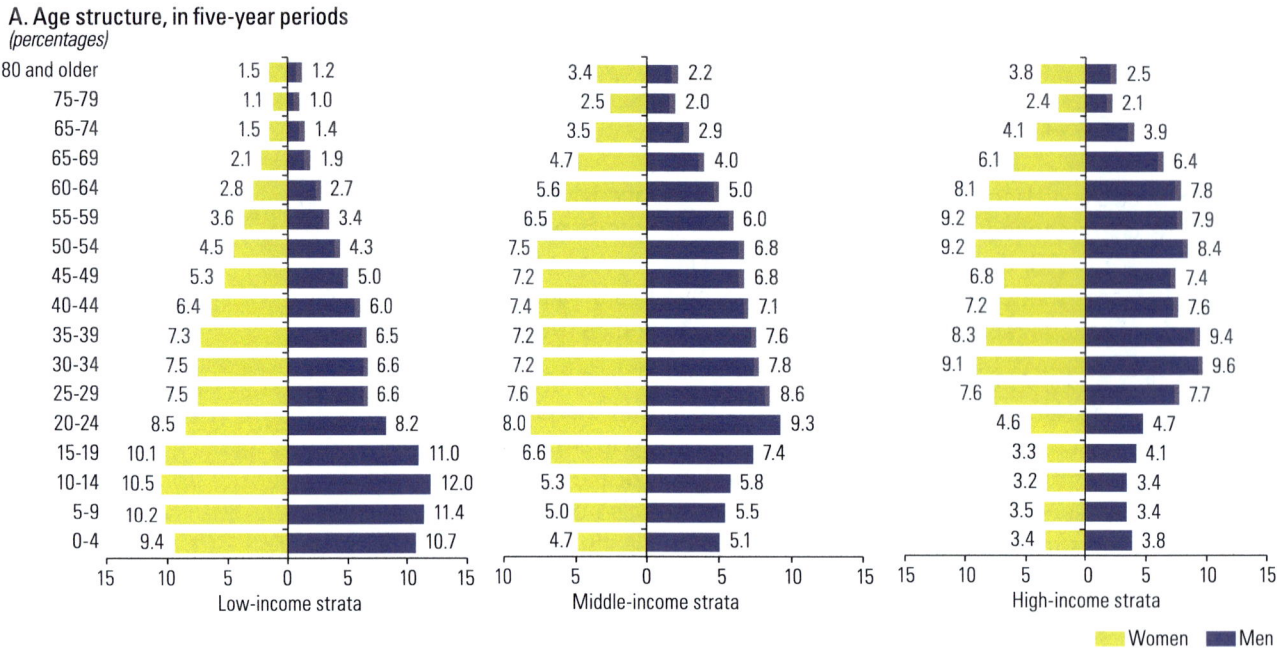

B. Stratification in urban and rural areas[b]
(percentages)

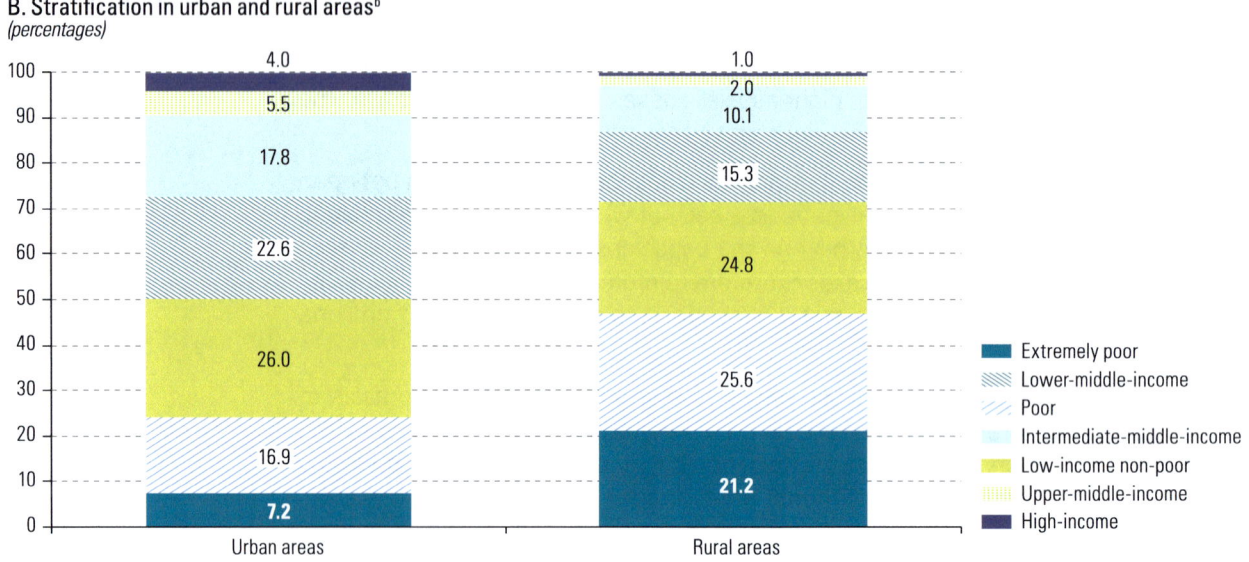

Figure I.16 (concluded)

C. Ethnicity[c]
(percentages)

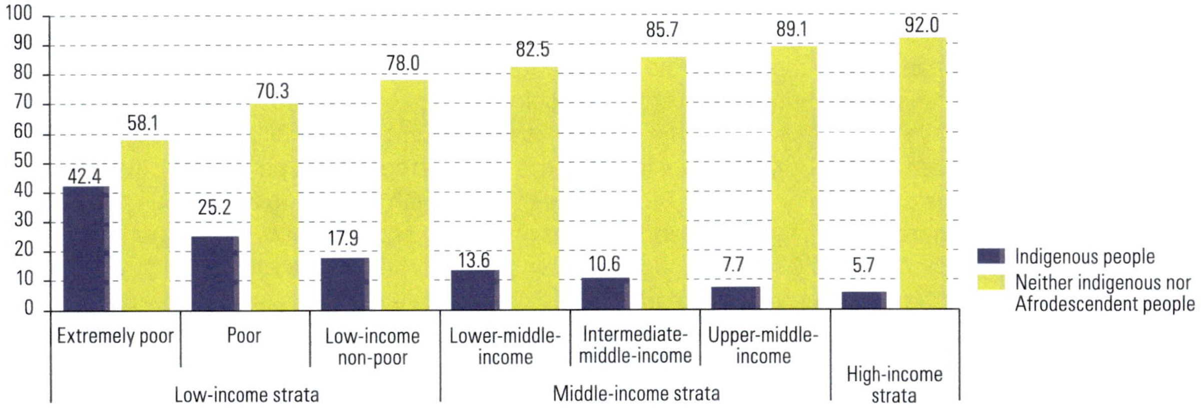

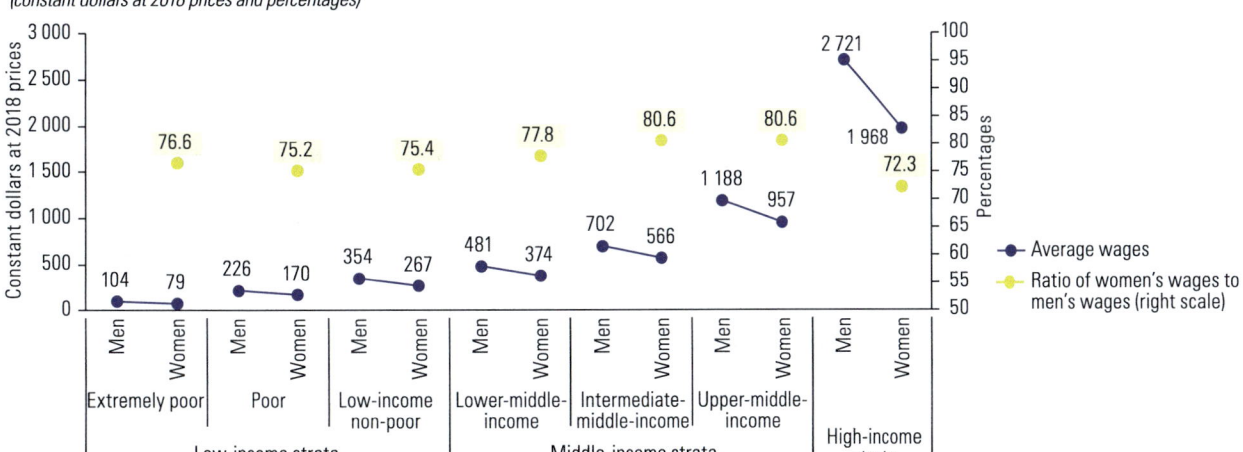

Indigenous people

Neither indigenous nor Afrodescendent people

(Chart C values by category:)
- Extremely poor: 42.4 / 58.1
- Poor: 25.2 / 70.3
- Low-income non-poor: 17.9 / 78.0
- Lower-middle-income: 13.6 / 82.5
- Intermediate-middle-income: 10.6 / 85.7
- Upper-middle-income: 7.7 / 89.1
- High-income strata: 5.7 / 92.0

Low-income strata | Middle-income strata | High-income strata

D. Race[c]
(percentages)

Afrodescendent people

Neither indigenous nor Afrodescendent people

(Chart D values by category:)
- Extremely poor: 22.7 / 48.7
- Poor: 22.5 / 59.6
- Low-income non-poor: 20.4 / 67.6
- Lower-middle-income: 18.2 / 73.8
- Intermediate-middle-income: 15.2 / 78.9
- Upper-middle-income: 12.1 / 83.9
- High-income strata: 8.6 / 88.7

Low-income strata | Middle-income strata | High-income strata

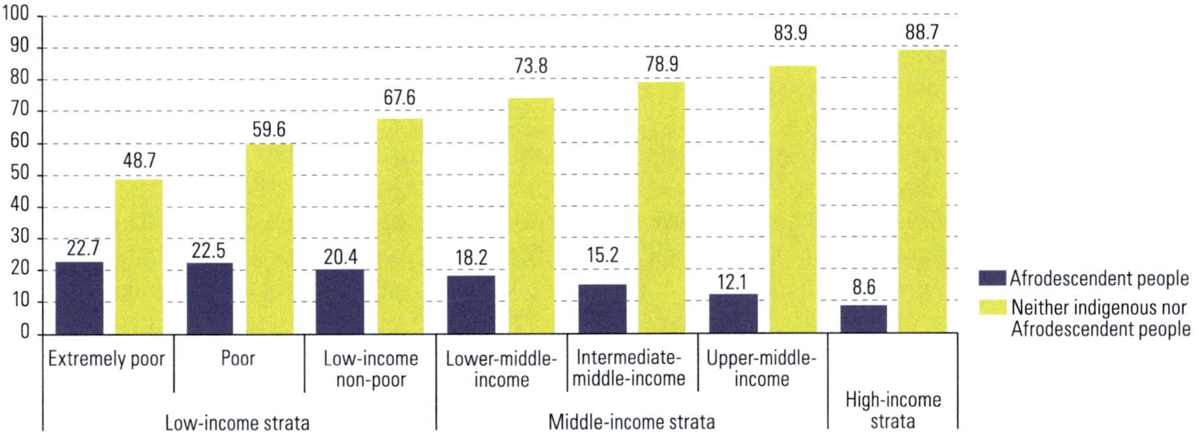

E. Monthly wages for persons aged 25–59 years working 20 hours or more per week[d]
(constant dollars at 2018 prices and percentages)

(Average wages Men/Women and Ratio of women's wages to men's wages:)
- Extremely poor: Men 104, Women 79 — 76.6
- Poor: Men 226, Women 170 — 75.2
- Low-income non-poor: Men 354, Women 267 — 75.4
- Lower-middle-income: Men 481, Women 374 — 77.8
- Intermediate-middle-income: Men 702, Women 566 — 80.6
- Upper-middle-income: Men 1 188, Women 957 — 80.6
- High-income strata: Men 2 721, Women 1 968 — 72.3

Average wages

Ratio of women's wages to men's wages (right scale)

Low-income strata | Middle-income strata | High-income strata

Source: Economic Commission for Latin America and the Caribbean (ECLAC), on the basis of Household Survey Data Bank (BADEHOG).
[a] The countries included are: Argentina, the Bolivarian Republic of Venezuela, Brazil, Chile, Colombia, Costa Rica, the Dominican Republic, Ecuador, El Salvador, Guatemala, Honduras, Mexico, Nicaragua, Panama, Paraguay, Peru, the Plurinational State of Bolivia and Uruguay.
[b] Does not include data for Argentina, the Bolivarian Republic of Venezuela or Uruguay.
[c] Simple averages. The comparison between the indigenous population and the rest of the population excludes Afrodescendants; the comparison between the Afrodescendent population and the rest of the population excludes indigenous peoples. For this reason, the sum of the bars is not equivalent to 100%. The figures on the indigenous population include data from Chile, Ecuador, Guatemala, Mexico, Nicaragua, Panama, Peru, the Plurinational State of Bolivia and Uruguay; those referring to the Afrodescendent population include data from Brazil, Ecuador, Panama, Peru and Uruguay.
[d] he Bolivarian Republic of Venezuela is not included owing to a lack of data for currency conversion.

There are also significant differences between the socioeconomic structures of urban and rural areas. In a comparison of 15 countries,[24] in urban areas the high-income strata represent 4% of the population, the upper-middle income segment accounts for 5.5% and the intermediate-middle and lower-middle income strata represent 40.4%. Meanwhile, in rural areas, the lower strata dominate (almost 72% combined), with 21.2% of this population being extremely poor, 25.6% poor and 24.8% low-income non-poor, while the high- and medium-income strata account for just 3% of the rural population (see figure I.16B). Geographic location is also related at least partly to another structural axis of inequality: ethnicity and race, especially with respect to indigenous populations. Figure I.16C, which is based on nine countries, shows that while indigenous people account for 17.6% of the population on average, they are notoriously overrepresented in the low-income strata, particularly among people living in extreme poverty, and have a comparatively small presence in the middle-income and especially the upper-middle income and high-income strata. A similar trend was reflected in five countries with respect to the Afrodescendent population (see figure I.16D).

Lastly, gender inequalities notably cut across all levels of the social structure. This is reflected in the wage gap between men and women wage earners aged 25–59 years who work 20 hours or more per week: women earn less than men, regardless of socioeconomic strata. Although the absolute differences in the low-income strata are slight, women earn wages accounting for around 75% of the amount earned by men. In high-income strata, where top managerial or professional positions are predominant, these differences are larger: wages earned by women represent, on average, slightly more than 70% of the amount earned by men (the famous "glass ceiling"). These differences diminish notably in the middle-income strata (particularly with respect to intermediate-middle and upper-middle income), although not significantly (women's wages are equivalent to roughly 80% of those earned by men), as shown in figure I.16E.

4.   The risk of falling into poverty owing to loss of labour income

One of the important processes included in the analysis of social structure relates to upward or downward social mobility, which was mentioned in previous sections. As underscored, in light of the overall improvements in the socioeconomic situation of the Latin American population, the information obtained from household surveys is not enough to conclude a massive upward mobility trend. Although all evidence points in this direction, estimation is impossible because it is not clear whether a large share of households (and people) saw their situation improve or whether a proportion of the population experienced a deterioration in position, offset by a larger percentage of households benefiting from upward mobility.

Meanwhile, the same methodology —using per capita income thresholds expressed as multiples of a country's poverty line— places certain limitations on determining the impoverishment or enrichment of the different strata, because if the shifts are significant (in terms of per capita income), the strata of households and people change. The information is only indirect as it shows increases or decreases in the different strata at various points in time.

In light of the analytical difficulties related to the type of measurement instrument and methodology used, an alternative is to use counterfactual microsimulation that measures, for example, the risk of deterioration in socioeconomic status. This section analyses the

---

[24]   Brazil, Chile, Colombia, Costa Rica, the Dominican Republic, Ecuador, El Salvador, Guatemala, Honduras, Mexico, Nicaragua, Panama, Paraguay, Peru and the Plurinational State of Bolivia. This list does not include Argentina, the Bolivarian Republic of Venezuela or Uruguay. The middle-income strata represent a significant share of the population in Argentina and Uruguay.

effect of the job loss of one or more members of a household on changes in households' per capita income. Naturally, any situation involving the loss of paid employment results in a deterioration in socioeconomic situation, so the focus is on the probability of maintaining the same socioeconomic position and the risk (at least temporary) of falling below the poverty line, in light of unemployment (or inactivity for various reasons).

As highlighted in the second part of section C, work is a crucial determinant of socioeconomic stratum for most households (in both the quantitative and qualitative dimensions, not limited solely to access to employment, but also including the conditions under which it is carried out, especially in terms of income and social protection). On average, labour income represents 64% of total household income. Hence, the better the job (and wages) and the larger the number of household members in paid employment, the more likely it is to have a better social position, assuming that family structure and size and other sources of income remain constant.

Three major scenarios were established to analyse the risk of people falling into poverty (or the probability of them maintaining the same socioeconomic position), based on the effects of the following situations: no recipients of labour income in addition to the main breadwinner, unemployment of the main (and in many cases, the sole) breadwinner, and no member of the household in paid employment.

The first scenario, in which there are no recipients of labour income in addition to the main breadwinner, represents the least risk of people not living in poverty seeing their position deteriorate significantly —except among households with per capita income of less than 1.8 times the poverty line— given that women's increased labour participation has played a decisive role in these households exiting and remaining out of poverty. People living in middle- and high-income households face a 1.7% risk, on average, of falling into poverty for the abovementioned reason, and 60% probability of maintaining their original socioeconomic position (see figure I.17A). Clearly, people living in households that are low-income but non-poor, or in the lower-middle-income strata, face a greater risk of falling into poverty, while those in high-income strata are the most likely to maintain their position. The relatively low risk of falling into poverty in this scenario is related to the fact that only 44% of Latin American households have additional recipients of labour income (and 14% have no members in paid employment).

The scenario changes with the elimination of labour income for the main breadwinner (41% of households are made up of a single person): there is only 20% probability of maintaining the same position and the risk of falling into poverty increases to 30%. Low-income non-poor households are at the greatest risk in the event that their main breadwinner loses their job, more than 80%, which decreases to 35% for lower-middle-income households. For intermediate-middle-income households, this risk decreases to 15% and is lower than 10% in higher-income strata (see figure I.17B).

Lastly, in a scenario of no labour income whatsoever, the probability of maintaining socioeconomic status is low: just 14% of people would maintain their original position (with no major differences between strata, except for people belonging to high-income strata) and the risk of falling into poverty increases to 55%. As could be expected, this risk increases more and more as one moves down the socioeconomic scale (see figure I.17C). However, deterioration in socioeconomic status is still significant for all groups, as it would leave about 89% of the population in the lower strata, in other words, in poverty or close to poverty,[25] which indicates the importance of employment in socioeconomic stratification for the majority of households in Latin America. Table I.A1.5 in the annex provides a more complete regional picture of movement between strata associated with the previous simulations.

---

[25] This figure includes people already living in poverty or extreme poverty.

Figure I.17
Latin America (18 countries): probability of persons remaining in the same stratum and risk of falling into poverty
or extreme poverty owing to loss of labour income, around 2017[a]

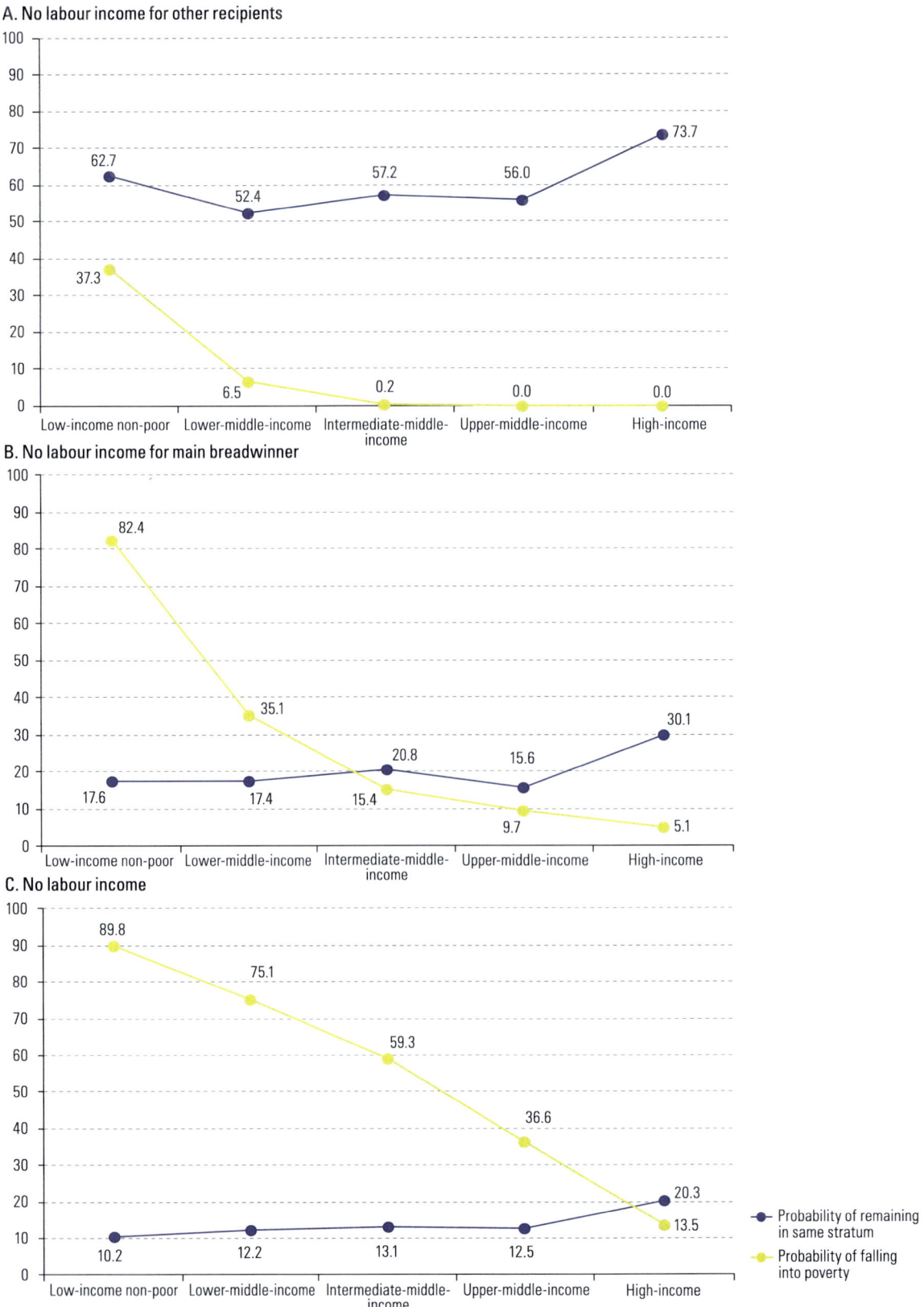

Source: Economic Commission for Latin America and the Caribbean (ECLAC), on the basis of Household Survey Data Bank (BADEHOG).
[a] The countries included are: Argentina, the Bolivarian Republic of Venezuela, Brazil, Chile, Colombia, Costa Rica, the Dominican Republic, Ecuador, El Salvador, Guatemala,
Honduras, Mexico, Nicaragua, Panama, Paraguay, Peru, the Plurinational State of Bolivia and Uruguay.

The risk of job loss and the resulting decline in the main source of income for most households is compounded by a considerable lack of social protection, which affects both the low-income and lower-middle income strata. In 2017, just 23.8% of the region's economically active population in the lower-income strata were affiliated with or contributed to a pension system, while the corresponding figures for the middle-income and high-income strata were 55% and 76%, respectively. The low- and middle-income strata, which account for 76.8% of the total population, represent pension system coverage (affiliation/contributions) of 31.8%, confirming that the lack of social protection does not only affect people living in poverty and extreme poverty, and the considerable sustainability challenges facing pension systems in the region (in terms of adequate coverage and benefits, and financial sustainability) (Arenas de Mesa, 2019). Also notable are the major differences —including in a context of limited access to pension systems— between workers (and unemployed people) who are in the non-poor low-income strata (32.8%) and those living in poverty (16.6%) and extreme poverty (4%), and between workers in the lower-middle-income strata (47.5%) and upper-middle-income strata (69.8%), which show a narrowing of the gap as one moves higher up the socioeconomic scale (see figure I.18A). The relationship between access to contributory social protection and socioeconomic stratification indicates, in turn, a link between job formality and adequacy of labour income.

The considerable lack of social protection and low labour income affecting much of the economically active population at the bottom and in the middle of the socioeconomic pyramid in Latin America has direct consequences for well-being in the long term: less than one third (31.7%) of persons aged 65 years and older in the low-income strata benefited from pension coverage, which was equivalent to US$ 234 per month, on average (at 2018 prices, slightly more than two times the poverty line). Coverage of the corresponding group in the middle-income strata was much higher —and with only slight differences within this group— and benefited more than two thirds of older persons, at an average of US$ 400 per month (3.6 times the poverty line), but with one major difference within that group: the average pensions of older persons in the lower-middle-income strata were equivalent to 43% of the average amount received by those in the upper-middle-income strata. Retirees in high-income strata received, on average, pensions that were twice the amount received by those in upper-middle-income strata and six times more than those in the low-income strata (see figure I.18B).

This indicates the importance of work and labour income in obtaining and maintaining a specific socioeconomic position, and the vulnerability to poverty of a large percentage of Latin American families facing situations that affect sources of work. It also indicates the importance of job quality in terms of access to social and labour protection systems, in terms of immediate effects (e.g. access to contributory health-care systems, unemployment insurance, sick leave and maternity or paternity leave) and long-term effects, which often involve pensions that are clearly unable to guarantee the living standards enjoyed prior to retirement and force older persons to continue working or make family arrangements to maintain the minimum decent living conditions.

Figure I.18
Latin America (18 countries): pension system contribution or affiliation among the active population aged 15 years and older, persons aged 65 years and older receiving pensions, and average monthly pensions by stratum based on per capita income, around 2017
(Percentages and constant dollars at 2018 prices)

A. Pension system contribution or affiliation among the active population aged 15 years and older[a][b]

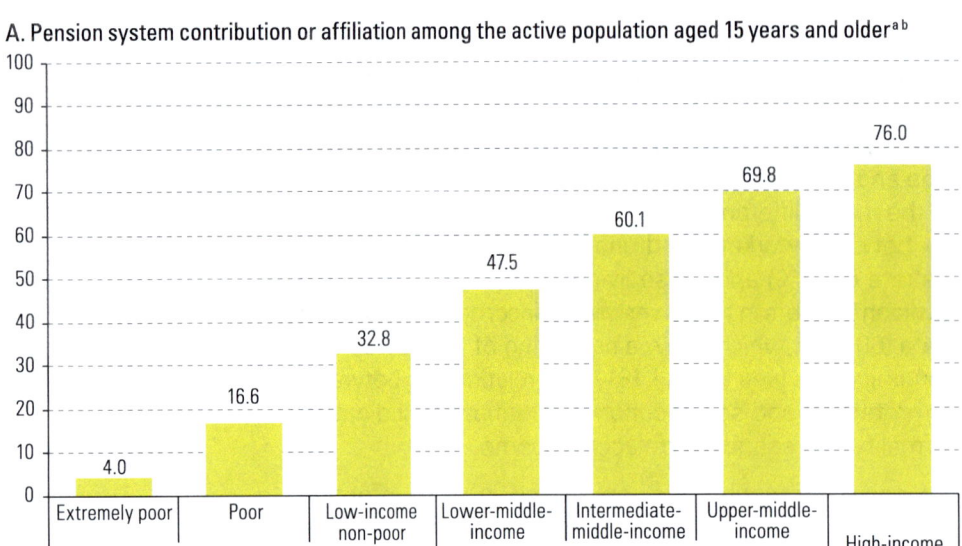

B. Persons aged 65 years and older receiving pensions and average monthly pensions[c][d]

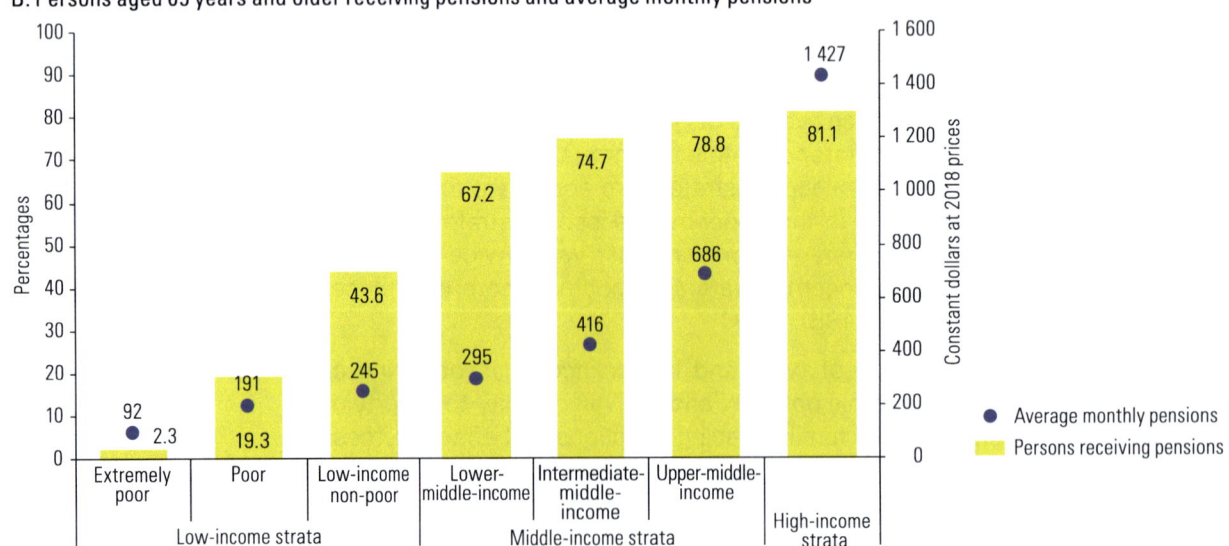

Source: Economic Commission for Latin America and the Caribbean (ECLAC), Household Survey Data Bank (BADEHOG).

[a] The indicator of access refers to affiliation with pension systems in the Dominican Republic, Ecuador, Panama and the Plurinational State of Bolivia.

[b] Includes unemployed people.

[c] Does not include Nicaragua. Refers to contributory pensions except where it is impossible to fully distinguish between contributory and non-contributory pensions (Chile and Costa Rica).

[d] The Bolivarian Republic of Venezuela is not included owing to a lack of data for currency conversion.

5.   Conclusions and research agenda

As discussed in the previous pages, the socioeconomic strata of most households and people depend heavily on paid employment and job quality (measured by remuneration) and the number of household members able to participate in the labour force. The social inequality matrix in Latin America is also determined by other elements, such as family structure and size and other characteristics, for example inequalities on the basis of gender, ethnicity, race, geographic location and life cycle stage which, because they affect access to education and paid work along with the quality of labour force participation, have an impact on the socioeconomic strata of households. Some of the factors that could foster upward social mobility and reduce vulnerability to poverty or, more generally, the deterioration in living conditions, could be addressed through public policies with short- and medium-term impacts: e.g., expansion of educational coverage, including technical and professional training; policies to keep students in school, to foster and formalize employment and to increase the minimum wage; expansion of contributory and non-contributory social protection and strengthening of care systems.

The strengthening of social protection policies includes the development of instruments that can benefit the low- and middle-income strata, by focusing on reducing the effects of unemployment (e.g., through unemployment insurance or basic citizen's income) and the excessive debt levels to which mainly middle-income strata are susceptible.

It is also necessary to develop or expand national care systems to foster shared responsibility in studies and the incorporation into the labour market of people —mainly women— who traditionally dedicate long hours to unpaid domestic work and care of dependents (children, older persons and persons with disabilities), thus strengthening the base of a family's labour income and increasing resilience in the event of the temporary unemployment of one of the household members. This could facilitate economic mobility and improve the prospects of the middle-income strata.

However, other factors require more complex, long-term measures, such as the transformation of the production structure, elimination of discrimination and fostering of gender equality or ethno-racial equality (including cultural change), or the strengthening of development of more depressed or less economically dynamic territories and geographic areas.

It is especially important to gradually eliminate the culture of privilege and its impact on society in general and on the labour market, for example, through mechanisms that foster wage equality between men and women, increase wages in the low- and middle-income strata, encourage freedom of association and collective bargaining, and promote hiring practices in the public and private sectors that strengthen selection processes based on merit and not on networks, especially for the top jobs in terms of required skills, responsibility and pay. This must also be accompanied by the improvement of the quality of education systems and increased access to post-secondary and university education (and its completion), in line with the present and future requirements of the region's production systems.

With respect to the knowledge required to improve the understanding of social realities and thus of the empirical evidence needed to improve public policy design, the countries of the region must resume studies on social classes. This implies not only addressing social stratification on the basis of monetary criteria (as is the case in this section), but also updating more traditional approaches which use occupation as the starting point, possibly combined with other criteria such as education, spending and lifestyle.

This poses major challenges:

- Gaining access to instruments to analyse social mobility, either through panel surveys or instruments that examine people's professional and economic background. These instruments could also be used to determine material and symbolic consumer patterns, and to measure the quality of social (and cultural) capital both in terms of investigating the mechanisms driving the culture of privilege and in reference to social networks that reduce families' vulnerability to different types of events such as unfavourable economic conditions, catastrophic illnesses and disasters relating to climate change and natural phenomena.

- Developing methodologies that help to understand the complexity of social stratification systems in which several members of a household are employed, especially when the status of their occupation differs; using criteria compatible with traditional classifications to categorize households (and people) in cases where no one is employed, for example, households in which the occupants are retirees. In this case, it makes sense to ask whether these households should be classified according to current income, past occupation, property ownership or other complementary criteria.

- Carrying out systematic and comparable research over time (and among countries, to the extent possible) which allows the monitoring of trends in class structure, and also allows the incorporation of new criteria of which the importance becomes clear with future economic, social and environmental changes, including technological changes and their effects on the structures of jobs, occupations and labour relations. In light of the foreseeable growth in consumption in the middle-income strata, it is important to reconsider which consumer patterns are sustainable in the context of the climate crisis, and the obstacles to fostering them.

- Developing research that reveals the relationship between changes in social structure and changes in the production structure. This also helps to anticipate the possible impacts of changes in the world of work associated with automation and robotization, and the changes needed in the production structure to ensure that it is more respectful of the environment.

Bibliography

Altimir, O. (1987), "Income distribution statistics in Latin America and their reliability", *Review of Income and Wealth*, vol. 33, No. 2.

___(1979), *La dimensión de la pobreza en América Latina*, Cuadernos de la CEPAL, Santiago, Economic Commission for Latin America and the Caribbean (ECLAC).

Alvaredo, F. (2007), "The rich in Argentina over the twentieth century: from the conservative republic to the Peronist experience and beyond 1932–2004", *Working Paper*, No. 2007-02, Paris, Paris School of Economics.

Alvaredo, F. and J. Londoño Vélez (2013), "High incomes and personal taxation in a developing economy: Colombia 1993-2010", *CEQ Working Paper*, No. 12, New Orleans, Commitment to Equity (CEQ).

Alvaredo F. and others (2017), "Distributional national accounts (DINA) guidelines: concepts and methods used in WID.world", *WID.world Working Paper*, No. 2016/2, World Inequality Lab.

Amarante, V. (2013), "Income inequality in Latin America: data challenges and availability from a comparative perspective", *Social Policy series*, No. 185 (LC/L.3695), Santiago, Economic Commission for Latin America and the Caribbean (ECLAC).

Anand, S., P. Segal and J. Stiglitz (2010), *Debates on the Measurement of Global Poverty*, New York, Oxford University Press.

Arenas de Mesa, A. (2019), Los sistemas de pensiones en la encrucijada: desafíos para la sostenibilidad en América Latina, Libros de la CEPAL, N 159 (LC/PUB.2019/19-P), Santiago, Comisión Económica para América Latina y el Caribe (CEPAL).

Atkinson, A. (2010), "Top incomes in a rapidly growing economy: Singapore", *Top Incomes: A Global Perspective*, A. Atkinson and T. Piketty (eds.), Oxford/New York, Oxford University Press.

Atkinson, A. and A. Leigh (2010), "The distribution of top incomes in five Anglo-Saxon countries over the twentieth century", *Discussion Paper*, No. 4937.

Atkinson, A. and T. Piketty (eds.) (2011), *Top Incomes over the 20th Century: A Contrast between Continental European and English-Speaking Countries*, Oxford, Oxford University Press.

Atkinson, A., T. Piketty and E. Saez (2011), "Top incomes in the long-run of history," *Journal of Economic Literature*, vol. 49, No. 1.

Atria, J. and others (2018), "Top incomes in Chile: a historical perspective of income inequality (1964-2015)", *WID.world Working Paper*, No. 2018/11, World Inequality Lab.

Banerjee, A. and E. Duflo (2008), "What is middle class about the middle class around the world?", *Journal of Economic Perspectives*, vol. 22, No. 2.

Birdsall, N. (2012), "A note on the middle class in Latin America", *Working Paper*, No. 303, Washington, D.C., Center for Global Development.

___(2010), "The (indispensable) middle class in developing countries; or, the rich and the rest, not the poor and the rest", *Working Paper*, No. 207, Washington, D.C., Center for Global Development.

Birdsall, N., C. Graham and S. Pettinato (2000), "Stuck in the tunnel: is globalization muddling the middle class?", *Working Paper*, No. 14, Washington, D.C., Center on Social and Economic Dynamics, The Brookings Institution.

Blackburn, M. and D. Bloom (1985), "What is happening to the middle class?", *American Demographics*, vol. 7, No. 1.

Blanchet, T., I. Flores and M. Morgan (2018), "The weight of the rich: improving surveys using tax data", *WID.world Working Paper*, No. 2018/12, Paris, World Inequality Database.

Blanchet, T., J. Fournier and T. Piketty (2017), "Generalized Pareto curves: theory and applications", *WID.world Working Paper*, No. 2017/3, Paris, World Wealth & Income Database.

Bourguignon, F. (2015), "Appraising income inequality databases in Latin America", *The Journal of Economic Inequality*, vol. 13, No. 4.

Brandolini, A. and A. Atkinson (2001), "Promise and pitfalls in the use of ‹secondary› data-sets: income inequality in OECD countries as a case study", *Journal of Economic Literature*, vol. 39, No. 3.

Bravo, D. and J. Valderrama (2011), "El impacto de los ajustes de ingresos realizados en la Encuesta CASEN sobre la medición de la desigualdad en Chile", *Estudios de Economía*, vol. 38, No. 1, Santiago, University of Chile, June.

Burdin, G., F. Esponda and A. Vigorito (2014), "Desigualdad y sectores de altos ingresos en Uruguay: un análisis en base a registros tributarios y encuestas de hogares para el periodo 2009-2011", *Documentos de Trabajo series*, No. 06/2014, Montevideo, Institute of Economics, University of the Republic.

Burkhauser, R., S. Feng and S. Jenkins (2009), "Using the P90/P10 index to measure U.S. inequality trends with current population survey data: a view from inside the census bureau vaults", *The Review of Income and Wealth*, vol. 55, No. 1, March.

Campos, R., E. Chávez and G. Esquivel (2014), "Los ingresos altos, la tributación óptima y la recaudación posible", *Finanzas Públicas*, vol. 6, No. 18.

Cárdenas, M., H. Kharas and C. Henao (2011), *Latin America's global middle class*, Washington, D.C., The Brookings Institution.

Carlson, B. (2001), "Education and the labour market in Latin America: why measurement is important and what it tells us about policies, reforms and performance", *Production Development series*, No. 114 (LC/L.1631-P), Santiago, Economic Commission for Latin America and the Caribbean (ECLAC).

Castellani, F. and G. Parent (2011), "Being 'middle class' in Latin America", *OECD Development Centre Working Paper*, No. 305, Paris, OECD Publishing.

Castellani, F., G. Parent and J. Zentero (2014), "The Latin American middle class: fragile after all?", *IDB Working Paper*, No. 557, Washington, D.C., Inter-American Development Bank (IDB).

Cortés, F. and D. Vargas (2017), "La evolución de la desigualdad en México: viejos y nuevos resultados", *Revista de Economía Mexicana. Anuario UNAM*, No. 2.

Costa Pinto, L. A. (1971), *Estructura de clases y cambio social*, Buenos Aires, Paidós.

Davies, J. C. and J. H. Huston (1992), "The shrinking middle-income class: a multivariate analysis", *Eastern Economic Journal*, vol. 18, No. 3.

Deaton, A. (1997), *The Analysis of Household Surveys: A Microeconometric Approach to Development Policy*, Washington, D.C., World Bank.

De Ipola, E. and S. Torrado (1976), *Teoría y método para el estudio de la estructura de clases sociales*, Santiago, Programa de Actividades Conjuntas ELAS/CELADE (PROELCE).

Del Castillo Negrete, M. (2017), "Income inequality in Mexico, 2004-2014", *Latin American Policy*, vol. 8, No. 1.

___(2015), "La magnitud de la desigualdad en el ingreso y la riqueza en México: una propuesta de cálculo", *Studies and Perspectives series-ECLAC Subregional Headquarters in Mexico*, No. 167 (LC/L.4108; LC/MEX/L.1199), Mexico City, Economic Commission for Latin America and the Caribbean (ECLAC).

___(2014), "Thomas Piketty para México", *Estudios*, No. 110, vol. XII.

Easterly, W. (2001), "The middle class consensus and economic development", *Journal of Economic Growth*, vol. 6, No. 4.

ECLAC (Economic Commission for Latin America and the Caribbean) (2019), *Social Panorama of Latin America, 2018* (LC/PUB.2019/3-P), Santiago.

___(2018), *Towards a regional agenda for inclusive social development: bases and initial proposal* (LC/MDS.2/2), Santiago.

___(2017), *Linkages between the social and production spheres: gaps, pillars and challenges* (LC/CDS.2/3), Santiago.

___(2016a), *Social Panorama of Latin America, 2015* (LC/G.2691-P), Santiago.

___(2016b), *The social inequality matrix in Latin America* (LC/G.2690(MDS.1/2)), Santiago.

___(2016c), *Inclusive social development: the next generation of policies for overcoming poverty and reducing inequality in Latin America and the Caribbean* (LC.L/4056/Rev.1), Santiago.

___(2014), *Compacts for Equality: Towards a Sustainable Future* (LC/G.2586(SES.35/3)), Santiago.

___(2010), *Time for Equality: Closing Gaps, Opening Trails* (LC/G.2432(SES.33/3)), Santiago

ECLAC/OIJ (Economic Commission for Latin America and the Caribbean/Ibero-American Youth Organization) (2004), *La juventud en Iberoamérica: tendencias y urgencias* (LC/L.2180), Santiago.

Feres, J. and A. León (1992), "Métodos y procedimientos para medir la pobreza en América Latina con el método de LP", *América Latina: el reto de la pobreza. Conceptos, métodos, magnitud, características y evolución*, L. Beccaria and others (comps.), Bogotá, United Nations Development Programme (UNDP).

Ferreira, F. H. and others (2013), *Economic Mobility and the Rise of the Latin American Middle Class*, Washington, D.C., World Bank.

Fesseau, M., F. Wolff and M. Mattonetti (2013), "A cross-country comparison of household income, consumption and wealth between micro sources and national accounts aggregates", *Statistics Working Papers*, No. 2013/03, Paris, OECD/Publishing.

Filgueira, C. (2001), "La actualidad de viejas temáticas: sobre los estudios de clase, estratificación y movilidad social en América Latina", *Social Policy series*, No. 51 (LC/L.1582-P), Santiago, Economic Commission for Latin America and the Caribbean (ECLAC).

Filgueira, C. and C. Geneletti (1981), *Estratificación y movilidad ocupacional en América Latina*, Cuadernos de la CEPAL, No. 39 (E/CEPAL/G.1122), Santiago Economic Commission for Latin America and the Caribbean (ECLAC).

Germani, G. (1968), *Política y sociedad en una época de transición: de la sociedad tradicional a la sociedad de masas*, Buenos Aires, Paidós.

Gómez Sabaini, J. C., J. P. Jiménez and R. Martner (eds.) (2017), *Consensos y conflictos en la política tributaria de América Latina*, ECLAC Books, No. 142 (LC/PUB.2017/5-P), Santiago, Economic Commission for Latin America and the Caribbean (ECLAC).

Hlasny, V. (2019), "Redistributive impacts of fiscal policies in Mexico: corrections for top income measurement problems", *LIS Working Papers*, No. 765, Luxembourg Income Study (LIS).

Jiménez, J. P. and D. Rossignolo (2019), *Concentración del ingreso y desigualdad en América Latina: el caso argentino*, Buenos Aires, Centro de Estudios para el Cambio Estructural (CECE).

Jorda, V. and M. Niño-Zarazúa (2016), "Global inequality: how large is the effect of top incomes?", *WIDER Working Paper*, No. 2016/94, World Institute for Development Economics Research (UNU-WIDER).

Kharas, H. and G. Gertz (2010), "The new global middle class: a cross-over from West to East", Washington, D.C., The Brookings Institution [online] https://www.brookings.edu/research/the-new-global-middle-class-a-cross-over-from-west-to-east/.

Kuznets, S. (1953), *Shares of Upper Income Groups in Income and Savings*, Cambridge, National Bureau of Economic Research (NBER).

Leyva-Parra, G. (2004), "El ajuste del ingreso de la ENIGH con la contabilidad nacional y la medición de la pobreza en México", *Documentos de Investigación*, No. 19, Mexico City, Secretariat of Social Development (SEDESOL), November.

López Calva, L. F. and E. Ortiz-Juárez (2014), "A vulnerability approach to the definition of the middle class", *Journal of Economic Inequality*, vol. 12, No. 1.

___(2011), "A vulnerability approach to the definition of the middle class", *Policy Research Working Paper*, No. 5902, Washington, D.C., World Bank.

Marinho, M. L. and V. Quiroz (2018), *Estratificación social: una propuesta metodológica multidimensional para la subregión norte de América Latina y el Caribe* (LC/MEX/TS.2018/28), Mexico City, Economic Commission for Latin America and the Caribbean (ECLAC).

Medina Echavarría, J. (1967), *Consideraciones sociológicas sobre el desarrollo económico de América Latina*, Buenos Aires, Solar/Hachette.

___(1973), *Aspectos sociales del desarrollo económico*, Santiago, Economic Commission for Latin America and the Caribbean (ECLAC).

Morgan, M. (2017), "Falling inequality beneath extreme and persistent concentration: new evidence for Brazil combining national accounts, surveys and fiscal data, 2001-2015", *WID.world Working Paper*, No. 2017/12.

OECD (Organization for Economic Cooperation and Development) (2019), *Under Pressure: The Squeezed Middle Class*, Paris, OECD Publishing.

___(2010), *Latin American Economic Outlook 2011: How middle-class is Latin America?*, Paris, OECD Publishing.

Paraje, G. and M. Weeks (2002), "How does income underreporting affect inequality measures?: a simulation approach", paper prepared for the seventh annual meeting of the Latin American and Caribbean Economic Association (LACEA), Madrid, 11–13 October.

Piketty, T. (2007), "Income, wage, and wealth inequality in France 1901-98", *Top Incomes over the 20th Century: A Contrast between Continental European and English-Speaking Countries*, A. Atkinson and T. Piketty (eds.), Oxford, Oxford University Press.

___(2001), "Income inequality in France 1901-98", *CEPR Discussion Papers*, No. 2876, Washington, D.C., Center for Economic and Policy Research (CEPR).

Piketty, T. and E. Saez (2003), "Income inequality in the United States, 1913-1998", *The Quarterly Journal of Economics*, vol. CXVIII, No. 1.

Piketty, T., E. Saez and G. Zucman (2018), "Distributional national accounts: methods and estimates for the United States", *The Quarterly Journal of Economics*, vol. 133, No. 2, May.

Ravallion, M. (2010), "The developing world's bulging (but vulnerable) 'middle class'", *World Development*, vol. 38, No. 4.

Reygadas, L. (2008), *La apropiación: destejiendo las redes de la desigualdad*, Barcelona, Anthropos.

Santaella, J., G. Leyva and A. Bustos (2017), "¿Quién se lleva los frutos del éxito en México?: una discusión sobre la verdadera distribución del ingreso", *Nexos*, 28 August [online] https://www.nexos.com.mx/?p=33425.

Sémbler, C. (2006), "Estratificación social y clases sociales: una revisión analítica de los sectores medios", *Social Policy series*, No. 125 (LC/L.2637-P), Santiago, Economic Commission for Latin America and the Caribbean (ECLAC).

Solimano, A. (2008), "The middle class and the development process", *Macroeconomics of Development series*, No. 65 (LC/L.2892-P), Santiago, Economic Commission for Latin America and the Caribbean (ECLAC).

Thurow, L. (1987), "A surge in inequality", *Scientific American*, vol. 256, No. 5.

Annex I.A1

Table I.A1.1
Latin America (18 countries): indicators of individual income distribution, 2001-2018[a]

Country	Year	Gini index[b]	Theil index[c]	Atkinson index[c]			Population with incomes below 50% of the median
				(e=0.5)	(e=1.0)	(e=1.5)	
Argentina[d]	2002	0.498	0.405	0.178	0.321	0.444	25.8
	2008	0.413	0.292	0.134	0.250	0.357	13.8
	2012	0.389	0.258	0.120	0.226	0.325	13.9
	2014	0.391	0.264	0.121	0.224	0.317	12.8
	2017	0.388	0.263	0.121	0.225	0.324	13.6
	2018	0.396	0.286	0.127	0.233	0.329	13.3
Bolivia (Plurinational State of)	2002	0.612	0.734	0.314	0.552	0.740	29.2
	2008	0.513	0.492	0.219	0.402	0.567	24.2
	2012	0.474	0.405	0.190	0.367	0.541	23.8
	2014	0.471	0.403	0.185	0.350	0.507	22.7
	2017	0.461	0.372	0.177	0.346	0.518	23.6
	2018	0.438	0.333	0.159	0.309	0.459	21.6
Brazil	2002	0.570	0.650	0.262	0.432	0.548	21.7
	2008	0.536	0.574	0.234	0.394	0.510	21.1
	2012	0.523	0.555	0.223	0.377	0.492	21.5
	2014	0.514	0.526	0.217	0.370	0.486	21.6
	2017[e]	0.539	0.570	0.235	0.400	0.524	22.9
	2018[e]	0.540	0.582	0.239	0.405	0.530	23.0
Chile	2003	0.507	0.514	0.211	0.359	0.478	18.7
	2009	0.478	0.453	0.188	0.323	0.434	15.8
	2011	0.469	0.430	0.181	0.313	0.419	15.1
	2013	0.466	0.424	0.178	0.306	0.408	14.2
	2015	0.453	0.408	0.170	0.293	0.392	14.1
	2017	0.454	0.417	0.172	0.295	0.394	14.1
Colombia	2002[f]	0.567	0.663	0.266	0.447	0.586	23.5
	2008[f]	0.572	0.652	0.268	0.456	0.600	25.1
	2012	0.539	0.573	0.240	0.414	0.553	23.3
	2014	0.540	0.577	0.240	0.412	0.547	23.0
	2017	0.511	0.515	0.216	0.375	0.504	21.5
	2018	0.520	0.537	0.224	0.386	0.516	21.8
Costa Rica	2002	0.497	0.462	0.198	0.349	0.475	20.0
	2008	0.491	0.461	0.195	0.339	0.451	18.7
	2012	0.502	0.450	0.200	0.359	0.493	21.4
	2014	0.498	0.440	0.197	0.356	0.488	21.1
	2017	0.496	0.445	0.197	0.351	0.478	20.1
	2018	0.493	0.430	0.193	0.348	0.478	20.5
Dominican Republic	2002	0.498	0.461	0.197	0.342	0.453	20.5
	2008	0.489	0.452	0.193	0.335	0.445	20.0
	2012	0.469	0.412	0.179	0.316	0.425	17.9
	2014	0.449	0.351	0.160	0.293	0.404	18.3
	2017[g]	0.441	0.379	0.158	0.274	0.368	15.6
	2018[g]	0.444	0.335	0.146	0.259	0.351	15.4
Ecuador	2001	0.538	0.643	0.244	0.395	0.502	18.1
	2008	0.496	0.461	0.196	0.340	0.452	18.9
	2012	0.468	0.405	0.174	0.308	0.419	19.2
	2014	0.449	0.391	0.165	0.288	0.387	16.5
	2017	0.444	0.370	0.161	0.287	0.394	17.6
	2018	0.454	0.386	0.167	0.296	0.401	17.8
El Salvador	2001	0.514	0.481	0.209	0.371	0.503	23.3
	2009	0.478	0.428	0.186	0.327	0.440	19.9
	2012	0.438	0.367	0.158	0.281	0.382	17.4
	2014	0.434	0.340	0.151	0.273	0.373	17.6
	2017	0.399	0.295	0.131	0.239	0.332	16.2
	2018	0.405	0.289	0.132	0.244	0.340	16.9

Table I.A1.1 (concluded)

Country	Year	Gini index[b]	Theil index[c]	Atkinson index[c]			Population with incomes below 50% of the median
				(e=0.5)	(e=1.0)	(e=1.5)	
Guatemala	2000	0.636	0.883	0.341	0.558	0.714	27.0
	2006	0.558	0.608	0.253	0.432	0.567	25.5
	2014	0.535	0.664	0.248	0.407	0.533	22.2
Honduras	2001	0.532	0.526	0.226	0.392	0.519	23.2
	2009	0.502	0.480	0.204	0.353	0.467	21.3
	2012	0.552	0.689	0.257	0.416	0.539	20.6
	2014	0.481	0.428	0.185	0.325	0.435	19.0
	2016	0.480	0.424	0.187	0.336	0.462	20.9
	2018	0.481	0.427	0.187	0.334	0.457	21.0
Mexico	2002	0.506	0.489	0.209	0.362	0.476	20.7
	2008	0.513	0.535	0.219	0.376	0.498	20.8
	2012	0.499	0.499	0.207	0.359	0.486	19.9
	2014	0.502	0.511	0.209	0.357	0.475	19.1
	2016	0.504	0.473	0.195	0.335	0.446	17.7
Nicaragua	2001	0.568	0.536	0.231	0.408	0.561	22.5
	2009	0.463	0.400	0.175	0.314	0.440	19.9
	2014	0.495	0.511	0.207	0.355	0.476	19.9
Panama	2002	0.572	0.622	0.270	0.472	0.623	27.3
	2008	0.528	0.518	0.229	0.410	0.553	24.9
	2011	0.528	0.520	0.228	0.404	0.543	25.0
	2014	0.509	0.470	0.212	0.386	0.531	24.3
	2017	0.508	0.480	0.212	0.382	0.523	24.8
	2018	0.498	0.459	0.204	0.371	0.511	24.4
Paraguay	2002	0.584	0.648	0.259	0.439	0.584	24.7
	2008	0.516	0.564	0.224	0.377	0.494	21.1
	2012	0.489	0.438	0.192	0.344	0.472	23.4
	2014	0.522	0.542	0.219	0.372	0.493	21.5
	2017	0.503	0.500	0.202	0.341	0.447	19.4
	2018	0.474	0.421	0.183	0.324	0.437	20.1
Peru	2002	0.544	0.610	0.248	0.422	0.560	24.4
	2008	0.495	0.450	0.201	0.364	0.500	24.7
	2012	0.457	0.383	0.173	0.318	0.445	22.3
	2014	0.446	0.369	0.165	0.303	0.424	21.5
	2017	0.448	0.368	0.165	0.303	0.422	20.9
	2018	0.439	0.345	0.157	0.290	0.406	20.0
Uruguay	2002[d]	0.474	0.393	0.177	0.322	0.448	21.1
	2008	0.453	0.382	0.166	0.295	0.397	18.7
	2012	0.391	0.262	0.122	0.228	0.320	16.5
	2014	0.392	0.271	0.124	0.229	0.319	16.3
	2017	0.390	0.272	0.123	0.225	0.311	15.8
	2018	0.391	0.269	0.123	0.225	0.312	15.6
Venezuela (Bolivarian Republic of)	2002	0.418	0.317	0.140	0.253	0.355	13.7
	2008	0.379	0.248	0.114	0.212	0.298	13.9
	2012	0.384	0.260	0.118	0.218	0.308	15.3
	2014	0.378	0.242	0.112	0.210	0.300	14.8

Source: Economic Commission for Latin America and the Caribbean (ECLAC), on the basis of Household Survey Data Bank (BADEHOG).
[a] Calculation based on the distribution of per capita personal income throughout the country.
[b] Includes persons with no income.
[c] To reduce the effect of extreme values, the Theil and Atkinson indices were calculated excluding values close to 0 and the three highest per capita incomes.
[d] Urban total.
[e] From 2016 onward, data from the PNAD-Continua survey are not comparable with those of previous years.
[f] Data prior to 2010 are not comparable with those of later years.
[g] Data based on the continuous national labour force survey (ENCFT) and are not comparable with previous years, which were based on the national labour force survey (ENFT).

Table I.A1.2
Latin America (18 countries): households by strata of per capita income, around 2002, 2008 and 2017
(Percentages)

| | Per capita income strata | | | | | | | | |
| | Low-income strata | | | | Middle-income strata | | | | High-income strata |
	Extremely poor	Poor	Low-income non-poor	Subtotal	Lower-middle	Intermediate-middle	Upper-middle	Subtotal	
ARG 2003[a]	8.7	31.0	30.1	69.8	17.0	9.9	2.5	29.4	0.9
ARG 2008[a]	3.3	16.2	31.5	51.0	23.0	19.4	4.8	47.2	1.7
ARG 2017[a]	2.4	10.9	26.2	39.5	28.8	23.5	6.2	58.5	1.9
BOL 2002	29.8	30.1	18.5	78.4	10.6	6.5	2.6	19.7	2.0
BOL 2008	17.0	22.6	26.5	66.1	17.2	11.9	2.9	32.0	1.9
BOL 2017	13.9	16.7	25.0	55.6	21.7	17.1	4.1	42.9	1.5
BRA 2001	5.8	25.1	26.2	57.1	17.8	14.3	5.6	37.7	5.2
BRA 2008	3.8	15.7	23.1	42.6	24.4	20.0	7.1	51.5	6.0
BRA 2017	5.1	10.8	18.8	34.7	25.1	24.2	8.5	57.8	7.4
CHL 2000	5.1	30.9	28.2	64.2	17.4	12.2	3.3	32.9	2.9
CHL 2009	3.6	20.2	30.5	54.3	23.2	14.9	4.5	42.6	3.2
CHL 2017	1.5	6.9	21.6	30.0	29.5	26.4	7.9	63.8	6.2
COL 2002	19.8	26.5	23.8	70.1	14.2	9.8	3.3	27.3	2.7
COL 2008	16.8	20.5	23.1	60.4	17.6	13.5	4.7	35.8	3.7
COL 2017	9.0	15.1	25.4	49.5	22.1	18.5	5.5	46.1	4.3
CRI 2002	4.9	20.2	25.5	50.6	21.2	18.3	6.3	45.8	3.5
CRI 2008	3.5	14.2	25.8	43.5	22.9	20.9	7.7	51.5	4.9
CRI 2017	3.0	9.6	20.6	33.2	22.9	24.5	10.8	58.2	8.7
DOM 2000	7.2	19.7	25.8	52.7	22.2	16.3	5.1	43.6	3.7
DOM 2008	11.5	22.7	27.7	61.9	18.9	13.1	3.8	35.8	2.4
DOM 2017	4.8	14.3	30.6	49.7	24.6	18.2	4.7	47.5	2.7
ECU 2001	18.0	29.9	25.0	72.9	13.8	8.5	2.6	24.9	2.1
ECU 2008	9.0	20.4	28.1	57.5	20.2	15.1	4.6	39.9	2.7
ECU 2017	5.4	13.7	27.3	46.4	24.5	20.6	5.7	50.8	2.8
SLV 2001	15.8	28.4	24.9	69.1	16.1	10.7	2.7	29.5	1.5
SLV 2009	13.5	29.6	29.0	72.1	15.5	8.7	2.5	26.7	1.2
SLV 2017	6.5	25.6	33.1	65.2	21.1	11.2	1.9	34.2	0.6
GTM 2000	14.4	32.5	21.3	68.2	14.0	10.5	3.9	28.4	3.5
GTM 2006	7.7	27.3	23.7	58.7	18.5	15.0	4.5	38.0	3.4
GTM 2014	11.8	31.3	26.5	69.6	15.3	10.7	2.8	28.8	1.7
HND 2001	23.6	27.7	21.7	73.0	14.0	9.3	2.4	25.7	1.3
HND 2009	16.1	28.7	25.9	70.7	15.4	10.2	2.4	28.0	1.4
HND 2016	16.7	31.6	25.4	73.7	14.1	9.5	1.9	25.5	0.8
MEX 2000	9.4	30.6	26.8	66.8	16.3	11.0	3.4	30.7	2.5
MEX 2008	9.2	26.9	27.0	63.1	18.2	12.7	3.5	34.4	2.4
MEX 2016	9.1	27.3	28.5	64.9	17.9	11.8	3.6	33.3	1.9
NIC 2001	29.3	28.1	21.7	79.1	11.5	6.3	2.0	19.8	1.0
NIC 2009	18.6	32.4	27.5	78.5	12.9	6.2	1.4	20.5	1.0
NIC 2014	16.1	24.8	29.8	70.7	16.7	8.8	2.2	27.7	1.6
PAN 2000	10.6	14.3	20.6	45.5	19.2	20.3	8.8	48.3	6.1
PAN 2008	8.8	11.7	21.0	41.5	22.1	22.5	8.4	53.0	5.5
PAN 2017	5.1	7.2	15.7	28.0	21.3	28.4	13.5	63.2	8.7
PER 2001	13.4	26.1	26.6	66.1	17.1	11.6	3.3	32.0	1.9
PER 2008	9.1	18.4	25.4	52.9	22.1	17.6	4.7	44.4	2.7
PER 2017	4.0	12.3	25.1	41.4	25.6	23.2	6.5	55.3	3.3

Table I.A1.2 (concluded)

| | Per capita income strata | | | | | | | | |
| | Low-income strata | | | | Middle-income strata | | | | High-income strata |
	Extremely poor	Poor	Low-income non-poor	Subtotal	Lower-middle	Intermediate-middle	Upper-middle	Subtotal	
PRY 2001	9.8	20.7	23.8	54.3	19.5	16.4	5.7	41.6	4.0
PRY 2008	9.2	18.9	25.9	54.0	20.6	17.3	4.9	42.8	3.2
PRY 2017	5.0	13.4	24.2	42.6	23.9	23.4	6.1	53.4	4.0
URY 2002[a]	3.3	10.6	19.2	33.1	23.6	27.6	10.0	61.2	5.7
URY 2008[a]	0.7	8.0	18.2	26.9	25.0	30.1	11.4	66.5	6.7
URY 2017[a]	0.1	1.5	9.6	11.2	19.8	39.3	18.9	78.0	10.8
VEN 2000	4.7	33.5	33.8	72.0	17.3	8.6	1.4	27.3	0.6
VEN 2008	4.5	16.3	32.1	52.9	25.0	17.9	3.3	46.2	1.0
VEN 2014	10.3	13.7	30.4	54.4	26.2	16.0	2.7	44.9	0.7
Latin America 2002	9.5	27.3	26.3	63.1	16.9	12.3	4.2	33.4	3.5
Latin America 2008	7.1	19.5	25.5	52.1	21.6	16.9	5.3	43.8	4.0
Latin America 2017	6.6	15.5	23.5	45.6	23.3	20.1	6.4	49.8	4.7

Source: Economic Commission for Latin America and the Caribbean (ECLAC), on the basis of Household Survey Data Bank (BADEHOG).
[a] Urban areas.

Table I.A1.3
Latin America (18 countries): population by stratum based on per capita income, around 2002, 2008 and 2017
(Percentages)

| | Strata based on per capita income | | | | | | | | |
| | Low-income strata | | | | Middle-income strata | | | | High-income strata |
	Extremely poor	Poor	Low-income non-poor	Subtotal	Lower-middle	Intermediate-middle	Upper-middle	Subtotal	
ARG 2003[a]	11.2	38.8	27.9	77.9	13.2	7.0	1.5	21.7	0.4
ARG 2008[a]	4.3	22.8	33.2	60.3	20.8	15.1	3.1	39.0	0.8
ARG 2017[a]	2.8	15.9	32.6	51.3	26.4	17.5	3.6	47.5	1.1
BOL 2002	35.1	31.7	17.2	84.0	8.6	4.5	1.8	14.9	1.1
BOL 2008	21.4	25.1	26.5	73.0	15.4	8.7	1.9	26.0	1.0
BOL 2017	16.4	18.8	27.4	62.6	21.3	12.8	2.6	36.7	0.7
BRA 2001	7.4	31.1	25.9	64.4	15.6	12.1	4.5	32.2	3.6
BRA 2008	4.3	21.1	25.8	51.2	21.8	17.0	5.8	44.6	4.3
BRA 2017	5.5	14.8	22.3	42.6	23.7	21.1	6.9	51.7	5.6
CHL 2000	6.3	36.5	28.5	71.3	14.9	9.4	2.5	26.8	2.0
CHL 2009	3.8	25.2	32.2	61.2	20.9	12.3	3.5	36.7	2.2
CHL 2017	1.4	9.3	26.5	37.2	29.8	22.5	6.1	58.4	4.4
COL 2002	23.8	30.1	23.2	77.1	12.0	7.2	2.2	21.4	1.6
COL 2008	20.7	23.9	23.9	68.5	15.6	10.3	3.2	29.1	2.3
COL 2017	10.9	18.9	28.1	57.9	21.2	14.4	3.9	39.5	2.6
CRI 2002	5.4	22.6	27.3	55.3	21.0	16.3	5.0	42.3	2.4
CRI 2008	3.6	16.5	27.3	47.4	23.3	19.3	6.5	49.1	3.5
CRI 2017	3.3	11.8	23.5	38.6	23.5	22.5	9.2	55.2	6.2
DOM 2000	9.5	23.0	27.1	59.6	20.0	13.8	4.2	38.0	2.5
DOM 2008	15.0	26.5	28.3	69.8	16.5	9.8	2.7	29.0	1.2
DOM 2017	6.4	18.6	33.7	58.7	22.5	13.9	3.3	39.7	1.5
ECU 2001	20.2	33.4	24.4	78.0	11.9	6.7	2.1	20.7	1.4
ECU 2008	10.8	23.9	29.5	64.2	18.6	12.0	3.4	34.0	1.8
ECU 2017	7.0	16.7	30.0	53.7	24.0	16.8	3.8	44.6	1.7
SLV 2001	19.1	31.5	24.3	74.9	13.8	8.6	1.9	24.3	0.9
SLV 2009	17.1	33.0	27.9	78.0	13.0	6.4	1.7	21.1	0.8
SLV 2017	8.3	29.5	33.9	71.7	18.8	7.8	1.2	27.8	0.4

Table I.A1.3 (concluded)

| | Strata based on per capita income | | | | | | | | |
| | Low-income strata | | | | Middle-income strata | | | | High-income strata |
	Extremely poor	Poor	Low-income non-poor	Subtotal	Lower-middle	Intermediate-middle	Upper-middle	Subtotal	
GTM 2000	16.9	36.8	20.9	74.6	12.0	8.1	2.8	22.9	2.5
GTM 2006	10.4	32.3	24.3	67.0	16.7	11.2	3.0	30.9	2.2
GTM 2014	15.4	35.1	25.8	76.3	13.0	7.9	1.8	22.7	1.0
HND 2001	27.3	30.1	21.0	78.4	11.7	7.2	1.7	20.6	0.9
HND 2009	19.6	31.4	25.0	76.0	13.5	7.9	1.8	23.2	0.9
HND 2016	18.8	34.5	25.2	78.5	12.3	7.4	1.4	21.1	0.4
MEX 2000	13.8	35.0	25.9	74.7	13.6	7.9	2.4	23.9	1.4
MEX 2008	11.8	31.2	27.5	70.5	16.0	9.6	2.4	28.0	1.4
MEX 2016	11.7	32.1	29.0	72.8	15.3	8.7	2.2	26.2	1.1
NIC 2001	35.8	29.3	19.4	84.5	9.3	4.3	1.3	14.9	0.6
NIC 2009	23.1	35.2	25.3	83.6	10.7	4.4	0.8	15.9	0.5
NIC 2014	18.3	28.0	30.3	76.6	14.3	6.5	1.5	22.3	1.0
PAN 2000	13.3	16.9	22.7	52.9	19.4	16.9	6.5	42.8	4.2
PAN 2008	12.2	14.0	23.8	50.0	21.9	18.3	6.1	46.3	3.7
PAN 2017	7.6	9.1	17.7	34.4	22.2	26.9	10.5	59.6	6.1
PER 2001	16.3	28.8	27.0	72.1	15.8	8.9	2.1	26.8	1.1
PER 2008	10.8	21.0	26.8	58.6	21.8	14.7	3.3	39.8	1.7
PER 2017	5.0	13.9	27.0	45.9	26.3	21.0	4.7	52.0	2.1
PRY 2001	13.2	24.5	25.1	62.8	17.9	12.8	4.0	34.7	2.5
PRY 2008	12.1	22.9	27.3	62.3	19.2	13.2	3.3	35.7	2.1
PRY 2017	6.0	15.6	26.9	48.5	23.9	20.2	4.6	48.7	2.8
URY 2002[a]	4.5	16.8	23.7	45.0	22.9	21.6	7.0	51.5	3.5
URY 2008[a]	1.2	13.3	23.3	37.8	24.6	24.7	8.4	57.7	4.4
URY 2017[a]	0.1	2.6	14.6	17.3	23.8	36.7	14.8	75.3	7.4
VEN 2000	4.8	39.4	33.8	78.0	14.8	6.1	0.8	21.7	0.3
VEN 2008	4.7	20.1	34.9	59.7	23.8	13.8	2.2	39.8	0.5
VEN 2014	11.9	16.3	33.5	61.7	24.3	11.8	1.8	37.9	0.4
Latin America 2002[b]	12.2	33.2	25.5	70.9	14.4	9.5	3.1	27.0	2.2
Latin America 2008[b]	9.1	24.4	27.2	60.7	19.3	13.4	3.9	36.6	2.6
Latin America 2017[b]	10.5	19.6	25.8	55.9	20.9	15.7	4.5	41.1	3.0

Source: Economic Commission for Latin America and the Caribbean (ECLAC), on the basis of Household Survey Data Bank (BADEHOG).
[a] Urban areas.
[b] Figures adjusted for population projections of World Population Prospects, 2019 revision, and estimated poverty trends in countries for which figures are not available for the years indicated.

Table I.A1.4
Latin America (17 countries): annual income and share of per capita income of different strata, around 2017[a]
(Millions of constant dollars at 2018 prices and percentages)

Country		Total	Strata								
			Low-income strata				Middle-income strata				High-income strata
			Extremely poor	Poor	Low-income non-poor	Subtotal	Lower-middle	Intermediate-middle	Upper-middle	Subtotal	
ARG 2017	Amount	163 707.6	475.2	8 866.8	31 677.6	41 019.6	43 204.8	49 856.4	18 949.2	112 010.4	10 678.8
	Share	100.0	0.3	5.4	19.3	25.0	26.4	30.5	11.6	68.5	6.5
BOL 2017	Amount	29 538.0	716.4	2 240.4	5 840.4	8 797.2	7 771.2	8 298.0	2 989.2	19 058.4	1 682.4
	Share	100.0	2.4	7.6	19.8	29.8	26.3	28.1	10.1	64.5	5.7
BRA 2017	Amount	974 815.2	3 477.6	30 734.4	84 771.6	118 983.6	155 372.4	241 584.0	146 857.2	543 813.6	312 018.0
	Share	100.0	0.4	3.2	8.7	12.3	15.9	24.8	15.1	55.8	32.0
CHL 2017	Amount	123 255.6	117.6	2 767.2	13 932.0	16 816.8	25 710.0	34 027.2	17 492.4	77 229.6	29 208.0
	Share	100.0	0.1	2.2	11.3	13.6	20.9	27.6	14.2	62.7	23.7
COL 2017	Amount	131 013.6	1 839.6	7 756.8	20 536.8	30 133.2	26 740.8	32 469.6	16 267.2	75 477.6	25 402.8
	Share	100.0	1.4	5.9	15.7	23.0	20.4	24.8	12.4	57.6	19.4
CRI 2017	Amount	29 898.0	66.0	721.2	2 666.4	3 453.6	4 479.6	7 712.4	5 863.2	18 055.2	8 389.2
	Share	100.0	0.2	2.4	8.9	11.5	15.0	25.8	19.6	60.4	28.1
DOM 2017	Amount	27 270.0	286.8	1 774.8	5 652.0	7 713.6	6 273.6	6 830.4	2 995.2	16 099.2	3 457.2
	Share	100.0	1.1	6.5	20.7	28.3	23.0	25.0	11.0	59.0	12.7
ECU 2017	Amount	48 856.8	528.0	2 690.4	8 385.6	11 604.0	11 385.6	14 068.8	6 057.6	31 512.0	5 739.6
	Share	100.0	1.1	5.5	17.2	23.8	23.3	28.8	12.4	64.5	11.7
GTM 2014	Amount	33 375.6	792.0	4 755.6	7 068.0	12 615.6	6 127.2	6 558.0	2 811.6	15 496.8	5 263.2
	Share	100.0	2.4	14.2	21.2	37.8	18.4	19.6	8.4	46.4	15.8
HND 2016	Amount	14 766.0	572.4	2 553.6	3 518.4	6 644.4	3 012.0	3 207.6	1 131.6	7 351.2	770.4
	Share	100.0	3.9	17.3	23.8	45.0	20.4	21.7	7.7	49.8	5.2
MEX 2016	Amount	253 011.6	5 026.8	32 538.0	54 168.0	91 732.8	49 819.2	50 229.6	24 373.2	124 422.0	36 858.0
	Share	100.0	2.0	12.9	21.4	36.3	19.7	19.9	9.6	49.2	14.6
NIC 2014	Amount	9 357.6	333.6	1 220.4	2 364.0	3 918.0	1 932.0	1 597.2	726.0	4 255.2	1 185.6
	Share	100.0	3.6	13.0	25.3	41.9	20.6	17.1	7.8	45.5	12.7
PAN 2017	Amount	21 866.4	139.2	375.6	1 333.2	1 848.0	2 886.0	6 277.2	4 502.4	13 665.6	6 351.6
	Share	100.0	0.6	1.7	6.1	8.4	13.2	28.7	20.6	62.5	29.1
PER 2017	Amount	94 461.6	548.4	3 490.8	12 762.0	16 801.2	21 757.2	30 873.6	12 867.6	65 498.4	12 162.0
	Share	100.0	0.6	3.7	13.5	17.8	23.0	32.7	13.6	69.3	12.9
PRY 2017	Amount	20 660.4	163.2	828.0	2 578.8	3 570.0	3 937.2	5 922.0	2 448.0	12 307.2	4 783.2
	Share	100.0	0.8	4.0	12.5	17.3	19.1	28.7	11.9	59.7	23.2
SLV 2017	Amount	1 516.8	26.4	202.8	434.4	663.6	409.2	298.8	87.6	795.6	55.2
	Share	100.0	1.8	13.4	28.6	43.8	27.0	19.7	5.8	52.5	3.6
URY 2017	Amount	32 488.8	1.2	153.6	1 473.6	1 628.4	4 017.6	11 030.4	7 905.6	22 953.6	7 906.8
	Share	100.0	0.0	0.5	4.5	5.0	12.4	34.0	24.3	70.7	24.3
Latin America	Amount	2 009 858.4	15 111.6	103 670.4	259 161.6	377 943.6	374 833.2	510 842.4	274 326.0	1 160 001.6	471 914.4
	Share	100.0	0.8	5.2	12.9	18.8	18.6	25.4	13.6	57.7	23.5

Source: Economic Commission for Latin America and the Caribbean (ECLAC), on the basis of Household Survey Data Bank (BADEHOG).
[a] The Bolivarian Republic of Venezuela is not included owing to a lack of data for currency conversion.

Table I.A1.5
Latin America (18 countries): simulation of changes in status owing to the elimination of labour income of the main breadwinner, that of additional recipients and all labour income, around 2017
(Percentages)

Original strata		Changes in socioeconomic position eliminating labour income of main breadwinner						High-income strata	Total
		Low-income strata			Middle-income strata				
		Extremely poor	Poor	Low-income non-poor	Lower-middle	Intermediate-middle	Upper-middle		
Low-income strata	Extremely poor	100.0	...	...	...	...	...	...	100.0
	Poor	74.9	25.1	...	...	...	...	...	100.0
	Low-income non-poor	35.2	47.2	17.6	...	...	...	...	100.0
Middle-income strata	Lower-middle	14.9	20.2	47.5	17.4	...	...	...	100.0
	Intermediate-middle	7.2	8.2	23.5	40.3	20.8	...	...	100.0
	Upper-middle	4.7	5.0	7.7	17.0	50.0	15.6	...	100.0
High-income strata	High-income strata	4.0	1.1	4.4	6.2	24.6	29.7	30.1	100.0
Total		37.2	23.5	19.2	11.2	6.4	1.6	0.9	100.0

Original strata		Changes in socioeconomic position eliminating labour income of additional recipients						High-income strata	Total
		Low-income strata			Middle-income strata				
		Extremely poor	Poor	Low-income non-poor	Lower-middle	Intermediate-middle	Upper-middle		
Low-income strata	Extremely poor	100.0	...	...	...	...	...	...	100.0
	Poor	16.8	83.2	...	...	...	...	...	100.0
	Low-income non-poor	2.9	34.4	62.7	...	...	...	...	100.0
Middle-income strata	Lower-middle	0.1	6.4	41.1	52.4	...	...	...	100.0
	Intermediate-middle	0.0	0.2	7.3	35.4	57.2	...	...	100.0
	Upper-middle	0.0	0.0	0.0	1.6	42.5	56.0	...	100.0
High-income strata		0.0	0.0	0.0	0.0	2.2	24.2	73.7	100.0
Total		12.3	27.1	26.7	17.1	11.2	3.3	2.3	100.0

Original strata		Changes in socioeconomic position eliminating all labour income						High-income strata	Total
		Low-income strata			Middle-income strata				
		Extremely poor	Poor	Low-income non-poor	Lower-middle	Intermediate-middle	Upper-middle		
Low-income strata	Extremely poor	100.0	...	...	...	...	...	...	100.0
	Poor	85.7	14.3	...	...	...	...	...	100.0
	Low-income non-poor	73.1	16.6	10.2	...	...	...	...	100.0
Middle-income strata	Lower-middle	56.6	18.4	12.8	12.2	...	...	...	100.0
	Intermediate-middle	31.6	27.8	15.3	12.3	13.1	...	...	100.0
	Upper-middle	14.1	22.5	20.0	13.0	18.0	12.5	...	100.0
High-income strata		10.6	3.0	17.0	17.2	20.5	11.4	20.3	100.0
Total		62.9	16.8	9.4	5.7	3.6	0.9	0.6	100.0

Source: Economic Commission for Latin America and the Caribbean (ECLAC), on the basis of Household Survey Data Bank (BADEHOG).

Poverty in Latin America: one of the critical obstacles to sustainable development

Introduction

A. Income poverty trends

B. Factors related to the recent poverty variations

Bibliography

Annex II.A1

Introduction

The persistence of poverty remains one of the critical obstacles to sustainable and more inclusive development in Latin America and the Caribbean (ECLAC, 2019a). The need to end poverty in all its forms, and thus fulfil the 2030 Agenda for Sustainable Development, has been widely recognized by the countries of the region.[1]

The increase in poverty and extreme poverty poses a major challenge when designing and implementing public policies in the vast majority of countries of the region, and the projected increase in 2019 only confirms that poverty and extreme poverty should remain at the centre of government discussions and efforts.

This chapter examines the extent of poverty in the region and its recent patterns, analyses trends in some related factors, and explores the possibilities countries have of eradicating extreme poverty by 2030 in order to fulfil the first Sustainable Development Goal (SDG).

Section A analyses the incidence and evolution of income poverty in the regional aggregate and in the different subregions on the basis of comparable measurements taken by the Economic Commission for Latin America and the Caribbean (ECLAC) (for more details of the methodology, see box II.1). It also describes changes in incidence and rates of poverty in each of the countries of Latin America. Lastly, it describes and compares the incidence of poverty among different subgroups of the population.

Box II.1
Income poverty measurement employed by the Economic Commission for Latin America and the Caribbean (ECLAC)

The poverty and extreme poverty figures presented in this chapter are calculated by ECLAC on the basis of a common methodology, which is intended to provide a regional perspective that is as comparable as possible, within the heterogeneity of the measurement tools and compilation procedures of each country's own data.

The approach used by ECLAC to estimate poverty consists of classifying a person as "poor" when the per capita income of his or her household is below the poverty line.

The poverty lines represent the level of income that enables each household to meet the basic needs of all its members. The basic basket for measuring poverty is formed from a selection of food, including the goods required to meet the nutritional needs of the population, taking into account their level of physical activity, consumption habits, effective availability of food and food prices in each country and geographical area.

To the value of this basic food basket, known as the "extreme poverty line", is added the amount required by households to satisfy basic non-food needs, in order to calculate the total value of the poverty line. To do this, the extreme poverty line is multiplied by a factor (called the Orshansky coefficient), which is the ratio of total spending to food spending for a reference population, and which has different values in each country and for urban and rural areas.

The extreme poverty and poverty lines are updated annually according to the cumulative variation in the consumer price index (CPI): the extreme poverty line is updated according to the variation in the CPI for food, while the part of the poverty line corresponding to spending on non-food is updated according to the variation in the CPI for non-food goods.

The percentages of households and of the population living in extreme poverty and poverty were obtained by contrasting the value of both poverty lines with the total per capita income of each household. Total household income is obtained by calculating the total income of household members (in cash and in kind) and includes income from work, income from retirement, pensions and other transfers, income from ownership of assets and other income (which includes imputed rent as part of total income).

Source: Economic Commission for Latin America and the Caribbean (ECLAC), *Income poverty measurement: updated methodology and results*, ECLAC Methodologies, No. 2 (LC/PUB.2018/22-P), Santiago, 2019.

---

[1] See, for example, resolution 3(III) of the third session of the Regional Conference on Social Development in Latin America and the Caribbean, held in October 2019 in Mexico City, [online] https://crds.cepal.org/3/sites/crds3/files/19-00900_cds.3_resolution_3-iii-ing_0.pdf.

Section B examines patterns in some factors relating to poverty trends. First, there is an analysis of the impact on poverty rates of variations in income averages and distribution, followed by an examination and comparison of the effect on poverty rates from changes in the various streams that make up household income (such as labour income, pensions and public and private transfers). This is followed by a continuation of the analysis presented in *Social Panorama of Latin America 2018* (ECLAC, 2019b) on the viability of eradicating extreme poverty and halving all poverty by 2030, as proposed in SDG 1. This exercise is performed for all the countries of the region, considering the variations in average income and income distribution between 2008 and 2018.

A.   Income poverty trends

Since 2015 there has been an increase in levels of poverty in the region, and especially extreme poverty, although this trend waned between 2017 and 2018. Nonetheless, in 2018, the incidences of poverty and extreme poverty were both higher than between 2012 and 2015. Despite the sombre panorama offered by the regional average, poverty declined in most countries between 2017 and 2018. For 2019, total poverty and extreme poverty are both expected to rise in the regional aggregate figures.

1.   Poverty and extreme poverty at the regional level and by subgroups of countries

In 2018, around 30.1% of the population of Latin America was below the poverty line, while 10.7% was below the extreme poverty line (see figure II.1). This means that, in that year, around 185 million people were living in poverty and 66 million people belonged to households with per capita incomes below the extreme poverty line.

Since 2015 there has been an increase in levels of poverty in the region, and especially extreme poverty, although this trend waned between 2017 and 2018. However, total poverty in 2018 was 2.3 percentage points higher than in 2014, an increase of about 21 million people. Extreme poverty grew by 2.9 percentage points and by around 20 million people between 2014 and 2018 (see figure II.1).

Regional aggregates for poverty and extreme poverty are projected to increase to 30.8% and 11.5%, respectively, in 2019 (see figure II.1). These projections are based on a forecast drop of 0.9% in the per capita economic growth rate for the region in 2019, and on the possibly sluggish economic performance expected from some countries in the region in 2019 (particularly Argentina and the Bolivarian Republic of Venezuela).[2]

The rise in poverty in the regional aggregate between 2014 and 2018 is essentially attributable to the increase in poverty in the Bolivarian Republic of Venezuela and Brazil. In Brazil, poverty and extreme poverty both grew from 2015 onward. Although poverty was lower in 2018 than in 2017, there was still a 3-percentage-point rise compared to 2014,[3] while the incidence of extreme poverty climbed 2 percentage points on 2014. As regards the Bolivarian Republic of Venezuela, the projections prepared by ECLAC indicate that people living in extreme poverty in the country as a percentage of the total regional population in that category increased from 8% in 2014 to 33% in 2018.[4]

---

[2]   The projected per capita GDP growth rate for 2019 is a weighted average.

[3]   In Brazil, the 2014 figures were adjusted according to the difference between the 2014 National Household Survey (PNAD) and Permanent National Household Survey (PNAD Continua), to make them comparable with those for 2018.

[4]   The poverty rates estimated by ECLAC for the Bolivarian Republic of Venezuela from 2015 onward are projections based on the growth rates of per capita GDP, as there are no data for household surveys for the country from 2015 onward.

Figure II.1

Latin America (18 countries): poverty and extreme poverty rates and persons living in poverty and extreme poverty, 2002–2019[a]

(Percentages and millions of persons)

A. Percentages

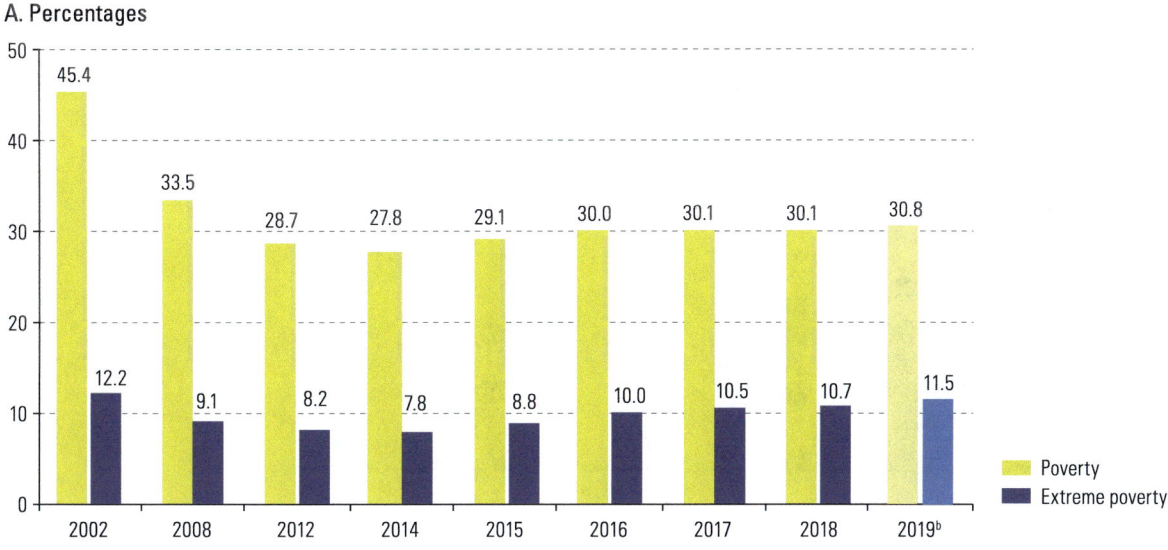

B. Millions of persons

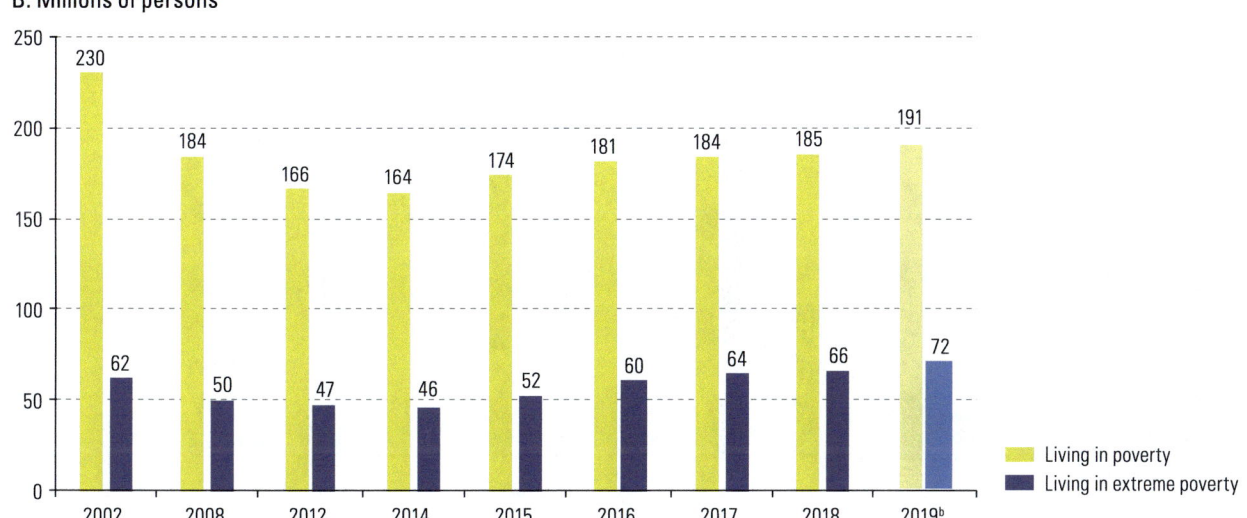

Source: Economic Commission for Latin America and the Caribbean (ECLAC), on the basis of Household Survey Data Bank (BADEHOG).
[a] Weighted average for the following countries: Argentina, Bolivarian Republic of Venezuela, Brazil, Chile, Colombia, Costa Rica, Dominican Republic, Ecuador, El Salvador, Guatemala, Honduras, Mexico, Nicaragua, Panama, Paraguay, Peru, Plurinational State of Bolivia and Uruguay.
[b] The values are projections.

Since 2014, however, there has been a decline in the incidence of total and extreme poverty in Central America. As a result, in 2018 the rate of overall poverty in the subregion was around 6.5 percentage points lower than in 2012 (see figure II.2). In Mexico, between 2014 and 2018, overall poverty declined, in a reversal of the country's trend of increases in poverty between 2008 and 2014. However, the decrease, in percentage point terms, was smaller than that in Central America. In South America (excluding the Bolivarian Republic of Venezuela and Brazil), overall poverty fell in 2015 and 2017, but in 2018 there was a slight increase, mainly owing to a rise in poverty in Argentina from 18.7% in 2017 to 24.4% in 2018.

Figure II.2

Latin America (17 countries): poverty and extreme poverty rates by country and subregion, 2008–2018
(Percentages)

A. Persons living in poverty

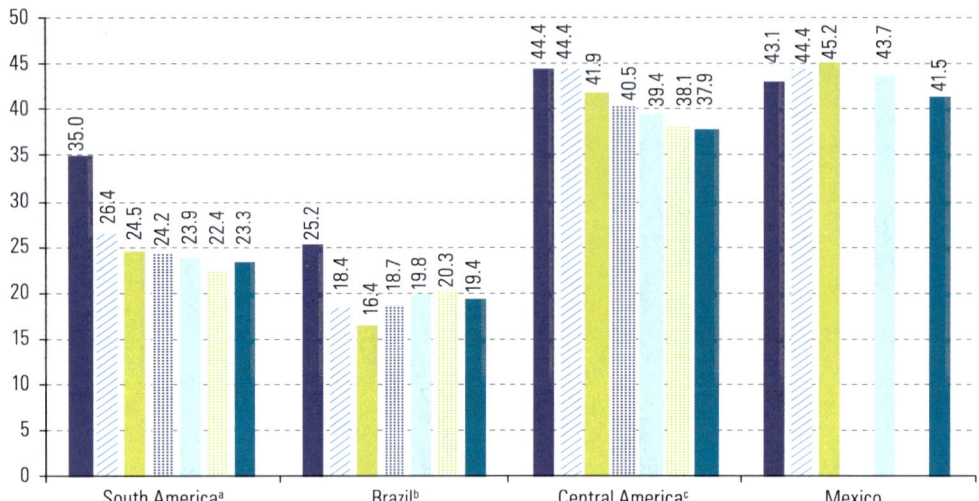

B. Persons living in extreme poverty

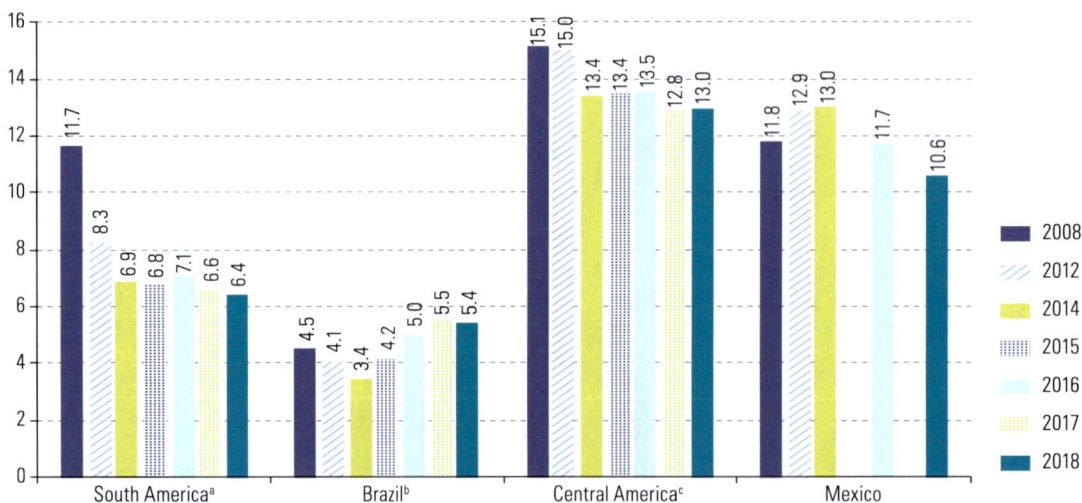

Source: Economic Commission for Latin America and the Caribbean (ECLAC), on the basis of Household Survey Data Bank (BADEHOG).

[a] Weighted average for: Argentina, Chile, Colombia, Ecuador, Paraguay, Peru, Plurinational State of Bolivia and Uruguay. Does not include the Bolivarian Republic of Venezuela, owing to the lack of data after 2014.

[b] Values between 2016 and 2018 correspond to the Permanent National Household Survey (PNAD Continua). Values between 2008 and 2015 correspond to the National Household Survey (PNAD), corrected for the difference between the two surveys in 2014.

[c] Weighted average for: Costa Rica, Dominican Republic, El Salvador, Guatemala, Honduras, Nicaragua and Panama. The values for Guatemala and Nicaragua are projections.

2. Poverty and extreme poverty by country

There is a broad heterogeneity among the countries of the region in the incidence of poverty and extreme poverty (see table II.1). In 2018, the best positioned countries were Uruguay and Chile, with overall poverty rates under 15% and incidences of extreme poverty under 5%. Below them stood Costa Rica, Peru and Panama. In the first two, total poverty rates were between 15% and 20%, and extreme poverty did not surpass 5%, while Panama's total poverty was less than 15% and its extreme poverty was between 5% and 10%. The worst situations were in Mexico, the Plurinational State of Bolivia, and above all Honduras.

Table II.1
Latin America (15 countries): classification of countries by poverty and extreme poverty rates, 2018[a]

		Poverty					
		Under 15%	15% to 20%	20% to 25%	25% to 30%	30% to 35%	Over 35%
Extreme poverty	Under 5%	Uruguay Chile	Costa Rica Peru	Argentina			
	5% to 10%	Panama	Brazil Paraguay	Ecuador Dominican Republic		El Salvador	
	10% to 15%				Colombia	Bolivia (Plurinational State of)	Mexico
	Over 15%						Honduras

Source: Economic Commission for Latin America and the Caribbean (ECLAC), on the basis of Household Survey Data Bank (BADEHOG).
[a] Includes only countries with available information for 2017 or 2018. Data refer to 2018 except in the case of Chile (2017).

Looking at changes in the incidence of total and extreme poverty between 2014 and 2018, the situation improved in seven countries (Chile, Colombia, Dominican Republic, El Salvador, Panama, Paraguay and Peru), and worsened in Brazil and the Dominican Republic (see table II.2). In Chile, Colombia, Panama and Paraguay there were reductions in total poverty. In Peru, the largest fall was in extreme poverty, and in El Salvador there were marked declines in both total and extreme poverty. In Brazil the deterioration is the result of a rise in extreme poverty, although the data series are not entirely comparable between 2014 and 2018.

Table II.2
Latin America (15 countries): classification of countries by poverty and extreme poverty rates, 2014[a]

		Poverty					
		Under 15%	15% to 20%	20% to 25%	25% to 30%	30% to 35%	Over 35%
Extreme poverty	Under 5%	Uruguay	Brazil Chile Costa Rica	Argentina			
	5% to 10%		Panama Peru	Ecuador Paraguay		Dominican Republic	
	10% to 15%					Bolivia (Plurinational State of) Colombia	El Salvador Mexico
	Over 15%						Honduras

Source: Economic Commission for Latin America and the Caribbean (ECLAC), on the basis of Household Survey Data Bank (BADEHOG).
[a] Includes only countries with available information for 2017 or 2018. Data refer to 2014 except in the case of Chile (2013).

As regards variations in the incidence of total poverty between 2017 and 2018, available information shows reductions in seven countries and increases in one country. There were no substantial changes in five countries (variations of less than one percentage point). In absolute terms, the main decreases in total poverty were recorded in El Salvador (3.3 percentage points), the Dominican Republic (3 percentage points), Mexico (2.3 percentage points, since 2016) and Panama (2.2 percentage points). In contrast, total poverty rose sharply in Argentina (5.6 percentage points) (see table II.3).

Table II.3
Latin America (15 countries): poverty and extreme poverty rates according to estimates by ECLAC and official national figures, 2015–2018[a]
(Percentages)

	ECLAC estimates									
	Extreme poverty				Total poverty				Variation 2017–2018	
	2015	2016	2017	2018	2015	2016	2017	2018	EP	P
Argentina[b]	...	2.9	2.8	3.6	...	21.5	18.7	24.4	0.8	5.6
Bolivia (Plurinational State of)	14.6	...	16.4	14.7	34.7	...	35.2	33.2	-1.7	-1.9
Brazil[c]	4.0	5.0	5.5	5.4	18.8	19.8	20.3	19.4	-0.1	-0.9
Chile	1.8	...	1.4	...	13.7	...	10.7	...	...	...
Colombia	11.3	12.0	10.9	10.8	30.6	30.9	29.8	29.9	-0.2	0.1
Costa Rica	4.6	4.2	3.3	4.0	17.4	16.5	15.4	16.2	0.7	0.8
Dominican Republic[d]	9.2	7.2	6.4	5.0	29.7	27.3	25.0	22.0	-1.5	-3.0
Ecuador	7.0	7.5	7.0	6.5	23.9	24.3	23.6	24.2	-0.5	0.5
El Salvador	10.4	10.7	8.3	7.6	42.6	40.5	37.8	34.5	-0.8	-3.3
Honduras	19.0	18.8	...	19.4	55.2	53.2	...	55.8	...	...
Mexico[e]	...	11.7	...	10.6	...	43.7	...	41.5	-1.0	-2.3
Panama	8.0	8.5	7.6	6.2	17.9	17.0	16.7	14.5	-1.4	-2.2
Paraguay	7.3	7.9	6.0	6.5	23.4	24.0	21.6	19.5	0.5	-2.1
Peru	5.4	5.2	5.0	3.7	19.0	19.1	18.9	16.8	-1.3	-2.1
Uruguay	0.2	0.2	0.1	0.1	4.2	3.5	2.7	2.9	0.0	0.3
	Official estimates by the countries									
	Extreme poverty				Total poverty				Variation 2017–2018	
	2015	2016	2017	2018	2015	2016	2017	2018	EP	P
Argentina[b]	...	6.1	4.8	6.7	...	30.3	25.7	32.0	1.9	6.3
Bolivia (Plurinational State of)	16.8	18.3	17.1	15.2	38.6	39.5	36.4	...	-1.9	...
Brazil[c]	4.9	5.8	6.4	6.5	23.7	25.5	26	25.3	0.1	-0.7
Chile	3.5	...	2.3	...	11.7	...	8.6	...		
Colombia	7.9	8.5	7.4	7.2	27.8	28.0	26.9	27.0	-0.2	0.1
Costa Rica[f]	7.2	6.3	5.7	6.3	21.7	20.5	20.0	21.1	0.6	1.1
Dominican Republic[d]	6.3	6.0	3.8	2.9	30.8	28.9	25.6	22.8	-0.9	-2.8
Ecuador	8.5	8.7	7.9	8.4	23.3	22.9	21.5	23.2	0.5	1.7
El Salvador[f]	8.1	7.9	6.2	5.7	34.9	32.7	29.2	26.3	-0.5	-2.9
Honduras[f]	40.0	38.4	40.7	38.7	63.8	60.9	64.3	61.9	-2.0	-2.4
Mexico[e]		17.5		16.8		50.6		48.8	-0.7	-1.8
Panama	10.2	9.9	9.8		23.0	22.1	20.7			
Paraguay	5.4	5.7	4.4	4.8	26.6	28.9	26.4	24.2	0.4	-2.2
Peru	4.1	3.8	3.8	2.8	21.8	20.7	21.7	20.5	-1.0	-1.2
Uruguay	0.3	0.2	0.1	0.1	9.7	9.4	7.9	8.1	0.0	0.2

Source: Economic Commission for Latin America and the Caribbean (ECLAC), on the basis of Household Survey Data Bank (BADEHOG) and official figures on poverty and extreme poverty.

[a] Countries for which ECLAC poverty estimates are available from 2015 onward.

[b] ECLAC estimates refer to the fourth quarter of each year. The official estimates refer to the second half of each year.

[c] From 2016 onward, the ECLAC estimates refer to the Permanent National Household Survey (PNAD-Continua) and are not comparable with those of previous years. The reported official data refer to estimates from the Brazilian Institute of Geography and Statistics (IBGE) (2019), based on the lines used by the World Bank for low- and medium-high-income countries.

[d] The ECLAC figures are based on the national labour force survey and refer to September of each year until 2015. From 2016 onward they are based on the continuous national labour force survey and are annual.

[e] The official poverty measurement is multidimensional. Therefore, the estimates published by the National Council for the Evaluation of Social Development Policy (CONEVAL) are used as an unofficial national reference, namely "population below the minimum welfare threshold", which is taken as a measure of "extreme poverty", and "population below the welfare threshold", which serves as a proxy for "total poverty".

[f] Official national measurement reported as a percentage of households.

Between 2017 and 2018, five countries recorded falls in the incidence of extreme poverty of more than one percentage point. The most significant declines occurred in the Plurinational State of Bolivia (1.7 percentage points), the Dominican Republic (1.5 percentage points), Panama (1.4 percentage points) and Peru (1.3 percentage points). In the remaining countries, there were no substantial absolute changes in the incidence of extreme poverty.

ECLAC and national official measurements generally coincide as regards the direction of estimated changes in poverty and extreme poverty between 2017 and 2018 (see table II.3). In the case of extreme poverty in Ecuador, however, is there a discrepancy between the two estimates, since the ECLAC measurement shows a drop of 0.5 percentage points, while the national data indicate an increase of the same magnitude. In Brazil, the estimate from the Brazilian Institute of Geography and Statistics (IBGE) (2019), which is not an official measurement of poverty, shows a rise in extreme poverty of 0.1 percentage points, while the ECLAC estimate indicates that extreme poverty declined by the same amount. In the remaining countries for which ECLAC measurements and official national measurements are available, the direction of the changes estimated by the two sources is the same, for both total and extreme poverty.

Figures II.3 and II.4 show the relative and absolute rates at which poverty and extreme poverty declined or increased in each country, considering two periods: 2008–2014 and 2014–2018. The absolute rate is the difference between the initial and final measurements of incidence of poverty. The relative rate takes into account the situation in the initial year, since it reflects the difference between the poverty rates in the initial and final year as a percentage of the incidence of poverty in the initial measurement.[5] Both rates are divided by the number of years between the initial and final measurements, to produce an estimate of the rate at which poverty declined or increased.

In 9 out of 15 countries in the region, the relative trend in total poverty was more positive between 2008 and 2014 than between 2014 and 2018. In seven of the nine countries, this was related to a faster reduction in poverty in the first period than in the second, and in two countries poverty declined between 2008 and 2014 and increased between 2014 and 2018 (the increase in poverty was much larger in Brazil than in Ecuador). In the Dominican Republic, El Salvador and Panama, poverty declined more rapidly between 2014 and 2018 than between 2008 and 2014, and in Mexico, the increase in poverty between 2008 and 2014 was reversed by a downward trend between 2014 and 2018.

In terms of absolute reductions in total poverty, the best performing countries between 2014 and 2018 were Chile, the Dominican Republic, El Salvador and Panama. In the Dominican Republic and El Salvador, the absolute decline in poverty was greater between 2014 and 2018 than between 2008 and 2014, while in Chile, the absolute reduction in poverty was smaller between 2014 and 2018 than between 2008 and 2014.

The tendency towards better performance in the 2008–2014 period than in 2014–2018 was more marked in the case of extreme poverty, as 10 countries performed better in the earlier period (see figure II.4). Considering only 2014–2018, the countries with the largest relative reductions in extreme poverty were Uruguay, the Dominican Republic and El Salvador. In absolute terms, between 2014 and 2018, extreme poverty decreased the most in the Dominican Republic and El Salvador.

---

[5]　For example, if in country "x" the poverty rate in the final measurement is 20% and the poverty rate in the initial measurement is 25%, the relative change in poverty is (20-25)/25. In this case, the relative change in non-annualized poverty is -20%. The absolute change in poverty (non-annualized) is -5 percentage points (20-25).

Figure II.3
Latin America (15 countries): poverty rate, relative and absolute annualized variations,
2008–2014 and 2014–2018[a]

A. Relative variation
(percentages)

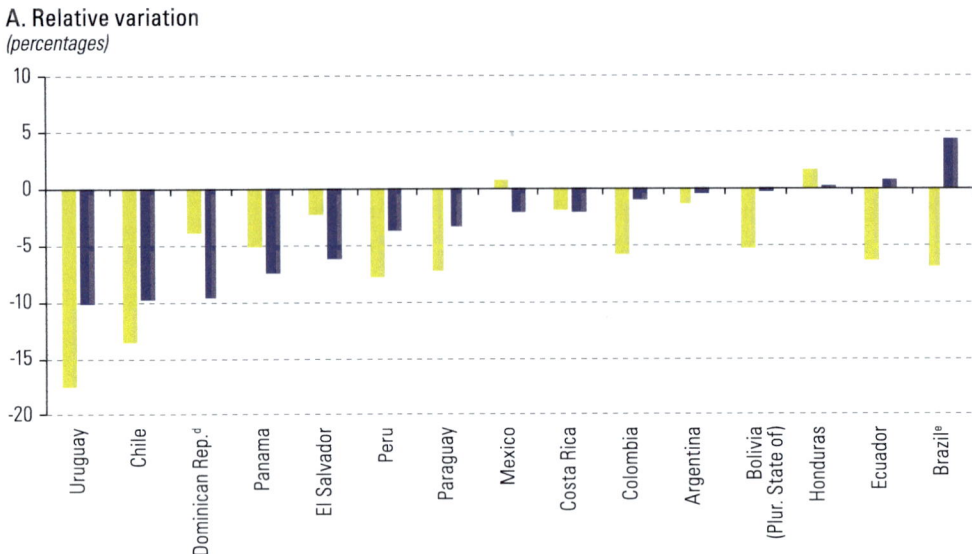

B. Absolute variation
(percentage points)

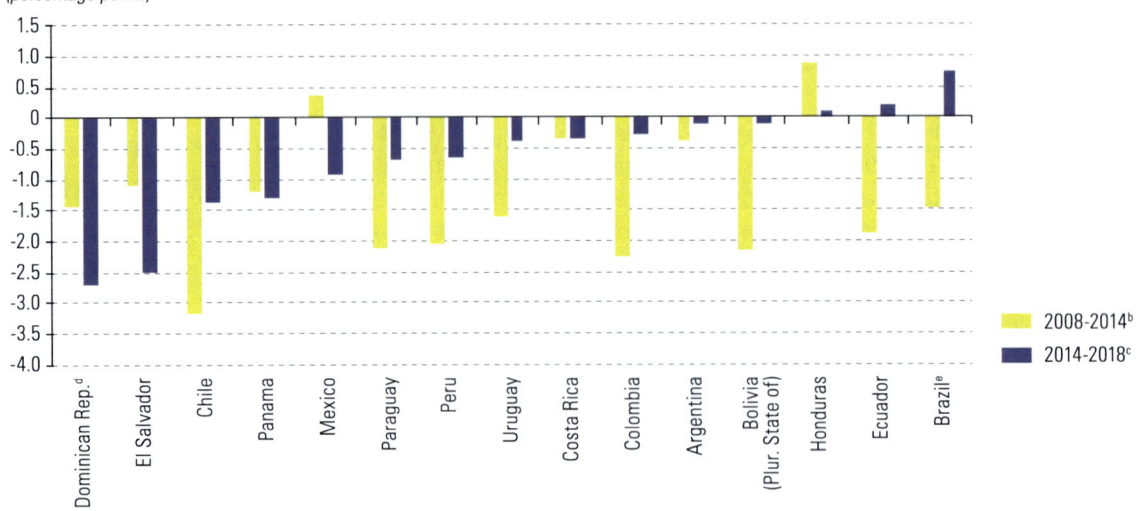

2008-2014[b]
2014-2018[c]

Source: Economic Commission for Latin America and the Caribbean (ECLAC), on the basis of Household Survey Data Bank (BADEHOG).
[a] The relative variation refers to the percentage variation in the poverty rate between the initial and end year. The absolute variation is the percentage-point difference
between the two years.
[b] The data refer to variations between 2008 and 2014, except in Chile (2009 and 2013), Costa Rica (2010 and 2014), El Salvador and Honduras (2009 and 2014).
[c] The data refer to the variations between 2014 and 2018, except for Chile (2013 and 2017).
[d] Figures are not strictly comparable over the period analysed.
[e] The 2008 and 2014 figures are adjusted for the difference between the National Household Survey (PNAD) and the 2014 Permanent National Household Survey
(PNAD Continua).

Figure II.4
Latin America (15 countries): extreme poverty rate, relative and absolute annualized variations, 2008–2014 and 2014–2018[a]

A. Relative variation
(percentages)

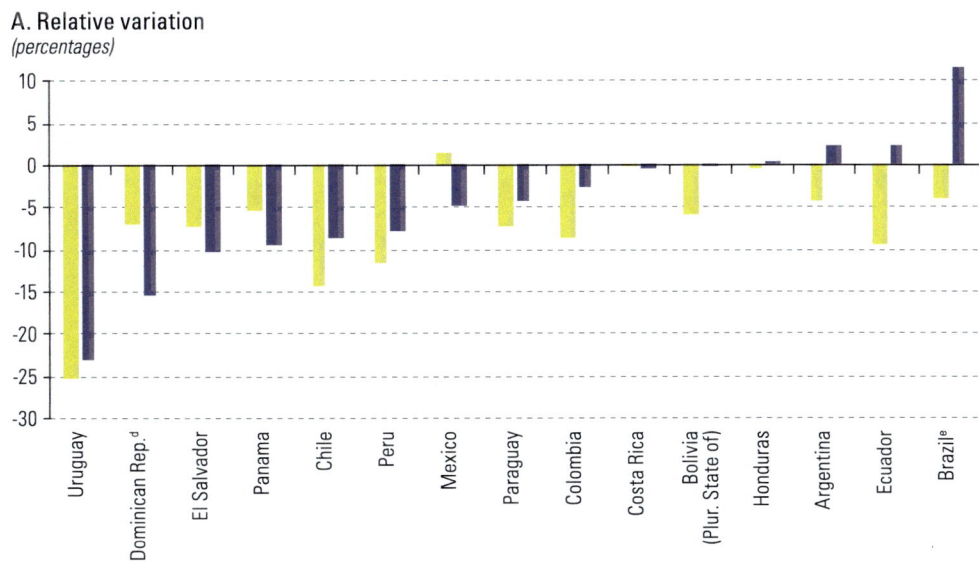

B. Absolute variation
(percentage points)

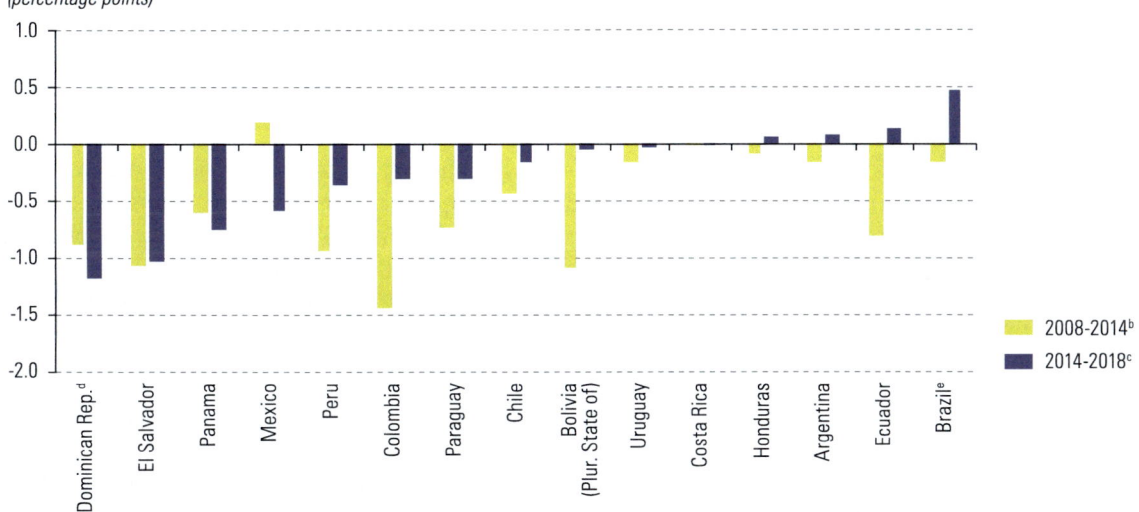

2008-2014[b]
2014-2018[c]

Source: Economic Commission for Latin America and the Caribbean (ECLAC), on the basis of Household Survey Data Bank (BADEHOG).

[a] The relative variation refers to the percentage variation in the poverty rate between the initial and end year. The absolute variation is the percentage-point difference between the two years.

[b] The data refer to variations between 2008 and 2014, except in Chile (2009 and 2013), Costa Rica (2010 and 2014), El Salvador and Honduras (2009 and 2014).

[c] The data refer to the variations between 2014 and 2018, except for Chile (2013 and 2017).

[d] Figures are not strictly comparable over the period analysed.

[e] The 2008 and 2014 figures are adjusted for the difference between the National Household Survey (PNAD) and the 2014 Permanent National Household Survey (PNAD Continua).

In Brazil and Argentina, the situation worsened between 2014 and 2018 compared to the period from 2008 to 2014. In Brazil, total poverty increased by 4.3% per year between 2014 and 2018, which contrasts sharply with the downward trend seen between 2008 and 2014 (6.9% per year). The trend in extreme poverty in Brazil is even more worrying, since between 2014 and 2018 it increased at a rate of 11.8% per year, while between 2008 and 2014 it decreased at an annual rate of 4%. In Argentina, poverty fell at a relative rate of 1.4% per year between 2008 and 2014, while between 2014 and 2018 it fell at a rate of 0.5% per year, mainly owing to the deterioration between 2017 and 2018 (see table II.3).

3.   Poverty and extreme poverty by population subgroups

Poverty does not affect the different subgroups of the Latin American population equally. For example, ECLAC (2019b), based on data from around 2017, indicates that the regional aggregates for incidence of poverty and extreme poverty were higher among persons living in rural areas, the younger population, those with the least schooling, women of working age, indigenous persons and Afrodescendants, among other groups. These disparities in incidence of poverty according to different sociodemographic characteristics were observed in previous studies of the region (ECLAC, 2014, 2016, 2018).

These inequalities still existed in 2018. The incidence of poverty was over 40% among those living in rural areas, children and adolescents aged 0–14, unemployed persons and indigenous persons. In contrast, poverty levels were lower among the urban population, older persons, wage earners, and among persons who are neither indigenous nor Afrodescendent.

Although the incidence of poverty and especially extreme poverty is much higher in rural areas (for example, in 2018 the rate of extreme poverty in rural areas was more than double that in urban areas), the trends between 2014 and 2018 were worse for urban areas (see figure II.5). Between 2014 and 2018, poverty and extreme poverty grew by 2.7 and 3.2 percentage points in urban areas, respectively, while in rural areas poverty and extreme poverty rose by 0.1 and 1.3 percentage points, respectively. In relative terms, in urban areas extreme poverty increased significantly more than poverty.

In terms of age groups, between 2014 and 2018, poverty and especially extreme poverty grew most in the younger population, particularly in the 0–14 age group (see figure II.6). Poverty and extreme poverty rates rose slightly more among women than among men in the 20–59 age group (see figure II.7),[6] and particularly increased —above all extreme poverty—among the unemployed (see figure II.8

---

[6]   The ratio between the poverty rates for women and men aged between 20 and 59 is the femininity index of poverty, which ECLAC regularly uses to portray gender gaps in poverty. Between 2014 and 2018, the femininity index of poverty held steady at 1.13 at the regional level, but the index for extreme poverty rose from 1.15 in 2014 to 1.18 in 2018.

Figure II.5
Latin America (18 countries): incidence of poverty and extreme poverty
by area of residence, 2014–2018[a]
(Percentages)

A. Poverty

B. Extreme poverty

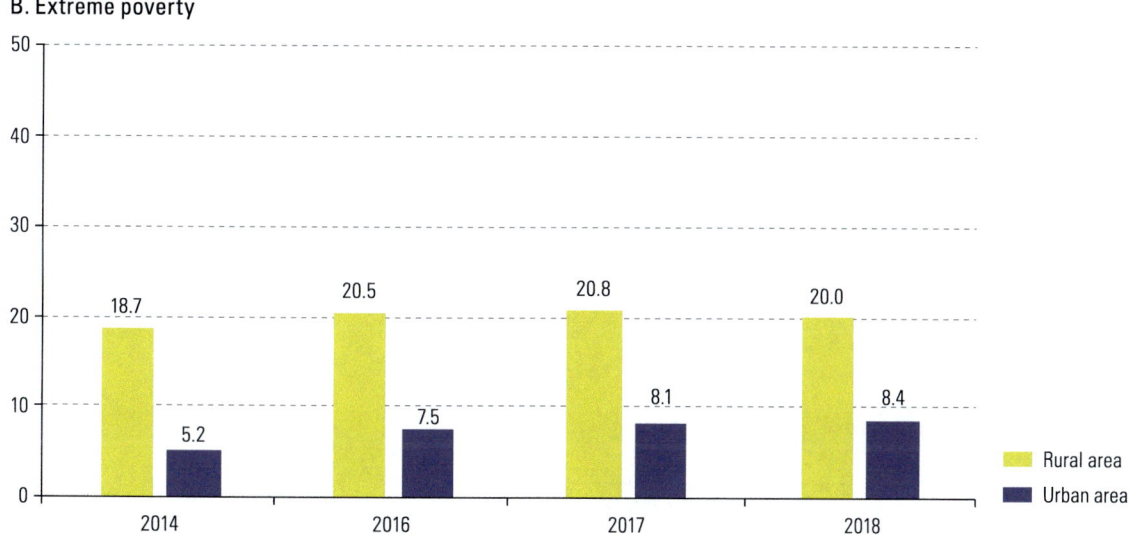

Source: Economic Commission for Latin America and the Caribbean (ECLAC), on the basis of Household Survey Data Bank (BADEHOG).
[a] Weighted average for the following countries: Argentina (urban), Bolivarian Republic of Venezuela, Brazil, Chile, Colombia, Costa Rica, Dominican Republic, Ecuador, El Salvador, Guatemala, Honduras, Mexico, Nicaragua, Panama, Paraguay, Peru, Plurinational State of Bolivia and Uruguay.

Figure II.6

Latin America (18 countries): incidence of poverty and extreme poverty by age group, 2014–2018[a]

(Percentages)

A. Poverty

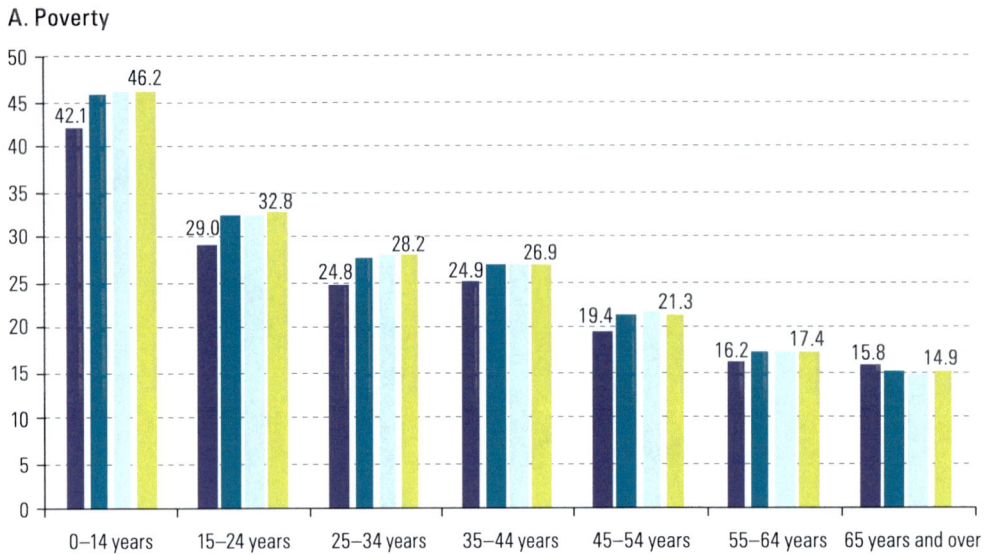

B. Extreme poverty

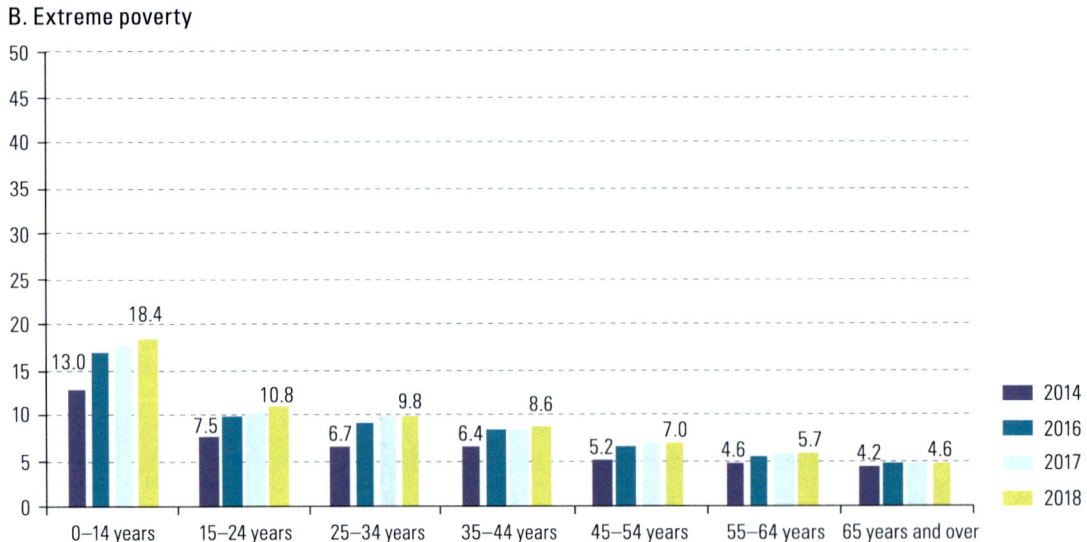

Source: Economic Commission for Latin America and the Caribbean (ECLAC), on the basis of Household Survey Data Bank (BADEHOG).

[a] Weighted average for the following countries: Argentina (urban), Bolivarian Republic of Venezuela, Brazil, Chile, Colombia, Costa Rica, Dominican Republic, Ecuador, El Salvador, Guatemala, Honduras, Mexico, Nicaragua, Panama, Paraguay, Peru, Plurinational State of Bolivia and Uruguay.

Figure II.7

Latin America (18 countries): incidence of poverty and extreme poverty by gender, 2014–2018[a]
(Percentage of population aged 20–59)

A. Poverty

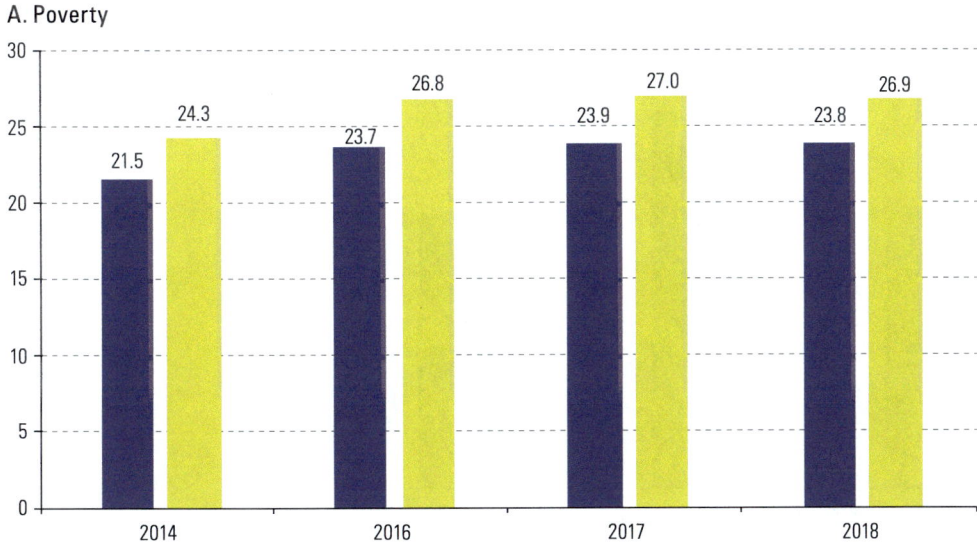

B. Extreme poverty

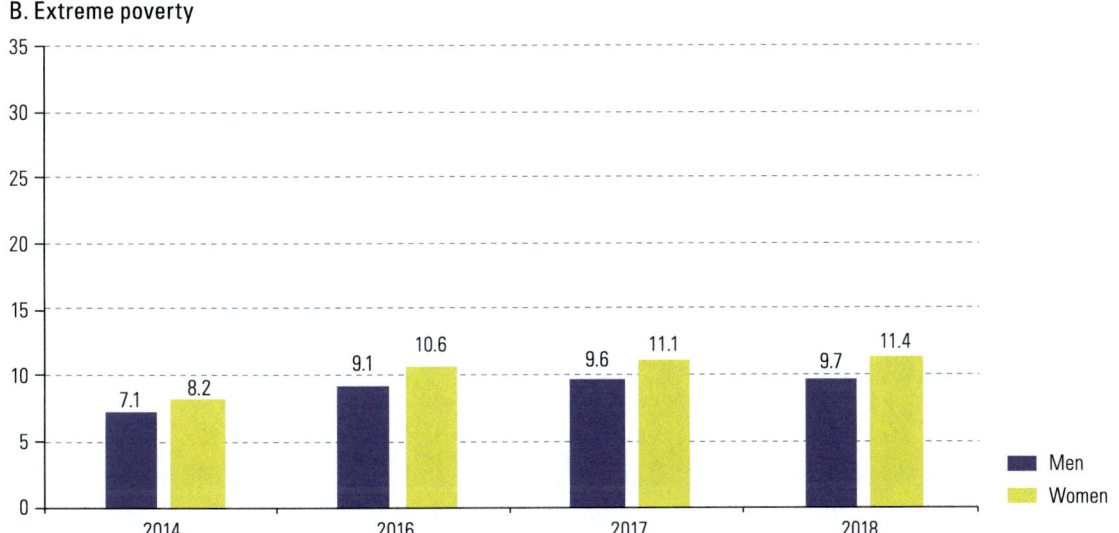

Source: Economic Commission for Latin America and the Caribbean (ECLAC), on the basis of Household Survey Data Bank (BADEHOG).
[a] Weighted average for the following countries: Argentina (urban), Bolivarian Republic of Venezuela, Brazil, Chile, Colombia, Costa Rica, Dominican Republic, Ecuador, El Salvador, Guatemala, Honduras, Mexico, Nicaragua, Panama, Paraguay, Peru, Plurinational State of Bolivia and Uruguay.

Figure II.8

Latin America (18 countries): incidence of poverty and extreme poverty by employment status, 2014–2018[a]
(Percentages of population aged 15 and over)

A. Poverty

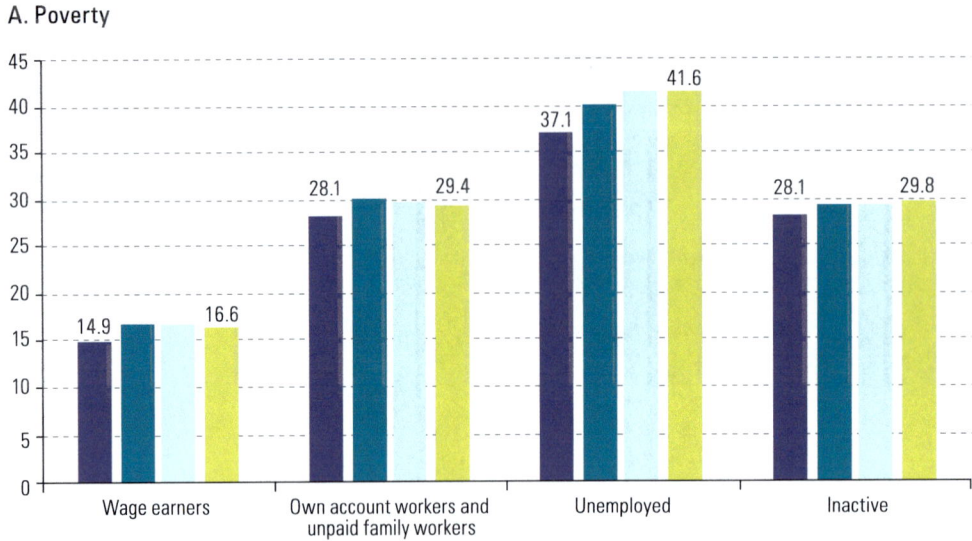

B. Extreme poverty

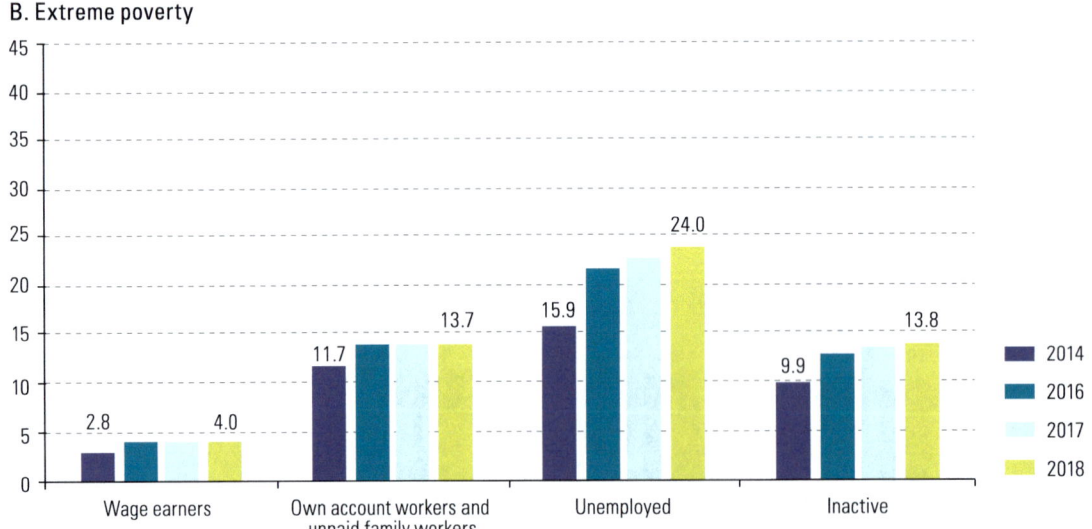

Source: Economic Commission for Latin America and the Caribbean (ECLAC), on the basis of Household Survey Data Bank (BADEHOG).
[a] Weighted average for the following countries: Argentina (urban), Bolivarian Republic of Venezuela (urban), Brazil, Chile, Colombia, Costa Rica, Dominican Republic, Ecuador, El Salvador, Guatemala, Honduras, Mexico, Nicaragua, Panama, Paraguay, Peru, Plurinational State of Bolivia and Uruguay.

An examination of the trend in poverty and extreme poverty according to ethnicity and race between 2014 and 2018, in the countries that make the relevant information available, shows significantly higher rates among indigenous persons and Afrodescendants compared with persons who are neither indigenous nor Afrodescendent in all the years considered (with the exception of Panama in the case of Afrodescendants) (see figure II.9).

Figure II.9
Latin America (5 countries): incidence of poverty by ethnicity and race, 2014 and 2018[a][b]
(Percentages)

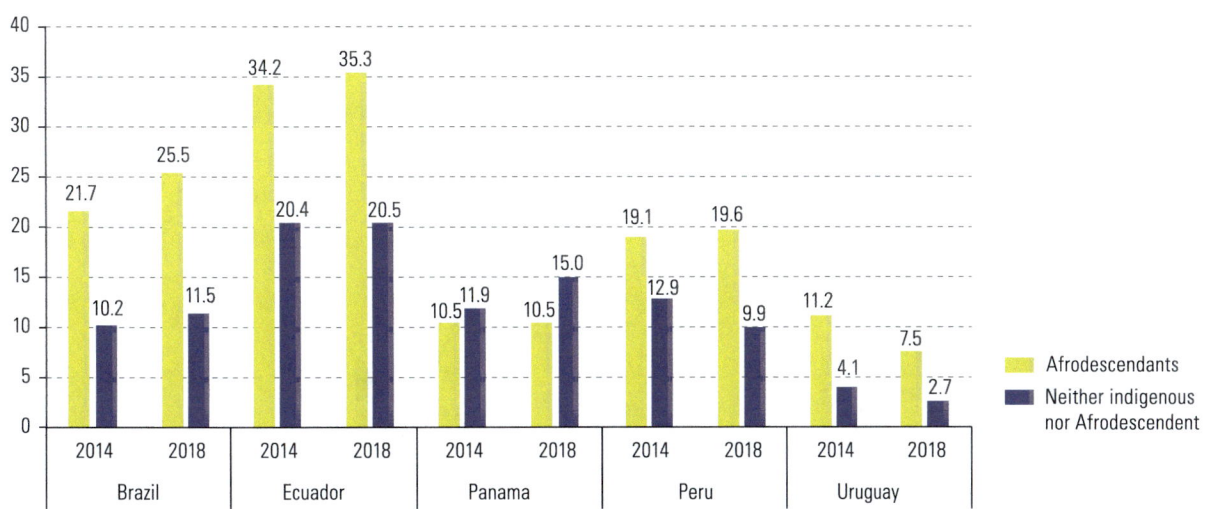

Source: Economic Commission for Latin America and the Caribbean (ECLAC), on the basis of Household Survey Data Bank (BADEHOG).
[a] Regional weighted averages were not used, owing to the low number of countries with available information and Brazil's high relative weighting in the weighted average.
[b] The years are as indicated, except for Ecuador (2015 is used for 2014) and Chile (2017 is used for 2018).

In the case of indigenous persons, despite a slight narrowing of the gaps in the period in question, in 2018 the poverty rate was 48.8% and the extreme poverty rate 17.9%, twice (2.2 times) and more than three times (3.4 times) the respective rates for the population that is neither indigenous nor Afrodescendent (see figure II.10).

In four of the five Latin American countries that have information through household surveys, the incidence of poverty by ethnicity was significantly higher among the Afrodescendent population than among the population that is neither indigenous nor Afrodescendent both in 2014 and around 2018 (see figure II.9). Between 2014 and 2018, the incidence of poverty among Afrodescendants increased by 3.8 percentage points in Brazil, and in Ecuador poverty increased by 1.1 percentage points between 2015 and 2018. In Peru, poverty among Afrodescendants increased by 0.5 percentage points. while among persons that are neither indigenous nor Afrodescendent it decreased by 3 percentage points. In Uruguay, the 2018 poverty rate for the Afrodescendent population was 2.8 times that of the population that is neither indigenous nor Afrodescendent, while in Brazil and Peru, the ratios were 2.2 and 2, respectively. The only country in which the rates of poverty and extreme poverty (as measured in household surveys) for Afrodescendants are lower than those for persons who are neither indigenous nor Afrodescendent is Panama.

Indigenous persons and Afrodescendants tend to be poorer than persons who are neither indigenous nor Afrodescendent in both rural and urban areas (see table II.4). The main difference is that in rural areas, the disparities are greater for the indigenous population, while in urban areas they affect Afrodescendants more. Around 2018, in rural areas the incidence of poverty among indigenous persons was on average 1.62 times that of non-indigenous and non-Afrodescendent persons, while for Afrodescendants it was 1.32 times that of non-indigenous and non-Afrodescendent persons. In urban areas, on average Afrodescendants are 1.94 times poorer than persons who are neither indigenous nor Afrodescendent, a higher ratio than for indigenous people (1.79 times). However, considering solely the four countries for which there is information for both groups (Brazil, Ecuador, Panama and Peru), the disparity in urban areas affects indigenous persons more than it affects Afrodescendants.

Figure II.10

Latin America (8 countries): incidence of poverty and extreme poverty by ethnicity, 2014–2018[a]

(Percentages)

A. Poverty

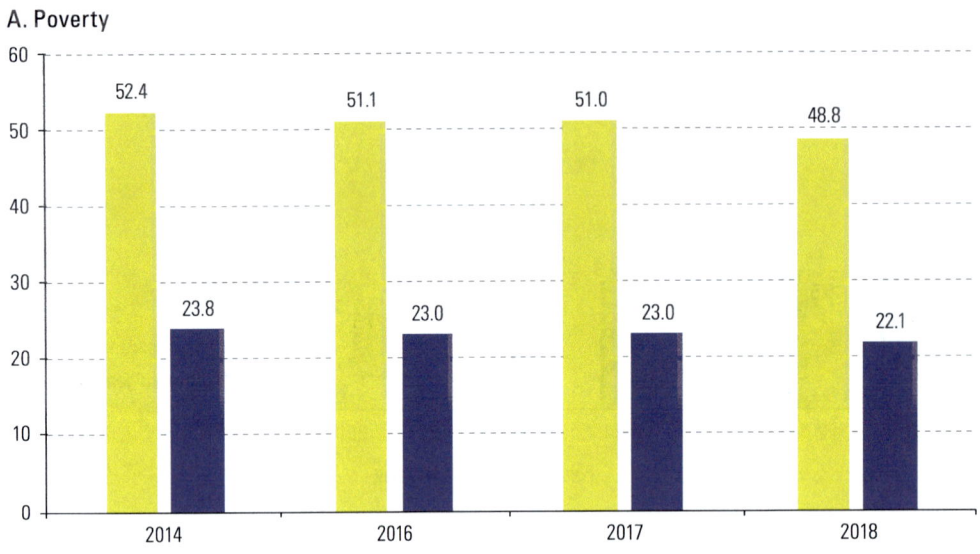

B. Extreme poverty

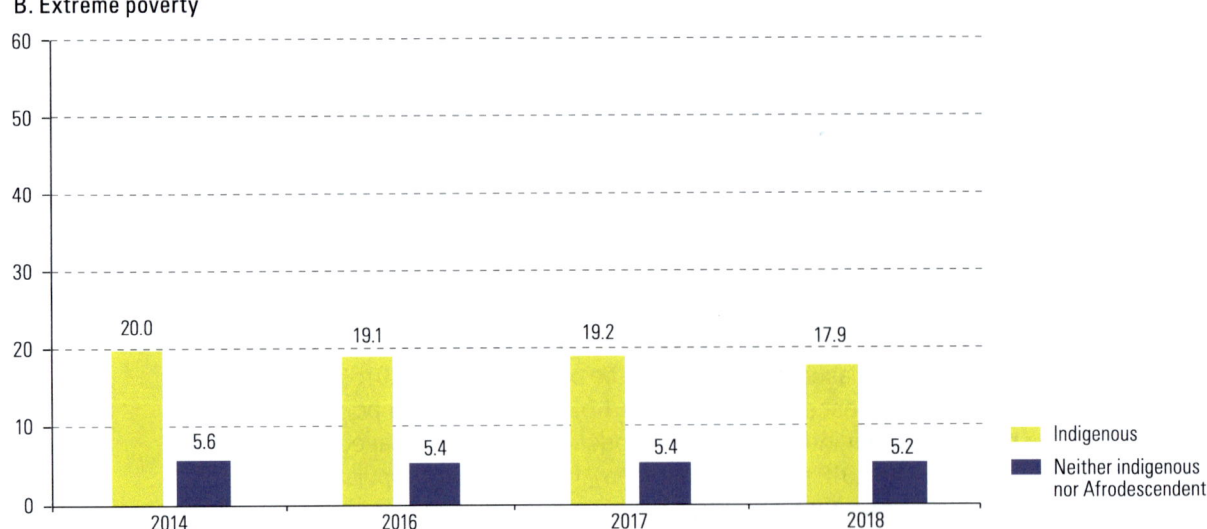

Source: Economic Commission for Latin America and the Caribbean (ECLAC), on the basis of Household Survey Data Bank (BADEHOG).

[a] Weighted average for Brazil, Chile, Ecuador, Mexico, Panama, Peru, the Plurinational State of Bolivia and Uruguay. The ethnicity indicator is constructed on the basis of ethnicity as reported by respondents and is not strictly comparable across countries.

Table II.4
Latin America (8 countries): incidence of poverty and by ethnicity and area of residence, 2018

Countries	Rural areas				
	Afrodescendants (A)	Indigenous persons (B)	Neither afrodescendent nor indigenous (C)	Disparity Afrodescendants (A/C)	Disparity Indigenous persons (B/C)
Bolivia (Plurinational State of)	-	65	48.2	-	1.35
Brazil	37.5	42.6	19.8	1.89	2.15
Chile	-	16.1	7.8	-	2.06
Ecuador	42.8	55.5	27.1	1.58	2.05
Mexico	-	64.4	48.6	-	1.33
Panama	16.6	37	32.3	0.51	1.15
Peru	34.4	32.8	26.7	1.29	1.23
Average rural disparity	-	-	-	1.32	1.62

Countries	Urban areas				
	Afrodescendants (A)	Indigenous persons (B)	Neither afrodescendent nor indigenous (C)	Disparity Afrodescendants (A/C)	Disparity Indigenous persons (B/C)
Bolivia (Plurinational State of)		28.1	22.5		1.25
Brazil	23.1	30.2	10.5	2.20	2.88
Chile		15.2	10.5		1.45
Ecuador	32.2	34.4	18	1.79	1.91
Mexico		45.4	32.6		1.39
Panama	8.2	11.3	7.1	1.15	1.59
Peru	13.5	15.3	7.5	1.80	2.04
Uruguay	7.7		2.8	2.75	
Average urban disparity				1.94	1.79

Source: Economic Commission for Latin America and the Caribbean (ECLAC), on the basis of Household Survey Data Bank (BADEHOG).

B. Factors related to the recent poverty variations

The role of redistribution has been fundamental, complementing economic growth and reductions in poverty during periods of prosperity, as well as preventing increases in poverty in phases of economic decline. Between 2014 and 2018, in 7 of the 13 countries in the region where poverty fell, there was a marked distribution effect.

In terms of sources of income, between 2014 and 2018, labour income was the item of income that had the greatest impact on changes in poverty rates. However, the best results in terms of reductions in poverty were seen in countries that experienced increases in public and private transfers in addition to rises in labour income.

1. Level and distribution of household income

Changes in the incidence of income poverty over time are linked to changes in average household income and in the distribution of income among households. A contraction in average household income, coupled with an increase in income concentration, produces a greater increase in the poverty rate than an equivalent fall in average household income that is not accompanied by a deterioration in distribution. Conversely, a reduction in levels of inequality (associated, for example, with redistributive policies in the area of social protection or the labour market) together with an increase in average household income leads to a greater reduction in the poverty rate than that which would occur with just one of these factors.

Changes in poverty rates are generally analysed by breaking them down into two elements: the effect of variations in average income (also known as the "growth effect") and the distribution effect (see box II.2). This is followed by an examination of impact of the income and distribution effects on changes in poverty rates in countries, using as a reference the subperiods 2008–2014 and 2014–2018.

Box II.2
Effect of changes in distribution and levels of household income on poverty

According to the traditional methodology for measuring poverty, based on income insufficiency, a country's poverty rate at a given moment is determined by three elements: the poverty line, average income and the structure of the income distribution. Hence, if the poverty line is kept constant in real terms, changes in the poverty indicator can be analysed from the perspective of variations in average income and in income distribution.

According to Datt and Ravallion (1992), a poverty indicator can be calculated using the initial-period income distribution and the average income level of the end period. The difference between this indicator and the initial-period poverty rate can be interpreted as a growth effect on average income. It is also possible to calculate the poverty rate that corresponds to the average income of the initial period, but with an income distribution similar to that of the end period. The difference between this indicator and the initial poverty rate is the distribution effect. Both effects can also be calculated by exchanging the initial and end periods.

In formal terms, if H(yt,dt) is the poverty indicator for period t, determined by average income (yt) and the shape of the distribution (dt), the growth and distribution effects can be decomposed as follows:

$$H(y_2,d_2) - H(y_1,d_1) = \underbrace{[H(y_2,d_1) - H(y_1,d_1)]}_{\text{Growth effect}} + \underbrace{[H(y_1,d_2) - H(y_1,d_1)]}_{\text{Distribution effect}} + R$$

In this decomposition, the strength of each effect depends on the base year used in the comparison (initial or end year), and it produces an unexplained residual. Both obstacles can be overcome by averaging the calculated effects using each of the two base years respectively (Kakwani,1997). This procedure is used to perform the calculations in this chapter.

The link between growth, distributive change and poverty can be used to simulate the trajectory of poverty rates in the future. For this, the methodology used generates a new income distribution (y^*) applying specific growth rates (β) and distributive change (α) to per capita household income (y) in each country, captured in household surveys, by means of the following equations:

If $y \geq \mu$: $y^* = (1+\beta)[(1-\alpha)y_i + \alpha\mu]$

If $y < \mu$: $y^* = (1+\beta)[\theta y_i]$, where θ is calculated in such a way that $\mu^* = (1+\beta)\mu$.

(where μ represents the average income distribution)

In other words, the methodology is to increase (or decrease) below-average incomes at a fixed rate and reduce (or increase) higher-than-average incomes at a rate proportional to the distance between each value and the mean.

Source: Economic Commission for Latin America and the Caribbean (ECLAC), on the basis of G. Datt and M. Ravallion, "Growth and redistribution components of changes in poverty measures", *Journal of Development Economics*, vol. 38, No. 2, Amsterdam, Elsevier, 1992, and N. Kakwani, "On measuring growth and inequality components of changes in poverty with application to Thailand", *Discussion Paper*, Sydney, University of New South Wales, 1997.

These subperiods, of 2008–2014 and 2014–2018, were chosen because they show different trends in poverty rates in the countries, since the rate of poverty reduction between 2014 and 2018 was 3.4% per year, while between 2008 and 2014 it was 5.5% per year.[7] Another reason for selecting longer time periods is that changes in poverty levels over very short intervals —for example two years— may not be large enough for the breakdown to produce robust results.

The results of this exercise confirm what has been observed in previous editions of the *Social Panorama* (ECLAC, 2018 and 2019b), that is to say that as the rate of reduction in poverty slows, the income effect weakens, and the distributive component acquires greater importance. This means that, even when the distribution effect has had a smaller impact on the trend in absolute poverty than the income effect, its role has been crucial, either by complementing the income effect on the reduction of poverty during periods of prosperity, or by preventing increases in poverty in situations of economic deterioration.

Between 2014 and 2018, when the pace of poverty reduction slowed, the distribution effect predominated in 5 of the 12 countries where poverty fell. Conversely, between 2008 and 2014, when poverty declined more rapidly, the distribution effect was greater in just 2 of the 13 countries with falls in poverty rates (see figure II.11).

In the countries with the largest relative reductions in poverty (5% to 10%) between 2014 and 2018, the income effect was more marked than the distribution effect (averages of 6.3% and 2.5%, respectively).[8] In contrast, in countries with more moderate decreases in poverty (2% to 3%) the average distribution effect was -2.4% and the average income effect was -0.4%.

The countries where poverty declined the most in in relative terms between 2014 and 2018 were, in order, Uruguay, Chile, the Dominican Republic and Panama. In the last three countries, the income effect was much more significant, while in Uruguay the distribution effect had a greater impact. In Colombia, Paraguay and the Plurinational State of Bolivia, changes in distribution counteracted the contraction in average household incomes, thereby reducing poverty. In Brazil, the increase in poverty was mainly caused by a worsening of distribution, as opposed to average incomes, which were almost unchanged.

With a longer-term perspective, the data for Uruguay and Chile, the countries with the largest relative reductions in poverty between 2008 and 2018, show two different stories. In Chile, the income effect is predominant, while in Uruguay, although the income effect was the larger of the two, the distribution effect contributed significantly to reducing poverty. Peru is the country with the second largest relative impact on poverty reduction from the distribution effect between 2008 and 2018. In Argentina and Mexico, the slight falls in poverty rates between 2008 and 2018 were essentially the result of the distribution effect, since average income tended to worsen over the period.

---

[7]　Simple averages of annualized rates of increase or decrease in poverty in 15 countries.
[8]　Simple averages of income and distribution effects for the group of countries in which poverty declined by 5%–10%.

Figure II.11

Latin America (15 countries): annual variation in poverty rate and relative contribution of growth and distribution effects, 2008–2014, 2014–2018 and 2008–2018

(Percentages)

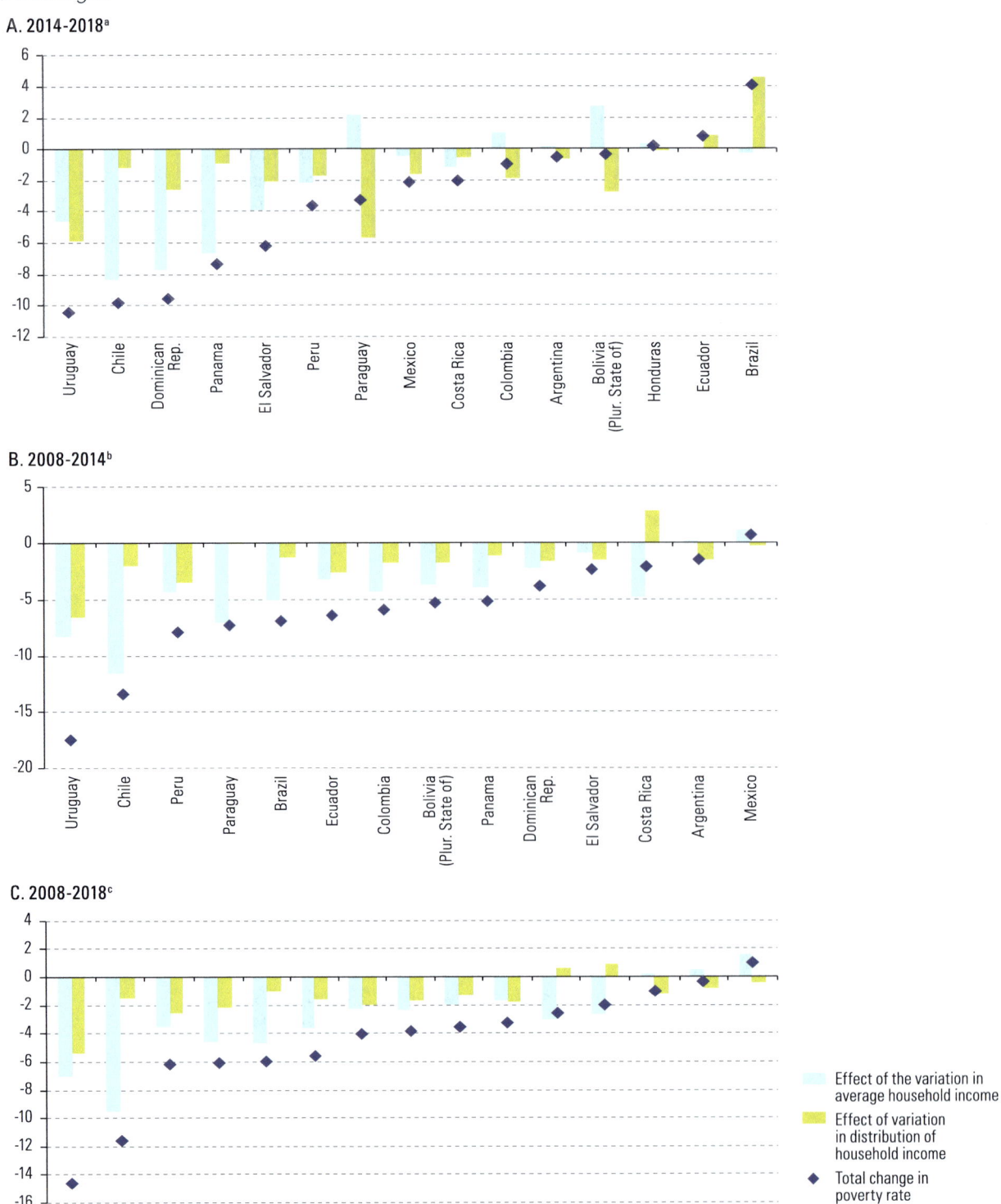

A. 2014-2018[a]

B. 2008-2014[b]

C. 2008-2018[c]

Effect of the variation in average household income

Effect of variation in distribution of household income

◆ Total change in poverty rate

Source: Economic Commission for Latin America and the Caribbean (ECLAC), on the basis of Household Survey Data Bank (BADEHOG).

[a] Data refer to the subperiod 2014–2018, except for Chile (2013–2017).

[b] Data refer to the 2008–2014 subperiod, except for Chile (2009–2013), El Salvador and Honduras (2009–2014), and Costa Rica (2010–2014).

[c] The data refer to the 2008–2018 subperiod, except for Chile (2009–2017), Costa Rica (2010–2018), El Salvador and Honduras (2009–2018).

2. Trends in the income sources of lower-income households

Monetary poverty inflows and outflows come from expansions or contractions in household income at the bottom end of the income distribution structure. Ideally, to identify the income flows that determine whether households emerge from or fall into poverty, the income of the same households must be assessed over different periods of time. As there are still few longitudinal surveys in the region that can capture variations in the income of the same households over time, this document analyses the changes in the different income streams in the same proportion of households from the bottom end of the income distribution structure, between 2014 and 2018.

To set the threshold in income distribution, for each country the poverty rate for the year in which the rate was highest was used —either the initial or end year— and 5 percentage points were added, to include households that are just above the poverty line. This makes it possible to analyse changes in the different income streams for the same percentage of households in the two years, regardless of changes in the incidence of poverty.[9]

The household income streams analysed in this exercise are: (a) labour income, including wages and income from self-employment; (b) public and private transfers, including pensions and contributory pensions, non-contributory transfers and other transfers (including remittances); and (c) other income, including income from ownership of assets and rent imputed for owned housing. Household income from different sources varies according to changes in the number of recipients and the average income per recipient from each source.

Labour income, including wages and income from self-employment, was the item of household income that had the greatest impact on variations in poverty rates between 2014 and 2018. In all the countries that were able to substantially reduce poverty (by 5% or more), and in almost all the countries with moderate declines in poverty, the increase in labour income was the main reason for growth in the income of low-income households. In Brazil, a country that experienced an increase in poverty, the drop in labour income was main driver of the contraction in income for low-income households (see figure II.12).

Income from public and private transfers also had an impact on changes in poverty rates between 2014 and 2018, but to a lesser degree than labour income. In 7 of the 10 countries with marked or moderate reductions in poverty, income from public or private transfers was second-ranked income stream in terms of contributions to the increase in income for low-income households. In one of these countries (Costa Rica), transfers were the topmost driver of the rise in incomes of low-income households.

The contribution of other income (mainly imputed rent and asset ownership) to changes in the total income of low-income households was generally smaller than that of labour income and transfers. The largest contributions from this income stream to increases in the income of low-income households were seen in Chile, Paraguay, Honduras and the Dominican Republic. In this group of countries, imputed rent accounted for 87% or more of the growth in the "other income" stream.[10]

---

[9]　If in a given country poverty fell from 20% to 16% between 2014 and 2018, the threshold would be 20% plus an additional 5% of households. If in another country poverty increased from 14% to 20% in the same period, the cut-off point would be the same. Thus, in both countries the analysis would be of the changes in different income streams for the 25% of households with the lowest per capita income.

[10]　Imputed rent is the income in kind allocated to households that own the dwelling in which they live. Therefore, it is not an unrestricted resource for households.

Figure II.12
Latin America (15 countries): annual variation in total per capita income among lower-income households,
by source of income, 2014–2018[a]
(Annualized figures)

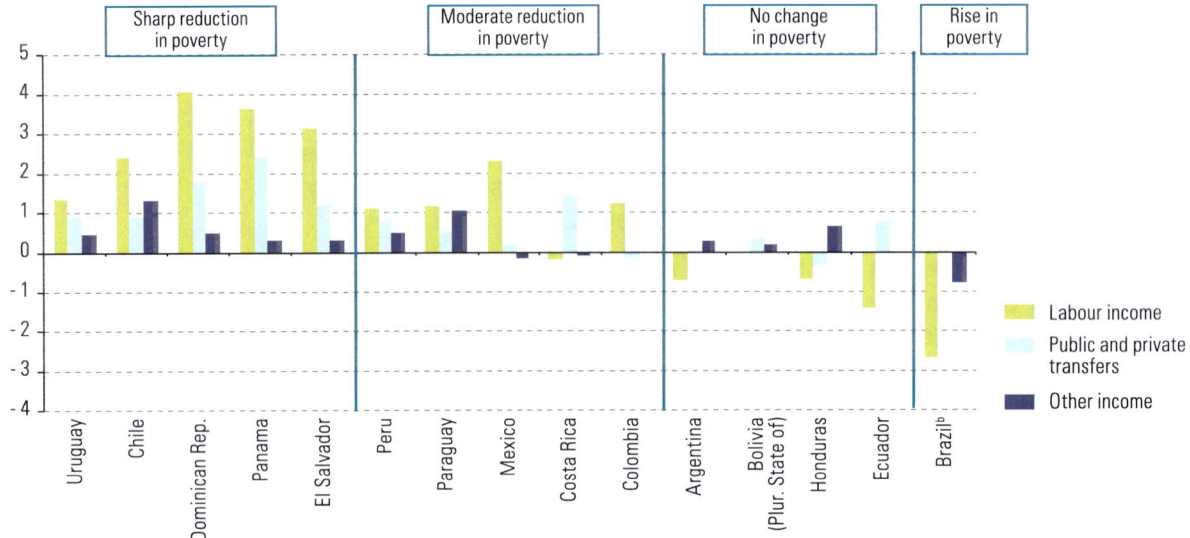

Source: Economic Commission for Latin America and the Caribbean (ECLAC), on the basis of Household Survey Data Bank (BADEHOG).
[a] Countries ranked by magnitude of reduction in poverty. Data refer to the subperiod 2014–2018, except for Chile (2013–2017).
[b] In Brazil, it is not possible to disaggregate transfers further for the entire period. Public and private transfers are therefore presented in the "other income" stream.

Thus, although changes in labour income contribute very significantly to variations in total household income at the bottom of the income distribution structure, they do not in themselves explain the differences between countries in the rates at which poverty increased or declined. For example, in countries with marked or moderate decreases in poverty, increases in labour income were accompanied by increases in other sources of income, especially public and private transfers. In the five countries with no significant changes or increases in poverty, the predominant situation was a fall in labour income.

(a) Trends in the labour income of lower-income households

In the countries that saw the largest reductions in poverty between 2014 and 2018, the increase in the labour income of low-income households was explained by an increase in the income of both wage earners and own account workers. In Panama and Uruguay, the rise in income from self-employment contributed most to the growth in labour income, while in the Dominican Republic and El Salvador the increase in wage income was more important (see figure II.13).

Within the group of countries with moderate decreases in poverty, the predominant situation was a somewhat larger increase in income from self-employment as compared to the rise in wage income (Colombia, Paraguay and Peru). In Mexico, the increase in labour income was primarily driven by the increase in wage income. In Costa Rica, both wages and income from self-employment declined slightly.

In three of the four countries with no changes in poverty (Argentina, Ecuador and the Plurinational State of Bolivia), there was a fall in the wage income of low-income households. As a counterbalance, in Ecuador and the Plurinational State of Bolivia, income from self-employment increased. In Honduras, income from self-employment fell and wage income grew slightly.

Figure II.13
Latin America (14 countries): contribution of wages and income from self-employment to total income variation among lower-income households, 2014–2018[a]
(Annualized figures)

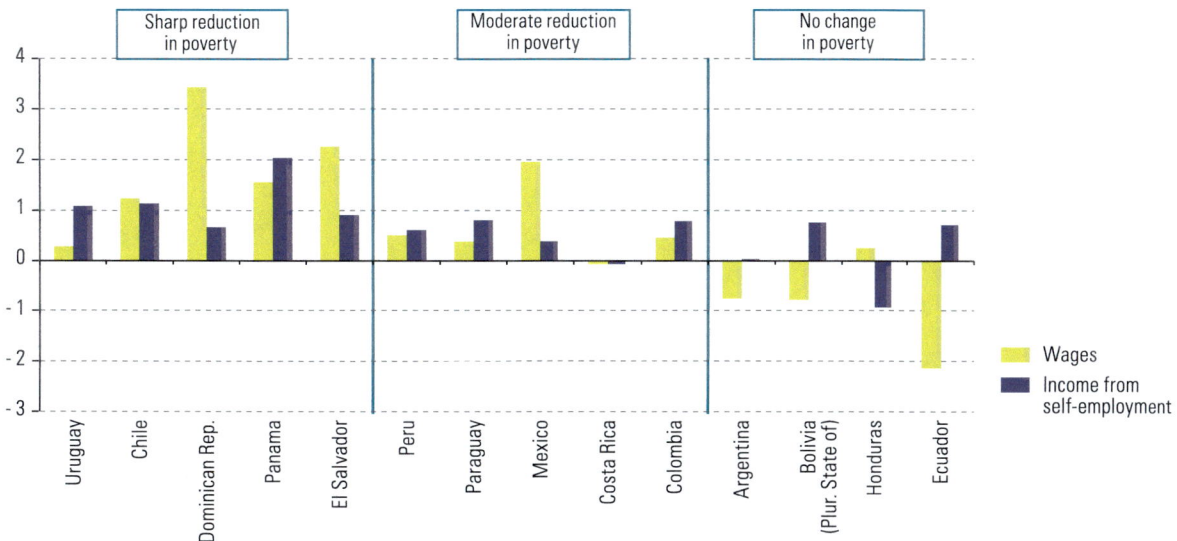

Source: Economic Commission for Latin America and the Caribbean (ECLAC), on the basis of Household Survey Data Bank (BADEHOG).
[a] Countries in order of magnitude of poverty reduction. Data refer to the subperiod 2014–2018, except for Chile (2013–2017).

Changes in labour income can come both from a variation in average income per recipient and from the number of recipients. In countries with sharp reductions in poverty between 2014 and 2018, the rise in labour income was attributable to a substantial increase in labour income per recipient, which was, on average, considerably higher than the number of recipients. The only exception to this pattern was Panama, where there was an almost equivalent increase in the number of recipients and in the average income per recipient.

In countries with moderate reductions in poverty, growth in labour income was related both to the increase in labour income per recipient and to the increase in the number of recipients. These increases were smaller than those recorded in countries with large reductions in poverty, especially for average income per recipient: the increase in the number of recipients in countries with large poverty reductions was on average 1.4 times that in countries with moderate decreases, while the increase in the average income per recipient in countries with large poverty reductions was 5.7 times that in countries with moderate reductions.[11]

In the group of countries with no change in poverty, the increase in the number of recipients was not enough to prevent a fall in household labour income, which was caused by a significant drop in average income per recipient, especially in Argentina, Ecuador and Honduras (see table II.5). In turn, in Brazil, labour income per recipient fell sharply, and it was the only country in which the number of recipients of labour income fell.

---

[11]   In countries with annualized poverty declines of 5% or more, labour income per recipient grew by 3.2% (simple average) and the number of recipients rose by 1.5%. In countries with moderate reductions (between 1% and 5%), labour income per recipient increased by just 0.6%, and the number of recipients grew by 1%.

Table II.5
Latin America
(15 countries): annual
variation in labour
income, in income per
recipient and in the
number of recipients,
lower-income
households, 2014–2018[a]
(Percentages)

	Labour income	Labour income per recipient	Recipients of labour income
Argentina	-0.7	-3.6	2.3
Bolivia (Plurinational State of)	0.0	-0.3	0.3
Brazil	-2.7	-3.0	-1.6
Chile	2.4	2.9	1.1
Colombia	1.2	1.3	0.3
Costa Rica	-0.2	-0.4	0.1
Dominican Republic	4.1	4.5	1.5
Ecuador	-1.4	-2.2	0.2
El Salvador	3.1	3.8	0.5
Honduras	-0.7	-2.6	1.6
Mexico	2.3	0.7	2.7
Panama	3.6	3.3	3.2
Paraguay	1.2	0.7	1.1
Peru	1.1	0.6	1.0
Uruguay	1.4	1.7	1.0

Source: Economic Commission for Latin America and the Caribbean (ECLAC), on the basis of Household Survey Data Bank (BADEHOG).
[a] Data refer to 2014–2018, except for Chile (2013–2017).

(b) Trends in public and private transfer income of lower-income households

Transfer income is broken down into pensions and retirement pensions, non-contributory transfers and other transfers, including remittances. In three of the five countries with large reductions in poverty (Dominican Republic, El Salvador and Chile, in that order), the increase in transfer income for low-income households was essentially the result of a rise in income from "other transfers". In El Salvador and the Dominican Republic, the increase is explained entirely by remittances, while in Chile, the increase may be caused by the trend in contributory transfers other than pensions and retirement pensions (see figure II.14).[12]

Figure II.14
Latin America (14 countries): contribution of pensions, non-contributory transfers and other transfers to total income variation among poor and vulnerable households, 2014–2018[a]
(Annualized figures)

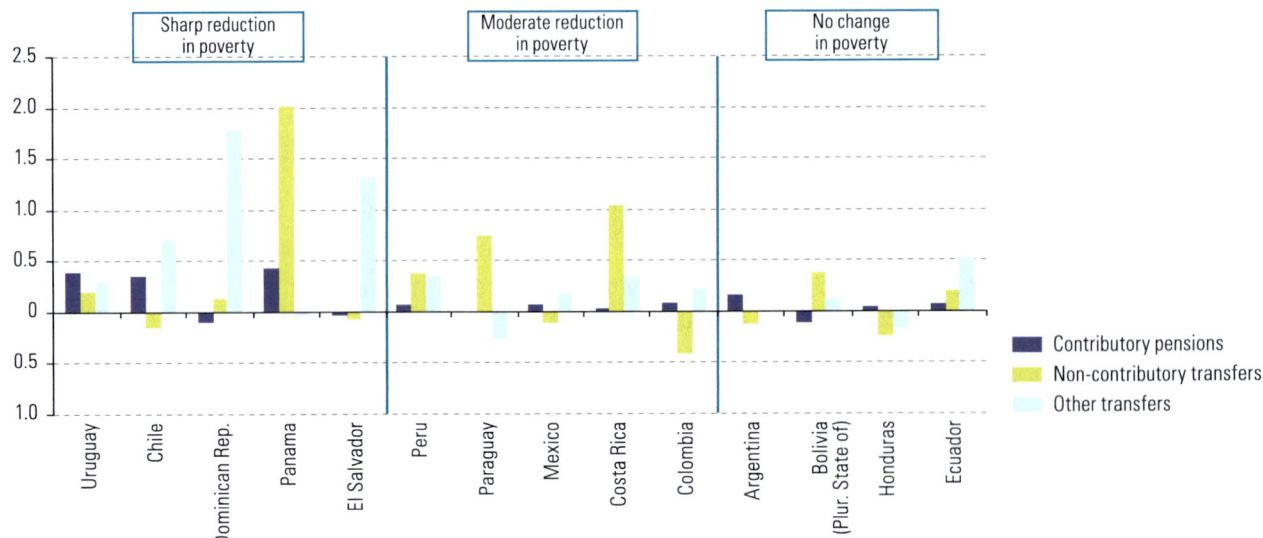

Source: Economic Commission for Latin America and the Caribbean (ECLAC), on the basis of Household Survey Data Bank (BADEHOG).
[a] Countries in order of magnitude of poverty reduction. Data refer to 2014–2018, except for Chile (2013–2017).

---

[12]   In the Dominican Republic, the annualized percentage change in remittances was 1.75%, versus a 1.72% increase in all income from public and private transfers. In El Salvador, the annualized variation in remittances was 0.52%, while growth in all public and private transfers was 0.45%.

Non-contributory public transfers include cash benefits that do not depend on participation in the formal labour market, and that are provided by States to alleviate poverty and reduce vulnerability.[13] Generally, non-contributory transfer programmes include conditional transfers and social pensions provided by States. The growth in income through this stream was the main factor behind the rise in the transfer income of poor households in Panama, Costa Rica and Paraguay, in that order. There has also been a decline in this income stream in Colombia, Mexico (countries with a moderate reduction in poverty), Argentina and Honduras (countries with no substantial changes in poverty rates).

In the vast majority of countries, income from retirement pensions and contributory pensions did not contribute to the increase in the income of low-income households through transfers. This may be explained by low levels of affiliation to contributory pension systems among such households. The exceptions were Chile, Panama and Uruguay. In low-income households in Uruguay, pension and retirement pension income contributed more to the increase in households' total transfer income from the bottom end of the income distribution structure than non-contributory transfers and other transfers.

3.   Possibility of achieving the Sustainable Development Goal of no poverty

The countries of the region must redouble their efforts to concurrently improve their performance in terms of economic growth and reductions in inequality, enabling them to meet the targets of reducing total poverty and eradicating extreme poverty by 2030.

In September 2015, 193 Member States of the United Nations pledged to advance an agenda to jointly work to end poverty, reduce inequality, preserve the environment and ensure the greatest possible well-being for all. This agenda was expressed in a set of SDGs, targets and indicators for monitoring the commitments made. The commitment of Latin American governments to the SDGs was reaffirmed at the first meeting of the Forum of the Countries of Latin America and the Caribbean on Sustainable Development (2017), when the countries of the region concluded that eradicating poverty is the greatest global challenge and a necessary condition for sustainable development.[14]

In terms of the goals and targets that specifically address poverty, SDG 1 proposes to end poverty in all its forms everywhere, and target 1.1 is to eradicate extreme poverty by 2030. The global indicator for target 1.1 is based on the international poverty line used by the World Bank, which is very low for the prevailing standards of living in most countries in the region.[15] In the regional context, it is more appropriate to use an extreme poverty threshold that is based on the cost of a basic food basket, determined specifically on the basis of nutritional needs, levels of physical activity and consumption patterns seen in Latin American countries.

This section analyses the possibilities for the region as a whole to meet the targets of halving total poverty and eradicating extreme poverty by 2030, considering different scenarios of change in the economic growth rate and in levels of distributive concentration between now and 2030. For total poverty, the target is to reach incidence

---

[13]   For more details, see Abramo, Cecchini and Morales (2019).

[14]   For more details, see the intergovernmentally agreed conclusions and recommendations of the first meeting of the Forum of the Countries of Latin America and the Caribbean on Sustainable Development [online] https://foroalc2030.cepal.org/2017/sites/default/files/final_text_of_the_conclusions_and_recommendations_3mayo.pdf.

[15]   The international poverty line corresponds to a daily purchasing power parity amount of US$ 1.90 in 2011. For reference purposes, of the 15 countries analysed in this section, the incidence of extreme poverty was below 3% in 8 of them in 2016 (see World Bank, "Poverty" [online] https://data.worldbank.org/topic/poverty).

of 14.5% by 2030, as the indicator stood at 29.1% in 2015. For extreme poverty, the target is 3%. Extreme poverty equal to zero is not used as a scenario because of certain methodological limitations of income measurements based on household surveys, which mean that even in a scenario in which extreme poverty is eradicated, measurements would continue to indicate an extreme poverty rate greater than zero.[16]

In a first scenario, with annual per capita GDP growth of 1% and no change in income concentration, the incidence of regional poverty would be 25.3% in 2030, well above the 14.5% required to meet the target (see figure II.15). This growth rate would produce an extreme poverty rate of 8.9% in 2030, also well above the 3% target for extreme poverty (see figure II.16). In this case, not only would the regional averages be far from the targets, but just 1 of 18 countries would manage to halve total poverty by 2030 (from 2015 levels) and only 3 countries would succeed in bringing the extreme poverty rate to 3% or less.

Policies that improve income distribution can crucially increase the chances of meeting poverty reduction targets. Assuming the same annual per capita GDP growth rate (1%), but also projecting a decline in inequality equivalent to a reduction in the Gini coefficient of 1% per year, the incidence of poverty would reach 20.1%. Although this is still above the target, it would represent an improvement in the region's performance of 5.2 percentage points compared to a scenario with no changes in distribution. In this scenario, the incidence of extreme poverty would be 7% in 2030, five countries would halve poverty and six countries would reduce extreme poverty to around 3%.

A more optimistic projection, with annual per capita GDP growth of 2% and a reduction in income distribution inequality of 1.5% per year through to 2030, would bring the region's poverty rate to 14.5%, meaning that the region as a whole would meet the target, as would 15 countries. However, the extreme poverty rate in 2030 would be 5.1%, indicating that even in this case the region as a whole would not meet the target. Only with per capita GDP growth of 5% and an annual Gini reduction of 1.5% would the region's extreme poverty rate fall to less than 3%, with 13 countries meeting the target.

Figure II.15
Latin America (18 countries): projected regional poverty rate in 2030 with different scenarios of per capita GDP growth and changes in income distribution
(Percentages)

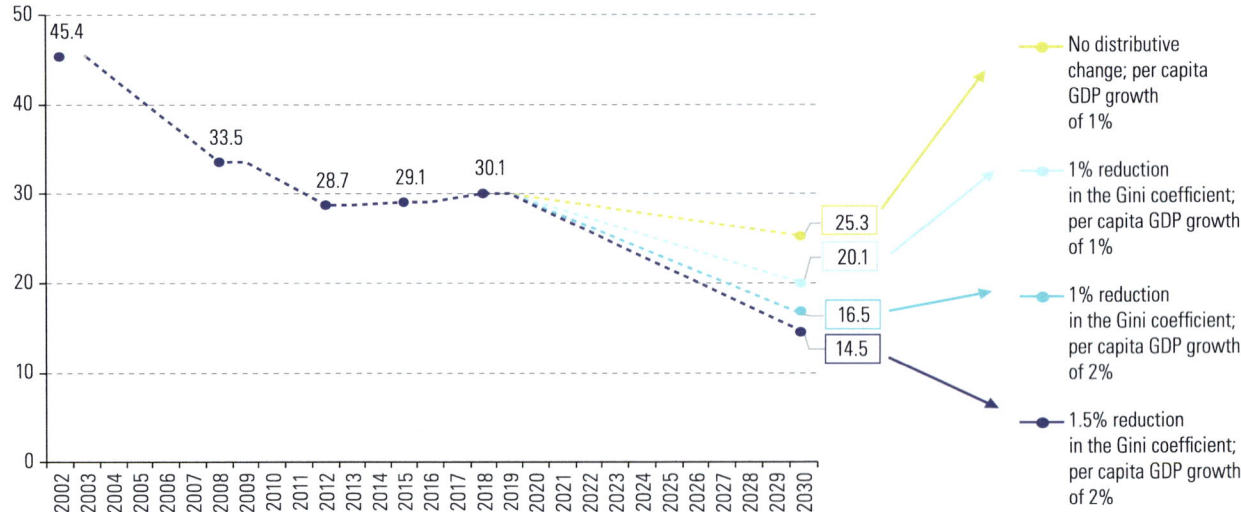

Source: Economic Commission for Latin America and the Caribbean (ECLAC), on the basis of Household Survey Data Bank (BADEHOG).

---

[16]   One of these limitations relates to reporting of income equal to or close to zero, which may be the result of fluctuations in current household income, as well as of the non-reporting or undercapturing of income.

Figure II.16
Latin America (18 countries): projected regional extreme poverty rate in 2030 with different scenarios of per capita GDP growth and changes in income distribution
(Percentages)

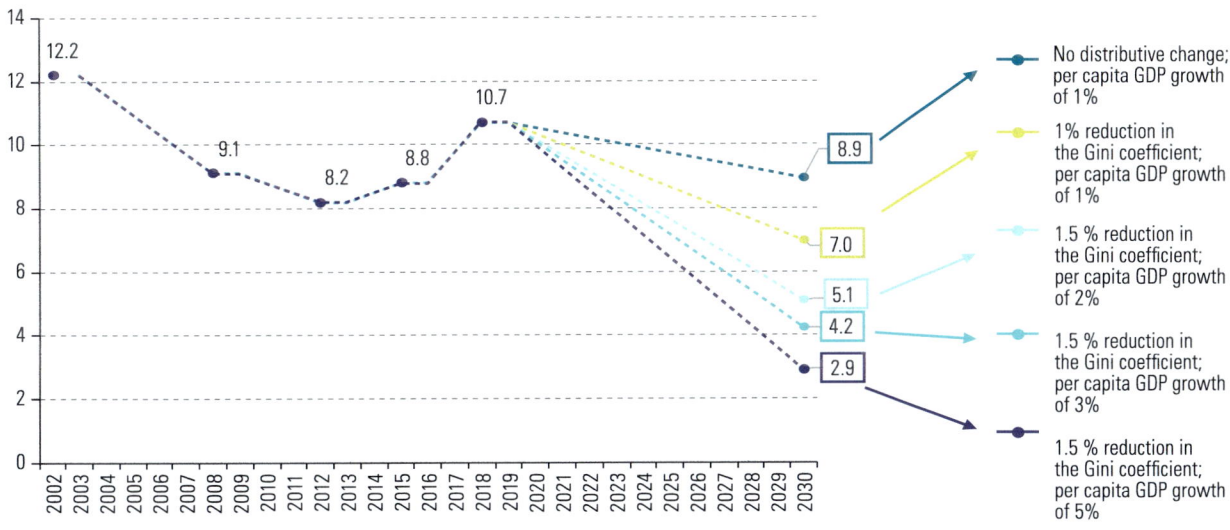

Source: Economic Commission for Latin America and the Caribbean (ECLAC), on the basis of Household Survey Data Bank (BADEHOG).

Bibliography

Abramo, L., S. Cecchini and B. Morales (2019), *Social programmes, poverty eradication and labour inclusion: lessons from Latin America and the Caribbean,* ECLAC Books, No. 1 155 (LC/PUB.2019/5-P), Santiago, Economic Commission for Latin America and the Caribbean (ECLAC).

ECLAC (Economic Commission for Latin America and the Caribbean) (2019a), *Critical obstacles to inclusive social development in Latin America and the Caribbean: background for a regional agenda* (LC/CDS.3/3), Santiago.

(2019b), *Social Panorama of Latin America, 2018* (LC/PUB.2019/3-P), Santiago.

(2018), *Social Panorama of Latin America, 2017* (LC/PUB.2018/1-P), Santiago.

(2016), *The social inequality matrix in Latin America* (LC/G.2690(MDS.1/2)), Santiago.

(2014), *Social Panorama of Latin America, 2014* (LC/G.2635-P), Santiago.

IBGE (Brazilian Institute of Geography and Statistics) (2019), "Síntese de indicadores sociais: uma análise das condições de vida da população brasileira 2019", *Estudos e Pesquisas,* No. 40, Rio de Janeiro.

Annex II.A1

Table II.A1.1
Latin America (18 countries): poverty and extreme poverty indicators, 2000–2018[a]
(In units of the corresponding indices)

| Country | Year | Poverty[b] | | | | Extreme poverty | | | |
| | | Households | | Individuals | | Households | | Individuals | |
		Poverty headcount ratio (H)	Poverty headcount ratio (H)	Poverty gap (PG)	Squared poverty gap index (FGT2)	Poverty headcount ratio (H)	Poverty headcount ratio (H)	Poverty gap (PG)	Squared poverty gap index (FGT2)
Argentina[c]	2002	52.8	62.4	31.0	21.3	17.3	21.1	12.1	9.4
	2008	19.5	27.1	8.6	4.4	3.3	4.3	1.8	1.2
	2012	15.2	21.8	6.5	3.1	2.6	3.3	1.4	0.9
	2014	17.5	24.9	7.2	3.4	3.0	3.3	1.4	1.0
	2017	13.3	18.7	5.5	2.7	2.4	2.8	1.2	0.8
	2018	17.6	24.4	7.6	3.8	2.9	3.6	1.6	1.1
Bolivia (Plurinational State of)	2002	59.9	66.8	37.7	26.5	29.8	35.1	19.2	13.6
	2008	39.6	46.5	21.4	13.2	17.0	21.4	9.7	6.2
	2012	31.1	35.9	16.0	9.9	14.0	16.5	7.8	5.1
	2014	28.6	33.7	13.9	8.1	12.5	14.9	6.5	4.0
	2017	30.6	35.1	15.0	9.1	13.9	16.4	7.5	4.8
	2018	27.8	33.2	13.3	7.6	12.3	14.7	6.1	3.6
Brazil	2002	30.1	37.8	14.4	7.6	4.8	6.2	2.7	1.9
	2008	19.4	25.3	8.9	4.7	3.8	4.3	2.0	1.5
	2012	14.4	18.5	6.6	3.7	3.8	3.9	2.0	1.5
	2014	12.6	16.5	5.5	2.9	3.0	3.3	1.4	1.0
	2017[d]	15.7	19.9	7.5	4.4	5.1	5.5	2.6	1.8
	2018[d]	15.1	19.4	7.5	4.4	5.0	5.4	2.5	1.8
Chile	2003	33.4	40.0	15.3	8.1	4.6	5.6	2.2	1.4
	2009	23.7	29.0	9.6	4.9	3.6	3.8	1.8	1.3
	2011	20.3	25.2	7.9	3.8	2.9	3.2	1.3	0.9
	2013	12.8	16.2	4.8	2.3	1.9	2.0	0.9	0.6
	2015	10.7	13.7	3.9	1.8	1.6	1.8	0.8	0.5
	2017	8.4	10.7	3.0	1.5	1.5	1.4	0.7	0.6
Colombia	2002[e]	46.3	53.8	25.2	15.4	19.8	23.8	10.1	6.0
	2008	37.3	44.6	20.3	12.5	16.8	20.7	9.1	5.7
	2012	29.3	35.5	14.6	8.3	11.8	14.5	5.7	3.3
	2014	25.4	31.1	12.4	6.9	9.9	12.0	4.7	2.7
	2017	24.2	29.8	11.3	6.2	9.0	10.9	4.1	2.4
	2018	24.2	29.9	11.5	6.3	8.9	10.8	4.2	2.5
Costa Rica	2002[e]	25.2	28.0	10.3	5.9	4.9	5.4	2.8	2.2
	2008[e]	17.7	20.1	6.6	3.4	3.5	3.6	1.7	1.2
	2012	15.1	18.6	6.7	3.7	3.9	4.7	2.0	1.3
	2014	14.4	17.5	6.4	3.6	3.7	4.1	1.9	1.2
	2017	12.5	15.1	5.3	2.9	3.0	3.3	1.5	1.0
	2018	13.1	16.1	6.0	3.4	3.4	4.0	1.8	1.2
Dominican Republic	2002	28.0	33.6	13.2	7.3	9.2	11.5	4.1	2.4
	2008	34.2	41.6	16.0	8.2	11.5	15.0	4.4	1.9
	2012	31.8	38.3	14.1	7.1	9.7	12.6	3.6	1.6
	2014	27.0	32.9	11.5	5.6	7.4	9.7	2.8	1.3
	2017[f]	19.1	25.0	8.0	3.9	4.8	6.4	2.1	1.2
	2018[f]	16.8	22.0	6.7	3.0	3.7	5.0	1.4	0.7
Ecuador	2001	48.0	53.5	21.8	11.9	18.0	20.2	6.7	3.6
	2008	29.4	34.7	12.1	6.1	9.0	10.8	3.6	1.9
	2012	23.2	26.6	8.9	4.3	7.8	8.7	2.7	1.4
	2014	19.2	23.4	7.0	3.1	4.7	5.9	1.7	0.8
	2017	19.1	23.6	7.4	3.5	5.4	7.0	2.2	1.1
	2018	18.6	24.2	7.4	3.4	4.8	6.5	2.0	1.0
El Salvador	2001	44.2	50.6	23.2	14.1	15.8	19.1	8.0	4.9
	2009	43.0	50.1	20.8	11.4	13.5	17.1	5.5	2.6
	2012	40.7	48.0	18.2	9.3	9.6	12.7	3.7	1.6
	2014	38.0	44.5	16.4	8.1	9.1	11.7	3.3	1.3
	2017	32.1	37.8	12.9	6.0	6.5	8.3	2.2	0.9
	2018	28.9	34.5	11.6	5.5	5.6	7.6	1.9	0.8

Table II.A1.1 (concluded)

Country	Year	Poverty[b] Households Poverty headcount ratio (H)	Poverty Individuals Poverty headcount ratio (H)	Poverty gap (PG)	Squared poverty gap index (FGT2)	Extreme poverty Households Poverty headcount ratio (H)	Poverty headcount ratio (H)	Individuals Poverty gap (PG)	Squared poverty gap index (FGT2)
Guatemala	2000	46.9	53.6	28.9	19.8	14.4	16.9	8.8	5.9
	2006	34.9	42.7	19.5	11.6	7.7	10.4	3.4	1.7
	2014	43.1	50.5	22.4	13.0	11.8	15.4	5.3	2.7
Honduras	2001	51.3	57.4	26.3	15.3	23.6	27.3	9.5	4.8
	2009	44.8	51.0	21.0	11.2	16.1	19.6	5.7	2.4
	2012	56.2	61.2	27.9	16.3	22.4	25.3	8.8	4.7
	2014	50.0	55.3	22.9	12.3	17.1	19.2	5.5	2.5
	2016	48.3	53.2	22.5	12.6	16.7	18.8	6.4	3.2
	2018	51.1	55.7	23.6	13.2	17.3	19.4	6.4	3.3
Mexico	2002	38.2	46.4	18.1	9.4	7.3	10.4	2.8	1.2
	2008	36.1	43.1	17.2	9.4	9.2	11.8	4.0	2.0
	2012	37.8	44.4	17.6	9.5	10.5	12.9	4.4	2.3
	2014	38.1	45.2	17.6	9.3	10.2	13.0	4.2	2.0
	2016[g]	36.4	43.7	16.2	8.2	9.1	11.7	3.5	1.6
	2018[g]	34.2	41.5	14.9	7.4	8.3	10.6	3.2	1.4
Nicaragua	2001	57.4	65.1	33.0	21.0	29.3	35.8	15.2	9.1
	2009	51.0	58.3	24.8	13.9	18.6	23.1	8.1	4.1
	2014	40.9	46.3	18.7	10.2	16.1	18.3	6.6	3.5
Panama	2002	27.7	34.0	15.7	9.5	12.2	16.2	6.7	3.8
	2008	20.5	26.8	11.5	6.6	8.8	12.8	5.0	2.6
	2011	16.6	23.1	9.3	5.1	6.7	10.5	3.6	1.8
	2014	14.3	19.7	8.1	4.6	5.9	9.2	3.6	1.9
	2017	12.3	16.7	6.5	3.5	5.1	7.6	2.7	1.4
	2018	10.5	14.5	5.4	2.8	4.0	6.2	2.1	1.1
Peru	2002	39.9	47.9	22.3	13.6	13.2	17.6	7.2	4.2
	2008	28.1	35.0	13.2	6.9	9.2	12.1	3.8	1.9
	2012	22.6	26.2	10.0	5.3	7.9	9.6	3.2	1.6
	2014	18.5	22.3	8.2	4.2	6.3	7.7	2.4	1.2
	2017	18.4	21.6	6.9	3.1	5.0	6.0	1.5	0.6
	2018	16.3	19.5	6.6	3.2	5.3	6.5	1.8	0.8
Paraguay	2002	37.4	43.3	18.2	10.2	12.1	14.9	5.6	3.0
	2008	27.5	31.8	12.4	6.6	9.1	10.8	3.6	1.7
	2012	18.5	20.9	7.3	3.6	5.3	6.3	1.9	0.9
	2014	16.7	19.5	6.4	3.1	4.2	5.1	1.5	0.6
	2017	16.3	18.9	6.1	2.8	4.0	5.0	1.4	0.6
	2018	14.3	16.8	5.1	2.3	2.9	3.7	1.0	0.4
Uruguay	2002	13.9	20.7	8.2	4.8	3.3	4.3	2.4	1.8
	2008	8.6	14.2	3.9	1.5	0.7	1.1	0.2	0.1
	2012	3.4	6.1	1.4	0.5	0.2	0.2	0.1	0.0
	2014	2.6	4.5	1.0	0.3	0.2	0.2	0.1	0.0
	2017	1.5	2.7	0.5	0.2	0.1	0.1	0.0	0.0
	2018	1.7	2.9	0.5	0.2	0.1	0.1	0.0	0.0
Venezuela (Bolivarian Republic of)	2002	45.3	51.7	19.9	10.6	6.8	7.2	3.5	2.6
	2008	20.8	24.7	7.6	3.6	4.5	4.7	1.6	1.0
	2012	17.6	20.9	6.7	3.4	4.6	5.1	1.9	1.3
	2014	24.0	28.3	9.3	4.6	10.3	12.0	3.7	2.0

Source: Economic Commission for Latin America and the Caribbean (ECLAC), on the basis of Household Survey Data Bank (BADEHOG).
[a] H = headcount ratio; PG = poverty gap; FGT2 = Foster, Greer and Thorbecke squared poverty gap index.
[b] Includes individuals and households living in extreme poverty.
[c] Urban total.
[d] From 2016 onward Permanent National Household Survey (PNAD Continua) data, not comparable with previous years (based on the National Household Survey (PNAD)).
[e] Data not comparable with subsequent years.
[f] Data based on the continuous national labour force survey (ECNFT), not comparable with previous years, based on the national labour force survey (ENFT).
[g] Figures estimated on the basis of the 2016 and 2018 statistical models for continuation of the social conditions module of the national household income and expenditure survey (MCS-ENIGH), prepared by the National Institute of Statistics and Geography (INEGI).

Table II.A1.2
Latin America (15 countries): non-contributory transfer programmes analysed in chapter II

Country	Programmes[a]		
	Conditional transfers	Social pensions	Other
Argentina	Universal Child Allowance (AUH)		Other State transfers[a]
Bolivia (Plurinational State of)	Juancito Pinto Grant Juana Azurduy Mother-and-Child Grant	*Renta Dignidad Universal* Old-age Pension	
Brazil[b]	*Bolsa Família*	Continuous Benefit Programme (BPC)	Other State transfers
Chile	Ethical Family Income (IEF) Solidarity Chile	Basic Solidarity Old-Age Pension Basic Solidarity Invalidity Pension	Consolidated Household Subsidy (SUF), Safe Water Subsidy, Permanent Family Contribution, Winter Grant, Youth Employment Subsidy, family allowances (mother, newborn, invalidity, mental disability), other State allowances
Colombia	More Families in Action Youth in Action	*Colombia Mayor* (older adult social protection programme)	
Costa Rica	*Avancemos*	Non-contributory Pension Scheme	Joint Institute for Social Aid (IMAS) Transfers (excluding Avancemos), State educational grants, subsidies
Dominican Republic	Progressing with Solidarity[c]	Development with Solidarity, Protection of Older Persons Living in Extreme Poverty (PROVEE)	
Ecuador	Human Development Grant (BDH)	Human Development Grant Old-age Pension	Joaquín Gallegos Lara Grant
El Salvador	Support for Solidarity in Communities (PACSES)	Basic Universal Pension	Other State transfers
Honduras	Better Life Grant Family Allowance Programme (PRAF)		Grant for persons with disabilities, grants, other government programmes
Mexico	*Prospera* (formerly *Progresa* and *Oportunidades*)	Elderly Welfare Pension	Programme of Direct Rural Support (PROCAMPO), Temporary Employment Programme (PET), government grants, No Hunger Card, other programmes for older persons, other social programmes
Panama	Opportunities Network Grant for Food Purchase programme	Special Cash Transfers Programme for Older Adults (120 at 65)	Guardian Angel Programme, Universal Grant, public institution grants
Paraguay	*Tekoporã*	Food Pension for Older Adults Living in Poverty	
Peru	National Programme of Direct Support for the Poorest *(Juntos)*	"Pension 65" National Solidarity Assistance Programme	
Uruguay	Family Allowances, Uruguay Social Card	Old age or disability pension	

Source: Economic Commission for Latin America and the Caribbean (ECLAC).

[a] The survey asks about receipt of government aid, without identifying specific programmes.

[b] The survey only captured Bolsa Família, the Continuous Benefit Programme (BPC) and other State transfers separately from 2016. For 2014 and 2015, recipients of both programmes were identified using an indirect method.

[c] To identify the recipients of Progressing with Solidarity in 2014 and 2015 it was assumed that all income from the government aid stream came from Progressing with Solidarity.

Social spending: recent trends and financing needs for achieving Sustainable Development Goal 1

Introduction

A. Social public spending in 2000–2018

B. Estimated resources needed to close the poverty and extreme poverty income gap in Latin America by 2030

C. Conclusions

Bibliography

Annex III.A1

Introduction

As indicated by the Economic Commission for Latin America and the Caribbean (ECLAC) in *Economic Survey of Latin America and the Caribbean 2019* (ECLAC, 2019b, pp. 27 and 28), the world is currently experiencing rising trade tensions, with estimates for global economic growth below 2018 levels. World trade growth has slowed significantly and turned negative in the year-on-year figures in early 2019, for the first time since the global financial crisis of 2008–2009. The developed economies will see the heaviest slowdowns in 2019, with growth projected at 1.2% in the eurozone and 2.5% in the United States, down 7 and 4 tenths of a percentage point, respectively, on 2018. Among the emerging economies, China is continuing to see gradual deceleration, with a rate of 6.2% expected for 2019, 4 tenths of a point less than in 2018 and the lowest rate for almost 30 years, owing to weak manufacturing activity and lower trade volumes, mainly relating to disputes with the United States.

In this context, it is estimated that global growth will be 2.6% in 2019, 4 tenths of a point below the 2018 rate, and that commodity prices (on which many of the region's economies depend for exports and even tax revenues) will fall by 5% from 2018, as a result of slacker economic activity (ECLAC, 2019b, p. 15). For the Latin American and Caribbean region, growth is projected at 0.5%, continuing the sustained downward path of the past five years (ECLAC, 2019b, p. 97). In the labour market, the urban open unemployment rate held stable in the first quarter of 2019, year-on-year; nevertheless, most new jobs were generated in the informal sector, which signals a deterioration in average employment quality (ECLAC, 2019b, p. 17).

Gross central government debt in Latin America increased in 2018, to 42.3% of GDP. In the Caribbean, this debt category remained significantly higher (at 72.4% of GDP), despite dropping by almost 2 GDP percentage points over the past year (ECLAC 2019c, pp. 16 and 17). By contrast, public revenues in Latin America overall remained constant from the previous year, but with differences between subregions, as they rose in South America but fell in Central America. The Caribbean saw a rise in public revenues of some 1.3% compared with 2018 (ECLAC, 2019c, p. 27). In addition, the cost of tax evasion and avoidance in Latin America, estimated at US$ 335 billion in 2017, or 6.3% of regional GDP (ECLAC, 2019c, p. 34), adds to the challenges faced by the countries in achieving social public spending levels capable of achieving their social policy goals and fulfilling the commitments of the 2030 Agenda for Sustainable Development.

This chapter analyses the volume and distribution of the public resources devoted to financing social policies in Latin America and in five countries of the English-speaking Caribbean. The first part reviews the evolution of social public spending, at both regional and subregional levels, using the Classification of the Functions of Government (COFOG). The second part provides an estimate of the quantity of resources that would be needed to achieve Sustainable Development Goal (SDG) 1 on eradicating poverty in all the countries of the region, including a projection of the costs over the next decade of closing the gaps by means of direct transfers to households.

A. Social public spending in 2000–2018

Investment in social policies in the region has slowed in relation to GDP and has slipped back to levels seen in earlier years. Social spending in the South American countries peaked in GDP terms in 2017, but fell in 2018. Meanwhile, the average for the group comprising the Central American countries, the Dominican Republic and Mexico has returned to pre-2011 levels, and for five English-speaking Caribbean countries, to 2014 levels. The instability of financing presents significant risks to the implementation of social policies and the achievement of the targets of the 2030 Agenda for Sustainable Development. This is particularly significant in the five countries of the Caribbean, which show a drop in the level of expenditure per capita, and in countries with a lower level of economic development, as these experience the greatest social challenges and have the lowest levels of social spending, with annual per capita outlays averaging less than US$ 230.

As detailed in previous editions of *Social Panorama of Latin America*, the volume of resources that countries allocate to social policy funding can be analysed by level of government or institutional coverage. As indicated in the International Monetary Fund (IMF) *Government Finance Statistics Manual 2001* and *Government Finance Statistics Manual 2014* (IMF, 2001 and 2014), central government coverage comprises a group of ministries, secretariats and administrative units that act under the authority of the central government, although they may have their own autonomous legal authority. Total public sector coverage is more complex, as it involves a combination of different types of institutional coverage, and figures for the different countries are not comparable: some report data for general government, but others include data for central government only, or refer to the non-financial public sector or the public sector overall.[1] This point is particularly important in the case of federal countries or those in which intermediate levels of government have greater autonomy in revenue collection and management, where subnational governments are responsible for much of social spending (ECLAC, 2017b, p. 94).

As in the 2016 and 2018 editions of (ECLAC, 2017b and 2019a), this section presents data on social expenditure by central government for the years between 2000 and 2018, including the most recent information available in each country for the whole period. In specific cases where information is available, the analysis is supplemented by wider institutional coverage. Along with information from Latin American countries, this edition contains data from five English-speaking Caribbean countries: Bahamas, Barbados, Guyana, Jamaica and Trinidad and Tobago. Thus, the series includes the same countries analysed in the 2018 edition of *Social Panorama*, but with updated data from official reports (see box III.1).

---

[1]   As the same document specifies, "a country's public sector is analysed by subsector or type of institutional coverage: (i) central government, which comprises the ministries, secretariats and public institutions exercising authority over the entire territory of the country; (ii) general government, which includes central government and subnational governments (first territorial subdivision and local governments); (iii) the non-financial public sector, which consists of general government and non-financial public corporations; and (iv) the public sector, which comprises the non-financial public sector plus financial public corporations" (ECLAC, 2017b, p. 94).

Box III.1
Statistical information on public social spending

This edition of *Social Panorama of Latin America* presents the information compiled in the ECLAC social expenditure database for the years between 2000 and 2018, for 20 Latin American and 5 Caribbean countries. The database has been constructed using the information available each year for the whole period under analysis, according to the methodology described in the International Monetary Fund (IMF) *Government Finance Statistics Manual 2014* (IMF, 2014), which allows public expenditure on specific functions or policy areas to be analysed over time and across different countries.

The analysis of recent trends in social spending in the region is performed at the central government level in each country in order to maintain consistency with the averages published over time in other ECLAC documents.[a] It is important to note that the total social spending effort of the region's governments is not necessarily captured by central government figures. In federal countries or countries with a high level of decentralization in particular, subnational government expenditures can be considerable. In addition, social security institutions in several countries, such as the Ecuadorian Social Security Institute, the Honduran Social Security Institute and the Social Security Bank in Uruguay, do not come within the central government purview.

The figures can be consulted in both the CEPALSTAT database and the ECLAC portal on social investment in Latin America and the Caribbean.

Latin America and the Caribbean (25 countries): availability of social public spending information by functional classification, institutional coverage and years

Country	Central government	Other coverage available		
		General government	Non-financial public sector	Public sector
Latin America				
Argentina	1993–2018		1990–2015	
Bolivia (Plurinational State of)	1990–2017[a]	1997–2008, 2010–2016		
Brazil	1995–2018	2000–2017		
Chile	1990–2018			
Colombia	1990–2018	2009–2017		
Costa Rica	1993–2018			1990–2018
Cuba	2002–2018	1996–2018		
Dominican Republic	1990–2018			
Ecuador	2000–2018			
El Salvador	1990–2018		2002–2018	
Guatemala	1995–2018			
Haiti	2012–2014			
Honduras	2000–2018			
Mexico	1999–2018			
Nicaragua	1998–2018			
Panama	2000–2017			
Paraguay	2000–2018	2003–2017		
Peru		1999–2018		
Uruguay	1990–2018			
Venezuela (Bolivarian Republic of)	1997–2014			
The Caribbean				
Bahamas	1990–2018			
Barbados	2006–2018			
Guyana	2008–2017			
Jamaica	1992–2018			
Trinidad and Tobago	2008–2018			

Source: Economic Commission for Latin America and the Caribbean (ECLAC), CEPALSTAT [online database] http://estadisticas.cepal.org/cepalstat/portada. html?idioma=english; Social Investment Portal in Latin America and the Caribbean [online] https://observatoriosocial.cepal.org/inversion/en; *Social Panorama of Latin America, 2016* (LC/PUB.2017/12), Santiago, 2017; International Monetary Fund (IMF), *Government Finance Statistics Manual 2014*, Washington, D.C., 2014.
[a] Central administration.

Source: Economic Commission for Latin America and the Caribbean (ECLAC), CEPALSTAT [online database] http://estadisticas.cepal.org/cepalstat/portada. html?idioma=english; Social Investment Portal in Latin America and the Caribbean [online] https://observatoriosocial.cepal.org/inversion/en; Social Panorama of Latin America, 2016 (LC/PUB.2017/12), Santiago, 2017; International Monetary Fund (IMF), Government Finance Statistics Manual 2014, Washington, D.C., 2014.
[a] See ECLAC (2017b) for more information on the indicators included in the Social Investment Portal in Latin America and the Caribbean [online] https://observatoriosocial. cepal.org/inversion/en.

1.   Recent evolution of social spending in the region

In 2017, as a simple average, central government social spending in 17 Latin American countries was 11.5% of GDP (see figure III.1), a small increase on 2015 and 2016 and a new peak from 2000.[2] However, the available data show a slight contraction in public social spending in 2018, to the level of the preceding biennium, with a setback in the average for the countries in particular.

Figure III.1
Latin America (17 countries): central government social spending, 2000–2018[a]
(Percentages of GDP and of total public spending)

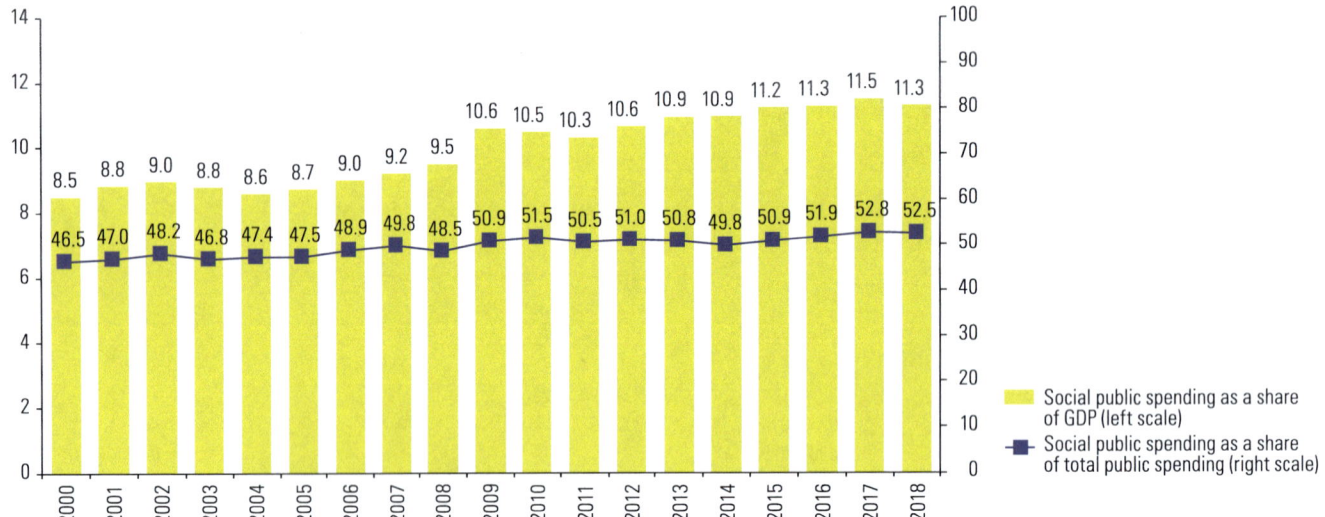

Source: Economic Commission for Latin America and the Caribbean (ECLAC), on the basis of official data from the countries.
[a] The averages are arithmetic means of the values for 17 Latin American countries: Argentina, Brazil, Chile, Colombia, Costa Rica, Dominican Republic, Ecuador, El Salvador, Guatemala, Honduras, Mexico, Nicaragua, Panama, Paraguay, Peru, the Plurinational State of Bolivia and Uruguay. The data for Peru are general government figures and those for the Plurinational State of Bolivia refer to the central administration.

Significant changes in the 2017–2018 biennium include a larger share of social functions in total public expenditure (around 53%). The higher public social spending in relation to GDP in the average for the countries in 2017 reflects stability in spending on the other functions that make up total government expenditure. Meanwhile, in 2018, public spending on both social and non-social functions decreased on average.

In the English-speaking Caribbean (see figure III.2), the average social expenditure of the central governments of five countries (Bahamas, Barbados, Guyana, Jamaica and Trinidad and Tobago), was 12.4% of GDP in 2017. This signals a downtrend since 2016, of 0.2 percentage points from the peak registered in 2015. The figures continue to show a downward trend in 2018, retreating to 2014 levels at 12.2% of GDP.

---

[2]   No information is included for the Bolivarian Republic of Venezuela, Cuba or Haiti because they do not have up-to-date figures for the whole series analysed.

Figure III.2
The Caribbean (5 countries): central government social spending, 2008–2018[a]
(Percentages of GDP and of total public spending)

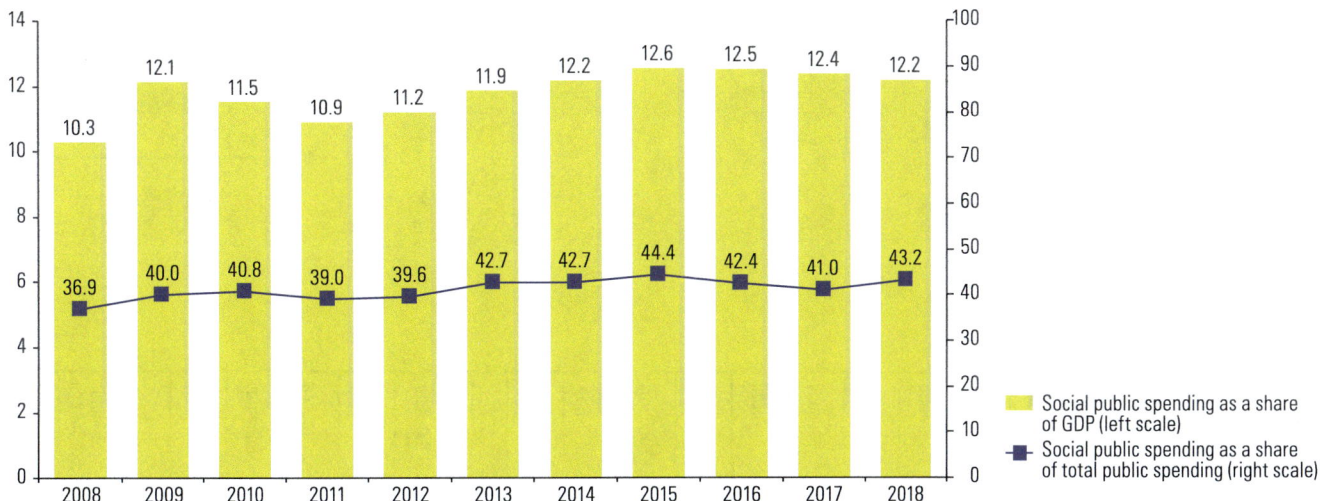

Social public spending as a share of GDP (left scale)

Social public spending as a share of total public spending (right scale)

Source: Economic Commission for Latin America and the Caribbean (ECLAC), on the basis of official data from the countries.
[a] The averages are arithmetic means of the values for five Caribbean countries: Bahamas, Barbados, Guyana, Jamaica and Trinidad and Tobago.

Analysis of the changes over the biennium in social public spending as a share of total central government spending shows that while, in the average figures for 2017 spending fell on social functions but rose slightly on the other functions of government, in 2018 it appears to have fallen on both social and non-social functions.

In light of this, in the group of five Caribbean countries, the proportion of resources devoted to social policy vis-à-vis other functions of government is, on average, significantly lower than the average for the Latin American countries (by 9.5 percentage points); nevertheless, the Caribbean countries present a level of social public spending almost 1 GDP percentage point higher than the Latin American countries and an average of total public expenditure 6.8 GDP points higher.

Analysis of the relative weight of central government social spending in 2018 in the various countries and subregions of Latin America (see figure III.3) shows that the average for the nine countries in South America was 13.2% of GDP. It was thus the subregion with the highest level of expenditure, although this was highly uneven between countries. Two countries (Ecuador and Paraguay) spend less than 10% of GDP on social functions, while Argentina, Brazil, Chile and Uruguay spend between 13.5% and 17.7% of GDP. The average for the six countries of Central America, the Dominican Republic and Mexico amounted to 9.1% of GDP. Among these, Costa Rica devotes the largest share of resources to social functions (12.1% of GDP), followed by Nicaragua and El Salvador (11.1% and 9.0% of GDP, respectively). Of all the Latin American countries, Guatemala devotes the lowest share of GDP to social policy (7.0%).

Figure III.3
Latin America and the Caribbean (22 countries): central government social spending by country and subregion, 2018[a] [b]
(Percentages of GDP)

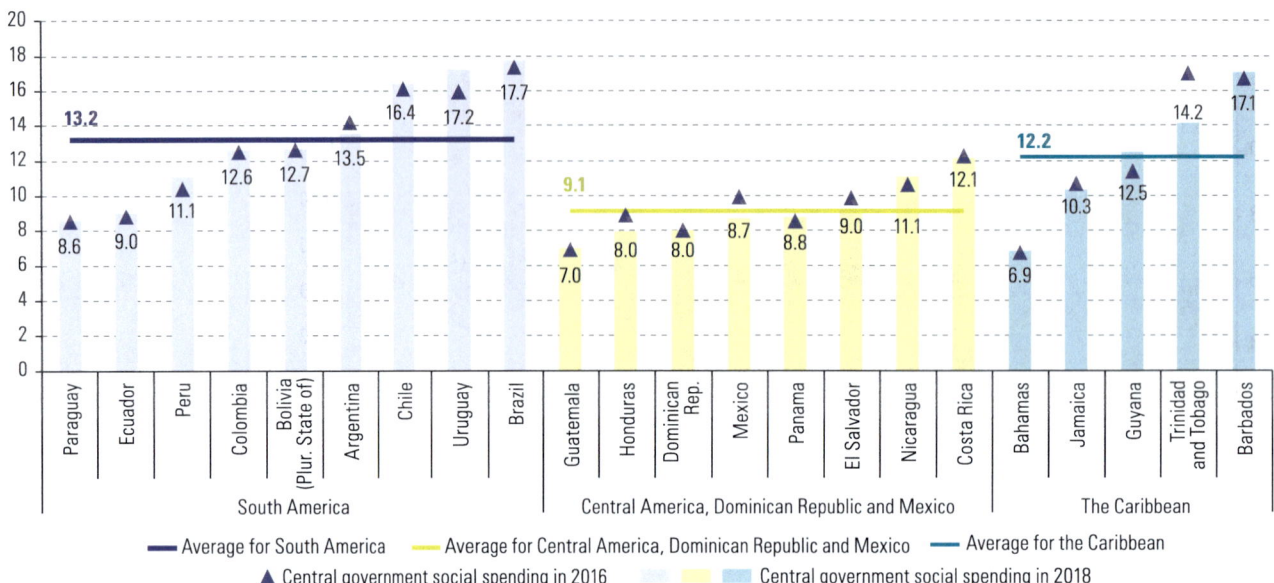

Source: Economic Commission for Latin America and the Caribbean (ECLAC), on the basis of official data from the countries.
[a] The data for Guyana, Panama and the Plurinational State of Bolivia refer to 2017. The data for Peru are general government figures and those for the Plurinational State of Bolivia refer to the central administration. The data for Uruguay do not include figures for the Social Security Bank.
[b] For the purposes of comparison, the public social spending levels in 2016, published in the 2018 edition of *Social Panorama of Latin America* (ECLAC, 2019a), are included as a reference.

The data presented here show that in Latin America, the proportion of resources allocated to social functions is still lower in countries with lower levels of wealth and greater poverty and vulnerability, as well as larger gaps in various areas of social development (ECLAC, 2019a). This evidently deepens the vulnerability to which their populations are exposed.

In the case of the five Caribbean countries, the most recent data show public social spending by the central government averaging 12.2% of GDP in 2018, ranging from 6.9% of GDP in Bahamas to 17.1% in Barbados.[3]

As may be seen in figure III.3, although the variations are generally small in terms of GDP points, the 2018 data for most countries show an increase over 2016.[4] The largest increases (by over 1 percentage point) occur in Guyana and Uruguay, followed by Peru (by 0.7 percentage points). The decrease of 0.2 GDP points in the average for Latin America and the Caribbean is due to significant falls in expenditure in relation to GDP in four countries: Trinidad and Tobago, Mexico, Honduras and El Salvador (by 2.8, 1.2, 0.9 and 0.8 percentage points, respectively).

Relative to 2016, the values reported here show growth of 9.5% in a single year in Guyana. It is followed by Uruguay and Peru, with rises of over 8% and nearly 7%, respectively, in a biennium, as well as Nicaragua, with 4% over the same period. Meanwhile, among the countries where central government social spending retreated most between 2016 and 2018, Trinidad and Tobago shows the heaviest fall, by 16.7%, followed by Mexico (12%), Honduras (10%) and El Salvador (8.5%), as well as Argentina, with a drop of 4.5%.

---

[3]   Data for some Caribbean countries are higher than those reported in the 2018 edition of *Social Panorama of Latin America*, owing to adjustments in the countries' official data.
[4]   Base year reported in the 2018 edition of *Social Panorama of Latin America* (ECLAC, 2019a).

2. Per capita social spending

Continuing the uptrend observed until 2016, average per capita social spending by the central government doubled between 2000 and 2018 in the Latin American countries, in terms of dollars at constant 2010 prices (see figure III.4). The trend shows a steady increase since 2003, with average growth of 5.2% per year, decreasing to 4.5% in the group comprising Central America, the Dominican Republic and Mexico and rising to 5.2% in the South American countries. In 2017, the regional average was US$ 941 per person, but with a great deal of heterogeneity between subregions and countries. While the average for South America was US$ 1,254 per capita, that for the group formed by the countries of Central America, the Dominican Republic and Mexico was only US$ 589. However, the trend for Latin America overall was broken in 2018, with a slight fall in the average. This was due mainly to a decline in the countries of Central America, Mexico and the Dominican Republic and stabilization in the South American average.

Figure III.4
Latin America and the Caribbean (22 countries): per capita central government social spending by subregion, 2018[a]
(Dollars at constant 2010 prices)

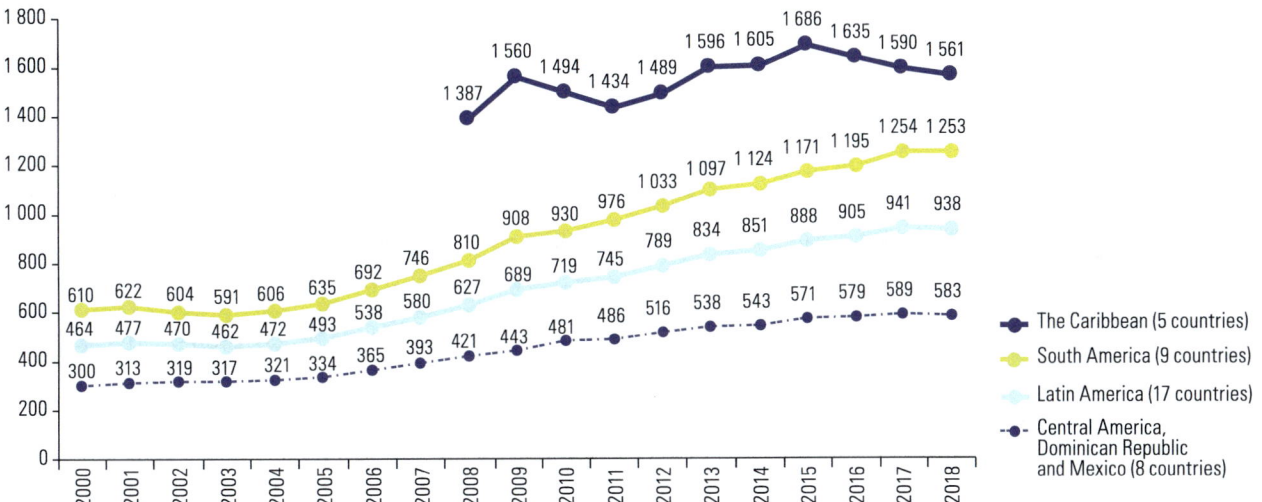

Source: Economic Commission for Latin America and the Caribbean (ECLAC), on the basis of official data from the countries.
[a] The averages for Latin America are arithmetic means of the values for 17 countries, which are divided into two groups: 9 in South America (Argentina, Brazil, Chile, Colombia, Ecuador, Paraguay, Peru, Plurinational State of Bolivia and Uruguay); and 8 in the group comprising Central America (Costa Rica, El Salvador, Guatemala, Honduras, Nicaragua and Panama), the Dominican Republic and Mexico. In the Caribbean, five countries are included (Bahamas, Barbados, Guyana, Jamaica and Trinidad and Tobago).

As shown in figure III.4, the five English-speaking Caribbean countries included in the analysis show growth that is lower on average (1.4% per year) and less stable, with a drop of 7% on average over the past four years. However, the average amount per capita is almost 1.7 times that of the Latin American countries.

The analysis by country shows that over the past two years, Chile and Uruguay allocated most resources per capita to social policy financing (US$ 2,538 and US$ 2,504, respectively), followed by Brazil (US$ 1,924), Argentina (US$ 1,924) and Costa Rica (US$ 1,209). Panama, Colombia and Mexico make up a third group of countries, with spending of between US$ 1,021 and US$ 884, followed by Peru and the Dominican Republic, with US$ 704 and US$ 604, respectively. Ecuador and Paraguay come next with less than US$ 500 per person (US$ 472 and US$ 470, respectively), followed by El Salvador and the Plurinational State of Bolivia with US$ 320 each, and lastly Guatemala, Nicaragua and Honduras with less than US$ 230 each[5] (see annex III.A1).

As indicated in previous editions of *Social Panorama of Latin America* (2015, 2016 and 2018), the region is still a long way behind the countries of the Organization for Economic Cooperation and Development (OECD) and the European Union in terms of the availability of resources for social spending, in both absolute and relative terms. At the same time, the detailed data reveal once again that the Latin American countries where the greatest efforts are required to combat poverty and which are most in need of services to ensure social rights and achieve the social targets of the 2030 Agenda for Sustainable Development (in areas such as health, education, social protection and access to drinking water, electricity and sanitation) have the fewest resources, both in absolute terms and as a proportion of their GDP.

3.   Social spending by function in the region

Analysis of the evolution of central government spending on social functions shows a similar distribution to that described in the 2018 edition of *Social Panorama of Latin America* (ECLAC, 2019a), with social protection, education and health standing out as the functions with most resources allocated. On average, spending on these functions represented 4.3%, 4.0% and 2.2% of GDP, respectively, in the Latin American countries in 2017 (see figure III.5). Between 2000 and 2017, these functions show the strongest spending growth in terms of GDP percentage points: growth of 1.1 GDP points in spending on social protection, 0.9 GDP points in education, and by 0.7 points in health, representing a 49% increase over the period.

Figure III.5
Latin America and the Caribbean (22 countries): central government social spending by function, 2000–2018[a]
(Percentages of GDP)

A. Latin America (17 countries)

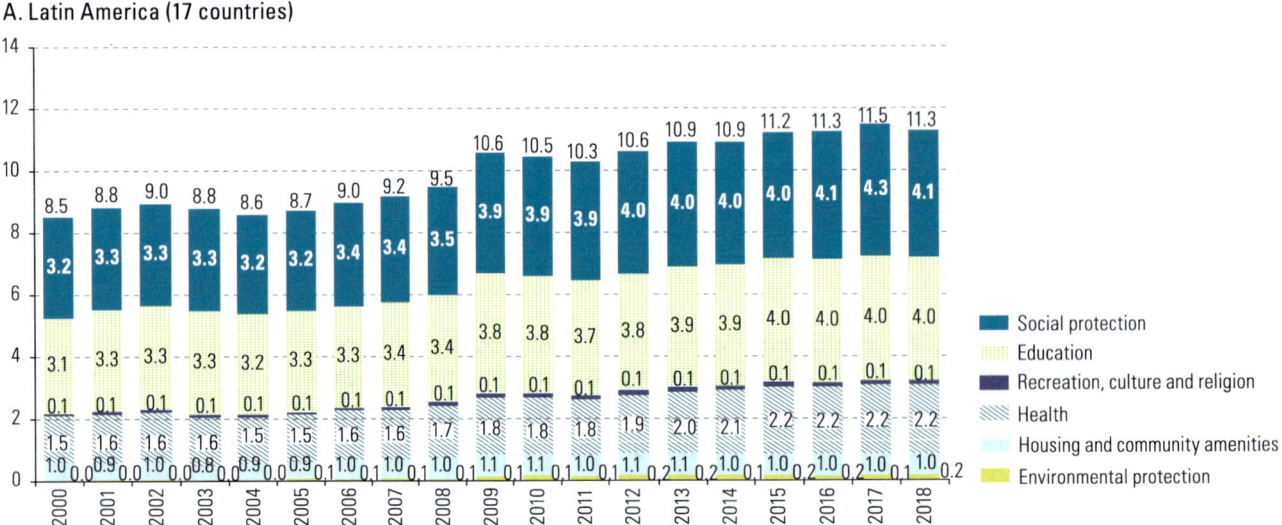

Figure III.5 (concluded)

B. South America (9 countries)

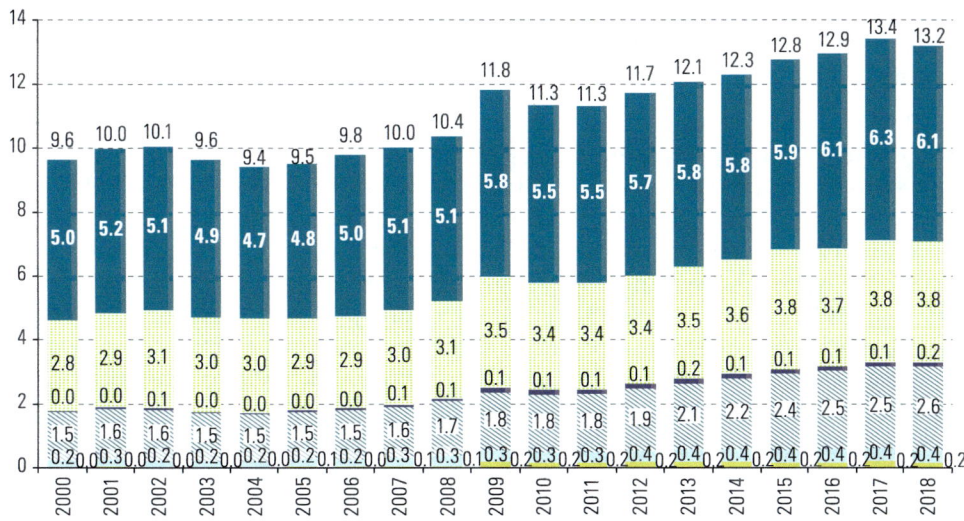

C. Central America, Dominican Republic and Mexico (8 countries)

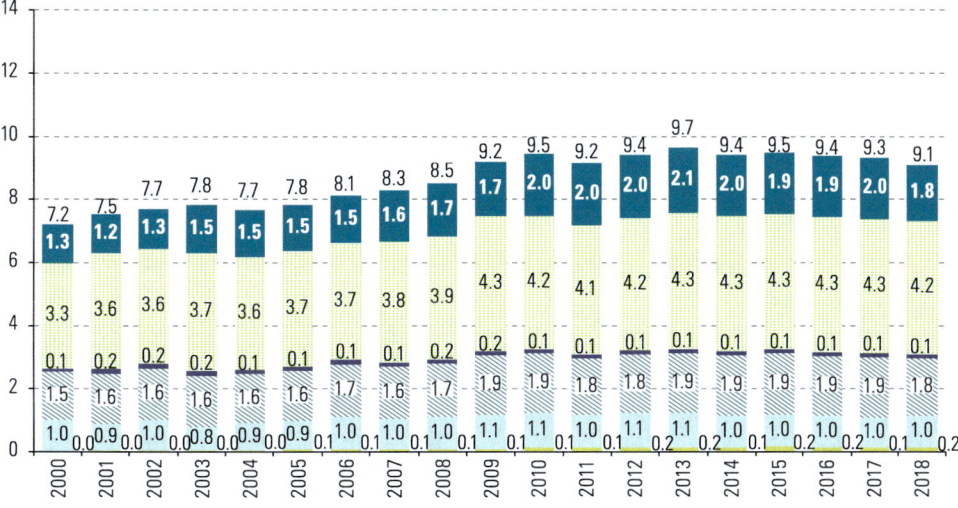

D. The Caribbean (5 countries)

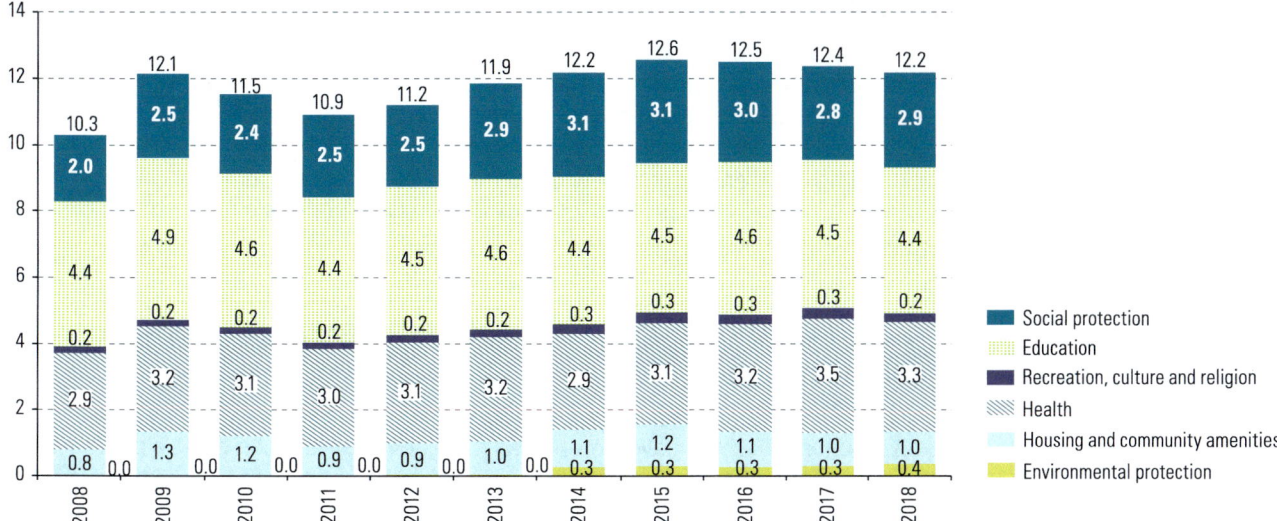

Legend:
- Social protection
- Education
- Recreation, culture and religion
- Health
- Housing and community amenities
- Environmental protection

Source: Economic Commission for Latin America and the Caribbean (ECLAC), on the basis of official information from the countries.

[a] The averages for Latin America (graph A) are arithmetic means of the values for 17 countries, which are divided into two groups (graphs B and C): 9 in South America (Argentina, Brazil, Chile, Colombia, Ecuador, Paraguay, Peru, Plurinational State of Bolivia and Uruguay); and 8 in the group comprising Central America (Costa Rica, El Salvador, Guatemala, Honduras, Nicaragua and Panama), the Dominican Republic and Mexico. In the Caribbean (graph D), five countries are included (Bahamas, Barbados, Guyana, Jamaica and Trinidad and Tobago).

In 2018, regional spending on social protection in Latin America fell on average by 0.2 GDP percentage points, back to 2016 levels, which in turn explained the reversal of the trend in public social spending. Meanwhile, spending on education and health remained at the same levels in GDP terms, on average, as in the preceding three years.

The functional distribution described is strongly influenced by the nine South American countries analysed, especially in the case of social protection spending, which reached an average of 6.3% of GDP in 2017, but fell to 6.1% of GDP in 2018. By contrast, in the group comprising Central America, the Dominican Republic and Mexico, social protection represented 2.0% of GDP on average, falling to 1.8% of GDP in 2018. In other words, the priority afforded to this function in this group of countries is, on average, less than a third of that of South America. Both the break in the trends seen in the South American countries and the low level of resources allocated to social protection in the group comprising the Central American countries, the Dominican Republic and Mexico call for reflection on the financial sustainability of policies and their potential effectiveness in driving progress towards eradicating poverty and achieving levels of pensions and access to goods and services consistent with a well-being threshold that ensures rights.

In the case of education, the average observed in the Central American countries, the Dominican Republic and Mexico is about half a GDP point higher than the average for the South American countries, at respectively 4.3% and 3.8% of GDP in 2017, and 4.2% and 3.8% of GDP in 2018.

In the health function, the difference between the two subregions is around 0.6 GDP points in 2017: South America has the higher average figure, at 2.5% of GDP in 2017, rising slightly to 2.6% in 2018. Meanwhile, in Central America, the Dominican Republic and Mexico, this function represented 1.9% of GDP on average in 2017, edging down to 1.8% in 2018.

In the case of spending on housing and community amenities, the observations made in the previous version of *Social Panorama of Latin America* (ECLAC, 2019a) still hold. In 2017 and 2018, the group comprising Central America, the Dominican Republic and Mexico spent, on average, more than twice the share of GDP spent by the South American countries.

The information for the five countries of the English-speaking Caribbean shows a relatively different functional distribution from that of the Latin American countries in 2017 and 2018. Education is the function allocated most resources (4.5% and 4.4% of GDP in 2017 and 2018, respectively), and has maintained a stable position in the past 10 years. The second function by resource allocation is health, which shows an upward trend since 2011, reaching 3.5% of GDP in 2017. This figure slipped slightly to 3.3% in 2018, although it was still higher than the 2016 value. Meanwhile, spending on social protection showed a downward trend until 2017, to 2.8% of GDP, and a slight upturn in 2018, to 2.9%, with a fall of 0.2 percentage points over the past four years. The function of housing and community amenities showed an expenditure level equivalent to 1.0% of GDP over the last two years of the analysis in the average for this group of countries, with an overall downtrend since 2015.

4. The distribution of functional social spending in the countries

The distribution of central government social spending by function gives a picture of the priorities and commitments in each of the countries, in terms of the allocation of public resources. As mentioned in *Social Panorama of Latin America 2018* (ECLAC, 2019a), in the last year the distribution of expenditure by social function shows that most countries allocate the largest proportions of resources to social protection, education and health, but also that there are significant differences in distribution (see figure III.6 and annex III.A1).

Figure III.6
Latin America and the Caribbean (23 countries): distribution of central government social spending by function, 2018[a]
(Percentages)

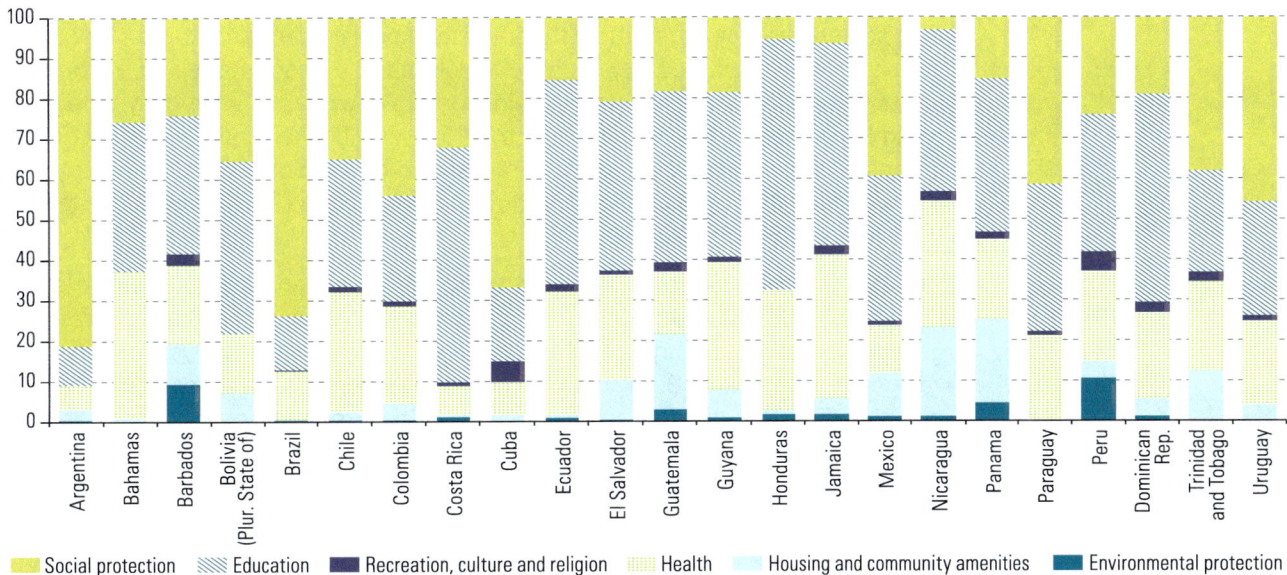

Social protection Education Recreation, culture and religion Health Housing and community amenities Environmental protection

Source: Economic Commission for Latin America and the Caribbean (ECLAC), on the basis of official information from the countries.
[a] The data for Guyana, Panama and the Plurinational State of Bolivia refer to 2017. The data for Peru refer to general government figures and those for the Plurinational State of Bolivia refer to the central administration.

The description given here focuses on central government data for 2018.[6] These amounts may vary significantly if broader coverages are analysed, such as general government or the non-financial public sector. This is particularly relevant in the case of countries with a federal structure or whose subnational governments have high levels of autonomy, such as Argentina, Brazil, Colombia and Mexico. Data on broader coverages of public social expenditure are available for some countries only (see box III.1). In those cases, complementary factors are included on the social spending situation observed in the 2017–2018 biennium.

The situation regarding each function in the different countries over the past biennium is briefly described below.

(a) Social protection

Resources spent on social protection policies include disbursements for services and transfers to individuals and families relating to illness and disability, old age, survivors,[7] families and children, unemployment, housing and social exclusion, in both the contributory and non-contributory social protection systems. This function encompasses policies and programmes designed to cover risks that may affect the whole population (related to disasters, sickness, old age and unemployment), as well as those aimed at facilitating inclusion and protecting against the consequences of poverty and inequality (such as conditional cash transfer programmes and social pensions).

On average, 23 Latin American and Caribbean countries for which information is available devoted resources equivalent to 3.9% of GDP to the social protection

---

[6] The data for Guyana, Panama and the Plurinational State of Bolivia refer to 2017.
[7] Spending associated with survivors is social protection in the form of cash and in-kind benefits for the survivors of deceased persons (such as the spouse, ex-spouse, children, grandchildren, parents and other family members).

function. Brazil and Argentina allocated the most resources to this function (over 13.1% and 11.0% of GDP, respectively). Uruguay ranks third, with 8.7% of GDP. At the other extreme, Honduras, Jamaica and Nicaragua allocated the fewest resources (less than 1% of GDP). In several countries the figures on social security spending may be higher than indicated here, owing to the different institutional models and forms of resource administration in each country; some models have management and accounting autonomy and others are privately administered. An example is Uruguay where, as noted in *Social Panorama of Latin America 2018*, consolidating central government data with those on contributory pensions administered by the Social Security Bank yields a significantly higher level of spending on social protection (13.3% of GDP according to 2016 figures) (ECLAC, 2019a, p. 117).

Comparing the resources allocated to social protection with total public social expenditure by the central government shows that Argentina and Brazil allocate the largest proportion of resources to this function, including in the analysis of expanded coverage presented later. Both countries prioritize this function in terms of expenditure distribution. This situation is strongly influenced by expenditure associated with old age, which accounts for over half of spending on social protection. This is also the case in Cuba, which allocates a significant share of social spending to this function. Consistently with the analysis in the previous paragraph, Uruguay is also among the countries that most prioritize this function within social spending.

Other countries that are notable for the large share of this function in total social spending are Colombia, Paraguay, Mexico, Trinidad and Tobago, the Plurinational State of Bolivia and Chile, with proportions of around 40%.[8] Meanwhile, Honduras, Jamaica and Nicaragua are among the countries allocating the smallest proportions of social spending to this function (6% or less).

(b) Education

The education function includes all expenditures made to finance education policies at the different levels of teaching, from pre-school to tertiary. It also includes ancillary services and research and development.

As indicated earlier, among the Latin American countries this is the second most important social function in terms of central government resources, but slightly exceeds the level of the social protection function in the average for the 23 Latin American and Caribbean countries analysed (equivalent to 4.0% of GDP). At the central government level, Costa Rica stands out as the country that allocates the largest share of its GDP to education (7%), followed by Barbados, the Plurinational State of Bolivia, Guyana, Chile, Jamaica, Honduras, Ecuador and Uruguay (all with around 5% of GDP).

Although the volume of resources allocated in each country does not necessarily meet its needs, several countries in the region spend a proportion of GDP that is in line with the recommendations of the Education 2030 Framework for Action: allocating at least 4% to 6% of gross domestic product (GDP) or at least 15% to 20% of public expenditure to education (UNESCO, 2015).

The latest data show that education is the function to which most resources are allocated in 15 of the 23 countries analysed. As observed in the 2018 edition of *Social Panorama*, this distribution does not necessarily reflect the quality of the outcomes, but reveals the preponderance of resources allocated to education policies in relation to the other social functions.

---

[8]   Distribution of data for 2017.

The country that allocates the greatest proportion of social spending to this function is Honduras (62%), closely followed by Costa Rica (58%), then the Dominican Republic (52%), Ecuador and Jamaica (both 50%). At the other extreme, and consistently with the significance of the social protection function within central government social spending, Brazil and Argentina allocate the lowest proportion of resources to education.[9] However, in the analysis by expanded coverage below, both countries report a higher level of resources going to education, at 6.2% and 4.9% of GDP, respectively.

(c) Health

The analysis of social expenditure on the health function includes disbursements made to finance services provided to individuals and groups at different levels of care, in both preventive and curative programmes.

Central government health funding averages 2.4% of GDP in the 23 countries analysed. This stands in contrast to the provisions of the *Sustainable Health Agenda for the Americas 2018–2030*,[10] which established that moving towards universal health[11] requires achieving "a level of public expenditure on health of at least 6% of GDP" (PAHO/WHO, 2017, p. 33, target 4.1). The magnitude of the resource gap to be closed to achieve this target is evident. Public social spending by the central government is not currently sufficient to meet this target in any country in the region. Chile allocates the most resources to health in relation to GDP (4.9%), followed by Guyana, Jamaica, Uruguay, Nicaragua, Barbados, Trinidad and Tobago and Colombia (all with over 3% of GDP). However, the expanded coverage analysis shows three countries meeting the target, with public spending on health standing at over 6% of GDP: Cuba (11% of GDP), Argentina (7% of GDP)[12] and Costa Rica (6.5% of GDP).

The Bahamas stands out for the proportion of resources devoted by the central government to social spending on health vis-à-vis other social functions; proportionally, it is the country that commits the most resources (36%). Another six countries allocate over 30% to this function: Jamaica (35%), Nicaragua (31%), and Guyana (31%), followed by Chile, Ecuador, Chile and Honduras (each with 30%). At the opposite extreme, the countries whose central governments allocate the smallest shares of social spending to health policies are Argentina, Costa Rica and Cuba, all with 8% or less, followed by Mexico, Brazil, Guatemala and the Plurinational State of Bolivia, all with under 16%.

It is also necessary to consider the weight of social protection spending in some of these countries and how it interacts with the health function. As noted in the 2018 edition of *Social Panorama*, the institutions involved in contributory social protection are often both providers and insurers of some health services. In view of this, more disaggregated data would be required to support an in-depth analysis. Yet another consideration is the effect of resource management at the subnational level, particularly in countries with autonomous state and subnational governments. Indeed, expenditure on the health function is significant in all cases where data are available with a broader coverage. In this regard, in addition to the countries mentioned above, the Plurinational State of Bolivia, Brazil and Colombia are very close to achieving the target proposed in *Sustainable Health Agenda for the Americas 2018–2030*, with expenditure of 5.5%, 5.2% and 4.9% of GDP, respectively.

---

[9]   This situation becomes more nuanced when broader institutional coverages are examined, such as general government (including subnational governments, which finance an important part of the education system in these two countries); however, the share of social spending devoted to the social protection function nonetheless remains at a significant distance from the other functions in both cases.

[10]   Prepared following a decision made at the 55th Directing Council of the Pan American Health Organization (PAHO) in 2016.

[11]   See Goal 4 of *Sustainable Health Agenda for the Americas 2018–2030* (PAHO/WHO, 2017, p. 33).

[12]   Data refer to 2015.

(d) Housing and community amenities

Public spending on housing and community amenities encompasses State resources devoted to urbanization (including the administration of urbanization issues, slum clearance for residential development, construction and remodelling of homes, and acquisition of land for housebuilding), community development, water supply and street lighting.

The countries of the region spend an average of 0.7% of GDP on this function. The highest level of expenditure is seen in Nicaragua (2.5% of GDP), followed by Trinidad and Tobago, Panama and Barbados (1.8% of GDP in each case). Accordingly, Nicaragua devotes the largest proportion of central government social spending to this function (22%), followed by Panama and Guatemala (21% and 19%, respectively). Fifteen of the 23 countries analysed devote less than 5% of all total central government social spending to this function.

(e) Recreation, culture and religion

Financing for recreation, culture and religion includes resources allocated to leisure (sports and cultural activities, radio and television) and religious services.

This function represented an average of 0.22% of GDP at the regional level in 2018, the lowest of all the social functions, equivalent to three quarters of the level agreed at the tenth Ibero-American Conference on Culture, held in Valparaiso (Chile) in July 2007, where the ministers and senior authorities of cultural affairs proposed progressively allocating a minimum of 1% of each State's general budget to the promotion of culture (ECLAC/OEI, 2014, p. 311). Although their central governments are far from fulfilling this commitment, Peru, Barbados and Cuba lead the way in resource allocation to this function (around 0.5% of GDP each). In four countries, central government public expenditure information makes no mention of funding for this function.

(f) Environmental protection

As part of the social functions, environmental protection includes spending on waste and wastewater management, pollution reduction, biodiversity and landscape protection, and research related to environmental protection.

At the central government level, expenditure on this function averaged 0.26% of GDP in the 23 countries analysed in 2018. Barbados and Peru allocate resources equivalent to 1.6% and 1.2% of GDP, respectively, followed by Panama (0.39%), Guatemala (0.2%) and Jamaica (0.17%).

However, these values may vary significantly when broader institutional coverage is considered, including subnational levels of government, given their role in waste management, and public wastewater treatment companies. This is reflected in the importance of the work done to consolidate these outlays in the satellite accounts for this area, which provide a fuller picture of the resources allocated and the actions taken by different actors within the framework of the countries' environmental protection policies.[13]

---

[13]   See further details on this subject in ECLAC, "Regional network of environmental statistics for Latin America" [online] https://comunidades.cepal.org/estadisticas-ambientales/es.

5.   Public social spending in broader institutional coverage than central government: selected countries

The data and analysis presented thus far refer to central government, which is the only level of institutional coverage available for all the countries in the region, and hence the level at which comparisons can be made regionwide. However, given that some countries' institutional structures include subsectors outside the central government (IMF, 2014) that have significant impacts on the execution of public social policies, this section complements the information using reports from nine countries on broader institutional coverage:[14]Argentina, Brazil, Colombia, Costa Rica, Cuba, El Salvador, Paraguay, Peru[15] and Plurinational State of Bolivia (see annex).

The most relevant elements for comparing data from the two levels of coverage are set forth below.

The level of public social spending as a proportion of GDP in each country changes significantly when data from the various levels of government are compared. The largest variation occurs in Argentina, where this level rises from 14.1% of GDP under central government coverage in 2015 to 30% in the figure for overall public spending, reaching US$ 3,175 per capita per year. Argentina is followed by Cuba and Brazil, whose expenditures rise to 28.5% and 27% of GDP (in 2018 and 2017, respectively) close to the average levels of social spending in OECD countries, where the average was 30.3% in 2017.[16]

The distribution of public social spending by function also changes significantly in the broader institutional coverage compared to central government coverage.

In the case of Argentina, the broader coverage in 2015 shows significant changes in relation to health and education spending, which account for 23.3% and 20.7% of public sector social spending, respectively, far above the 7% and 12% corresponding to central government social spending that year. This brings spending on social protection to 46.3% of social spending by the public sector, still the function to which most resources are allocated, but proportionally much less than the 76% it represents in the social expenditure of the central government. In turn, the weight of broader public spending on housing and community amenities is 4 percentage points higher than central government spending on this function.

In the Plurinational State of Bolivia, education is the priority function in general government spending, as it is in central administration spending, in 2016. A change occurs in the distribution of resources, however, as health moves to second place, with 24.8% of social spending, followed by social protection with 21% (versus 15% and 37%, respectively, in the central government distribution).

The case of Brazil is similar to Argentina. Spending on social protection accounts for a smaller share of total public social spending in the general government coverage in 2017 (58% compared to 74% in the central government coverage), while spending on health and education acquire larger shares, with figures of around 19% for both, compared with around 11% and 13% in the central government distribution.

---

[14]   Increasing the availability of datasets with coverage broader than the central government requires a major effort of public finance consolidation between levels of government. For this reason, information is not available for all the countries, and in some cases the review years differ.

[15]   In the case of Peru, the series reported is the same in the previous sections, as data are available for general government coverage only.

[16]   For more details, see Organization for Economic Cooperation and Development (OECD), OECDStat.

Colombia maintains a similar distribution between the functions in the different levels of coverage in the 2017 data, as the amount allocated to each grows in proportion to the rise in public social spending in relation to GDP from 13% at the central government level to 20% at the general government level.

In Costa Rica, education remains the function attracting the most resources in public sector coverage in 2018, although its overall share falls to 31%, from 58% in the central government coverage. The opposite occurs with the health function, which accounts for 7% of central government social public spending as against 27% of consolidated public sector social spending. In turn, the weight of housing and community amenities rises from 0.5% in the narrower coverage to 9.9% in the broader coverage. Social protection shows virtually no difference between the two categories of coverage.

For Cuba, in the general government coverage in 2018, health spending is the priority, with 38%, compared to third place for this function, at 8%, in central government coverage. Health is followed by education, whose allocation in the general government coverage is 11 percentage points higher than in the central government public social spending. By contrast, social protection moves from first place at the level of central government expenditure to third place at the general government level (with its allocation falling from 67% to 22%, respectively). Lastly, expenditure on housing and community amenities gains two percentage points in the allocation in the broader coverage of analysis.

El Salvador is a particular case, with revealing differences in the wider coverage. Spending on housing and community amenities is the highest in the region in relation to GDP (2.82%) and in relation to total social spending, accounting for 19.3% of the public sector coverage, versus 10% at the central government level, where it is the third priority, ahead of the health function. This structure is similar to that of Guatemala, Nicaragua and Panama, analysed earlier in relation to central government coverage, which afford priority to housing and community amenities over health (Guatemala and Panama) and social protection (Nicaragua). In the expanded coverage, social protection has a larger share, up from 21% to 37% of total public social spending. By contrast, education and health account for a smaller share, down from 42% and 26%, respectively, of central government social spending, to 26% and 17%, respectively, of broader public sector social spending.

Finally, Paraguay shows no change in the structure of the functions. Social protection remains the priority, followed by education and health, but the concentration of resources is slightly different in two functions. Expenditure on social protection is 4 percentage points higher in the general government distribution than in the central government one. The functions of housing and community amenities and health also have a greater share in the expanded coverage, by around 2 and 3 points, respectively. The opposite occurs with education, which shows a 9-percentage-point drop in share in the distribution compared to the central government figures.

B. Estimated resources needed to close the poverty and extreme poverty income gap in Latin America by 2030

Ensuring that all households have the necessary resources to close the income gap in extreme and total poverty in the next decade seems an attainable goal for most countries of the region. However, to that end, progress must be made in addressing the social footprint of the current development model, maintaining adequate levels of economic growth and labour inclusion, and adopting a clear political decision on tax rates and the financing social policies, particularly in those countries that have lower levels of social spending and wider gaps. Reducing levels of tax evasion appears to be an alternative, which would provide resources for the development of social protection systems including income transfers to universalize adequate levels of well-being, closing gaps and expanding opportunities.

As stated in chapter II, it is estimated that there were 184 million people living in poverty in the region in 2017, of whom 64 million were living in extreme poverty. In addition, there were 158 million people living above the poverty line but with low incomes, making them highly vulnerable to falling into poverty (with incomes equivalent to between 1 and less than 1.8 times the poverty line). To achieve Sustainable Development Goal (SDG) 1 concering income poverty, these people's earnings must exceed the poverty line in the next 10 years, and they must achieve a level of income sustainability that minimizes their vulnerability to falling back into poverty.

This section provides an estimate of the resources needed to bridge the income gaps in order to achieve SDG 1 by 2030 in 16 countries of the region.[17] These gaps reflect the average income deficit of populations living in poverty with respect to the poverty and extreme poverty lines and, therefore, the amount of resources required by those populations to end poverty. Regardless of whether the resources are generated by the households themselves in the labour market, come from transfers between households or are the result of public policy actions, the objective is to quantify this amount.

1. Household resources needed to bridge poverty income gaps

Taking as a reference the estimates from household surveys for 2017 (or the most recent year available for each country)[18] of the 16 Latin American countries analysed, the income gaps[19] to be bridged for extreme poverty reached a simple average per country of US$ 223 at constant 2010 prices per person per year (see figure III.7). Seven countries have an average gap ranging from US$ 112 to US$ 158 per person (Ecuador,

---

[17] Argentina is not included in this analysis because poverty data is only available for urban areas. The Bolivarian Republic of Venezuela is not included either because of difficulties in estimating the gaps to be bridged in the years ahead.

[18] Estimates for Guatemala and Nicaragua are for 2014, while those for Honduras and Mexico are for 2016.

[19] The monthly amount needed for each person living in poverty or extreme poverty to have a per capita income equivalent to the value of the poverty or extreme poverty line.

El Salvador, Honduras, Guatemala, Paraguay, Peru and Nicaragua). Meanwhile, the average gap per person is between US$ 209 and US$ 287 dollars in six countries (Colombia, Costa Rica, the Dominican Republic, Mexico, Panama and the Plurinational State of Bolivia). Brazil, Chile and Uruguay have average gaps between US$ 342 and US$ 485 per person.[20]

Figure III.7
Latin America (16 countries): average annual gaps per person for extreme poverty, poverty and 1.8 poverty lines, by country, 2017[a]
(Dollars per capita at constant 2010 prices)

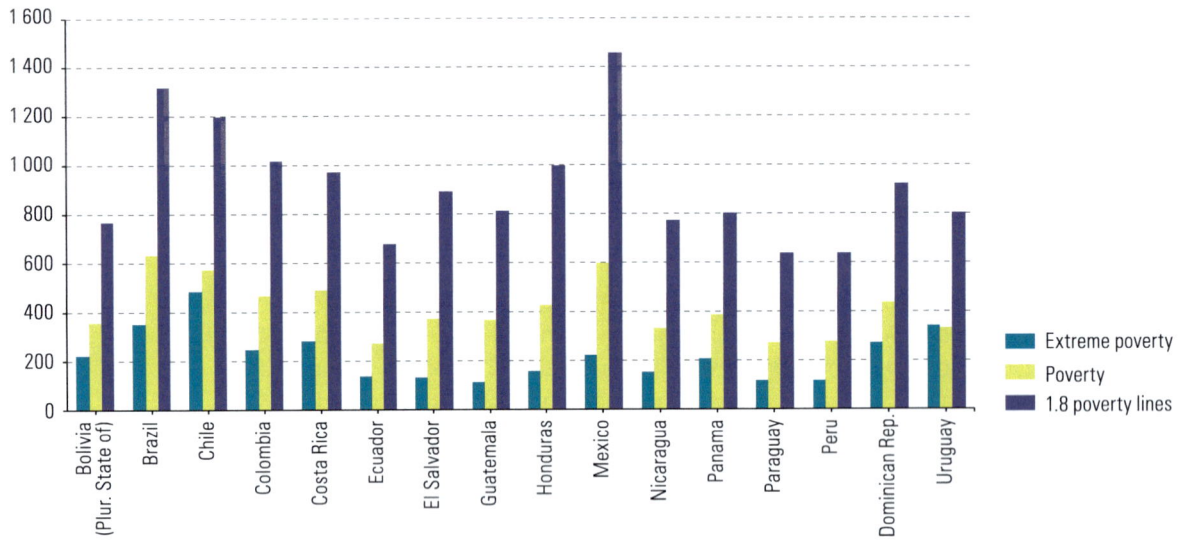

Source: Economic Commission for Latin America and the Caribbean (ECLAC), on the basis of special processing of household surveys conducted in the respective countries.
[a] Data for Guatemala and Nicaragua are for 2014, those for Honduras and Mexico are for 2016.

With regard to total poverty, the gap to be bridged to ensure that all inhabitants' earnings will exceed the poverty line (including those living in extreme poverty) is an average of US$ 412 per capita per year. The countries with the lowest average amounts are Paraguay, Peru and Ecuador (between US$ 273 and US$ 279). They are followed by Guatemala, El Salvador, Panama, the Plurinational State of Bolivia and Uruguay (between US$ 332 and US$ 385 per person). In Colombia, Costa Rica, the Dominican Republic and Honduras, the poverty gap is between US$ 424 and US$ 467 per person. Meanwhile, in Brazil, Chile and Mexico, it is between US$ 575 and US$ 632.

The average income gap that would need to be bridged so that the entire population has an annual income equal to or greater than 1.8 times the poverty line is US$ 918. The value of this gap ranges from US$ 639 to US$ 774 per person in five countries (Ecuador, Nicaragua, Paraguay, Peru and the Plurinational State of Bolivia), followed by Costa Rica, El Salvador, Guatemala, Honduras, Panama and Uruguay, with between US$ 801 and US$ 998 per person. Brazil, Chile, Colombia and Mexico have average vulnerability gaps of between US$ 1,017 and US$ 1,456.

---

[20]   The differences in the average gaps among countries expressed in 2010 dollars are due to both the extent of poverty (how poor the poor or extremely poor are) and the value of the poverty and extreme poverty lines. The specific mechanisms used to reduce poverty or extreme poverty in a country may either narrow or widen the average gaps with respect to the poverty line, depending on whether those who are lifted out of poverty (or extreme poverty) are those who are furthest from the poverty line or closest to it.

By multiplying the values indicated by the estimated number of people living with per capita incomes below the extreme poverty line, the poverty line and 1.8 times the poverty line, the additional amount of resources that would need to increase the income of those households in each country to ensure that the entire population reaches at least those thresholds can be calculated.

According to ECLAC data on the gaps and population estimates (2019 revision), the projected amounts needed to eradicate extreme poverty in the 16 Latin American countries analysed comes to a regional total of US$ 10.667 billion (at constant 2010 prices), rising to US$ 79.696 billion to end poverty. When these figures are compared with the GDP of the countries studied, they account for 0.4% and 2.9% of GDP,[21] respectively.

As figure III.8 shows, the resources needed for the income of all households to exceed the extreme poverty and poverty lines are highly heterogeneous across countries. The country facing the greatest challenge to eradicate extreme poverty is Nicaragua, with 1.6% of GDP (as of 2014), followed by the Plurinational State of Bolivia and Honduras (more than 1.4% of GDP) and then, some way behind, is Guatemala, with 0.6% of GDP. Other countries' needs do not exceed 0.4% of GDP for the year under consideration.

Figure III.8
Latin America (16 countries): total resource increase needed in the population income to end extreme poverty and poverty, by country, 2017[a]
(Percentages of GDP)

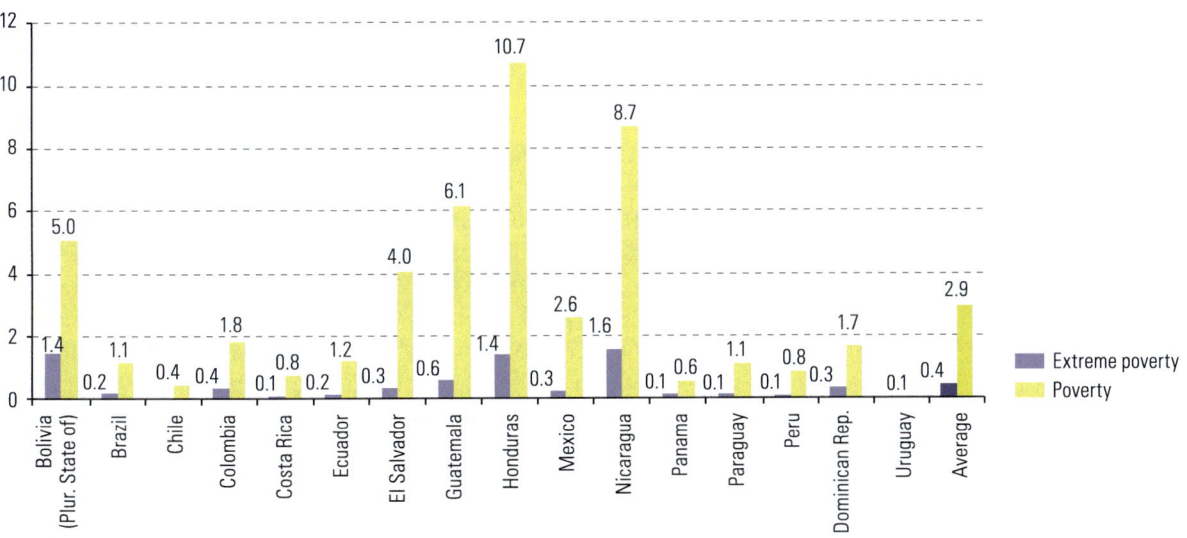

Source: Economic Commission for Latin America and the Caribbean (ECLAC), on the basis of special processing of household surveys conducted in the respective countries.
[a] Data for Guatemala and Nicaragua are for 2014, those for Honduras and Mexico are for 2016.

Heterogeneity is more marked when the challenge of closing monetary poverty gaps in each of the countries is analysed. Central America is home to four of the five countries facing the greatest challenges. Data for Honduras from 2016 indicate that the income in poor households in this country need to increase by an aggregate value equivalent to almost 11% of GDP, more than 1.4 times annual national social spending. It is followed by Nicaragua and Guatemala, which needed the equivalent of 8.7% and 6.1% of GDP, respectively, in 2014. The fourth Central American country facing a considerable challenge is El Salvador, which needed 4.0% of GDP in 2017, one percentage point lower than that of the Plurinational State of Bolivia.

---

[21] To calculate the aggregate annual gaps as a percentage of GDP, the values corresponding to the year of estimation of the annual gap was used, based on household surveys and fiscal statistics for each country.

A second group of countries would need poor households to raise their incomes by around 2 percentage points of GDP. These are Mexico (2.6% of GDP), Argentina (2.0% of GDP), Colombia (1.8% of GDP) and the Dominican Republic (1.7% of GDP). The incomes of those living in poverty in Brazil, Costa Rica, Ecuador, Paraguay and Peru need to increase by around 1% of GDP, while 0.6% is needed in Chile, Panama and Uruguay. To close poverty and extreme poverty gaps in Uruguay, no more than 0.1% of GDP is needed.

The values indicated here reflect the annual effort the countries of the region need to make in order to attain the Goal of ending poverty by 2030, if the number of poor people remains constant.

2. Comparing resource requirements, social public spending, tax revenues, and levels of tax evasion and avoidance

This section compares the resources needed to increase the incomes of the poorest households in order to bridge gaps in monetary poverty, regardless of how it is achieved (improvement in the labour market; transfers between private individuals, for example, remittances; increase in the transfer of income or assets from the State; subsidies, or another mechanisms), using three reference parameters to gauge the magnitude of the challenge posed by SDG 1, namely central government social spending in each country, national tax revenue, and estimates of the scale of tax evasion and avoidance at the regional level.

As can be seen in table III.1, when analysing the additional requirements together with the current volume of central government social spending, the first thing that stands out is that in several countries the estimated amounts are relatively lower than the resources currently allocated to social policies, while in others they are equivalent to a significant proportion. On average, bridging the extreme poverty income gap through public policies requires an amount equivalent to 4.5% of central government social spending in 2017 (see table III.1). The difference is less than 1% in four countries (Chile, Costa Rica, Peru and Uruguay), between 1% and 2% would be required in another four (Brazil, Ecuador, Panama and Paraguay) and between 2% and 4% would be needed in Colombia, Dominican Republic, El Salvador and Mexico. Meanwhile, in four countries, the difference represents between 8% and 17% of central government social spending in 2017 (Guatemala, Honduras, Nicaragua and the Plurinational State of Bolivia).

The incremental amount needed to bridge the income gap to close the total poverty income gap in all the countries of the region represents 2.9% of GDP on average, equivalent to 30.8% of central government social expenditure of the Latin American countries analysed. The relative magnitude of the growth needed shows a distribution similar to that required to eradicate extreme poverty. In Uruguay, this amount is equivalent to less than 1% of central government social spending, while in Honduras it exceeds 125%, in Guatemala it is estimated to be 89% and in Nicaragua it is 81%.

But the magnitude of the growth needed refers not only to the amounts involved, but also to the amount of resources available. The average increase that would be required in the income of people living in extreme poverty is equivalent to 2.9% of tax revenue in 2017 (see figure III.9). At the country level, this value ranges from 0.01% of Uruguay's tax revenues to 7.5% of Nicaragua's, with eight countries needing less than 1% and four requiring 4.5% or more.

Table III.1
Latin America (16 countries): amount needed to bridge gaps and as a percentage of central government social expenditure, around 2017[a]
(Percentages of GDP)

Country	Additional resources		Central government social expenditure (C)	Additional resources needed as a percentage of social public spending	
	To close extreme poverty gap (A)	To close poverty gap (B)		To close extreme poverty gap (A/C)	To close poverty gap (B/C)
Bolivia (Plurinational State of)	1.4	5.0	12.7	11.4	39.8
Brazil	0.2	1.15	17.6	1.0	6.5
Chile	0.0	0.4	16.4	0.3	2.6
Colombia	0.4	1.8	13.4	2.6	13.6
Costa Rica	0.1	0.8	12.5	0.8	6.1
Dominican Republic	0.3	1.7	8.5	3.8	19.8
Ecuador	0.2	1.2	9.2	1.8	13.0
El Salvador	0.3	4.0	10.0	3.2	40.4
Guatemala	0.6	6.1	6.9	8.3	88.9
Honduras	1.4	10.7	8.5	16.6	125.9
Mexico	0.3	2.6	8.8	2.9	29.1
Nicaragua	1.6	8.7	10.7	14.8	81.0
Panama	0.1	0.6	8.8	1.6	6.3
Paraguay	0.1	1.1	8.6	1.6	13.0
Peru	0.1	0.8	11.4	0.8	7.3
Uruguay	0.0	0.1	16.8	0.0	0.4
Average	0.4	2.9	11.3	4.4	30.8

Source: Economic Commission for Latin America and the Caribbean (ECLAC), on the basis of special processing of household surveys conducted in the respective countries.
[a] Data for Guatemala and Nicaragua are for 2014, those for Honduras and Mexico are for 2016.

Figure III.9
Latin America (16 countries): percentage of general government tax revenues[a] that would need to be allocated to bridging gaps, around 2017[b]
(Percentages of tax revenue)

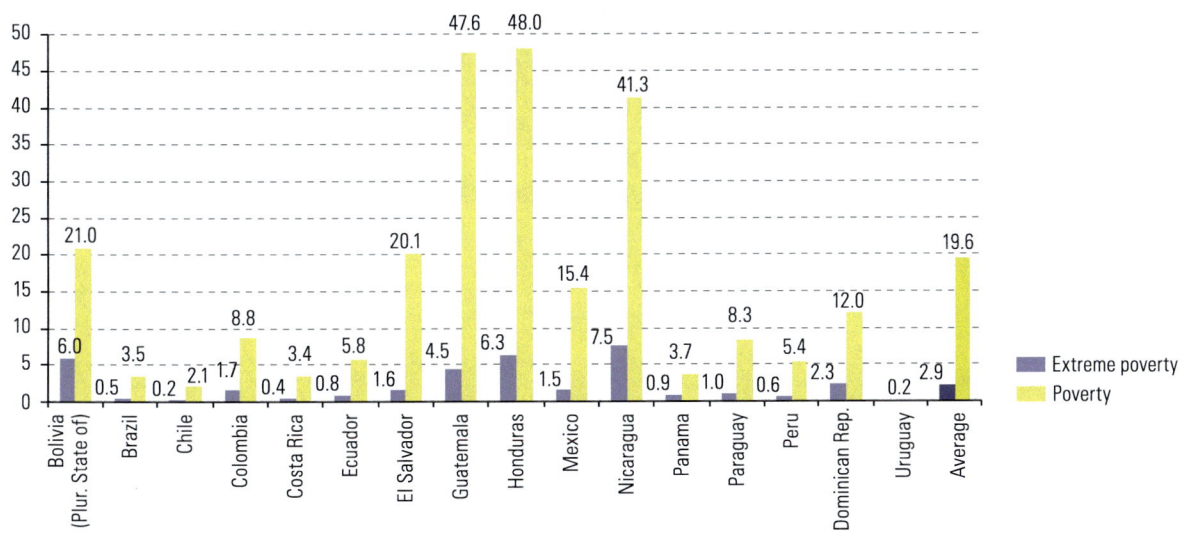

Source: Economic Commission for Latin America and the Caribbean (ECLAC), on the basis of official information from the countries.
[a] Data for El Salvador and the Dominican Republic correspond to the central government.
[b] Data for Guatemala and Nicaragua are for 2014, those for Honduras and Mexico are for 2016.

In the case of the amounts required to bridge the poverty gap, this proportion represents 19.6% of countries' tax revenues as a simple average. Uruguay is again the country that needs the lowest proportion (0.2%), followed by Brazil, Chile, Costa Rica and Panama (between 2% and 4%). In contrast, the income required to bridge the gap is equivalent to almost half of total revenues of Honduras and Guatemala (48%) and to 41% in Nicaragua. They are followed by the Plurinational State of Bolivia and El Salvador (around 20%), with Mexico and the Dominican Republic bringing up the rear (15% and 12%, respectively).

In order to fully analyse the feasibility of financing the aforementioned incremental resources, it is useful to compare the needs to tax evasion estimates. The financial requirements needed to bridge the extreme poverty gaps in these 16 countries are equivalent to 4.6% of regional evaded tax income; 34% would be needed to close the total poverty gap. Thus, improving the efficiency of existing tax systems could be a source of financing to cover both the extreme poverty and total poverty income gaps.

3.   Estimates of the costs of achieving the Goal on poverty over a 10-year period through income transfers

SDG 1 of the 2030 Agenda for Sustainable Development is to end poverty in all its forms everywhere by the year 2030. To achieve this, incomes must be increased, and the aforementioned gaps bridged. In addition to increases resulting from work and transfers between private individuals (through remittances or donations), subsidies and income transfers from social protection are public policy tools that have been shown to be effective in the region in recent decades (Cecchini, S. and others, 2015).

This section presents estimates of the annual increases in resources that would be needed in the region to bridge the entire poverty and extreme poverty gap by 2030 through income transfers, taking into account both existing gaps, population and economic growth estimates, and the projected poverty and extreme poverty trends in each of the countries (see box III.2).[22]

To eradicate extreme poverty within 10 years in households in this situation,[23] the region would need to progressively increase social spending by an average of US$ 865 million per year (at constant 2010 prices), to spend around US$ 1.037 billion in the first year and US$ 8.655 billion in 2029. As shown in figure III.10, this would mean allocating the equivalent of 0.02% of regional GDP in 2020, and progressively increasing this expenditure to reach a total equivalent to 0.13% of regional GDP by 2029.

---

[22] This is a comparison for reference purposes only, assuming perfect coverage and allocation. It does not include administration costs.
[23] This estimate only refers to the population living below the poverty and extreme poverty lines. It does not include the operational challenges and costs resulting from changes in the population's status, derived from the income variability of those living in poverty and vulnerable to falling into poverty.

Box III.2
Method for estimating
the resources needed
to end poverty

The projected cost of income transfers to gradually eradicate extreme poverty and total poverty by 2030 is based, as a starting point, on the estimated incidence of poverty and extreme poverty, as well as the average per capita income gaps with respect to the various poverty lines of a group of 17 countries of the region using the updated ECLAC methodology (ECLAC, 2018) applied to household surveys carried out around 2017. Surveys were carried out in 2017 in Argentina (urban areas), Brazil, Chile, Colombia, Costa Rica, the Dominican Republic, Ecuador, Panama, Paraguay, Peru, the Plurinational State of Bolivia and Uruguay. The surveys in Mexico and Honduras date from 2016, and in Guatemala and Nicaragua from 2014.

In order to estimate poverty and extreme poverty rates to 2030, economic growth was first projected on the basis of estimates produced by The Economist Intelligence Unit for 10 countries between 2019 and 2023 (Argentina, Brazil, Chile, Colombia, Costa Rica, Dominican Republic, Ecuador, El Salvador, Mexico and Peru). From 2019 to 2030, the trend growth rate is estimated using moving averages of the last five years, based on the projected variation rates in these 10 countries, and on those observed between 2014 and 2018 in the other countries. These annual growth estimates were used to calculate the total volumes of annual GDP in constant 2010 dollars, based on the most recent estimates available from CEPALSTAT.

In order to obtain annual projections of the population living in poverty and extreme poverty until 2030, the number of people living in poverty was adjusted for the years in which it was measured, using population estimates and projections (the latter were prepared using an average variant of fertility) published in United Nations (2019).

The projected poverty and extreme poverty rates and, therefore, the corresponding population volumes were based on the calculation of the elasticity of extreme poverty and total poverty (variation in percentage points) with respect to GDP variation rates, using linear regression methods by country, taking as a reference the period between 2009 and 2016 or 2017. The exceptions were Guatemala and Nicaragua, whose reference period was 2004–2014. In the case of discontinuous series of extreme poverty and total poverty data, linear interpolations were used and then the annual variations were calculated.

The average monthly extreme poverty and total poverty gaps were annualized and, based on the reference (or application) period of each survey, calculated at constant 2010 prices in the local currency according to the official monthly consumer price index (CPI) in CEPALSTAT. These figures were then converted into 2010 dollars using the average annual exchange rate of the International Monetary Fund (IMF).

Lastly, the annual resources needed to cover poverty and extreme poverty gaps through transfers were estimated by multiplying the projected size of the population living in poverty (or extreme poverty) by the annualized poverty and extreme poverty gaps (based on the assumption that the gaps will remain constant, i.e. that reductions in the poverty or extreme poverty rate from one year to the next will be the result of people from of all income levels beneath the poverty or extreme poverty line of the previous year being lifted out of poverty or extreme poverty). The evolution of these transfers to gradually bridge all the gaps was estimated on the basis of a 10-year period (2020–2029), based on an increase in coverage of 10 percentage points per year, taking the projected size of the population living in poverty or extreme poverty in each year as the reference population for this trend, expressed in percentage points (10% in the first year, 20% in the second, 30% in the third and so on until reaching 100% in 2029). Estimated resource requirements do not include direct or indirect administrative costs.

Source: Economic Commission for Latin America and the Caribbean (ECLAC), *Social Panorama of Latin America, 2017* (LC/PUB.2018/1-P), Santiago, 2018; *Social Panorama of Latin America, 2018* (LC/PUB.2019/3-P), Santiago, 2019; United Nations, World Population Prospects 2019 [online database] https://population.un.org/wpp/; The Economist Intelligence Unit [online] https://www.eiu.com/ and CEPALSTAT [online database] https://estadisticas.cepal.org/cepalstat/portada.html?idioma=english; International Monetary Fund (IMF), *International Financial Statistics* (IFS) [online] https://data.imf.org/regular.aspx?key=61545862.

Figure III.10
Latin America
(16 countries): increase in
resource transfers needed
to close poverty and
extreme poverty gaps
in 10 years, 2020–2030
(Percentages of GDP)

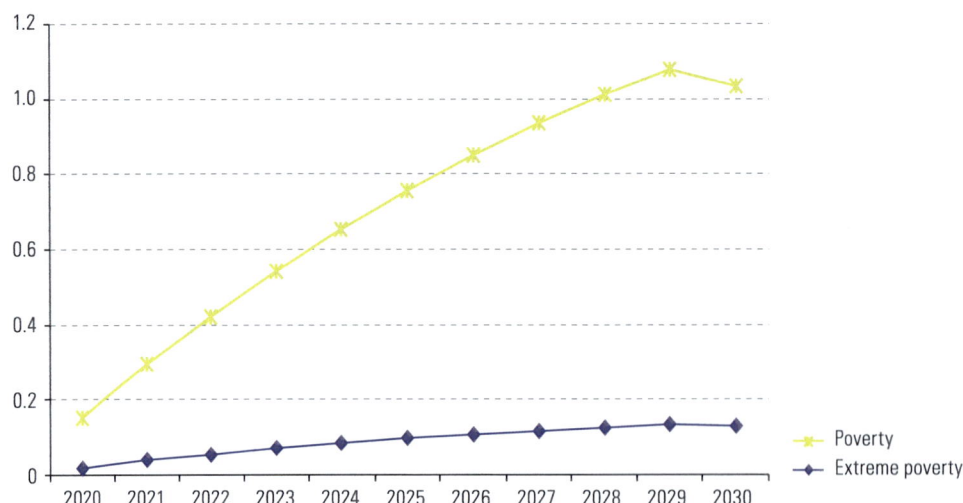

Source: Economic Commission for Latin America and the Caribbean (ECLAC), on the basis of official information from the countries.

Ensuring that, in the 16 countries of the region analysed, all households have incomes above the poverty line through the progressive expansion of coverage over 10 years, will require an average annual increase of US$ 6.982 billion (at constant 2010 prices), starting with US$ 7.891 billion in 2020 and amounting to US$ 69.825 billion by 2029.

In accordance with the parameters indicated in box III.2, once total coverage has been reached in 10 years, the income transfer resources needed to lock in achievements regarding poverty and total poverty should start to decrease.

Strategies for expanding transfers are highly heterogeneous across the countries, owing to the size of the total gaps to be bridged, population and economic growth projections, and the resulting magnitude of the reductions needed in poverty and extreme poverty linked to these factors. If the economic conditions in Chile and Uruguay are maintained, these countries should attain SDG 1 before 2030. Meanwhile, costs in 2029 would be less than 1% of GDP in several countries, including Brazil, Colombia, Costa Rica, the Dominican Republic, Panama, Peru, and Paraguay, followed by the Plurinational State of Bolivia and El Salvador, with amounts between 2% and 2.5% of GDP. Three countries face significant financing challenges, requiring improvements on both the revenue and expenditure sides, namely Guatemala, Honduras and Nicaragua (between 5% and 9% of GDP).

It must be recalled that the estimates described here are merely a reference for the purposes of analysis. Both their feasibility and the sustainability of their outcomes are subject to changing circumstances and great variability in the income of the poor population. Transfer tools have direct impacts on income only, with no guarantee of affecting other dimensions of poverty. In view of the data shown in chapter I and the agreements of the governments of the region enshrined in the Regional Agenda for Inclusive Social Development, adopted at the third session of the Regional Conference on Social Development in Latin America and the Caribbean, [24]progress is needed in developing universal, rights-based and difference-sensitive social protection systems.

---

[24]   See report of the third session of the Conference [online] https://repositorio.cepal.org/bitstream/handle/11362/44346/
       S1801178_en.pdf?sequence=1&isAllowed=y.

C. Conclusions

As in previous editions of the *Social Panorama of Latin America*, this chapter analyses social public spending at the central government level, which has been trending upward over the last five years. However, the last year saw a reversal of that trend, with a return to 2011 levels in the average for Central America, Mexico and Dominican Republic, and 2014 levels among the five countries of the English-speaking Caribbean analysed.

While the central governments of Brazil, Chile and Uruguay, in Latin America, and Barbados and Trinidad and Tobago, in the Caribbean, allocate more than 14% of GDP to social policy financing, the central governments of most of the Central American countries (El Salvador, Guatemala, Honduras and Panama), in addition to Mexico, the Dominican Republic, Ecuador, Paraguay and the Bahamas, spend less than 10% of GDP on social policies. Thus, the heterogeneity iand inadequacy of the allocation of public resources to social policies remains a characteristic of the region, both in terms of total amounts and their distribution, although social protection, education and health remain the priority areas in terms of resources.

As indicated in the *Social Panorama of Latin America, 2018*, it remains the case that those Latin American countries that will struggle the most to achieve the social goals of the 2030 Agenda for Sustainable Development are the ones that allocate the least resources to policies in this area, both as a percentage of GDP and in amounts per person.

Average spending per person among Latin American countries stabilized between 2017 and 2018, remaining at the highest levels of the last 18 years, double the amounts available per person at the beginning of the twenty-first century. However, the countries of the region remain far from meeting the intergovernmental commitments they have undertaken in various forums in areas such as health, education and culture, and lag well behind developed countries. The trend in per capita spending in the five English-speaking Caribbean countries for which information is available continues its downward trajectory, even though they spend more than Latin American countries, and they face challenges related to the sustainability of social policy financing and of debt levels.

The incorporation of data on broader government coverage in some countries has made it possible to supplement the information presented here. The countries for which information is available show increases of between 5 and 10 percentage points of GDP compared to their central government coverage reports, thus reaffirming the importance of increasing the availability of data at the general government level, particularly among countries that have subnational tax collection and public expenditure systems that are independent of the central government.

The data presented in section B reveal that, on average, the estimated volume of resources needed to bridge the extreme poverty gap does not seem as large when compared to the current level of average central government social expenditure in the countries of the region. Meanwhile, closing the total poverty gap does require a considerable amount of resources. Heterogeneity once again emerges as a key characteristic, as countries with higher poverty rates, lower levels of social spending and lower tax rates face greater challenges. The simulation of the extent to which the coverage of income transfer programmes needs to be expanded over a 10-year period shows that it is highly unlikely that some countries will end poverty by 2030 unless they broaden policy efforts to change the current poverty rate trends. However, the vast majority of countries of the region should be able to attain SDG 1 if steps are taken to make possible financing to support minimum levels of well-being, especially if regional efforts to reduce tax evasion are stepped up.

Bibliography

Cecchini, S. and R. Martínez (2011), *A Comprehensive, Rights-Based Approach*, ECLAC Books, No. 111 (LC/G.2488-P), Santiago, Economic Commission for Latin America and the Caribbean (ECLAC), March.

Cecchini, S. and others (eds.) (2015), *Towards universal social protection: Latin American pathways and policy tools*, ECLAC books, No. 136 (LC/G.2644-P), S. Cecchini and others (eds.), Santiago, Economic Commission for Latin America and the Caribbean (ECLAC), July.

ECLAC (Economic Commission for Latin America and the Caribbean) (2019a), *Social Panorama of Latin America, 2018* (LC/PUB.2019/3-P), Santiago, February.

___(2019b), *Economic Survey of Latin America and the Caribbean, 2019* (LC/PUB.2019/12-P), Santiago, July.

___(2019c), *Fiscal Panorama of Latin America and the Caribbean, 2019* (LC/PUB.2019/8-P), Santiago, March.

___(2018a), *The Inefficiency of Inequality* (LC/SES.37/3-P), Santiago, May.

___(2018b), *Economic Survey of Latin America and the Caribbean, 2018* (LC/PUB.2018/17-P), Santiago, October.

___(2018c), *Social Panorama of Latin America, 2017* (LC/PUB.2018/1-P), Santiago, February.

___(2017a), *Linkages between the social and production spheres: gaps, pillars and challenges* (LC/CDS.2/3), Santiago, October.

___(2017b), *Social Panorama of Latin America, 2016* (LC/PUB.2017/12-P), Santiago, August.

___(2016a), *Social Panorama of Latin America, 2015* (LC/G.2691-P), Santiago, October.

___(2016b), *The social inequality matrix in Latin America* (LC/G.2690(MDS.1/2)), Santiago, October.

ECLAC/OEI (Economic Commission for Latin America and the Caribbean/Organization of IberoAmerican States for Education, Science and Culture) (2014), *Cultura y desarrollo económico en Iberoamérica*, E. Espíndola (coord.), Madrid.

IMF (International Monetary Fund) (2014), *Government Finance Statistics Manual 2014*, Washington, D.C.

___(2001), *Government Finance Statistics Manual 2001*, Washington, D.C.

Martínez, R. (2015), "Monitoring and evaluation of social protection policies and programmes", *Towards universal social protection: Latin American pathways and policy tools*, ECLAC Books, No. 136 (LC/G.2644-P), S. Cecchini and others (eds.), Santiago, Economic Commission for Latin America and the Caribbean (ECLAC), July.

PAHO/WHO (Pan American Health Organization/World Health Organization) (2017), *Sustainable Health Agenda for the Americas 2018-2030: A Call to Action for Health and Well-Being in the Region*, Washington, D.C., September.

___(2014), "Resolution CD53.R14: strategy for universal access to health and universal health coverage", Washington, D.C., October [online] http://iris.paho.org/xmlui/bitstream/handle/123456789/7652/CD53-R14-s.pdf.

UNESCO (United Nations Educational, Scientific and Cultural Organization) (2015), *Education 2030. Incheon Declaration and Framework for Action: Towards Inclusive and Equitable Quality Education and Lifelong Learning for All*, Paris.

United Nations (2007), *Convention on the Rights of Persons with Disabilities* (A/RES/61/106), New York, January.

___(2001), "Classifications of expenditure according to purpose", *Statistical Papers: Series M*, No. 84, New York.

World Bank (2012), "Resilience, equity, and opportunity: The World Bank's social protection strategy 2012-2022", Board Report, No. 73235, Washington, D.C.

Annex III.A1

Table III.A1.1
Latin America and the Caribbean (24 countries): central government social spending by function, 2018
(Percentages of GDP, dollars at 2010 prices and percentages)

Country	Social spending				Distribution of social spending by function *(percentages)*						
	Percentages of GDP		Constant 2010 dollars per capita		Social protection	Education	Health	Housing and community amenities	Recreation, culture and religion	Environmental protection[a]	Total
	2017	2018	2017	2018							
Argentina	14.6	13.5	1 531	1 368	81.1	9.7	6.0	2.8	0.0	0.4	100
Bahamas	7.6	6.9	1 984	1 809	25.8	36.8	36.5	0.9	0.0	0.0	100
Barbados	16.5	17.1	2 715	2 783	24.2	34.0	19.4	9.9	3.0	9.5	100
Bolivia (Plurinational State of)	12.7	...	320	...	35.4	42.6	14.7	7.3	0.0	0.0	100
Brazil	17.6	17.7	1 908	1 924	73.6	13.4	11.9	0.4	0.3	0.4	100
Chile	16.4	16.4	2 456	2 538	34.9	31.6	29.9	1.9	1.1	0.5	100
Colombia	13.4	12.6	1 016	975	43.9	26.4	24.0	4.1	1.2	0.5	100
Costa Rica	12.5	12.1	1 225	1 209	32.1	57.8	7.2	0.5	1.2	1.2	100
Cuba	14.6	9.6	963	641	66.7	18.2	8.1	1.8	5.2	0.0	100
Dominican Republic	8.5	8.0	602	604	19.1	51.6	21.4	4.3	2.3	1.3	100
Ecuador	9.2	9.0	484	472	15.5	50.5	30.4	0.7	1.8	1.0	100
El Salvador	10.0	9.0	347	320	20.9	41.8	26.0	9.8	0.9	0.5	100
Guatemala	6.9	7.0	222	228	18.2	42.3	15.3	18.9	2.4	2.9	100
Guyana	12.5	...	481	...	18.6	40.7	31.4	6.9	1.4	1.1	100
Haiti[b]	5.2	...	38	...	11.0	56.8	16.1	0.9	8.7	6.4	100
Honduras	8.5	8.0	192	185	5.5	61.9	29.9	1.0	0.0	1.6	100
Jamaica	10.7	10.3	516	508	6.5	50.0	35.2	4.2	2.5	1.6	100
Mexico	8.8	8.7	885	884	39.4	35.8	11.8	10.9	1.0	1.1	100
Nicaragua	10.7	11.1	215	212	3.2	40.1	31.2	22.1	2.3	1.2	100
Panama	8.8	...	1 021	...	15.2	37.9	19.8	20.7	1.9	4.5	100
Paraguay	8.6	8.6	458	470	40.9	35.9	20.7	0.3	0.8	0.0	100
Peru[c]	11.4	11.1	703	704	24.1	33.9	22.4	4.0	4.9	10.7	100
Trinidad and Tobago	14.6	14.2	2 253	2 225	38.1	25.1	22.1	12.5	2.2	0.0	100
Uruguay[d]	16.8	17.2	2 407	2 504	45.6	28.2	21.0	3.7	1.3	0.2	100

Source: Economic Commission for Latin America and the Caribbean (ECLAC), on the basis of official data from the countries.
[a] Environmental protection data may not match the estimates in environmental satellite accounts.
[b] Data for Haiti refer to 2014.
[c] Coverage is general government in the case of Peru.
[d] Data for Uruguay do not include disbursements by the Social Security Bank.

Table III.A1.2
Latin America (9 countries): social expenditure by institutional coverage, by function, 2018
(Percentages of GDP, dollars at constant 2010 prices and percentages)

Country	Coverage	Social spending		Distribution of social spending by function, 2018 (percentages)						
		Percentages of GDP	Constant 2010 dollars per capita	Social protection	Education	Health	Housing and community amenities	Recreation, culture and religion	Environmental protection[a]	Total
Argentina[b]	Public sector	30.0	3 175	46.3	20.7	23.3	8.9	0.0	...	100
Bolivia (Plurinational State of)[c]	General government	22.2	545	21.0	38.9	24.8	8.0	0.0	0.0	100
Brazil[d]	General government	27.0	2 921	58.2	19.8	19.3	0.3	0.8	1.7	100
Colombia[d]	General government	20.4	1 548	43.9	23.7	23.9	2.4	3.3	2.7	100
Costa Rica	Public sector	24.0	2 389	30.5	30.8	27.6	9.9	0.8	0.5	100
Cuba	General government	28.5	1 904	22.4	29.0	38.1	3.9	6.5	0.0	100
El Salvador	Public sector	14.6	516	36.7	26.4	16.7	19.3	0.5	0.4	100
Paraguay[d]	General government	13.5	720	46.0	26.9	23.5	2.9	0.5	0.0	100
Peru	General government	11.1	704	24.1	33.9	22.4	4.0	4.9	10.7	100

Source: Economic Commission for Latin America and the Caribbean (ECLAC), on the basis of official data from the countries.
[a] Environmental protection data may not match the estimates in environmental satellite accounts.
[b] Data for Argentina refer to 2015.
[c] Data for the Plurinational State of Bolivia refer to 2016.
[d] Data for Brazil, Colombia y Paraguay refer to 2017.

Migration in the region and its main dimensions

Introduction

A. Changes and continuities in migration

B. Migration and its problems in the subregions

Bibliography

Introduction

This chapter presents data on the characteristics of Latin American and Caribbean migration, including recent background information on the trends of flows, and on the changes and continuities in migratory patterns. It also describes some of the characteristics of migrants and certain national and subregional specifics, drawing on information obtained from different sources.

It is very important to note that the regional analysis presented has shortcomings related to the lack of reliable, timely and adequate information. This issue is significant given the recent changes that have occurred within the region, because data sources are not comparable between countries. It is therefore necessary to wait for the 2020 round of censuses, the methodological development of records and improvements to household surveys in the different countries. Nonetheless, it is possible to discern general migration scenarios by drawing on information sources from the destination countries and data provided by the United Nations Population Division (United Nations, 2019).

The current juncture: a call for multilateral cooperation to protect migrants

According to the latest estimates made by the United Nations Population Division, published in July 2019, the migrant population of Latin America and the Caribbean is estimated at 40.5 million, representing about 15% of the world's migrant population of nearly 272 million (United Nations, 2019). This figure does not include recent migratory movements, temporary migration, circular or return migration, among other dimensions.

Given the current complex regional migration panorama, and considering both the historical presence of migration in all nations and its current characteristics, the region should take steps to strengthen multilateral cooperation and address the most visible and pressing needs, such as the protection of migrants and the provision of policy instruments and resources to deal with "humanitarian crises".

It is well known that migration both from and between the countries of northern Central America, along with that of the population of the Bolivarian Republic of Venezuela —especially in South America— present worrying situations and challenges that are generating responses through different mechanisms of cooperation between countries, with various initiatives such as the Comprehensive Development Plan for the Countries of Northern Central America and Mexico (ECLAC, 2019b) platforms for dealing with the Venezuelan emigrant population, dialogues on migrant children in South America, political processes, inter-American working groups and national initiatives in all countries, all of which should be encouraged and continuously evaluated.

In reality, these crises are nothing more than the expression of the heterogeneity of migratory flows that have been present for at least two decades, especially in the case of extraregional emigration. Today, there is a clear presence of "mixed migrations", since movements by asylum seekers, economic migrants, unaccompanied children and adolescents, environmental migrants, irregular migrants, trafficked persons, victims of trafficking and stranded migrants,[1] among others, are increasingly forced upon them. The main characteristic of this type of migration is the vulnerability of the individuals involved, as well as their differentiated profile and their specific needs. The key issue in this case is the need to increase protection for migrants, as the countries agreed to do in the Montevideo Consensus on Population and Development in Latin America and the Caribbean (ECLAC, 2013).

---

[1]   While there is no international definition for the term "*stranded migrants*", it is often used to describe migrants who are detained for lengthy periods, have had their asylum applications rejected, or are of irregular migration status. The term "stranded migrants" has been used in the framework of the Regional Conference on Migration and in numerous documents issued by reliable sources, such as those of various United Nations agencies (UNODC, 2011).

Many migrants currently face serious situations of vulnerability caused by violence, racism and xenophobia in the countries of northern Central America and Mexico —either on their journeys or when arriving at their destinations outside the region— and also in South American countries —especially Venezuelan populations in border areas. In addition, other groups, such as Haitians, suffer dual discrimination based on their national origin and on race. Young people, women and children, for example, have difficulties in accessing social protection, either because of the forced nature of their migration, its large-scale, or the fact that it raises crosscutting and emerging issues. The links between migration and crises, climate change and disasters, demographic ageing and the care crisis are permanent; and they are areas that will need further analysis and policy action in the future.

Migration processes contribute to the well-being and development of communities and countries in the region, so they should be encouraged from a long-term perspective. This should encompass various issues, such as the creation of more inclusive labour markets, the possibility of building more diverse and rejuvenated societies, and the challenges of interculturality. In the countries of Latin America and the Caribbean, it may be appropriate to emphasize the role of immigration in promoting generational replacement and counteracting demographic ageing processes in the first world, as well as recognizing the possibilities offered by migration for poverty alleviation, the configuration of more democratic societies (through the forces of transnationalism, appreciation of cultural diversity and the pursuit of social cohesion), the implementation of new forms of development aid and regional cooperation (Martínez, 2011).

This is clearly a matter of encouraging a critical, positive and purposeful vision when analysing the many issues that intersect with international migration, rights and development (ECLAC, 2002). In many of these debates and analyses, it is imperative to adopt gender, ethno-racial, generational, territorial and cross-cutting human rights approaches. This is an opportunity to study how migration can foster equality and thus contribute towards building fairer societies (see box IV.1).

A.   Changes and continuities in migration

International migration in Latin America and the Caribbean is a particularly relevant issue today, since its continuities and changes occupy a prominent place in public opinion and in the political and development agendas of the countries in question. Migration patterns and corridors reflect long-term continuities (such as the prevalence of Argentina as one of the countries with the highest number of migrants), as well as changes in the volume and direction of flows (for example, intense immigration into Chile and the mixed nature of current Central American and Venezuelan emigration). These have led to changes in the profile of the migrants (such as the participation of more men and children and adolescents in the migration cycle), which provide the backdrop to the trends in Latin American and Caribbean migration.

1.   Patterns and trends

The three most salient patterns of international migration in Latin America and the Caribbean since the second half of the twentieth century have been outward migration from the region, historical overseas immigration and intraregional exchanges. A fourth, often less prominent, pattern is return to the countries of origin, either planned or forced (Martínez Pizarro, Cano and Soffia, 2014).

Box IV.1
The importance of achieving the objectives of the Global Compact for Safe, Orderly and Regular Migration 2018

The Global Compact for Safe, Orderly and Regular Migration, adopted in December 2018 following lengthy negotiations, provides an opportunity to enhance multilateral cooperation on international migration through a collective commitment. It recognizes the need to protect the rights of migrants, since migration is a source of prosperity, innovation and sustainable development in our globalized world. The Compact has 23 objectives, guided by the following principles: people-centred, international cooperation, national sovereignty, rule of law and due process, sustainable development, human rights, gender-responsive, and the best interests of the child, among others. The Compact is closely related to the 2030 Agenda for Sustainable Development, since both instruments call for protection of the rights and social inclusion of migrants. In the region, nearly all countries have created institutions and allocated resources to achieve the Sustainable Development Goals (SDGs), which augurs well for the implementation of the Compact. Its 23 objectives are organized according to the sequence of the migration cycle, from emigration to return and re-emigration, taking into account all age groups, from children to working-age populations. The various issues addressed are well summarized in the objectives, which call for multilateral cooperation and an international commitment. The following table provides a preliminary classification of these objectives.

Preliminary classification of the objectives of the Global Compact for Safe, Orderly and Regular Migration

Information and cooperation	Access to social protection and services	Regularization	Sovereignty and safety of migrants	Social inclusion
(1) Collect and utilize accurate and disaggregated data as a basis for evidence-based policies	(4) Ensure that all migrants have proof of legal identity and adequate documentation	(2) Minimize the adverse drivers and structural factors that compel people to leave their country of origin	(8) Save lives and establish coordinated international efforts on missing migrants	(16) Empower migrants and societies to realize full inclusion and social cohesion
(3) Provide accurate and timely information at all stages of migration	(14) Enhance consular protection, assistance and cooperation throughout the migration cycle	(5) Enhance availability and flexibility of pathways for regular migration	(9) Strengthen the transnational response to smuggling of migrants	(17) Eliminate all forms of discrimination and promote evidence-based public discourse to shape perceptions of migration
(23) Strengthen international cooperation and global partnerships for safe, orderly and regular migration	(15) Provide access to basic services for migrants	(6) Facilitate fair and ethical recruitment and safeguard conditions that ensure decent work	(10) Prevent, combat and eradicate trafficking in persons in the context of international migration	(18) Invest in skills development and facilitate mutual recognition of skills, qualifications and competences
	(20) Promote faster, safer and cheaper transfer of remittances and foster financial inclusion of migrants	(7) Address and reduce vulnerabilities in migration	(11) Manage borders in an integrated, secure and coordinated manner	(19) Create conditions for migrants and diasporas to fully contribute to sustainable development in all countries
	(22) Establish mechanisms for the portability of social security entitlements and earned benefits	(12) Strengthen certainty and predictability in migration procedures for appropriate screening, assessment and referral	(13) Use migration detention only as a measure of last resort and work towards alternatives	(21) Cooperate in facilitating safe and dignified return and readmission, as well as sustainable reintegration

Source: C. Maldonado Valera, J. Martínez Pizarro and R. Martínez, "Protección social y migración: una mirada desde las vulnerabilidades a lo largo del ciclo de la migración y de la vida de las personas", *Project Documents* (LC/TS.2018/62), Santiago.

Source: C. Maldonado Valera, J. Martínez Pizarro and R. Martínez, "Protección social y migración: una mirada desde las vulnerabilidades a lo largo del ciclo de la migración y de la vida de las personas", *Project Documents* (LC/TS.2018/62), Santiago.

While recently been signs of a slowdown in some emigration flows to major extraregional destinations, the pace of immigration from other regions of the world has been slackening. The negative migration balance —that is, the predominance of emigration over immigration— continues to be a defining feature of the region's exchanges with the rest of the world, with current estimates reporting six emigrants for every two immigrants (see table IV.1).

Table IV.1
Latin America and the Caribbean: immigrants and emigrants relative to the total population,
by country of residence and birth, 2019
(Minimum estimates of number of persons and percentages)

Region/country	Total population	Immigrants		Emigrants	
		Number	Percentage of total population	Number	Percentage of total population
Total Latin America and the Caribbean	**648 094 978**	**11 657 804**	**1.8**	**40 440 504**	**6.2**
South America	**424 393 617**	**8 220 807**	**1.9**	**14 821 322**	**3.5**
Argentina	44 780 677	2 212 879	4.9	1 013 414	2.3
Bolivia (Plurinational State of)	11 513 100	156 114	1.4	878 211	7.6
Brazil	211 049 527	807 006	0.4	1 745 339	0.8
Chile	18 952 038	939 992	5.0	650 151	3.4
Colombia	50 339 443	1 142 319	2.3	2 869 032	5.7
Ecuador	17 373 662	381 507	2.2	1 183 685	6.8
Falkland Islands	3 377	1 902	56.3	1 623	48.1
French Guiana	782 766	15 699	2.0	520 196	66.5
Guyana	290 832	117 372	40.4	520 196	66.5
Paraguay	7 044 636	160 519	2.3	871 638	12.4
Peru	32 510 453	782 169	2.4	1 512 920	4.7
Suriname	581 372	46 157	7.9	423 517	72.8
Uruguay	3 461 734	81 482	2.4	633 439	18.3
Venezuela (Bolivarian Republic of)	28 515 829	1 375 690	4.8	2 519 780	8.8
Central America	**177 586 526**	**1 927 688**	**1.1**	**16 465 784**	**9.3**
Belize	390 353	59 998	15.4	68 144	17.5
Costa Rica	5 047 561	417 768	8.3	150 400	3.0
El Salvador	6 453 553	42 617	0.7	1 600 739	24.8
Guatemala	17 581 472	80 421	0.5	1 205 644	6.9
Honduras	9 746 117	38 933	0.4	800 707	8.2
Mexico	127 575 529	1 060 707	0.8	11 796 178	9.2
Nicaragua	6 545 502	42 172	0.6	682 865	10.4
Panama	4 246 439	185 072	4.4	161 107	3.8
The Caribbean	**43 309 006**	**1 509 309**	**3.5**	**9 135 349**	**21.1**
Anguilla	14 869	5 679	38.2	2 707	18.2
Antigua and Barbuda	97 118	29 207	30.1	55 089	56.7
Aruba	106 314	36 532	34.4	19 640	18.5
Bahamas	389 482	62 962	16.2	46 467	11.9
Barbados	287 025	34 807	12.1	112 925	39.3
British Virgin Islands	3 003	20 778	691.9		
Cayman Islands	64 948	28 985	44.6	1 973	3.0
Cuba	11 333 483	4 886	0.0	1 654 684	14.6
Curaçao	163 424	40 883	25.0	123 132	75.3
Dominica	71 808	8 264	11.5	78 634	109.5
Dominican Republic	10 738 958	567 648	5.3	1 558 668	14.5
Grenada	112 003	7 124	6.4	75 784	67.7
Guadeloupe	447 905	100 030	22.3	11 856	2.6
Haiti	11 263 077	18 756	0.2	1 585 681	14.1
Jamaica	2 948 279	23 468	0.8	1 111 021	37.7
Martinique	375 554	61 647	16.4	13 919	3.7
Montserrat	4 989	1 375	27.6	22 838	457.8
Puerto Rico	2 933 408	266 828	9.1	2 007 347	68.4
Saint Kitts and Nevis	52 823	7 587	14.4	124 941	236.5
Saint Lucia	18 279	8 383	45.9	63 605	348.0
Saint Vincent and the Grenadines	110 589	4 692	4.2	60 655	54.8
Sint Maarten	42 388	28 260	66.7	29 209	68.9
Trinidad and Tobago	1 394 973	59 249	4.2	334 304	24.0
Turks and Caicos Islands	38 191	24 534	64.2	31 033	81.3
United States Virgin Islands	104 578	56 745	54.3	25 863	24.7

Source: United Nations, "International migrant stock 2019" [online] https://www.un.org/en/development/desa/population/migration/data/estimates2/estimates19.asp; and
J. Martínez, M. V. Cano and M. Soffia, "Tendencias y patrones de la migración latinoamericana y caribeña hacia 2010 y desafíos para una agenda regional", *Population and Development series*, No. 109 (LC/L.3914), Santiago, Economic Commission for Latin America and the Caribbean (ECLAC), 2014.

Note: The total figures are current estimates.

Nonetheless, it is exchanges within the region that have intensified the most. While intraregional migration accounted for 50% of the migrant population as early as 1990, by 2010 its share had grown to 63% of the total (see figure IV.1). Moreover, in recent years, the number of countries of origin has increased, and new destinations have appeared as a result of Venezuelan emigration to several countries in the region —especially Colombia, Chile, Ecuador and Peru— as well as in some Caribbean countries.

Figure IV.1
Latin America and the Caribbean: immigrant population by place of origin, 1970–2019
(Percentages)

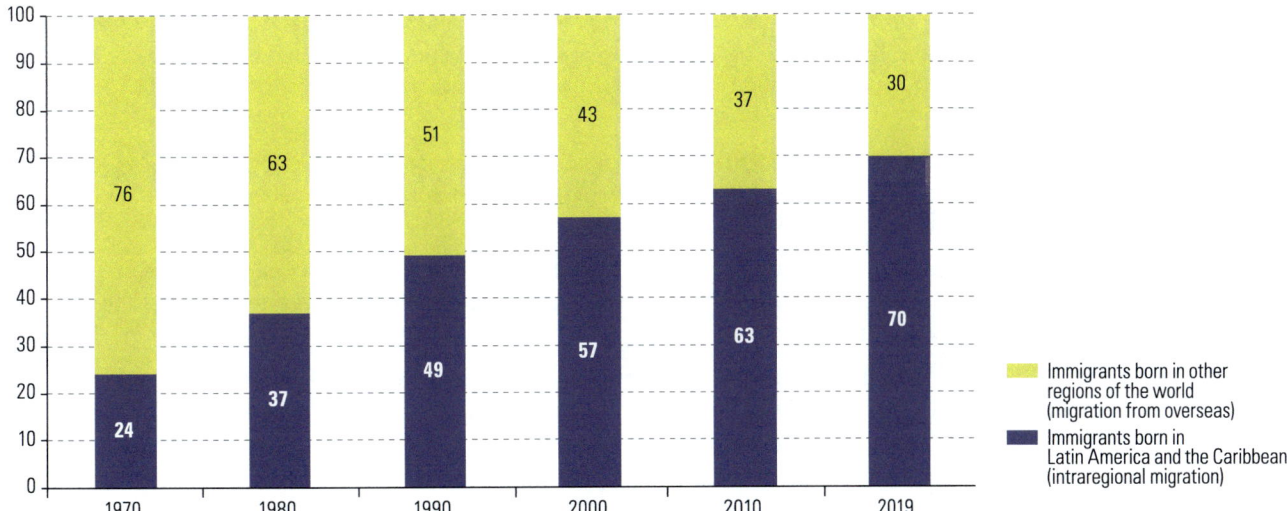

Source: United Nations, "International migrant stock 2019" [online] https://www.un.org/en/development/desa/population/migration/data/estimates2/estimates19.asp; and J. Martínez, M. V. Cano and M. Soffia, "Tendencias y patrones de la migración latinoamericana y caribeña hacia 2010 y desafíos para una agenda regional", *Population and Development series*, No. 109 (LC/L.3914), Santiago, Economic Commission for Latin America and the Caribbean (ECLAC), 2014.

A common denominator in the analysis of migratory trends is the insufficiency of reliable, timely information that is appropriate to the complexity of the phenomenon. Most of the available data come from the following sources: the 2010 round of censuses (which, given their age, are unable to capture the most recent trends), administrative records of varying types, household surveys that are appropriate in a few countries and specific national surveys on migration in a few others (see box IV.2).[2]

Box IV.2
Possibilities and shortcomings of household surveys for estimating migration

Household surveys, along with population censuses and administrative records, are the three main sources supporting migration research, analysis and diagnostic assessment, and for providing empirical data to different areas of knowledge, especially on economic, demographic and social issues. Each of these instruments is subject to different measurement and design errors, which impose limitations.

Household surveys in Latin American countries generally have a complex, probabilistic, stratified and multi-stage sample design, with non-uniform probabilities of inclusion. Hence, the estimates produced from these statistical exercises are subject to sampling error; and their statistical validity needs to be evaluated using various quality indicators that describe their accuracy and reliability. It is also necessary to warn the user when the accuracy of the estimate is unreliable. The quality indicators include: confidence intervals, sample size, design effect, effective sample size, coefficient of variation, degrees of freedom, logarithmic coefficient of variation, and unweighted case counts (Gutiérrez and others, 2019).

---

[2]   The most recent examples are the 2018 Survey of the Venezuelan Population Residing in Peru (ENPOVE) which receives multilateral technical and financial support (INEI, 2019), and the 2016 National Survey of Immigration and Emigration in Costa Rica (ENIE), conducted with support from the International Organization for Migration (IOM) (CCP/UCR, 2016).

Box IV.2 (concluded)

In some of the estimations contained in this edition of *Social Panorama of Latin America*, the indicators mentioned have been calculated from the specific parameters of each sample design, and they have been contrasted with a set of limits established in keeping with the recommendations and international usage of the statistics institutes. The application of these criteria imposes a constraint on the use of surveys, because it restricts the inferences that can be made from the estimated value of a statistic. On the other hand, it can also be seen as a contribution, by allowing certain degree of confidence to be established regarding the accuracy with which such an estimate is made.

There is also the problem of out-of-date sampling frameworks, which are usually based on population censuses and may be significantly affected by large-scale migration processes occurring in the intercensal period, as has happened in recent years in the countries of the region. Similarly, in cases where immigrants initially settle in collective households, or even live at their places of work, they will be outside the normal perimeter of household surveys and are therefore not included in their estimates. Lastly, underestimation may increase owing to omissions such as the concealment of migrant status for various reasons.

An additional difficulty may arise as a result of a lack of comparability between concepts of "migrant" as defined in some of the surveys. Although most countries include questions on migration that comply with international recommendations, in some cases this set of questions may not be sufficient.

In 13 of the 16 countries for which information is available from their latest survey, the place of birth of the household members is known; and, in several cases, additional information is available on their place of residence before the survey was undertaken. In 12 of the 16 countries, information on the place of residence five years earlier is available.

The following table reports an exercise to estimate the proportion of migrants in each of the countries for which information is available, as well as the bounds of the respective confidence interval. It also includes a warning when the estimate presented does not satisfy any of the established quality criteria.

Latin America (selected countries): estimated proportion of immigrants and upper
and lower bounds of the confidence interval, latest available survey
(Percentages)

	Immigrants	Lower bound	Upper bound	Recent immigrants	Lower bound	Upper bound
Argentina	4.75	4.50	4.99	0.39		
Bolivia (Plurinational State of)[a]	0.27[b]	0.17	0.42	0.08[b]	0.06	0.10
Brazil	0.38	0.33	0.43	0.08	0.07	0.10
Chile	3.91	3.38	4.52	2.58	2.11	3.15
Colombia	1.12	1.09	1.15	...	...	...
Costa Rica	8.67	8.00	9.40	0.53	0.41	0.68
Dominican Republic	3.04	2.54	3.62	...	...	...
Ecuador	1.18			...	...	...
Guatemala	3.53	2.81	4.43	...	...	...
Honduras	0.71			0.09[b]		
Mexico[a]	...	...	...	0.11	0.08	0.15
Nicaragua	0.82			0.21[b]		
Panama	4.42	3.88	5.03	2.13		
Paraguay	1.33	1.07	1.65	0.29	0.20	0.43
Peru	0.34	0.28	0.41	0.07[b]	0.05	0.10
Uruguay	2.31	2.2	2.4	0.47	...	...

Source: Economic Commission for Latin America and the Caribbean (ECLAC), on the basis of Household Survey Data Bank (BADEHOG).
[a] Approximate measure, not strictly comparable.
[b] The estimate does not attain the required level of accuracy.

Source: Economic Commission for Latin America and the Caribbean (ECLAC), on the basis of Household Survey Data Bank (BADEHOG).

In view of these shortcomings, the United Nations Population Division estimates that, in 2019, 40.5 million Latin American and Caribbean people were living outside the countries in which they were born (United Nations, 2019), which represents a significant increase from the 30 million recorded in the 2010 round of censuses (Martínez Pizarro, Cano and Soffia, 2014). As table IV.1 shows, 6% of the total population of Latin America and the Caribbean are not living in their country of birth.

The total volume of emigrants consists firstly of the population born in Latin American and Caribbean countries living in other regions of the world, and, secondly, of the native population resident in countries of the region other than that of their birth. According to national censuses, the total foreign population residing in Latin American and Caribbean countries amounted to 7.6 million people in 2010. Estimates for 2019 indicate a total of 11.7 million, equivalent to almost a quarter of the number of emigrants and only 1.8% of the region's total population. The immigrants originate both from overseas and from the region itself. In the first case, extraregional immigration continued to lose ground, retreating from 37.2% of the total immigrant population to 30% in 2019, while in the second case the figure advanced from 62.8% to 70% (see figure IV.1).

Figure IV.2 shows that the ratio of immigrants to the native population is broadly homogeneous in the various subregions of Latin America and the Caribbean, ranging from 1.1% in Central America and Mexico to 3.5% in the Caribbean. In contrast, the ratio of emigrants to national populations is higher and varies more between subregions: the Caribbean and Central America and Mexico have the largest proportion of immigrants relative to the native population (21.1% and 9.3%, respectively).

Mexico has the largest absolute number of emigrants, although the relative share of regional emigration from this country has declined from 40% in 2010 (when some 12 million of its citizens were living abroad) to 29% in 2019 (about 11.8 million). Colombia, with almost 2.9 million, has the next largest number of emigrants. In total, 14 countries report more than 1 million emigrants (Argentina, Brazil, the Bolivarian Republic of Venezuela, Colombia, Cuba, the Dominican Republic, Ecuador, El Salvador, Guatemala, Haiti, Jamaica, Mexico, Peru and Puerto Rico). The countries with the largest proportion of emigrants in their national population are El Salvador (24.8%), Jamaica (37.7%) and Puerto Rico (68.4%) along with several Caribbean nations (see table IV.1).

The recent emigration from the Bolivarian Republic of Venezuela, which is discussed below, is one of the most significant changes to have occurred in recent years. This particularly affects estimated immigration figures in Chile, Colombia, Ecuador and Peru in absolute terms, and in some Caribbean nations in relative terms.

Bearing in mind the shortcomings mentioned in table IV.1, Argentina continues to report the largest volume of immigration, with its 2.2 million immigrants accounting for 19% of all immigrants registered in the region. Four countries have more than 1 million immigrants (Argentina, the Bolivarian Republic of Venezuela, Colombia and Mexico, along with the Caribbean as a whole).[3] In terms of the relative impact on national populations, immigration exceeds 10% in two countries (Belize and Guyana) and in many Caribbean nations, where migratory exchanges are intense, as measured by the percentages of immigrants and emigrants (see figures IV.2 and IV.3). Chile has also reported that it had more than 1 million immigrants in 2018, according to an estimate based on a combination of sources, including data from the 2017 census (INE, 2018) and administrative records.[4]

---

[3]   Apart from Colombia, these countries have recorded high figures on previous occasions. In Mexico, it is widely recognized that over half of the immigrant population is actually of Mexican origin (children of returnee parents who were born in Mexico), which reflects the dynamics of life on the United States border and the effects of migratory processes. The vast majority are children and adolescents who live in border states or those with a long emigration tradition (Rodríguez, 2010).

[4]   See [online] https://www.ine.cl/estadisticas/demograficas-y-vitales.

Figure IV.2
Latin America and the Caribbean: share of immigrants and emigrants in national populations by subregion, around 2010 and 2019
(Percentages)

A. Immigrants

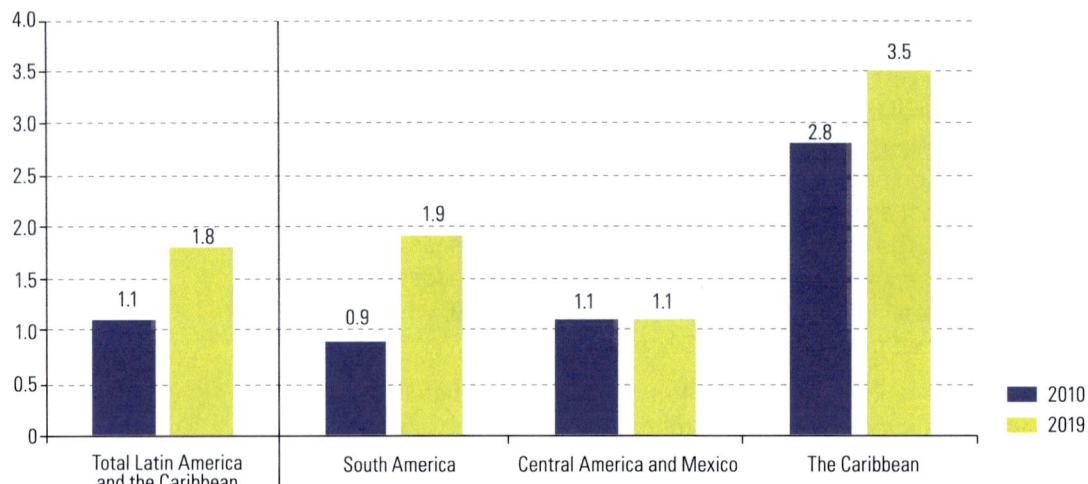

B. Emigrants

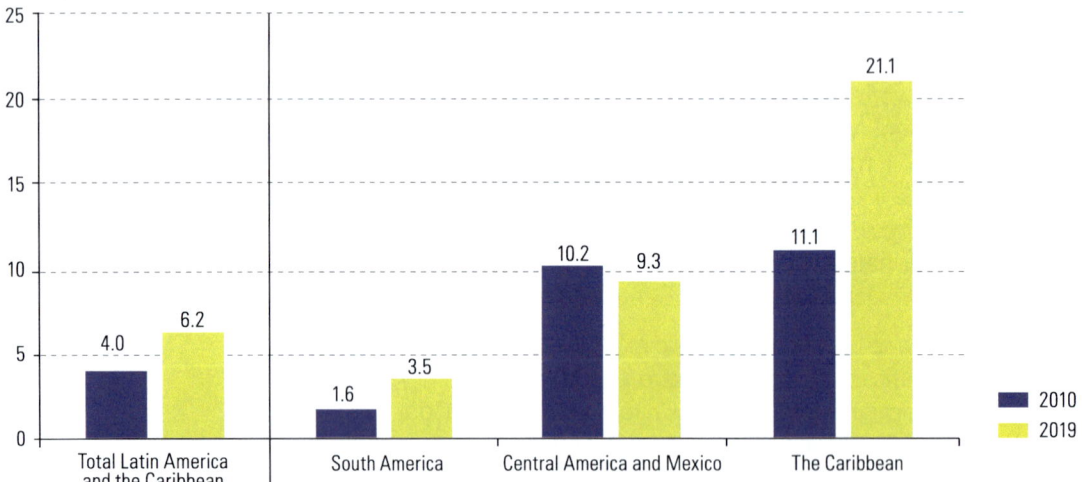

Source: Latin American and Caribbean Demographic Centre (CELADE) – Population Division of ECLAC United Nations, "International migrant stock 2019" [online] https://www.un.org/en/development/desa/population/migration/data/estimates2/estimates19.asp.

Figure IV.3
The Caribbean (26 countries): share of immigrants and emigrants in national populations, 2019

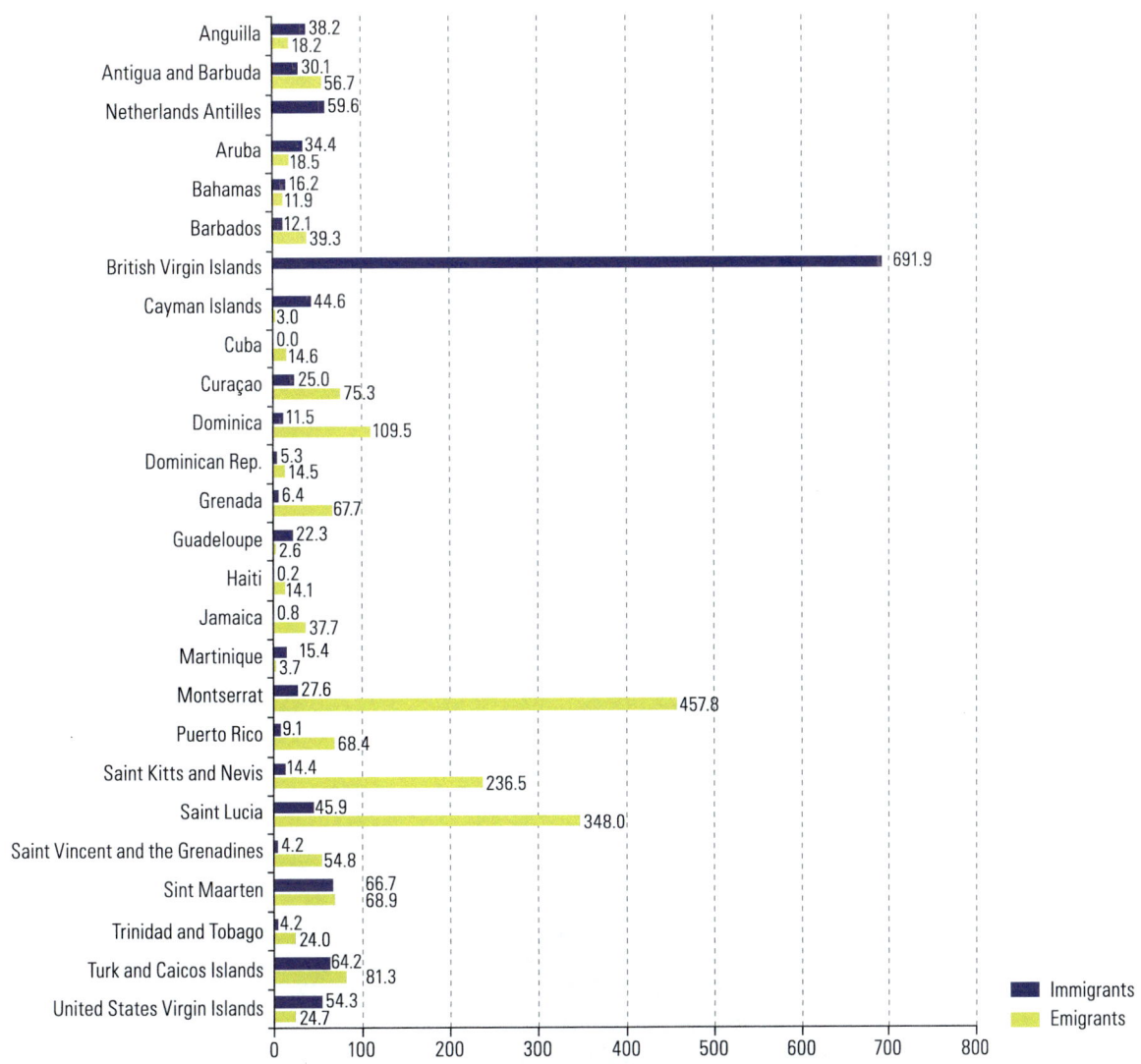

Source: United Nations, "International migrant stock 2019" [online] https://www.un.org/en/development/desa/population/migration/data/estimates2/estimates19.asp.

2.   Declining extraregional emigration: a short-term trend?

The United States is the main destination for regional emigration (see figures IV.4 and IV.5) While this does not apply to all countries, it does reflect a long-term trend. Around 2010, this country accommodated three quarters of the Latin American and Caribbean migrant population, while other countries of the Organization for Economic Cooperation and Development (OECD) —Canada, Spain and Japan— attracted only 13% (OECD, 2016).

Figure IV.4
Latin America and
the Caribbean:
principal emigrant
destinations, 2019
(Percentages)

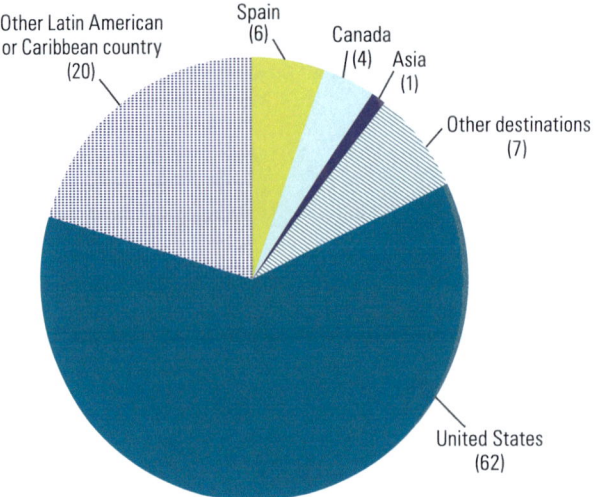

Source: United Nations, "International migrant stock 2019" [online] https://www.un.org/en/development/desa/population/migration/data/estimates2/estimates19.asp.

Figure IV.5
Latin America and the
Caribbean: principal
emigrant destinations,
excluding Mexicans in
the United States, 2019
(Percentages)

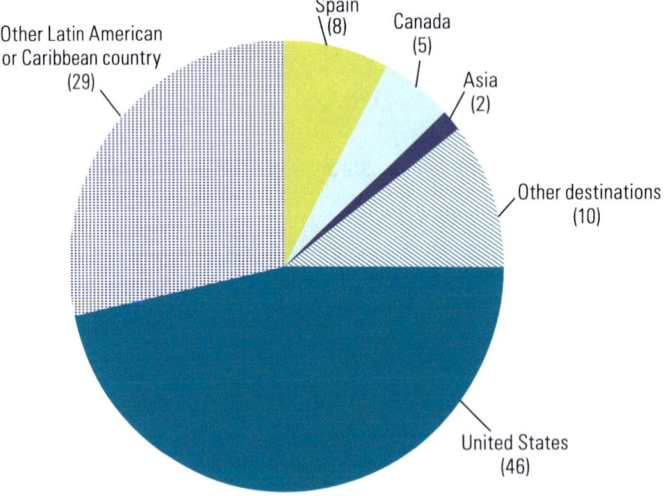

Source: United Nations, "International migrant stock 2019" [online] https://www.un.org/en/development/desa/population/migration/data/estimates2/estimates19.asp.

Since the global financial crisis of 2008–2009, migrant flows from the region to the United States have decreased. Nonetheless, that country remains a very important destination: even excluding migrants from Mexico, is still accounts for nearly 50% of all regional migrants (see box IV.3 regarding unpaid female domestic workers).

Box IV.3
Latin American female
domestic employees in
the United States

Official figures show that 46% of paid domestic workers in the United States were born abroad; and the real figure could be higher owing to the difficulty of counting undocumented migrants in that sector. Various studies have highlighted the racially biased nature of this occupation, which is performed mostly by women of African descent, and by migrant workers from Latin America and the Caribbean and, to a lesser extent, from Asia. Paid domestic work is one of the fastest growing occupations in the United States.[a]

A survey of paid domestic employees in 14 metropolitan areas of the United States found that it was an occupation performed almost exclusively by women (97%) and with a very high prevalence of migrants: 78% of paid domestic workers were born abroad. Of the individuals surveyed, 60% were identified as "Latino", 23% as white, 9% as black, and 9% as Asian. Nearly half of the migrant workers (47%) had irregular migratory status (undocumented and, therefore, at risk of being deported). A large proportion of the paid domestic workers interviewed spoke very poor English or none at all (41%) and had a low level of education (39% had not completed secondary school). The survey also showed that "Latino" workers of either sex consistently received lower wages, and undocumented workers even less. The latter, moreover, faced worse working conditions and limited bargaining power. They often agreed to perform tasks not included in the contract and without pay, and most did not enjoy any social benefit. Workers living in their employer's home experienced higher levels of vulnerability and abuse; and a large proportion had to work longer hours than agreed upon, and had to interrupt their rest breaks without being paid overtime.

Source:Burnham, Linda y Theodore, Nik (2012) Home economics. The invisible and unregulated world of domestic workers. National Domestic Workers Alliance, New York. Disponible en: http://www.idwfed.org/en/resources/home-economics-the-invisible-and-unregulated-world-of-domestic-work/@@display-file/attachment_1.

[a] An example of this increase can be seen in figures from the State of Oregon Department of Employment, which estimated that the number of households hiring domestic service support increased more than six-fold between 2001 and 2018 (State of Oregon Employment Department, 2019).

The dwindling annual flow of Mexican emigrants to the United States since the 2008–2009 crisis and the increase the number of emigrants returning is notable. This process has caused the number of Mexican immigrants in United States to either decrease or stabilize in recent years —a trend that is still difficult to define, according to the American Community Survey[5] and other sources (Passel and Cohn, 2016; González-Barrera, 2015). In contrast, larger numbers of immigrants have been arriving in the United States from countries in the north-east of Central America (El Salvador, Guatemala and Honduras) and the Caribbean, mainly Cuba, the Dominican Republic and Haiti.

Estimates made by the United Nations (see figures IV.6 and IV.7) show that the United States remains the leading migratory destination for countries in the region, and Spain the second. They also reveal significant differences between subregions, since the tendency to migrate to the United States is much greater in Mexico, Central America and the Caribbean, while the countries of South America display a much stronger trend towards intraregional migratory movements.

---

[5]   See United States Census Bureau, "American Community Survey (ACS)", [online] at http://www.census.gov/programs-surveys/acs/.

Figure IV.6
Latin America and the Caribbean: distribution of emigrants in other continents and subregions
of the world, by subregion of origin, 2019
(Percentages)

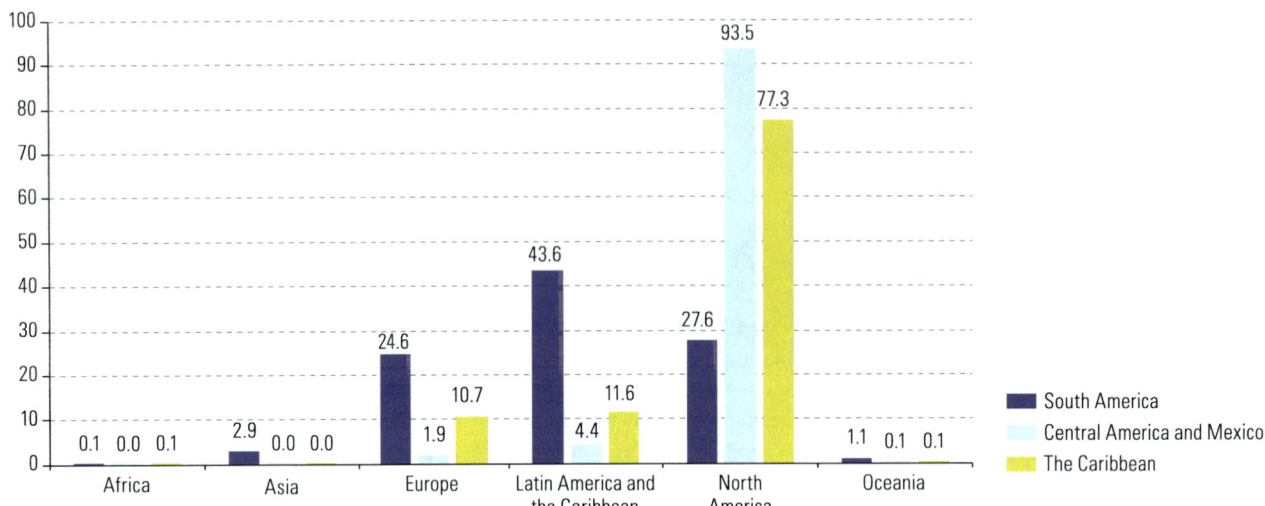

Source: United Nations, "International migrant stock 2019" [online] https://www.un.org/en/development/desa/population/migration/data/estimates2/estimates19.asp.

Figure IV.7
Latin America and the Caribbean: distribution of migrants in traditional destination countries
elsewhere in the world, by subregion of origin, 2019
(Percentages)

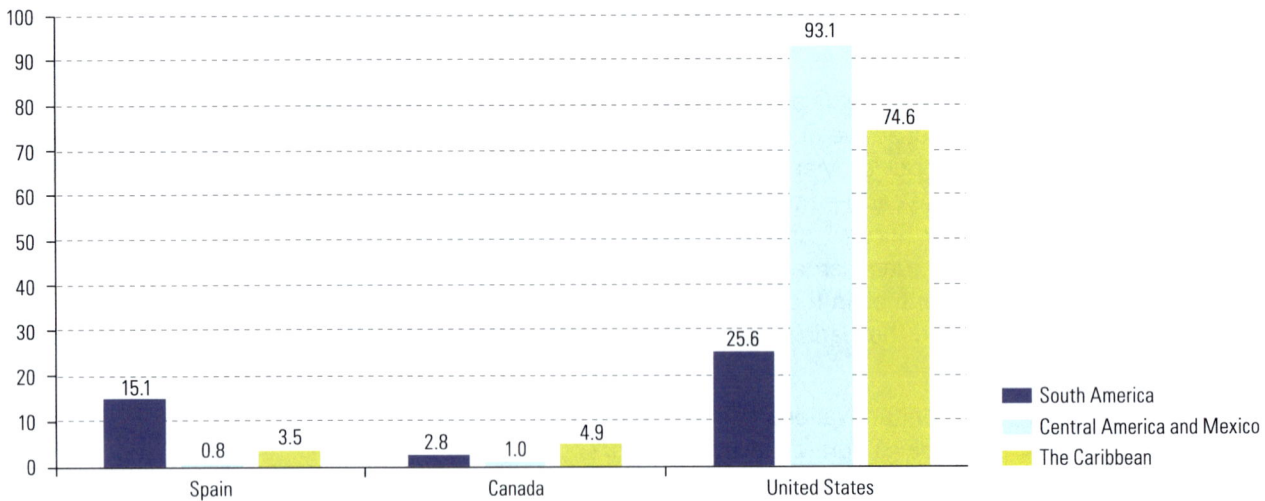

Source: United Nations, "International migrant stock 2019" [online] https://www.un.org/en/development/desa/population/migration/data/estimates2/estimates19.asp.

3.   The growing trend of intraregional migration

Intraregional migration has increased sharply in the last five years, represented by
flows of Central Americans to Mexico. Apart from the United States and Mexico, the
other cross-border migratory flows that have traditionally existed within the region
(South-South migration flows) involve migrants from Haiti to the Dominican Republic,
from Nicaragua to Costa Rica and from Colombia to the Bolivarian Republic of Venezuela,
in which the majority of migrants were from neighbouring countries.

Before the current five-year period 2014-2019, population exchanges between countries of the region had been increasing, owing to the combined effect of restrictions and the high costs involved in emigration to developed countries. This was further encouraged by easier travel, especially between neighbouring countries, in terms of communications and means of transport. While this continues to be the case, the picture has become more complex, as several countries have experienced significant increases in the volume of immigrants, and immigration from neighbouring countries has tended to combine with immigration from elsewhere.

The need to provide humanitarian and political assistance to Venezuelan emigration, in particular, has given rise to several initiatives, especially in South America (International Organization for Migration (IOM), 2018; R4V, 2019; Organization of American States (OAS), 2019), and estimating the number of emigrants is a central item on the regional agenda. Table IV.2 and figure IV.8 show the magnitude of this phenomenon and the increase in growth rates.[6] In view of this situation, the Regional Interagency Coordination Platform for Refugees and Migrants from Venezuela (R4V), coordinated by the Office of the United Nations High Commissioner for Refugees (UNHCR) and the International Organization for Migration (IOM) (R4V, 2019), is expected to provide a concerted response. The increase in Venezuelan emigration has been heavily concentrated in recent years, although emigration from the country had been in evidence for some time (Freitez, 2011 and 2017; Martínez and Orrego, 2016).

Year	Number (thousand people)	Proportion of the national population (percentages)	Annual growth rate (per 100 inhabitants)
1990	185	0.9	5.2
1995	240	1.1	5.5
2000	317	1.3	5.4
2005	416	1.6	5.5
2010	550	1.9	1.9
2015	606	1.9	39.6
2017	1 400	4.8	75.6
2018	3 100	10.7	46.9
2019	5 000	17.5	36.1
2020	7 200	25.4	

Table IV.2
Bolivarian Republic of Venezuela: estimations of population living abroad, 1990–2019[a]

Source: United Nations, "Workbook" [online] UN_MigrantStockByOriginAndDestination_2017, para 1990 a 2015; A. Freitez, "ENCOVI. Encuesta sobre Condiciones de Vida, Venezuela 2017. Emigración", Caracas, Institute of Economic and Social Research of the Catholic Andrés Bello Catholic University (IIES-UCAB), 2017; Coordination Plataform for Refugees and Migrants fromVenezuela (R4V), "Response for Venezuelans. Latin America and the Caribbean Venezuelan Refugees & Migrants in the region", 2019 [online] https://data2.unhcr.org/en/documents/download/69837, for 2018 and Organization of American States (OAS), *OAS Working Group to Address the Regional Crisis Caused by Venezuela's Migrant and Refugee Flows* (OAS/ Ser.D/XV.21), June 2019, on the linear projection for 2020.
[a] Figures for the 2000 decade subject to revision.

At the same time, in recent years the scale and visibility of Central American migration has increased (see figure IV.9), especially towards the United States and during the transit through Mexico. This includes migration by unaccompanied children and adolescents, as well as movements in caravans, which triggered successive "humanitarian crises" owing to the lack of protocols to deal with massive and unprecedented migration and, subsequently, the massive displacement of entire families caused by deportations. In this subregion, the need to influence the economic, environmental, and social factors fuelling migration, as well as the growing violence and political crises that are forcing people to migrate, has become clear.

---

[6]　The data come from various sources and combine different "migrant" concepts. While the estimates of the United Nations Department of Economic and Social Affairs (DESA) refer to persons born in the Bolivarian Republic of Venezuela who are living in other countries, other sources are based on records of legal stays (R4V, 2019), or else refer to former members of a household who are now living abroad (Freitez, 2017), among other alternatives. The Venezuelan Migration Observatory, based on IOM estimates, calculates that there are some 4 million emigrants (see [online] https://www.observatoriovenezolanodemigracion. org/). Bahar and Barrios (2018) project a figure of over 8 million emigrants in 2020.

Figure IV.8
Bolivarian Republic
of Venezuela: annual
growth of emigration,
1990–2020
(Rate per 100 inhabitants)

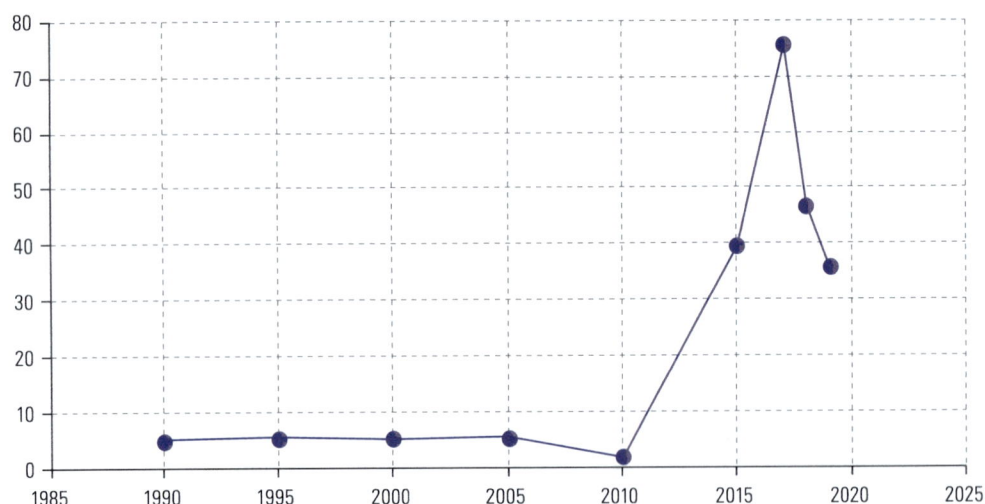

Source: United Nations, "Workbook" [online] UN_Migrant Stock by Origin and Destination_2017, para 1990 a 2015; A. Freitez, "ENCOVI. Encuesta sobre Condiciones de Vida, Venezuela 2017. Emigración", Caracas, Institute of Economic and Social Research of the Catholic Andrés Bello Catholic University (IIES-UCAB), 2017; Coordination Platform for Refugees and Migrants from Venezuela (R4V), "Response for Venezuelans. Latin America and the Caribbean Venezuelan Refugees & Migrants in the region", 2019 [online] https://data2.unhcr.org/en/documents/download/69837, para 2018 and Organization of American States (OEA), *OAS Working Group to Address the Regional Crisis Caused by Venezuela's Migrant and Refugee Flows* (OEA/Ser.D/XV.21), June 2019, on the linear projection for 2020.

Figure IV.9
United States: immigrants from Mexico and Central America living in the country, January 1995–July 2017
(Millions of people)

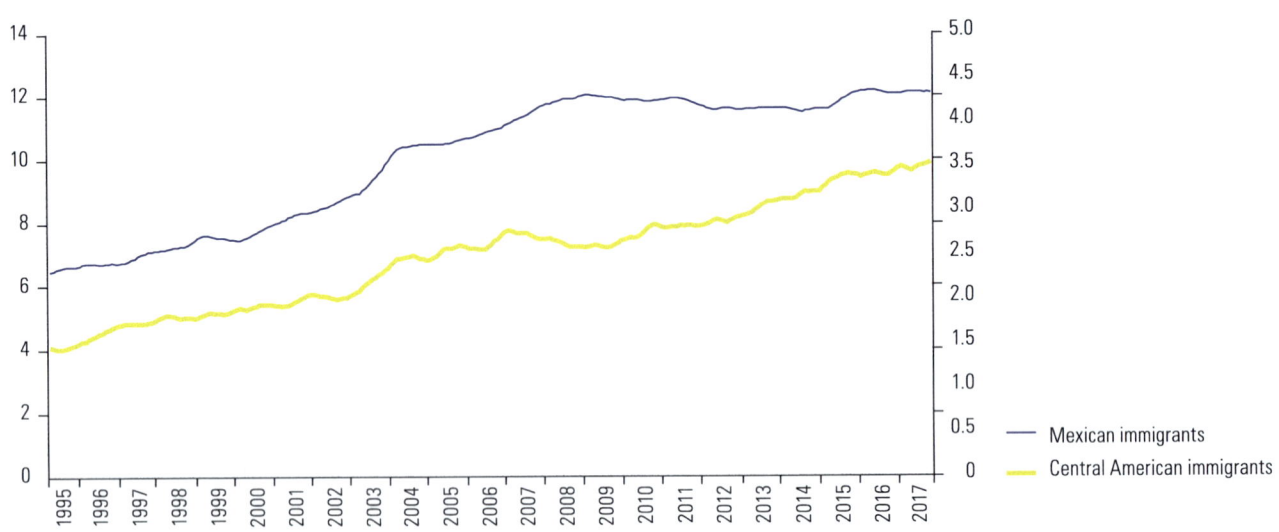

Source: A. Canales and M. Rojas, "Panorama de la migración internacional en México y Centroamérica", *Population and Development series*, No. 124 (LC/TS.2018/42), Santiago, Economic Commission for Latin America and the Caribbean (ECLAC), 2018.

This subregion also displays new migratory flows to Panama (of extra-continental origin) and two other flows that pose special challenges: firstly, the migration of Nicaraguans to Costa Rica; and secondly, migration in the border region between Mexico and Guatemala.

As the figures reported in table IV.1 suggest, migration plays a very significant role in the Caribbean, given the size of the territories and populations involved. The proportions of migrants relative to native populations tend to be higher in smaller territories. The Caribbean migrant population is concentrated in the United States and Canada (Mejia, 2018).

4.   Recent Venezuelan migration: imperative cooperation needs

Venezuelan migration is a priority issue at the regional, national, and local levels. Political processes such as the Quito Process,[7] R4V,[8] OAS working groups, an increasing number of research groups, and the Venezuelan Migration Observatory, are just a sample of the numerous cooperation and knowledge dissemination responses that are emerging.

This migration is expanding rapidly in the region, and the patterns are changing in both immigration and emigration. Data from the 2010 round of censuses showed that the Bolivarian Republic of Venezuela remained one of the main recipient countries in terms of absolute numbers, as a consequence of the traditional arrival of Colombian populations and the influx, in past decades, of people from other origins seeking opportunities and refuge. The situation began to change in the 2000s, however, as Freitez (2011) warned in an analysis of trends, owing to the political, social and economic context in which the country was living through; and it became more pronounced in subsequent years, when emigration started to increase (Martínez and Orrego, 2016). Faced with the social, political and economic instability of the Bolivarian Republic of Venezuela, emigration from this country has grown vigorously in recent years, posing a challenge for government responses in the recipient countries.

According to R4V data, in recent years and up to November 2019, approximately 657,405 Venezuelans had requested protection and formal recognition of their refugee status (see [online] https://r4v.info/es/situations/platform).

B.   Migration and its problems in the subregions

Some specific characteristics of international migration in the region can be analysed by distinguishing subregions consisting of Central America and Mexico, the Caribbean, and South America. Although these three subregions share the main migration patterns already highlighted, each has specific features, either because of the trends and magnitudes of the migration, or because of their link with places of destination and return processes, or the intensity of intraregional mobility, among other factors. The following analysis highlights just a few aspects of this complex problem.

1.   Central America and Mexico

In this subregion, migration has been one of the key social processes of recent decades. The close relationship between these countries and the United States has already been noted, as have the opportunities and challenges that migratory exchanges represent for

---

[7]   The Quito Process is an initiative launched by a group of Latin American countries to respond to the migration crisis in the Bolivarian Republic of Venezuela, following the Quito Declaration on Human Mobility and Venezuelan Citizens in the Region of 4 September 2018. In November of the same year, the Quito Process Plan of Action on the Human Mobility and Venezuelan Nationals in the Region was signed by Argentina, Brazil, Chile, Colombia, Costa Rica, Ecuador, Mexico, Panama, Paraguay, Peru and Uruguay. The declaration seeks to deepen international financial cooperation mechanisms and coordination with international organizations (see [online] https://r4v.info/es/documents/download/68101).

[8]   The Regional Coordination Platform for Refugees and Migrants from Venezuela was set up in April 2018 at the request of the United Nations Secretary General, to direct and coordinate the response to the needs of refugees and migrants from the Bolivarian Republic of Venezuela. It aims to attend to the protection, assistance and integration needs of Venezuelan refugees and migrants in affected Latin American and Caribbean, by complementing and strengthening the national and regional responses of governments, in line with the principles outlined in the New York Declaration for Refugees and Migrants (see [online] https://r4v.info/es/situations/platform).

migrants, their communities and their families. Emigration is a crucial issue in Mexico, along with immigration, return and transit. In Central America, the greatest concern is emigration from the north of the subregion, although Costa Rica has received a large contingent of Nicaraguan migrants, and there is a traditional cross-border flow of Guatemalans into Mexico. The changes resulting from the demographic transition in Central America are less advanced in El Salvador, Guatemala, Honduras and Nicaragua, where their populations are younger.

All of these situations presage a reality that will become increasingly complex in the coming years, and is becoming the priority issue on the agenda of many countries.

Migration from this subregion to the United States has been increasing for some time, albeit with different phases. Flows from the countries of northern Central America grew on a sustained basis until early 2007, and until November 2008 in the case of Mexico. Central American migration slowed initially in the wake of the international economic crisis, and then receded before resuming its growth trend. In the case of Mexico, the economic crisis brought migration to a halt for a longer period that lasted until early 2014 (Canales and Rojas, 2018).

The countries of northern Central America have negative net migration. The number of people born in one of these countries who are living abroad rose to over 3.1 million in 2015. El Salvador has the highest rate of emigration (22.1%), followed by Honduras (6.9%) and Guatemala (5.8%). Of these migrants 86.7% are living in the United States; in the case of Guatemala, 5% live in Mexico, while large numbers of migrants from Honduras and El Salvador are living in Europe (see table IV.3).

Table IV.3
North Central American countries: indicators of absolute migration, 2017
(Number of persons)

Indicator	El Salvador	Guatemala	Honduras
Population	6 312 478	16 252 429	8 960 829
Emigrants	1 436 158	1 017 517	648 520
Immigrants	42 045	76 352	28 070
Net migratory balance	-1 394 113	-941 165	-620 450
Absolute migration rate (percentages)	-22.1	-5.8	-6.9
Emigrants in the United States	1 276 489	881 191	530 645
Emigrants in Mexico	10 054	53 128	15 027
Emigrants in Europe	29 995	19 918	44 292

Source: Economic Commission for Latin America and the Caribbean (ECLAC), on the basis of United Nations, "World Population Prospects: The 2017 Revision", 2017 [online] https://esa.un.org/unpd/wpp/ and United Nations, *Trends in International Migrant Stock: The 2015 Revision* (POP/DB/MIG/Stock/Rev.2015), New York, 2015 [online] http://www.un.org/en/development/desa/population/migration/data/estimates2/estimates15.shtml.
Note: An absolute migrant is defined as a person who resides in a country other than that in which he or she was born.

Transit migration is a distinctive feature of migratory processes in the countries of northern Central America. Although there are no official figures on the number of migrants from these countries who pass through Mexico on their way to the United States, in 2015 the number was estimated at around 417,000, of whom only 19% completed their journey successfully and managed to reach their destination (Canales and Rojas, 2018, p. 72). These migrants are exposed to varying degrees of vulnerability and risks along the way: 14.5% were assaulted or robbed, 10.2% suffered extreme cold, 8.4% suffered from food shortages, and 1.6% were run the risk of drowning in a river or canal.[9]

The number of forced migrants from the countries of northern Central America who have applied for asylum and whose applications are being considered has grown in both Mexico and the United States. In the latter country, 91,000 Salvadorans, 71,000 Guatemalans and 54,000 Hondurans applied for asylum in 2017. Mexico received a smaller number: 5,400 asylum applications from migrants from El Salvador and Honduras

---

[9]   Migrants returned by United States authorities (data from El Colegio de la Frontera Norte and other sources (2013)).

in 2017. In 2018, UNHCR estimates that 29,000 asylum applications were received in Mexico and that the number is set to rise to 59,000 by 2019. In recent years, the profile of asylum-seekers in Mexico has changed from single men to whole families, as well as women and unaccompanied children and adolescents (ECLAC, 2019b).

In the countries of northern Central America (El Salvador, Guatemala and Honduras), the main factors driving emigration are: firstly, insufficient productive capacity combined with lack of employment; and, secondly, the widespread adverse effects of disasters and climate change. These factors are intertwined with violence and insecurity. Social networks facilitate new migrations and refuge seeking, as evidenced by the migrant caravans of recent months. It is increasingly recognized that the bulk of this migration is driven by the lack of alternatives for remaining in the countries of origin.

The profile of these migratory flows is mainly male, young (28% of migrants are under 20 years of age) and low levels of schooling; and it is clearly job-seeking. In fact, about 87% of these migrants are of working age, a higher percentage than the other immigrant groups present in the United States (Canales and Rojas, 2018), which enables them to make a special contribution to the economy and society of this country.

Nonetheless, the restrictive policy and large-scale deportations implemented by the United States Government since the second half of the 2000 decade have had serious consequences for migrant communities and families. Between 2007 and 2016, more than 840,000 migrants from the countries of northern Central America were deported (Canales and Rojas, 2018). A major problem is the response capacity of the authorities of these countries of origin to the needs of returnees, many of whom have spent long periods abroad and no longer have family ties. Several initiatives have been designed to address this situation; however, new needs are emerging, such as psychosocial support and reintegration into a labour market with few employment opportunities and low wages.

Migrants from northern Central American countries sent back by the United States authorities are mostly men (88.4% on average). The education level of those from Guatemala is low (53% have primary education or lower), while among Hondurans and Salvadorans it is higher: 38.9% of Honduran migrants have secondary, technical or higher education, and the proportion is 43.7% among migrants from El Salvador. Nearly one third of returnee migrants from Guatemala belong to an indigenous community or people. The largest proportion of migrant children under 15 years of age accompanied by non-relatives comes from El Salvador (11%) and Guatemala (8.5%)[10] (see box IV.4).

In recent years, there has been an increase in the flow of Central American migrants passing through Mexico (Rodríguez Chávez, 2016) in highly vulnerable conditions and exposed to various dangers, such as organized trafficking gangs. Of particular concern is the increase in the number of unaccompanied children and adolescents in transit, who are fleeing their countries of origin, to escape violence, poverty and social exclusion (Orozco and Yansura, 2015).

---

[10] Estimations by ECLAC on the basis of data from El Colegio de la Frontera Norte; Ministry of Labour and Social Security; National Population Council; Unit for Migration Policy, Registration and Personal Identity (UPMRIP); Ministry of Foreign Relations; National Council for the Prevention of Discrimination (CONAPRED); Ministry of Social Development; "Survey of Migration at Mexico's Northern Border" (EMIF) [online] www.colef.mx/emif.

Box IV.4

Central America: unaccompanied migrant children and adolescents

Unaccompanied migrant children and adolescents (defined by UNHCR —cited in Maldonado Valera, Martínez Pizarro and Martínez (2018)— as any child under the age of 18 who is separated from both parents and is not being cared for by an adult who by law or custom has responsibility to do so, as well as those who are left alone after entering a country) have become an increasingly visible phenomenon as their numbers have grown since 2013. By 2017 a total of 180,000 unaccompanied children and adolescents from the north of Central America had been detained on the southwestern border of the United States. If Mexican children and adolescents are added to this figure, the number of detentions totals 244,000. The situation of Mexico is notable for the fact that it is a country of origin, transit, destination and return of unaccompanied children and adolescents. According to data from the Ministry of the Interior, between 2015 and 2017, Mexico's Migration Policy Unit had about 45,000 registered cases of migrants from the countries of northern Central America.

Among the vectors motivating the migration of children and adolescents, empirical data reveal the importance of the search for work, family reunification, the need to escape from situations of domestic or social violence, the consequences of natural disasters and poverty. The sociodemographic profile indicates that 71.4% are men and 28.6% are women, with average ages of 15.5 and 14.3 years, respectively.

Several studies on migration legislation in Central America and Mexico have encountered major shortcomings in the development of an institutional framework for the protection of migrant rights. Nonetheless, important regulatory and legal initiatives include the following: in El Salvador, the Law for the Comprehensive Protection of Children and Adolescents was enacted in 2009; in Mexico, the Law for the Protection of Children and Adolescents was strengthened as from 2006; and in 2008 the Roundtable for Dialogue on Unaccompanied Migrant Children and Adolescents and Migrant Women was established; Guatemala has the Law on the Protection of Unaccompanied Migrant Children and Adolescents Separated from their Families, and on the Combating of the Illicit Trafficking of Migrants.

Northern Central American countries and Mexico: unaccompanied children, adolescents and family units on the south-western border of the United States, October 2017 to June 2018
(Number)

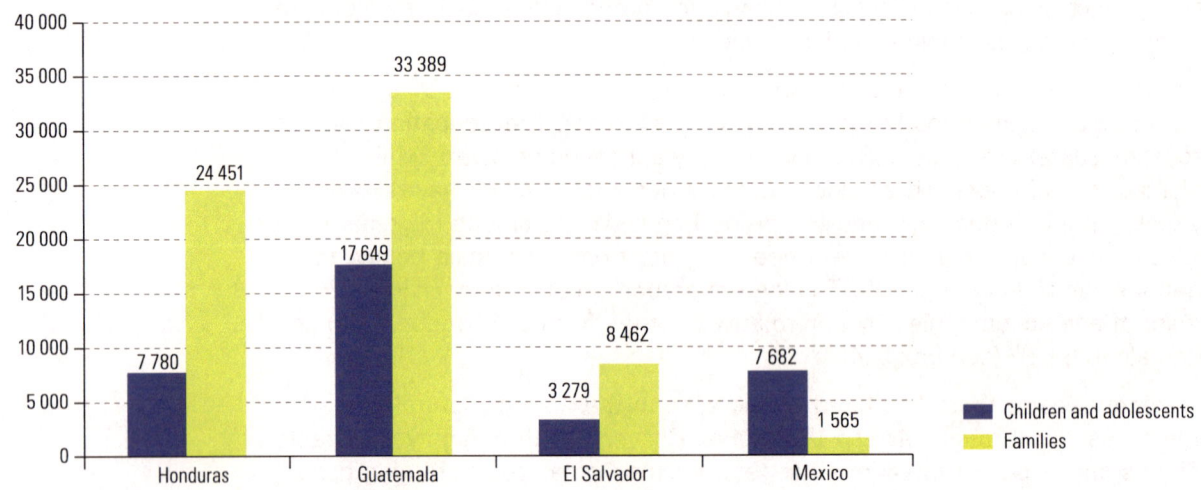

Source: C. Maldonado Valera, J. Martínez Pizarro and R. Martínez, "Protección social y migración: una mirada desde las vulnerabilidades a lo largo del ciclo de la migración y de la vida de las personas", *Project Documents* (LC/TS.2018/62), Santiago 2018 and J. Martínez Pizarro and C. Orrego Rivera, "Nuevas tendencias y dinámicas migratorias en América Latina y el Caribe", *Population and Development series*, No.114 (LC/L.4164), Santiago, Economic Commission for Latin America and the Caribbean (ECLAC) 2016.

(a) Migrant's motivations interact with structural determinants

It is widely known that migration from and in the north of Central America is one component of worrying situations and challenges that are generating responses from various aspects of cooperation between the countries, through initiatives such as the Comprehensive Development Plan for Central America sponsored by ECLAC.

Although the reasons that motivate individuals and families to change their place of residence are multiple, it is possible to identify the main causes that people from the countries of northern Central America (El Salvador, Guatemala and Honduras) state as the main factors driving them to migrate to the United States. According to a survey coordinated by the Colegio de la Frontera Norte in 2016, these include lack of employment, economic crisis, low incomes or poor working conditions in their countries of origin (see figure IV.10).

Figure IV.10
Northern Central American countries: reasons for migrating declared by migrants sent back by the United States authorities, 2016
(Percentages)

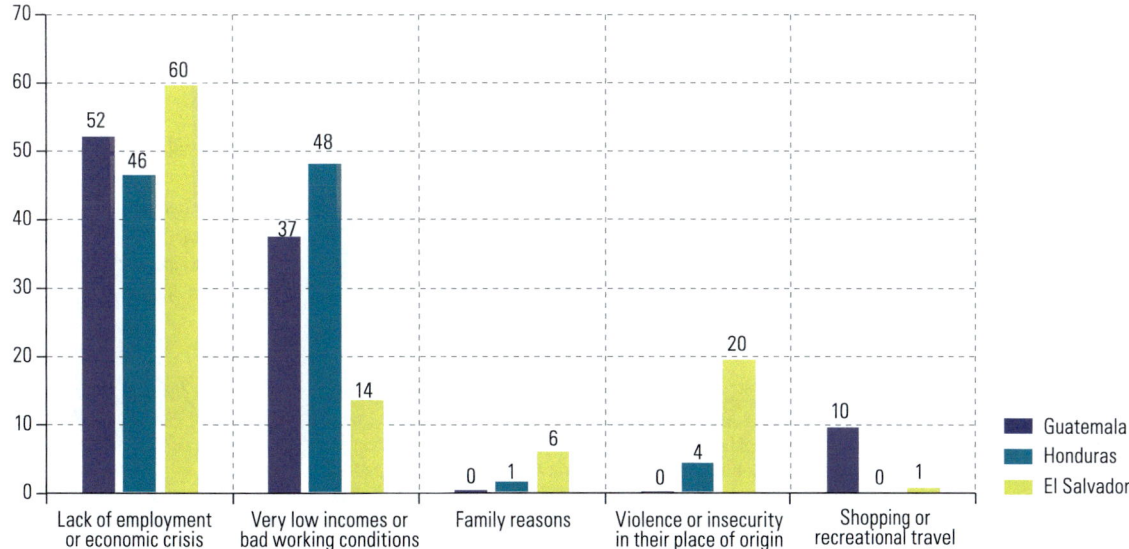

Source: Economic Commission for Latin America and the Caribbean (ECLAC), on the basis of El Colegio de la Frontera Norte; Ministry of Labour and Social Security; National Population Council; Unit for Migration Policy, Registration and Personal Identity (UPMRIP); Ministry of Foreign Relations; National Council for the Prevention of Discrimination (CONAPRED); Ministry of Social Development; "Survey of Migration at Mexico's Northern Border" (EMIF) [online] www.colef.mx/emif.

In the case of migrants from El Salvador, violence is ranked second among the reasons for migrating (20% mentioned it as their main reason). Family reunification ranks third with 6% of responses.

Another factor that motivates the decision to migrate to the United States is the search for work, because of the wage gap that exists between the countries of origin and destination of the migration. In 2018, the minimum wage in the United States was six times higher than the mean minimum wage across the countries of northern Central America and Mexico. In the case of the average wage, the difference was even greater: 12 times higher in the United States (see figure IV.11). While Central American and Mexican migrants in the United States receive less than the average, they still earn more than they would in their countries of origin.

Demography also plays a major role in this subregion. Between 1950 and 1975, the countries of northern Central America experienced high population growth due to a reduction in the mortality rate, and their population increased at an average rate of 2.8% per year. When a population grows at this rate, it doubles every 25 years: the number of inhabitants in the three countries increased from 6.9 million in 1950 to 13.7 million in 1975. While the growth rate subsequently slackened as a result of declining fertility, their combined population will reach 34.3 million by 2020. In the period of high population growth, the public policy challenge was to provide for the growing child population, mainly in the areas of primary education and health.[11]

[11] In 1970, children under 15 years of age represented 45.6% of the total population in El Salvador, 45.8% in Guatemala and 47.4% in Honduras. As a result of demographic change, by 2020 the share of this age group is expected to fall to 26.5% in El Salvador, 33.3% in Guatemala and 30.5% in Honduras (author's calculations on the basis of information from the United Nations (2017b)).

Figure IV.11
Mexico, the United States and northern Central American countries: minimum and average monthly wages, 2017–2019
(Dollars)

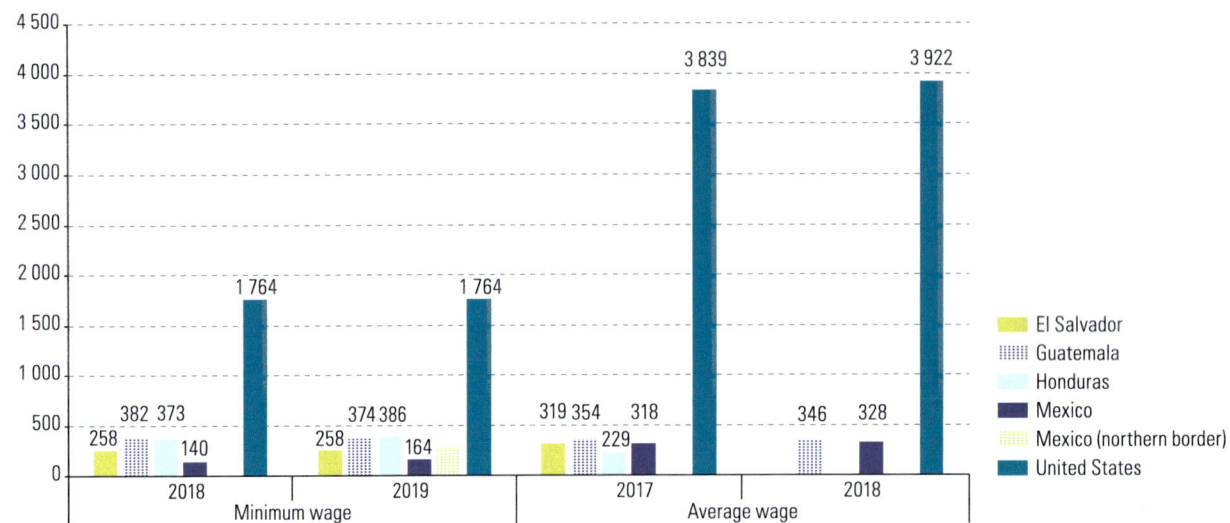

Source: Economic Commission for Latin America and the Caribbean (ECLAC), on the basis of International Labour Organization (ILO), ILOSTAT database [online] http://www.ilo.org/ilostat; United States Census Bureau, Current Population Survey (CPS) [online] www.census.gov/programs-surveys/cps.html; World Bank, World Bank Open Data [online] data.worldbank.org; El Salvador, Ministry of Labour and Social Security, "Tarifas de salarios mínimos vigentes a partir del 1° de enero del 2018" [online] www.mtps.gob.sv/avisos/salarios-minimos-2018/; Guatemala, *Diario de Centro América*, "Ministerio de Trabajo y Previsión Social, Acuerdo Gubernativo Número 297-2017", December 2017; Honduras, Secretariat of Labor and Social Security, Wages Department, "Tabla de salario mínimo, vigente a partir del 1 de enero del año 2018" [online] www.trabajo.gob.hn/wp-content/uploads/2018/01/Tabla-SM-2018-ipc-4-73.pdf and "Tabla de salario mínimo, vigente a partir del 1 de enero del año 2019" [online] http://www.trabajo.gob.hn/wp-content/uploads/2019/01/Tabla-Salario-2019.pdf; Mexico, National Commission on Minimum Wages, "Salarios mínimos vigentes a partir del 1° de enero del 2018" [online] www.gob.mx/cms/uploads/attachment/file/285013/TablaSalariosMinimos-01ene2018.pdf and "Salarios mínimos vigentes a partir del 1° de enero del 2019" [online] www.gob.mx/cms/uploads/attachment/file/426395/2019_Salarios_Minimos.pdf, United States, Department of Labor, "Minimun Wage" [online] www.dol.gov/general/topic/wages/minimumwage.

The demographic transition has generated the "demographic dividend" in the countries of northern Central America[12]. While this means that fewer resources need to be transferred from the economically active to the non-active age group (those under 15 and over 65); it also generates an urgent need to create jobs. However, the economic growth of these countries has not created enough jobs, and those that exist are precarious, offering offer low wages and poor working conditions.

In the countries of northern Central America, nearly 700,000 young people reach working age (15 years old) every year. While not everyone wants or needs to work at that point in their life cycle, some are looking for a job; and, at some point most of them can be expected to need work. In addition, every year roughly 120,000 people reach retirement age in these countries; so, to achieve the labour inclusion demanded by current demographics would require about 580,000 jobs to be created annually, and this is not happening. As a result, the youth unemployment rate in El Salvador is 16% for men and 15.1% among women; in Honduras it is 9.5% for men and 15.6% for women; and in Guatemala it is about 8% for both sexes.[13]

[12]   In 2020, the population aged 15-49 years will represent 52.6% of the total population in El Salvador, 53.5% in Guatemala and 55.1% in Honduras (United Nations, 2017b).
[13]   Figures from CEPALSTAT [online] interwp.cepal.org/cepalstat.

The unemployment rate only captures part of the problem, however. Many young people have stopped looking for work because they do not have the education required for the job, or because they have suffered some form of discrimination, or because there is no work available where they live. Discouraged jobseekers in the countries of northern Central America total 205,000; half of them are young people aged 15–24, and two thirds are women.[14]

The shortage of jobs in the countries of northern Central America, combined with the robust demand for labour in the United States economy, is one of the key structural drivers migration in the subregion. In El Salvador, Guatemala and Honduras, more than two thirds of job seekers are forced either to work in the informal economy or to migrate.

2.   The Caribbean

In the Caribbean, migration plays a predominant role owing to the size of the territories in question and the impact it can have on population dynamics and structure. The combined data on immigrants and emigrants, expressed as a proportion of the total national population of each country, shows that migration in this subregion has major impacts, although there are significant differences according to the population size of the individual countries.

The United States and Canada accounted for 77% of the Caribbean emigrant population in 2019.

There is also a substantial flow of migrants from Haiti to South America, mainly to Brazil and Chile (Mejía, 2018). Chile quickly became one of the preferred destinations for Haitian emigration, but this trend slowed in 2018 when the requirements for Haitians to enter the country changed. The increase in migration from Haiti following the 2010 earthquake and other natural disasters (in particular Hurricane Matthew), call for an active and effective cooperation strategy for that country.

(a) Main challenges and migration trends in the Caribbean

High rates of emigration are not a new challenge for the Caribbean subregion. Their migratory flows have been determined by historical and cultural links, as well as geographical factors. However, the traditional socioeconomic motivation to seek better opportunities for education, employment and living standards is now being augmented by migratory forces arising from natural disasters and climate change.

The region has one of the largest diasporas in the world relative to its population: the number of migrants from the Caribbean is estimated at 9 million, which even in 2017 represented 19.8% of the subregion's total population.[15] The largest diasporas are those of Puerto Rico, Cuba, the Dominican Republic, Haiti, Jamaica, French Guiana and Trinidad and Tobago. In the smaller islands, the proportion of emigrants is usually very large. For example, emigrants from Montserrat are estimated to far outnumber the resident national population; in Dominica emigrants represent 96.7% of its population, and in Antigua and Barbuda, Grenada, French Guiana, Puerto Rico, Saint Kitts and Nevis, Sint Maarten and Saint Vincent and the Grenadines emigrants are equivalent to at least half of the resident national population (see table IV.1).

[14] Average from 2012 to 2016. Estimated using figures from the International Labour Organization (ILO), "Discouraged job-seekers by sex and age" [online] https://ilostat.ilo.org/data/#summarytables.
[15] The data include all member countries of the Caribbean Development and Cooperation Committee (CDCC) plus French Guiana (30 countries altogether).

(b) Skilled migration: positive and negative effects

Managing skilled migration is always a challenge; the steady loss of human capital undermines progress in education, health and many other areas (ECLAC, 2018). Migration policy must therefore consider how to address this loss of professional skills: provide incentives to encourage people to stay in the Caribbean, and endeavour to take advantage of this emigration, by maintaining links with diaspora communities and facilitating return migration, among other measures.

Migration, and more particularly the emigration of skilled persons, is both a challenge and an opportunity for Caribbean countries. These countries have one of the highest rates of skilled emigration in the world, and the diaspora has greatly influenced economic, social and political developments in the subregion. Far from being a short-term phenomenon, it is one of the key trends and one of the patterns that characterize the scenario of population movements in the Caribbean.

The emigration of highly qualified people has been a sensitive issue in several countries of the subregion for decades (Thomas-Hope, 2002). In Jamaica, for example, large numbers of professionals continually emigrate, particularly skilled women working in the health and education sectors. This has caused labour shortages in these important sectors, which threaten the sustainability of quality education and health care in the country (IOM, 2018b).

The departure of skilled personnel in search of better economic opportunities hinders the accumulation of institutional knowledge and prevents the transfer and exchange of knowledge with less skilled workers. In addition to the loss of tax revenue resulting from emigration, the country of origin also suffers indirectly by being unable to benefit from professionals who have received highly subsidized education and training and who could repay this investment by contributing to their nation's development.

Nonetheless, skilled emigration also has positive effects on the countries of origin, of which the most important for the Caribbean countries is the receipt of remittances.[16] These are crucial for financing and facilitating private consumption; and, through a multiplier effect, for enhancing the stability of the financial sector and boosting tax revenues. Their crucial capacity to reduce poverty and improve the lives of both the migrants themselves and their families has been recognized (IOM, 2017a). Migrant networks also encourage trade and investment and, when effectively harnessed, can promote human capital formation through the exchange of experiences abroad or upon return to the subregion. While there is a growing trend of return migration in the form of retirees to the Caribbean, except in Cuba and Haiti (IOM, 2017b), the rate of emigration far outweighs the rate of return; and the highly skilled labour force of Caribbean countries is reduced by an average of 70%.

To mitigate the adverse impacts of highly skilled migration and improve its positive effects, Caribbean States need to design policies that create and maintain a balance between these positive and negative consequences; policies that encourage highly skilled potential migrants to stay, or encourage them to return, or engage the diaspora with various initiatives (investment, trade or research) in the country of origin.

---

[16]   World Bank data show that remittances represented more than 5% of GDP in six Caribbean countries in 2018: Haiti (30.9%), Jamaica (15.9%), Dominica (9.2%), the Dominican Republic (8.4%), Guyana (7.9%) and Saint Vincent and the Grenadines (5.1%). See also chapter V.

An analysis of the United Nations World Population Policies Database[17] concludes that only two Caribbean Member States wanted to reduce immigration (Barbados and Belize); five wanted to increase skilled immigration (Barbados, Guyana, Jamaica, Suriname and Trinidad and Tobago); and four wanted to reduce emigration (Barbados, Dominica, Guyana and Suriname) (Jones, Camarinhas and Gény, 2019).

In the context of Caribbean migration policies, the Government of Jamaica has developed a national policy and action plan on international migration and development, with a view to enhancing the development impact. The policy promotes short- and medium-term measures such as reducing the costs of remittances, adopting international agreements to facilitate labour migration, regulating recruitment agencies, negotiating bilateral agreements on pension portability and transfer, and providing incentives for the diaspora to invest in Jamaica.

(c) Climate-related migration

Migratory movements triggered by disaster situations and climate change tend to have major impacts in the Caribbean. While the connection between rural-urban migration and environmental degradation has been demonstrated, migration still needs to be addressed as an extreme adaptation strategy for coping with the impact of climate change.[18] In addition, migration, including from rural to urban areas, affects land use, infrastructure, housing and social cohesion, forming complex interrelationships. Urban population growth continues to take place largely in low-lying, disaster-prone, coastal areas (ECLAC, 2019a). Policies to address climate-related migration are only at an incipient stage.

Well-planned relocation can serve as a means of reducing disaster risk, as well as a way of adapting to climate change. One possible preventive measure would be to address inequalities related to territorial development —particularly in view of the impacts of climate change— through practical programmes and coordination mechanisms to address the risks in question. Given the relationship between disasters, poverty and displacement, disaster risk reduction and adaptation plans could include natural disaster preparedness measures and a proactive climate change adjustment strategy that takes migration into account.

Population resettlement or relocation, traditionally more associated with urban development, are adopting new forms that will need to be taken into account in regional development and spatial planning policies. A large proportion of the Caribbean population lives near the coast, often in low-lying areas, where coastal flooding, storm surges and inland flooding can cause serious problems of population displacement. Some countries have started to consider the issue of internal migration and population location in the context of preventing natural disasters —Haiti, for example, following the 2010 earthquake— as well as mitigating the effects of climate change. In fact, the migration, environment and development component is one of the four main components of migration policy in Haiti, which was the first Central American and Caribbean country to incorporate the link between the environment and internal migration in its 2015 migration policy project (IOM, 2019a) (see box IV.5).

---

[17] Based on the United Nations Inquiry among Governments on Population and Development (2015 revision).
[18] In this connection, see the discussion of extreme risk and adaptive capacity in Belize in ECLAC (2019a, pp. 60-63).

Box IV.5
Haiti and the impact of
disasters on mobility

With a population of just under 11 million, Haiti is the second largest Caribbean country and also the most vulnerable in terms of natural hazards (storms, floods, landslides and droughts). In 2010, the devastating effects of the earthquake were compounded by the displacement of 2.3 million people; and in 2016 the drought caused by the El Niño weather pattern affected more than 3.5 million. This was followed by Hurricane Matthew in the same year, which affected 2.1 million people in the country and displaced around 176,000, according to IOM data. In response, some countries in the region suspended the deportation of Haitians, offered them humanitarian visas to regularize their situation, and provided them with protection and humanitarian assistance. On the other hand, before Hurricane Matthew made landfall many had tried to take refuge in the Dominican Republic, but they were sent back to Haiti. The Governments of Panama and Costa Rica have expressed their intention to seek third countries to relocate Haitians from their territory. It is unclear whether this relocation will be forced or voluntary, which will affect monitoring.

Data gaps and inconsistencies in documentation have been identified throughout this process, in relation to the number of beneficiaries of humanitarian visas and the number of persons in temporary shelters or collective centres, in both transit and host countries. For example, the lack of systematic documentation of population departures from Haiti makes it difficult to identify which disaster triggered the cross-border movement. Moreover, media reports on cross-border movements make indiscriminate use of terms such as "migrants", "refugees" or "asylum seekers", which complicates the analysis.

Source: Economic Commission for Latin America and the Caribbean (ECLAC).

The impact of the 2017 hurricane season exemplifies the challenges faced by Caribbean islands and the consequences for internal and international displacement. The worst affected islands included Anguilla, Antigua and Barbuda, the Bahamas, Dominica, the British Virgin Islands and the Turks and Caicos Islands. The socioeconomic impact of disasters in the Caribbean tends to be particularly severe given the size of their economies: in the 2017 hurricane season, the damage caused by hurricanes Irma and Maria in the British Virgin Islands and Sint Maarten cost more than 100% of their GDP (ECLAC, 2019a). Governments in the region, together with international agencies, provided shelter and humanitarian assistance to people who had lost their homes. Hurricane Irma damaged 90% of the structures on the island of Barbuda, leading to its complete evacuation; and roughly 1,500 people were evacuated to Antigua. The Government handled the reception and registration of these evacuees and provided accommodation, food and psychosocial support. Six months later, only 22% of Barbuda's former inhabitants had returned. After Hurricane Maria, Antigua, Guyana and Saint Kitts and Nevis also received displaced persons (IOM, 2017c).

In addition to direct migratory movements caused by natural disasters and extreme events, considerable migratory impact is also expected as a result of the long-term effects of climate change, such as losses in the tourism sector, agriculture or quality of life, by disrupting access to fundamental goods such as water, which exacerbates the vulnerability caused by other existing problems.

(d) Prospects for intergovernmental cooperation on migration policy in the Caribbean

In the Caribbean, there is a complex and multi-causal relationship between population movements —both within countries and across borders— and political, demographic, environmental and social factors. Natural disasters uprooted more than 6.5 million people (mainly within the subregion) in 2008–2017; most of the displaced being Cubans or Haitians (IOM, 2019a). More recently, many Caribbean countries and territories experienced both internal displacement and migration to nearby countries following Hurricanes Irma and Maria in 2017.

As reported in the review of the implementation of the Montevideo Consensus on Population and Development in the Caribbean subregion, the protection of refugees, asylum-seekers and other vulnerable migrants has been the focus of the Caribbean Migration Consultations (CMC). The aim of these consultations is to establish a framework for regional cooperation in addressing population movements in response to disasters and climate change. The consultations will focus on issues such as climate change mitigation, reducing exposure to its effects, planned relocation and enhanced resilience.

Assistance and protection also pose challenges for Caribbean countries. According to UNHCR and IOM estimates, 40,000 Venezuelans are currently living in Trinidad and Tobago, of whom 11,512 are registered as asylum-seekers (R4V, 2019). In response to the Venezuelan immigration crisis, in June 2019 the Government of Trinidad and Tobago launched a two-week regularization process in which 16,523 Venezuelans were registered and granted a work permit exemption —initially valid for six months— to enable them to work and gain access to health and education services.

3.   South America

In South America, migratory dynamics predominantly involve movements between countries, although the subregion is also going through transformations in which many of the countries are becoming scenarios of emigration, immigration, transit and return. In addition, the migration of Venezuelans to various countries, both traditional and new destinations, has intensified.

One of the key features of migration in this subregion is the participation of women, especially the employment of many female migrants in paid domestic work.

(a) Paid domestic work and migration in the subregion

In Latin America, paid domestic work has traditionally been a major source of employment for women, especially those from poor, indigenous and Afrodescendent households. Paid domestic work has historical roots linked to slavery, the *hacienda* tradition and the employment of women in their employers' homes. These women performed domestic tasks that were usually paid for in kind; or else they simply worked without pay, since their wage was considered to be included in the pay of their father or husband, as the case may be (Kuznesof, 1989). Since colonial times and persisting well into the twentieth century, many women from poor families in rural areas moved to the cities in search of a livelihood. They worked in a variety of trades, predominantly paid domestic work (Hutchinson, 2014). The increase in the number of women migrating to the city in search of work made it possible to expand paid domestic work into the middle-income sectors. As a result, in the second half of the twentieth century, the proportion of paid domestic work in total female employment in Latin America was the highest anywhere in the world.

In recent years, the number of women migrating to neighbouring countries in search of work has been increasing; and a large proportion of them find employment in the destination country as paid domestic workers. This type of work, which is valued lowest on the occupational social scale and carries a stigma, is one of the few alternatives available to a group that already suffers stigmatization —and often a devaluation of qualifications— owing to its migrant status. Women migrants also tend to remain in this occupation without being able to develop an occupational mobility project, owing to the lack of networks and recognition of their qualifications, or else because of the negative stamp imposed on their employment history by having worked in domestic service.

Female domestic employees perform household management tasks (cleaning, preparing meals, shopping, caring for pets, among others) as well as child and elderly care, without their contribution to the well-being of the family necessarily being recognized. Paid domestic work remains socially undervalued and associated with low social status.

(b) Global care chains

The global care chain concept has been widely used to explain female migration from lower-income countries. Along with the flows of capital, information and goods that circulate as part of globalization, international circuits of caregivers that underpin social reproduction in destination countries are also formed (Ehrenreich and Hochschild, 2003, Parreñas, 2001).

International migration for care motives is an expression of the global processes of capital accumulation, which are structural and based not only on the transnationalization of capital or production, but also of reproduction (Bakker and Gill, 2003).

International migration poses a new challenge for analysing care. Women migrate to undertake care tasks in the destination countries; but, at the same time, they also assume the burden of economic provision for their home and undertake care tasks at a distance (transnational care) within the framework of a new social organization of family life imposed by their absence. Female migration thus triggers major changes in households: care work is redistributed among the family members who remain in the country of origin; and transnational households develop whose members maintain frequent relations with each other, despite living separated by national borders, thus linking their societies of origin with those of destination (Acosta, 2015). The transnational family gives rise to new care practices: distance motherhood being one of the most studied. Emotional care —which involves listening, talking and counselling— is not interrupted by distance, but takes place through phone calls, emails, and other media based on the new technologies (Gonzálvez, 2013).

(c) Formation of migratory corridors for care in Latin America

The formation of migratory corridors for care revolves around urban centres that have generated high-paying jobs in specialized services. This implies a significant potential demand for care services. The professionals who live in these areas require support for their daily subsistence, so they outsource the tasks of house-cleaning, preparing meals or caring for children and older people, to ensure a certain level of labour productivity. This demand is met by low-cost labour, which increasingly consists of migrants since local female workers tend not to be available for this type of work.

The effects of this phenomenon include a widening of the inequality gap within and between countries, greater labour market segregation, and the transfer of tasks that are shunned by the local population to women from other countries who are willing to fulfil them for a minimum wage (Soto and others 2016).

The main destination countries for migrant women in care work are Argentina, Chile and Costa Rica. Most female migrant domestic employees traditionally come from neighbouring countries. Geographical proximity is an important factor in the decision to migrate, especially when the migrants leave their family behind in their country of origin. Various studies (Messina, 2015; Magliano and Barral, 2017; Gonzálvez, 2013;

Stefoni, 2002) have shown that, while economic motivation prevails over other reasons, the desire for fulfilment and greater economic independence, and the flight from domestic violence and situations of oppression within the family, also act as powerful factors compounding economic difficulties. Migration can give the worker more independence, as she assumes a provider role that potentially gives her greater authority in making decisions regarding her household.

Female migrant domestic employees come from a variety of social sectors and situations that have motivated their migration project. In many cases, their previous work histories are not related to paid domestic work. They tend to be better educated than their national counterparts, and they are younger. Specific data processed from the latest Household Survey Data Bank (BADEHOG) surveys show that the age difference in Chile is almost 11 years and in Costa Rica it is nearly four.

For many women migrant workers, especially those who have travelled alone and left their children in their country of origin, their first job in paid domestic work involves accommodation in the workplace. Although this modality is not without its problems —associated, for example, with long working hours— it has the advantage of offering a higher wage and, at the same time, guaranteeing maximum savings, since there are no housing, transport or sustenance expenses. This enables them to accumulate a larger sum of money to send back to their family or to hasten family reunification. In addition, some female workers consider that live-in employment affords them greater personal safety in an environment that is alien and unknown to them.

The live-in work modality is generally temporary, and its duration depends on the worker's migratory project. If she plans to settle in the destination country more permanently, and especially if there is a family reunification process, she will probably choose to work externally.

(i) Peru-Paraguay-Argentina migrant corridor

Argentina's current migration policy is based on Migration Law No. 25.871, which has been in force since January 2004. This is supplemented by Decree No. 616 of 2010 and the *Patria Grande* (Greater Homeland) regularization program, which is intended for citizens of countries that are members of the Southern Common Market (MERCOSUR) and its associate states. Argentine law allows these citizens to enter Argentina on the basis of their national identity document, and to apply for temporary residence for two years with no requirement other than entry through legal channels and a police record. At the end of the two years, they obtain permanent residency by virtue of settled status. Persons from countries outside MERCOSUR can apply for a one-year temporary residence (renewable) if they satisfy the requirements specified for each category residence.

In Argentina, many Paraguayan and Peruvian women workers are engaged in paid domestic work (69% of Paraguayan and 58% of Peruvian women, according to the latest household surveys), although qualitative studies indicate that some Peruvian women workers see it as a job they hope to move out of (Jaramillo, 2017).

The contingent of female migrant domestic employees in Argentina is heterogeneous and includes women with a variety of migratory and labour histories and different levels of education and vocational training. In contrast, Paraguayan female domestic employees come mainly from rural areas, are young and tend to have low levels of education. These workers value not only having more job opportunities than in their country of origin, but also higher wage levels and, especially, easier and lower-cost access to essential public health services (and, when they are able to bring their children, access to an education system they consider to be of good quality). They also value the social policy measures applicable to them (even though a minimum number of years of residence is required to qualify for the benefits) and the possibility of retirement when they reach the requisite age, thanks to the Law on Retirement of Female Domestic Workers (Messina, 2015) (Messina, 2015); Dobré and others, 2015).

Peruvians are currently the fourth largest group of migrants in Argentina, and is heavily concentrated in paid domestic work. Peruvian women workers have higher levels of education, many of them with full secondary schooling and even post-secondary studies (Rosas, 2010). Before migrating, many had skilled or semi-skilled jobs (such as secretaries, nursing technicians, or occupations in the beauty sector), and a large proportion worked in commerce. There are also female migrant domestic workers with tertiary and university degrees (such as social workers, graduates in nursing or obstetrics, teachers, among others) who, despite this, were unable to choose other career paths. Difficulties in gaining recognition for their qualifications appear to be one of the main factors preventing them from practising their profession in the destination country.

Argentina has launched major initiatives to improve the situation of female domestic employees. In 2013, a new law was adopted that equates them to other wage-earners in nearly all respects; and this was supported by a policy of promoting labour formalization targeting both national and migrant workers.

(ii) Peru-Chile migratory corridor

Chile started to receive immigrants following the return to democracy in 1990 and in a subsequent context of political stability and economic growth; and today it has become one of the countries with the highest rates of immigration from the region (Martínez, 2011; Martínez and Orrego, 2016). This is a new phenomenon, which has caused the number of migrants to more than quadruple in less than 30 years. The largest groups originally came from neighbouring countries; but migrants from Colombia, the Dominican Republic, Haiti and particularly the Bolivarian Republic of Venezuela have recently joined the inflow.

In Chile, 13% of employed migrant women are working in domestic service, according to information obtained from special processing of the latest BADEHOG household surveys, compared to 8% of Chilean women. Chile's migration law dates from 1975; it was drafted in the context of military dictatorship and conceived under the influence of a national security rationale. The law grants huge discretion to the border authority and requires special clauses for granting a work visa. The country is about to approve a reform of the migration law in order to adapt it to the current migration reality. Since the return to democracy, three migration regularization processes, or "amnesties" have taken place in 1998, 2007 and 2018.

Despite the difficulty in reaching a domestic consensus that would allow migratory legislation to be amended, various administrative programmes and initiatives have been implemented to manage migration in recent years.

A large proportion of migrant women are concentrated in domestic work, an occupation that has a significant degree of labour protection, since Law 20.786 gives them equal rights with any other wage-earner in nearly all respects. In Chile, a major effort has also been made to formalize domestic work, ensuring that over half of the workers in this sector have employment contracts and social security coverage. Female migrant domestic employees know that they need an employment contract to obtain the temporary visa. Obtaining that contract is a key element in the terms of negotiation when entering an employment relationship. For this reason, most migrant female domestic employees pay social security contributions (65.2% according to data from special processing of the latest BADEHOG household surveys) and the level of labour formality they achieve is higher than that of their Chilean counterparts.

Migration from Peru to Chile started to gather pace in the mid-1990s. According to the 2002 census, the Peruvian community in Chile represented 20.5% of the total number of migrants and was the second largest after the Argentine community. The largest flows occurred in the 2000 decade. The importance of paid domestic work as a source of employment marked the feminized nature of migration from Peru, a situation that persists to this day. According to the 2017 National Socioeconomic Characterization Survey (CASEN), 56.2% of all immigrants from Peru were women. The rate of growth of migration from Peru slowed from the 2010 decade onwards, while the source countries of migration to Chile diversified to include Colombia, Ecuador and the Plurinational State of Bolivia. The pattern of feminized migration (with a larger proportion of women) persisted in these cases, as paid domestic work also became an important source of employment for email migrant workers from these countries.

Stefoni (2002) and Acosta (2015) note that the arrival of Peruvian workers in Chile not only responded to an unsatisfied demand for paid domestic workers in the host country, but also, in some cases, to an attempt to postpone the establishment of more modern and formal labour relations. Employers' testimonies reveal their preference for Peruvian women workers as a way to maintain the servile hierarchical patterns that had historically characterized paid domestic work and which Chilean women workers no longer respect.

(iii) Circular migration: Bolivian female domestic workers in Chile

According to data from Chile's foreign national registration and migration department (Departamento de Extranjería y Migración), immigration from the Plurinational State of Bolivia has increased in recent years. Female domestic employees arrive in Chile pursuing circular migration strategies —in other words temporary, repetitive and cyclical migration; they do not intend to settle in Chile permanently. This is a survival strategy in the face of the need to provide income to the household. They travel by land from various Bolivian cities, mainly from the departments of La Paz, Oruro and Potosí, located along the 800 km border with Chile; they concentrate in the northern part of Chile close to the Bolivian border. This is an unusual pattern as most women migrant workers from elsewhere move to the central part of the country, where there are more sources of employment.

The women migrant workers enter the country as tourists, with an identity card issued by the Plurinational State of Bolivia, which allows them to stay in the country for 90 days. At the end of that period they return to their country, some for a few days and others for longer (a few months or a year), and then return to Chile again to work. Most of them are not covered by the Residency Agreement for Nationals of the States Parties of MERCOSUR, the Plurinational State of Bolivia and Chile, which would allow them to stay for one year; nor do they apply for a work permit. The explanation for this circularity strategy includes ignorance of the regulations on the circulation of nationals from MERCOSUR and associate countries and the economic costs involved in regularization of their status. The temporary visa costs US$ 283 and the work permit costs US$ 150. Another reason for not obtaining the temporary visa is the fear that it will force them to stay in Chile for a year (as a condition for permanent residency), thereby preventing them from returning to their country of origin every three months to visit their children. As they do not have a work permit, they also do not have a contract, and the work relationship is established under conditions of extreme vulnerability and risk of abuses and rights violations. Given this situation, they feel unable to complain (Leiva and Ross, 2016). However, they are not interested in having an employment contract either, because for fear that their wages will decrease when their pension contributions are deducted.

These migrants prefer live-in work (they spend the night in their employers' home), in order to save as much of their income as possible to send to their families in the Plurinational State of Bolivia. The wages they receive in Chile are twice what they would receive in their country. Despite not having a contract, their pay is similar to that of their Chilean peers, and almost their entire wage goes on remittances. Due to the circular nature of migration, their trajectories are fragmented, and they have to seek work again each time they return to Chile. They receive significant support from *Pastoral Migratoria,* a Catholic Church organization which maintains a job bank and provides guidance on their labour rights (Leiva, Mansilla and Comelin, 2017).

Bibliography

Acosta, E. (2015), *Cuidados en crisis: mujeres migrantes hacia España y Chile*, Bilbao, Universidad de Deusto.

Acosta, D., C. Blouin and L. Freier (2019), *La emigración venezolana: respuestas latinoamericanas*, Fundación Carolina.

Bahar, D. and D. Barrios (2018), "¿Cuántos migrantes y refugiados más podemos esperar de Venezuela?", Brookings [online] https://www. brookings.edu/blog/up-front/2018/12/10/how-many-more-migrants-and-refugees-can-we-expect-out-of-venezuela/.

Bahar, D. M. Dooley and C. Huang (2018), "Integración de los venezolanos en el mercado laboral", Brookings Global Economy & Development, December.

Bakker, I. and S. Gill (eds.) (2003), *Power, Production, and Social Reproduction: Human In/Security in The Global Political Economy*, New York, Palgrave Macmillan.

Burnham, L. and N. Theodore (2012), *Home Economics: The Invisible and Unregulated World of Domestic Work National Domestic Workers Alliance*, New York, National Domestic Workers Alliance.

Canales, A. and M. Rojas (2018), "Panorama de la migración internacional en México y Centroamérica: documento elaborado en el marco de la Reunión Regional Latinoamericana y Caribeña de Expertas y Expertos en Migración Internacional preparatoria del Pacto Mundial para una Migración Segura, Ordenada y Regular", *Population and Development series*, No. 124 (LC/TS.2018/42), Santiago, Economic Commission for Latin America and the Caribbean (ECLAC).

CCP/UCR (Central American Population Centre/University of Costa Rica) (2016), *Encuesta Nacional de Inmigración y Emigración en Costa Rica (ENIE 2016). Informe General (versión preliminar)*, San Jose, International Organization for Migration (IOM).

Dobrée, P., M. González and C. Soto (2015), *Perfil de Paraguay con relación al trabajo doméstico de personas migrantes en Argentina*, Asunción, International Labour Organization/United Nations Entity for Gender Equality and the Empowerment of Women (ILO/UN-Women).

ECLAC (Economic Commission for Latin America and the Caribbean) (2019a), *Planificación para el desarrollo territorial sostenible en América Latina y el Caribe* (LC/CRP.17/3), Santiago.

___(2019b), *Hacia un nuevo estilo de desarrollo. Plan de Desarrollo Integral El Salvador-Guatemala-Honduras-México. Diagnóstico, áreas de oportunidad y recomendaciones de la CEPAL* (LC/MEX/TS.2019/6), Mexico City.

___(2018), *The Caribbean Outlook*, 2018 (LC/SES.37/14/Rev.1), Santiago.

___(2013), *Montevideo Consensus on Population and Development* (LC/L.3697) [online] http://repositorio.cepal.org/bitstream/handle/11362/21860/S20131039_en.pdf?sequence=4&isAllowed=y.

___(2002), *Globalization and Development* (LC/G.2157(SES.29/3)), Santiago.

Ehrenreich, B. and A. Hochschild (eds.) (2003), *Global Woman: Nannies, Maids, and Sex Workers in the New Economy*, New York, Henry Holt and Company.

El Colegio de la Frontera Norte and others (2017), "Encuesta sobre Migración en la Frontera Sur de México" [online] www.colef.mx/emif.

Freitez, A. (2017), "ENCOVI. Encuesta sobre Condiciones de Vida, Venezuela 2017. Emigración", Caracas, Institute of Economic and Social Research of the Catholic Andrés Bello Catholic University (IIES-UCAB).

___(2011), "La emigración desde Venezuela durante la última década", *Temas de Coyuntura*, vol. 63, July [online] http://w2.ucab.edu.ve/tl_files/IIES/recursos/Temas%20de%20Coyuntura%2063/1.La_emigracion_Venezuela_Freitez..pdf.

González-Barrera, A. (2015), "More Mexicans Leaving Than Coming to the US", Washington, D.C., Pew Research Center, 19 November.

Gonzálvez Torralbo, H. (2013), "Los cuidados en el centro de la migración: la organización social de los cuidados transnacionales desde un enfoque de género", *Migraciones. Publicación del Instituto Universitario de Estudios sobre Migraciones*, vol. 33.

Gutiérrez, A. and otros (2019), "Criterios de calidad en la estimación de indicadores sociales usando encuestas de hogares: una aplicación a la medición de la migración internacional", *serie Estudios Estadísticos*, Santiago, Economic Commission for Latin America and the Caribbean (ECLAC), in press.

Hutchinson, E. (2014), *Labores propias de su sexo. Género, políticas y trabajo en Chile urbano, 1900-1930*, Santiago, LOM.

ILO (International Labour Organization) (2016a), *Políticas de formalización del trabajo doméstico remunerado en América Latina y el Caribe*, Lima, ILO Regional Office for Latin America and the Caribbean/Programme for the Promotion of Formalization in Latin America and the Caribbean (FORLAC).

___(2016b), *Estadísticas de migración laboral: mapeo y análisis de 5 países de América Latina y el Caribe*, Brasilia.

INE (National Institute of Statistics) (2018), *Características de la inmigración internacional en Chile, Censo 2017*, November [online] https://www.ine.cl/docs/default-source/demogr%c3%a1ficas-y-vitales/inmigraci%c3%b3n/documento-inmigraci%c3%b3n.pdf?sfvrsn=7a5659d2_4.

INEI (National Institute of Statistics and Informatics) (2019), *Condiciones de vida de la población venezolana que reside en Perú: resultados de la "Encuesta dirigida a la población venezolana que reside en el país" ENPOVE 2018*, Lima.

IOM (Organization for Migration) (2019a), "Caribbean Migration Consultations" [online] https://www.iom.int/caribbean-migration-consultations-cmc.

___(2019b), *Monitoreo de flujo de población venezolana en el Perú DTM ronda 5*, Lima.

___(2018a), "Tendencias migratorias nacionales en América del Sur: República Bolivariana de Venezuela", February [online] http://robuenosaires.iom.int/sites/default/files/Informes/Tendencias_Migratorias_Nacionales_en_America_del_Sur_Venezuela.pdf.

___(2018b), *Migration in Jamaica: A Country Profile 2018*.

___(2018c), "Triángulo Norte: retornos", Iniciativa de Gestión de Información de Movilidad Humana en el Triángulo Norte (NTMI) [online] https://mic.iom.int/webntmi/ triangulo-norte/.

___(2017a), *Migration in The Caribbean: Current Trends, Opportunities and Challenges*.

___(2017b), *Migration Governance in the Caribbean: Report on the islands of the Commonwealth Caribbean*, San Jose.

___(2017c), "Report on the Caribbean migration consultations", *Refugee Protection Hosted by the Government of the Bahamas, Regional Office for Central America, North America and the Caribbean*, San Jose.

Jaramillo, V. (2019), "Acceso a la justicia: trabajadoras domésticas migrantes en la ciudad de Buenos Aires", *Estado & Comunes, Revista de Políticas y Problemas Públicos*, No. 8, vol. 1, Quito, Institute of Higher National Studies (IAEN), January-June.

Jones, F., C. Camarinhas and L. Gény (2019), "Implementation of the Montevideo Consensus on Population and Development in the Caribbean: a review of the period 2013–2018", *Studies and Perspectives series-ECLAC Subregional Headquarters for the Caribbean*, No. 76 (LC/TS.2019/8; LC/CAR/TS.2018/4), Santiago, Economic Commission for Latin America and the Caribbean (ECLAC).

Koechlin, J. and J. Eguren (eds.) (2018), *El éxodo venezolano: entre el exilio y la emigración*, Colección OBIMID, vol. 4.

Kuznesof, E. (1989), "A history of domestic service in Spanish America, 1492-1980", *Muchachas no more: household workers in Latin America and the Caribbean*, Temple University Press.

Leiva, S. and C. Ross (2016), "Migración circular y trabajo de cuidado: fragmentación de trayectorias laborales de migrantes bolivianas en Tarapacá", *Psicoperspectivas*, vol. 15, N° 3, Valparaíso, Pontificia Universidad Católica de Valparaíso (PUCV).

Leiva, S., M. Mansilla and A. Comelin (2017), "Condiciones laborales de migrantes bolivianas que realizan trabajo de cuidado en Iquique", *Si Somos Americanos. Revista de Estudios Fronterizos*.

Magliano, M. J. and A. I. M. Barral (2017), *Las mujeres latinoamericanas y sus migraciones*, Eduvim.

Maldonado Valera, C., J. Martínez Pizarro and R. Martínez (2018), "Protección social y migración: una mirada desde las vulnerabilidades a lo largo del ciclo de la migración y de la vida de las personas", *Project Documents* (LC/TS.2018/62), Santiago.

Martínez Pizarro, J. (ed.) (2008), "América Latina y el Caribe: migración internacional, derechos humanos y desarrollo", *ECLAC Books*, N° 97 (LC/G.2358-P), Santiago, Economic Commission for Latin America and the Caribbean (ECLAC).

___(2011), *Migración internacional en América latina y el Caribe: nuevas tendencias, nuevos enfoques*, Santiago, Economic Commission for Latin America and the Caribbean (ECLAC).

Martínez Pizarro, J. and C. Orrego Rivera (2016), "Nuevas tendencias y dinámicas migratorias en América Latina y el Caribe", *Population and Development series*, No. 114 (LC/L.4164), Santiago, Economic Commission for Latin America and the Caribbean (ECLAC).

Martínez J., V. Cano and M. S. Contrucci (2014), "Tendencias y patrones de la migración latinoamericana y caribeña hacia 2010 y desafíos para una agenda regional", *Population and Development series*, No. 109 (LC/L.3914), Santiago, Economic Commission for Latin America and the Caribbean (ECLAC).

Martínez Pizarro, J., L. Reboiras and M. Soffia (2009), "Los derechos concedidos: crisis económica mundial y migración internacional", *Population and Development series*, No. 89 (LC/L.3164-P), Santiago, Economic Commission for Latin America and the Caribbean (ECLAC).

Mazuera-Arias, R. and others (2019), *Venezuelan Human Mobility Report II: Realities and Perspectives of those who Emigrate*, San Cristobal, Jesuit Refugee Service (JRS) Venezuela/ FundaciónCentro Gumilla/UCAT.

Mejía, W. (2018), "Panorama de la migración internacional en el Caribe: documento elaborado en el marco de la Reunión Regional Latinoamericana y Caribeña de Expertas y Expertos en Migración Internacional preparatoria del Pacto Mundial para una Migración Segura, Ordenada y Regular", *Population and Development series*, No. 122 (LC/TS.2018/28), Santiago, Economic Commission for Latin America and the Caribbean (ECLAC).

Messina, G. (2015), "Inserción de las trabajadoras domésticas paraguayas a partir de las reformas laborales y migratorias en Argentina", *serie Documentos de Trabajo*, No. 10, Buenos Aires, International Labour Organization (ILO).

OAS (Organization of American States) (2019), *OAS Working Group to Address the Regional Crisis Caused by Venezuela's Migrant and Refugee Flows* (OEA/Ser.D/XV.21), June.

OECD (Organization for Economic Cooperation and Development) (2016), *International Migration Outlook 2016*, Paris, OECD Publishing.

Orozco, M. and J. Yansura (2015), *Centroamérica en la mira: la migración en su relación con el desarrollo y las oportunidades para el cambio*, Buenos Aires, Teseo.

Parreñas, R. S. (2001), "Women, migration and domestic work", *Región y Sociedad*, vol. 15.

Passel, J. S. and D. Cohn (2016), "Overall number of U.S. unauthorized immigrants holds steady since 2009", Washington, D.C., Pew Research Center [online] http://www.pewhispanic. org/2016/09/20/overall-number-of-u-s-unauthorized-immigrants-holds-steady-since-2009/.

Rodríguez Chávez, E. (2016), "Migración centroamericana en tránsito irregular por México: nuevas cifras y tendencias", *CANAMID Policy Brief Series*, PB14, Guadalajara, CIESAS.

___(2010), "La inmigración en México a inicios del siglo XXI", *Extranjeros en México. Continuidades y aproximaciones*, Mexico City, DGE Ediciones.

Rosas, C. (2010), "Jóvenes migrantes: sueños y desilusiones entre Perú y Argentina", *Arzate Salgado y Trejo Sánchez (coords.): desigualdades sociales y ciudadanía desde las culturas juveniles en América Latina*, Ed Porrúa/Autonomous University of the State of Mexico.

R4V (Coordination Plataform for Refugees and Migrants from Venezuela) (2019), "Response for Venezuelans. Latin America and the Caribbean Venezuelan Refugees & Migrants in the region" [online] https://data2.unhcr.org/en/documents/download/69837.

State of Oregon Employment Department (2019), "Private Households: Employing the Nation's Invisible Workforce" [online] https://www.qualityinfo.org/-/private-households-employing-the-nation-s-invisible-workforce.

Soto, C. and others (2016), *Panorama regional sobre trabajadoras domésticas migrantes en América Latina*, Asunción, International Labour Organization/United Nations Entity for Gender Equality and the Empowerment of Women (ILO/UN-Women).

Stefoni, C. (2002), "Mujeres inmigrantes peruanas en Chile", *Papeles de Población*, vol. 8, No. 33, Mexico City, Autonomous University of the State of Mexico.

Thomas-Hope, E. (2002), "Skilled labour migration from developing countries: study on the Caribbean Region", *International migration papers*, vol. 50, Geneva, International Labour Organization (ILO).

United Nations (2019), "International migrant stock 2019" [online] https://www.un.org/en/development/desa/population/migration/data/estimates2/estimates19.asp.

___(2017a), "Workbook" [online] UN_MigrantStockByOriginAndDestination_2017.

___(2017b), "World Population Prospects: The 2017 Revision" [online] https://esa.un.org/unpd/wpp/.

___(2015), "World Population Policies Database" [online database] https://esa.un.org/PopPolicy/wpp_datasets.aspx.

UNODC (United Nations Office on Drugs and Crime) (2011), *Toolkit to Combat Smuggling of Migrants*, New York.

World Bank (2018), *Migración desde Venezuela a Colombia: impactos y estrategia de respuesta en el corto y mediano plazo*, Washington, D. C.

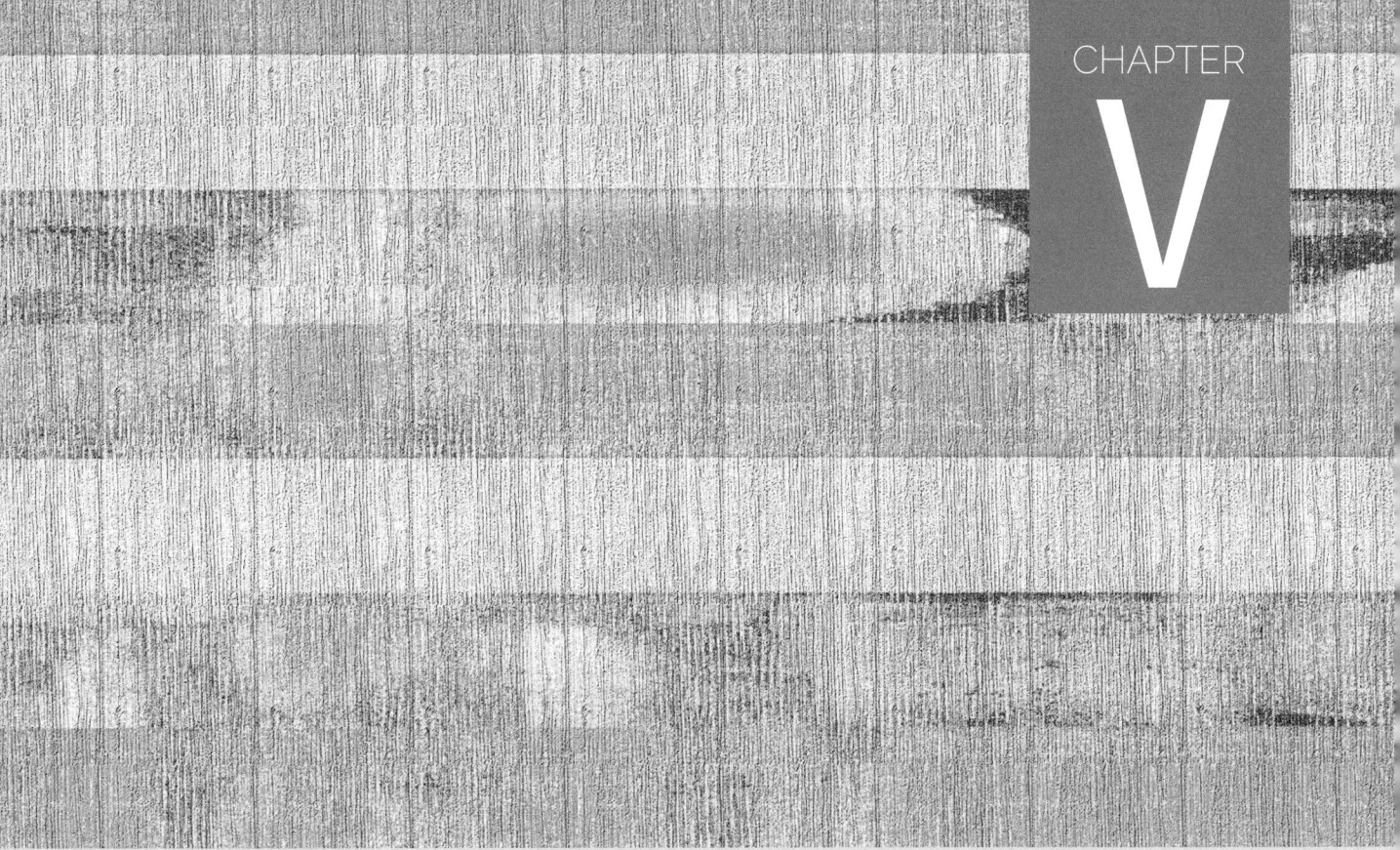

Migration and social and labour inclusion for equality

A. The complex relationship between migration, poverty and international remittance flows

B. Migration and social and labour inclusion

C. Racism, discrimination and migration

D. The institutional framework for migrants in the region

E. Migration cycle and challenges for inclusion and social protection: some priority policy areas

F. Concluding remarks

Bibliography

Annex V.A1

A. The complex relationship between migration, poverty and international remittance flows

The relationship between poverty and migration differs among the different destination countries where it can be examined. The region's nine countries where the significant statistical data are available are distributed equally among those where international migrants report lower poverty rates than people born in the country, those where they report higher poverty rates and, finally, those where are no significant differences. However, controlling for a series of sociodemographic factors (age, sex, education, employment, area of residence, household structure and others), in five countries migrants report higher poverty rates than their native-born counterparts. Similarly, there are a large number of Latin America and Caribbean countries that receive significant remittance flows from other countries, sent back by emigrants to their families. Those flows are distributed across all sectors of society and represent a form of protection against poverty in the beneficiary households, particularly in those countries where incoming remittances account for a large share of GDP.

As explained in the previous chapter, migration is a phenomenon of growing complexity that involves economic, political and social factors and, increasingly, personal and family security concerns. This section examines the relationship between migration, international remittances and poverty. The first part analyses the relationship between migration and poverty in the countries of Latin America, while the second part showcases the role that migrant remittances play in alleviating family poverty and, as is the case of some Central American and Caribbean countries, their increasing participation in the economy as a whole.

1. Poverty and immigration: unequal relationships from one country to the next

An analysis of the relationship between poverty and migration in destination countries based on household survey data indicates, first of all, the existence of different situations. A comparison of poverty rates among immigrants[1] and among people born in the country,[2] for the nine countries where the information is statistically representative, reveals three situations (see table V.1):

- Countries in which poverty does not differ significantly between migrants and non-migrants: Argentina, Ecuador and the Dominican Republic.

- Countries where poverty is higher among migrants: Chile, Colombia and Costa Rica.

- Countries where poverty is lower among migrants: Brazil, Guatemala and Panama.

---

[1] Household surveys define an immigrant as a person resident in the country who was born in a different country.

[2] Of the 15 countries for which information is available, in nine the poverty rate among migrants reaches the minimum level of precision set for the analysis: a set of limit values established on the coefficient of variation (lower than 20%), sample size (greater than 100), effective sample size (greater than 50) and the degrees of freedom of the estimate (greater than 10). With respect to the relationship between recent migration (over the past five years) and poverty, the usefulness of the surveys is even lower. Thus, of the 11 surveys in which this variable can be calculated, in only two is the estimate of the proportion of poverty among migrants significant: Chile and Colombia. In the remaining countries it does not reach the levels of quality needed to draw inferences about this segment of the population, and so its use for analytical purposes is not advised.

Table V.1
Latin America
(9 countries): poor
persons, by country
and migrant status, most
recent year available
(specific estimate, lower
and upper limits of the
confidence interval)
(Proportions of the poor)

Country	Year	Migrants			Non-migrants		
		Proportion of poor	Lower limit	Upper limit	Proportion of poor	Lower limit	Upper limit
Argentina	2017	0.20	0.15	0.25	0.19	0.18	0.20
Brazil	2015	0.08	0.06	0.10	0.19	0.18	0.19
Chile	2017	0.13	0.11	0.16	0.11	0.10	0.11
Colombia	2017	0.40	0.37	0.43	0.30	0.29	0.30
Costa Rica	2017	0.20	0.16	0.24	0.15	0.14	0.16
Dominican Republic	2016	0.33	0.27	0.40	0.27	0.25	0.29
Ecuador	2017	0.20	0.14	0.25	0.23	0.22	0.24
Guatemala	2014	0.21	0.15	0.27	0.52	0.50	0.53
Panama	2017	0.08	0.05	0.11	0.17	0.16	0.18

Source: Economic Commission for Latin America and the Caribbean (ECLAC), on the basis of Household Survey Data Bank (BADEHOG).

In light of the countries' differing results for poverty rates among immigrants and non-immigrants, one useful exercise is to analyse more closely the sociodemographic characteristics associated with poverty. This allows the relationship between migrant status and poverty to be established, once a series of sociodemographic factors —such as age, sex, schooling, nature of employment, area of residence, household characteristics and a set of basic shortcomings associated with housing and employment— have been controlled for.

Table V.2 shows the results of a probit regression model for poverty, which includes those socioeconomic variables and the subjects' migrant status among the explanatory factors. The estimated marginal effect corresponds to the probability of a migrant person being in conditions of poverty compared to the poverty probability of a non-migrant in the same socioeconomic situation. A positive effect indicates a higher level of poverty among migrants, with the value of the effect being the difference between the two proportions.[3]

Table V.2
Latin America (9 countries): estimated marginal effort of migrant status on poverty
(Proportion of poor as a function of migrant status)

Country	Marginal effect	Standard error	z	P>z	Lower confidence limit	Upper confidence limit
Argentina (2017)	0.013	0.009	1.460	0.145	-0.004	0.030
Brazil (2015)	-0.034	0.012	-2.870	0.004	-0.058	-0.011
Chile (2017)	0.059	0.005	12.440	0.000	0.050	0.068
Colombia (2017)	0.048	0.004	11.200	0.000	0.040	0.057
Costa Rica (2017)	0.046	0.007	6.480	0.000	0.032	0.059
Dominican Republic (2016)	0.059	0.016	3.730	0.000	0.028	0.090
Ecuador (2017)	0.039	0.010	3.920	0.000	0.020	0.059
Guatemala (2014)	-0.081	0.013	-6.100	0.000	-0.107	-0.055
Panama (2017)	0.004	0.011	0.350	0.728	-0.018	0.026

Source: Economic Commission for Latin America and the Caribbean (ECLAC), on the basis of Household Survey Data Bank (BADEHOG).
Note: Estimated by means of a probit model that adjusts the probability of being poor according to a series of determining factors, including migrant status, age, sex, education, employment conditions, area of residence, age and sex of the head of the household, type of household and a series of shortcomings related to basic services and housing structures, employment status and social protection within the household.

---

[3]   The quality indicators of the probability adjustment model are summarized on table V.A.1 in the annex, which shows that the proposed model offers a good power of prediction in most of the countries, judging by the percentage of cases that are classified correctly. In some countries the model performs better because it predicts those people not in poverty, which is reflected in the specificity parameter. The model correctly identifies a higher percentage of poor people (sensitivity) in countries with higher poverty rates, while its predictive power is lower in countries such as Chile and Uruguay.

Using the information from the nine countries analysed, it can be seen that five report a higher incidence of poverty among migrants once the set of associated factors have been controlled for. Those five include Chile, with a poverty rate that is 5.9 percentage points higher among migrants; Colombia, 4.8 percentage points higher; Costa Rica, 4.6; Ecuador, 3.9; and the Dominican Republic, 5.9. Note that when the other variables were controlled for, the estimated effects for Ecuador and the Dominican Republic went from neutral (as indicated by table V.1) to positive.

In two countries, migrant status entails a lower incidence of poverty. Those countries are Brazil, where the incidence of poverty among migrants is 3.4 percentage points lower than among non-migrants, and Guatemala, where it is 8.1 percentage points lower. Finally, Argentina and Panama report no significant differences in the incidence of poverty between migrants and non-migrants.[4]

2. International remittance flows and their impact on poverty in the countries of Latin America

This section analyses the contribution made by international remittances to household well-being in the region's countries. Those funds are generally included as part of households' non-labour income, although in most cases they are earned through the paid work of emigrants in their destination countries. This analysis pays particular attention to the contribution those transfers make to household incomes and poverty reduction. The analysis is based on two different sources of information: The first basically comprises statistics on national accounts and balances of payments, and allows remittance levels and trends —both incoming and outgoing— to be examine for a specific country over a lengthy period. The second source is household surveys which, while they use a more restricted definition of international remittances, allow correlations to be established with household well-being and conditions of poverty.

(a) International remittance flows in the countries of Latin America

The previous chapter examined in depth some of the main issues in international economics that indicate the importance of analysing migratory flows in general and the contribution of international remittances to household well-being in the region's countries in particular.[5] The growing checks and regulations imposed by some States, along with their mass deportation policies and the closing of their borders, could ultimately hamper the conditions under which international remittances currently flow, which could in turn impact household incomes and lead many families down a swift descent into poverty.

Of the countries examined, this situation could be particularly dramatic in Mexico, the Dominican Republic and the countries of Central America. In 2018, those countries received international remittances in an amount equal, on average, to 9.7 points of GDP, with highs of over 20 points of GDP in Honduras and El Salvador and around 12 points in Guatemala and Nicaragua (see table V.3). Observing the evolution over time of the weight of international remittances in the domestic economies of those four countries reveals that between 1990 and 2018, remittance flows grew by between two- and sixteen-fold. That result highlights not only the countries' vulnerability to fluctuations in that source of income, but also the loss of their working-age populations that they have suffered, with the inevitable short-, medium- and long-term impact on the economic system and the social fabric. The Economic Commission for Latin America

---

[4]   In the remaining countries the poverty estimates for the migrant subsector of the population are not significant.

[5]   The importance of remittances to developing countries was acknowledged in the 2030 Agenda for Sustainable Development, in which the signatory countries undertook to reduce remittance transaction costs to less than 3% and eliminate remittance corridors with costs in excess of 5% by 2030 (target 10.7 of the Sustainable Development Goals).

and the Caribbean (ECLAC) has called this phenomenon the dependence of economies and households on remittances.

In contrast, dependence on international remittances is much lower in South America: on average, remittance flows account for less than 1.5 points of GDP, with results of 3.45 points in the Plurinational State of Bolivia, 2.8 points in Ecuador and between 1 and 2 points in Colombia, Paraguay and Peru. In most of these countries, remittance flows have remained stable over time, although Ecuador and the Plurinational State of Bolivia did report decreases between the start of the century and 2018.

Table V.3
Latin America
(18 countries): workers'
remittances and
employees' earnings
received, 1990–2018[a]
(Percentages of GDP)

Country	1990	2000	2010	2015	2018
South America					
Argentina	0.02	0.03	0.15	0.08	0.10
Bolivia (Plurinational State of)	0.09	1.51	4.89	3.61	3.45
Brazil	0.12	0.21	0.14	0.16	0.16
Chile	0.00	0.02	0.03	0.02	0.02
Colombia	1.03	1.61	1.41	1.59	1.93
Ecuador	0.33	7.21	3.74	2.40	2.80
Peru	0.33	1.39	1.72	1.44	1.46
Paraguay	0.58	1.71	1.51	1.53	1.67
Uruguay	...	...	0.31	0.16	0.17
Venezuela (Bolivarian Republic of)	0.00	0.01	0.04	...	...
Average	0.31	1.71	1.53	1.36	1.46
Minimum	0.36	1.52	1.39	1.22	1.31
Maximum	1.03	7.21	4.89	3.61	3.45
Mexico and Central America					
Costa Rica	0.21	0.91	1.42	1.01	0.89
Dominican Republic	4.45	7.57	7.20	7.55	8.38
El Salvador	7.60	14.97	18.82	18.24	20.68
Guatemala	1.55	3.09	10.24	10.31	12.10
Honduras	1.28	6.68	16.64	17.61	20.07
Mexico	1.19	1.06	2.09	2.24	2.91
Nicaragua	...	6.27	9.42	9.39	11.47
Panama	1.71	0.13	1.39	1.02	0.83
Average	2.57	5.09	8.40	8.42	9.67
Minimum	0.21	0.13	1.39	1.01	0.83
Maximum	7.60	14.97	18.82	18.24	20.68

Source: Economic Commission for Latin America and the Caribbean (ECLAC), on the basis of World Bank, Data Bank [online] https://databank.worldbank.org.
[a] Calculated from the total remittances sent by workers abroad, employees' earnings and transfers from emigrants received by the country. Employees' earnings means the income of borderland, seasonal and other short-term workers employed in an economy where they are not residents and that of residents employed by non-resident entities. Calculations based on countries' balance of payments data from the International Monetary Fund (IMF) and on information provided by central banks and the national statistics offices. For some countries, the years given are approximate.

International remittances can also be analysed by breaking them down into remittances received in the country from abroad and remittances sent abroad by residents in the country. That approach reveals patterns in their evolution depending on whether the countries in question are net receivers or remitters of transfers at any given time. In the latter case, the available information is somewhat more limited, primarily on account of the difficulties in calculating outgoing remittances.

In South America, one group of countries were net recipients over the entire 1990–2017 period: Brazil, Colombia, Ecuador, Peru and Uruguay. The Plurinational State of Bolivia has been a net recipient since 1995, after being a net sender prior to that year. Argentina, in contrast, has swapped between the two: it has primarily been a net sender, although the difference between the two flows has been minimal, particularly since 2000. That situation can be explained by the fact that Argentina was traditionally a destination for emigrants from its neighbouring countries (primarily the Plurinational State of Bolivia, Paraguay and Uruguay) and from Peru. The Bolivarian Republic of Venezuela went from being a net sender to a net recipient of remittances, most markedly after 2014 because of the factors already identified that gave rise to the mass emigration of Venezuelans. Finally, Chile is the only country in the subregion that remained a net sender, probably as a result of the economic growth it has experienced in recent decades, which has made it a final destination for emigrants first from Peru, then from Colombia and Haiti and, more recently, from Venezuela (see figure V.1).

Meanwhile, the Central American countries for which information is available are clearly remittance recipients. That holds true in El Salvador, Guatemala and Honduras. Mexico has also followed a similar pattern, although information is only available about its outgoing remittances for the most recent years. Panama, which was a net recipient of remittances before 2000, after which both flows stabilized at similar levels, is the sole exception in this group of countries (see figure V.2).

Figure V.1
South America (9 countries): workers' remittances and employees' earnings, incoming and outgoing, 1990–2017[a] [b]
(Millions of dollars per year, logarithmic scale)

Remittances sent —— Remittances received ——

Figure V.1 (concluded)

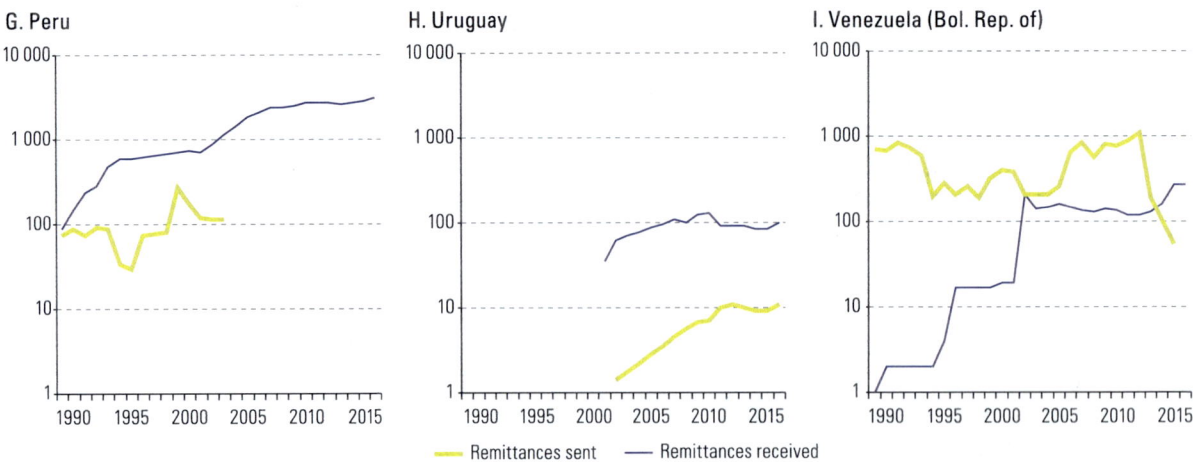

Source: Economic Commission for Latin America and the Caribbean (ECLAC), on the basis of World Bank, Data Bank [online] https://databank.worldbank.org.
[a] Calculated from the total remittances sent by workers abroad, employees' earnings and transfers from emigrants received by the country. Employees' earnings means the income of borderland, seasonal and other short-term workers employed in an economy where they are not residents and that of residents employed by non-resident entities. Calculations based on countries' balance of payments data from the International Monetary Fund (IMF) and on information provided by central banks and the national statistics offices.
[b] A logarithmic scale has been used because of the differences in remittance volumes between the countries.

Figure V.2
Mexico and Central America (5 countries): workers' remittances and employees' earnings, incoming and outgoing, 1990–2017[a][b]
(Millions of dollars per year, logarithmic scale)

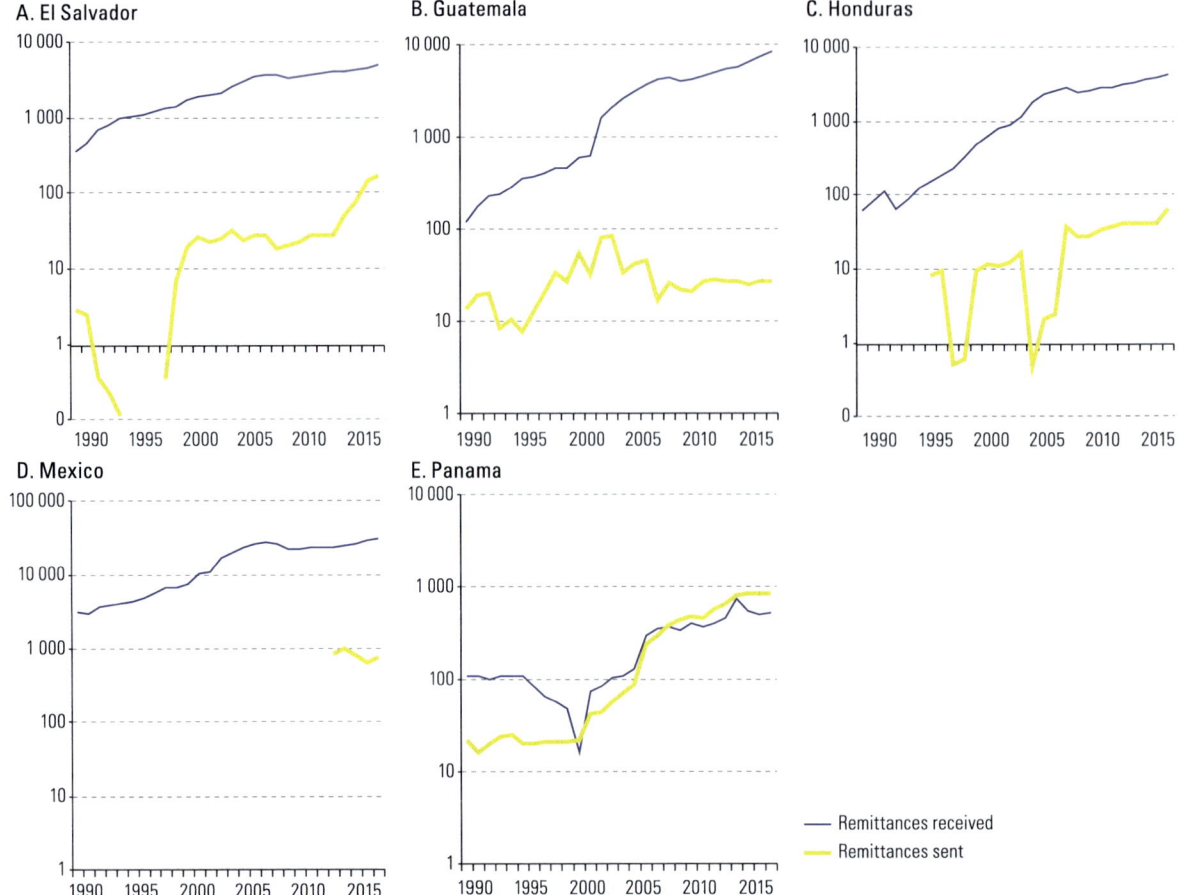

Source: Economic Commission for Latin America and the Caribbean (ECLAC), on the basis of World Bank, Data Bank [online] https://databank.worldbank.org.
[a] Calculated from the total remittances sent by workers abroad, employees' earnings and transfers from emigrants received by the country. Employees' earnings means the income of borderland, seasonal and other short-term workers employed in an economy where they are not residents and that of residents employed by non-resident entities. Calculations based on countries' balance of payments data from the International Monetary Fund (IMF) and on information provided by central banks and the national statistics offices.
[b] A logarithmic scale has been used because of the differences in remittance volumes between the countries.

(b) International remittance flows in the countries of the Caribbean

In the Caribbean, the remittances situation is similar to that seen in Latin America, with some countries where remittances account for a high proportion of GDP and where many households are critically dependent on them. In this subregion, remittances have on average remained stable at around 6 points of GDP over the past decade, about 2 points higher than in the 1990s and 2000s. Haiti and Jamaica are the countries where remittances account for the largest shares of GDP: almost 31% in the former, and close to 16% in the latter. Those shares have both increased over time: in Haiti the figure doubled between 2000 and 2018 to reach almost a third of total GDP, whereas between 1990 and 2018 Jamaica's incoming remittances tripled (see table V.4). In the remaining countries, remittances account for high shares of GDP in Dominica (9.22 points), Guyana (7.9), Curaçao (5.1), Saint Vincent and the Grenadines (5.1), Belize (4.81) and Grenada (4.0).

As seen in Latin America, different profiles for incoming and outgoing remittances are found among the countries of the Caribbean. Three of the countries for which information is available (Aruba, Sint Maarten and Suriname) have been and remain net remittance senders, the first two on a permanent basis and the third alternating at different times between being a sender and a recipient. With respect to the first two, this could be on account of the high numbers of immigrants in their population: in 2015 immigrants accounted for more than a third of the total population of Aruba and more than 70% of Sint Maarten's.

Guyana reported a shift in the early 2000s, when it changed from being a sender to become a net recipient. The region's remaining countries are net recipients of remittances, on account of the high numbers of individuals born in those countries who decide to emigrate. That group includes Antigua and Barbuda, whose emigrants represented 40% of the population in 2015; Barbados (28%), Dominica (51%), Jamaica (28%), and Saint Kitts and Nevis (44%), as the countries with the highest proportions of emigrants as a share of the local population (see figure V.3).

Table V.4
The Caribbean (16 countries): workers' remittances and employees' earnings received, 1990–2018[a]
(Percentages of GDP)

Country	1990	2000	2010	2015	2018
Aruba	...	0.06	0.21	0.30	0.28[b]
Antigua and Barbuda	2.73	2.09	1.75	2.30	2.16
Belize	4.48	2.99	5.59	4.81	4.81
Barbados	1.87	3.63	1.81	2.36	2.32[b]
Curaçao	...	...	...	4.52	5.14[b]
Dominica	6.91	4.06	4.64	10.34	9.22
Grenada	6.46	4.66	3.69	4.34	4.00
Guyana	...	3.83	16.18	9.47	7.91
Haiti	...	14.62	22.25	25.17	30.92
Jamaica	4.98	9.77	15.35	16.69	15.92
Saint Kitts and Nevis	8.88	5.60	6.13	2.16	2.19
Saint Lucia	3.11	2.86	2.07	2.29	1.71
Saint Vincent and the Grenadines	6.50	4.87	4.27	5.52	5.12
Suriname	0.13	0.13	0.10	0.14	0.02
Trinidad and Tobago	0.07	0.47	0.41	0.62	0.61
Turks and Caicos Islands	· ...	...	...	0.68	0.73
Average	4.19	4.26	6.03	5.73	5.82
Minimum	0.07	0.06	0.10	0.14	0.02
Maximum	8.88	14.62	22.25	25.17	30.92

Source: Economic Commission for Latin America and the Caribbean (ECLAC), on the basis of World Bank, Data Bank [online] https://databank.worldbank.org.
[a] Calculated from the total remittances sent by workers abroad, employees' earnings and transfers from emigrants received by the country. Employees' earnings means the income of borderland, seasonal and other short-term workers employed in an economy where they are not residents and that of residents employed by non-resident entities. Calculations based on countries' balance of payments data from the International Monetary Fund (IMF) and on information provided by central banks and the national statistics offices. For some countries, the years given are approximate.
[b] 2017 figure.

Figure V.3
The Caribbean (15 countries): workers' remittances and employees' earnings, incoming and outgoing, 1990–2017[a] [b]
(Millions of dollars per year, logarithmic scale)

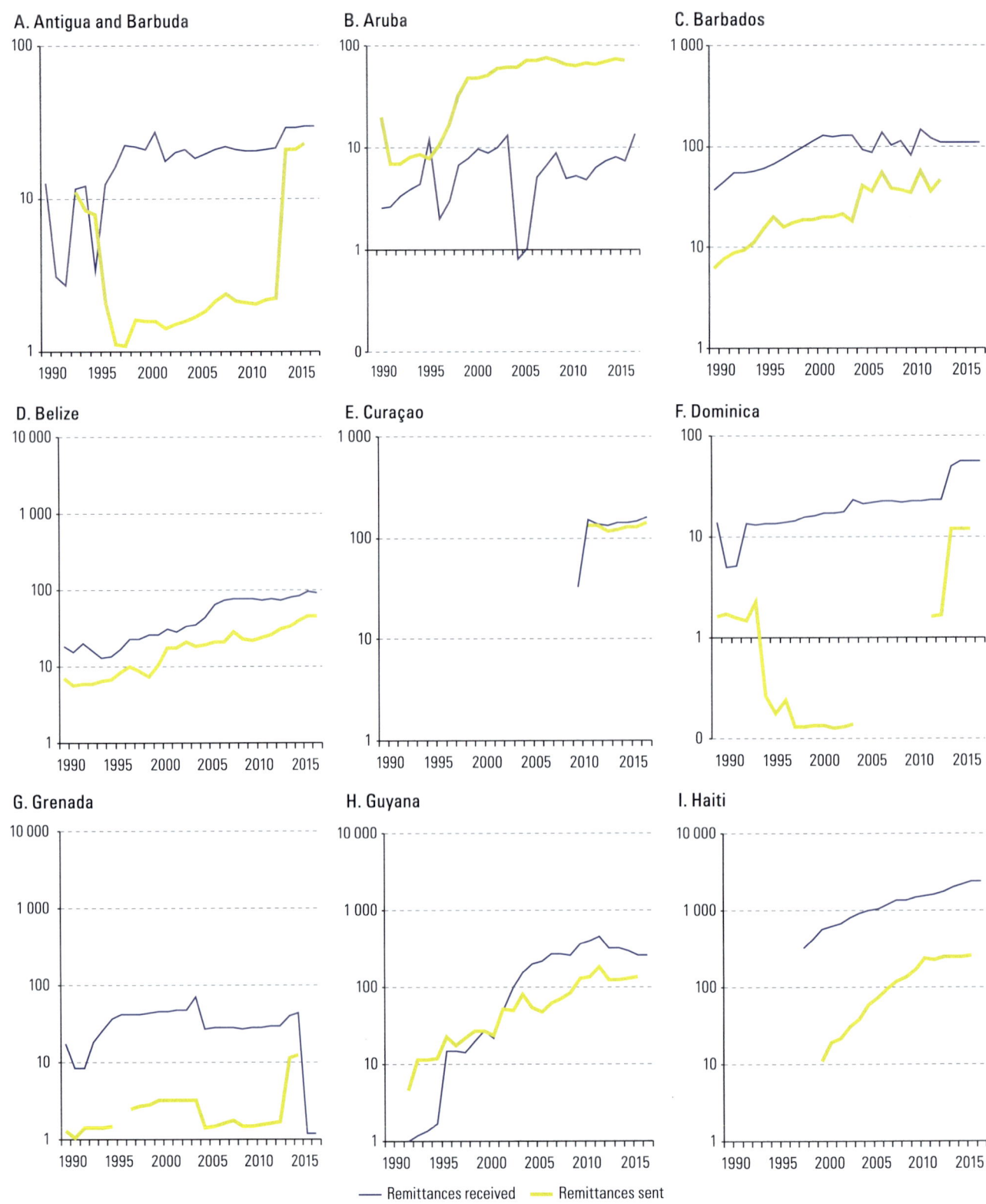

Figure V.3 (concluded)

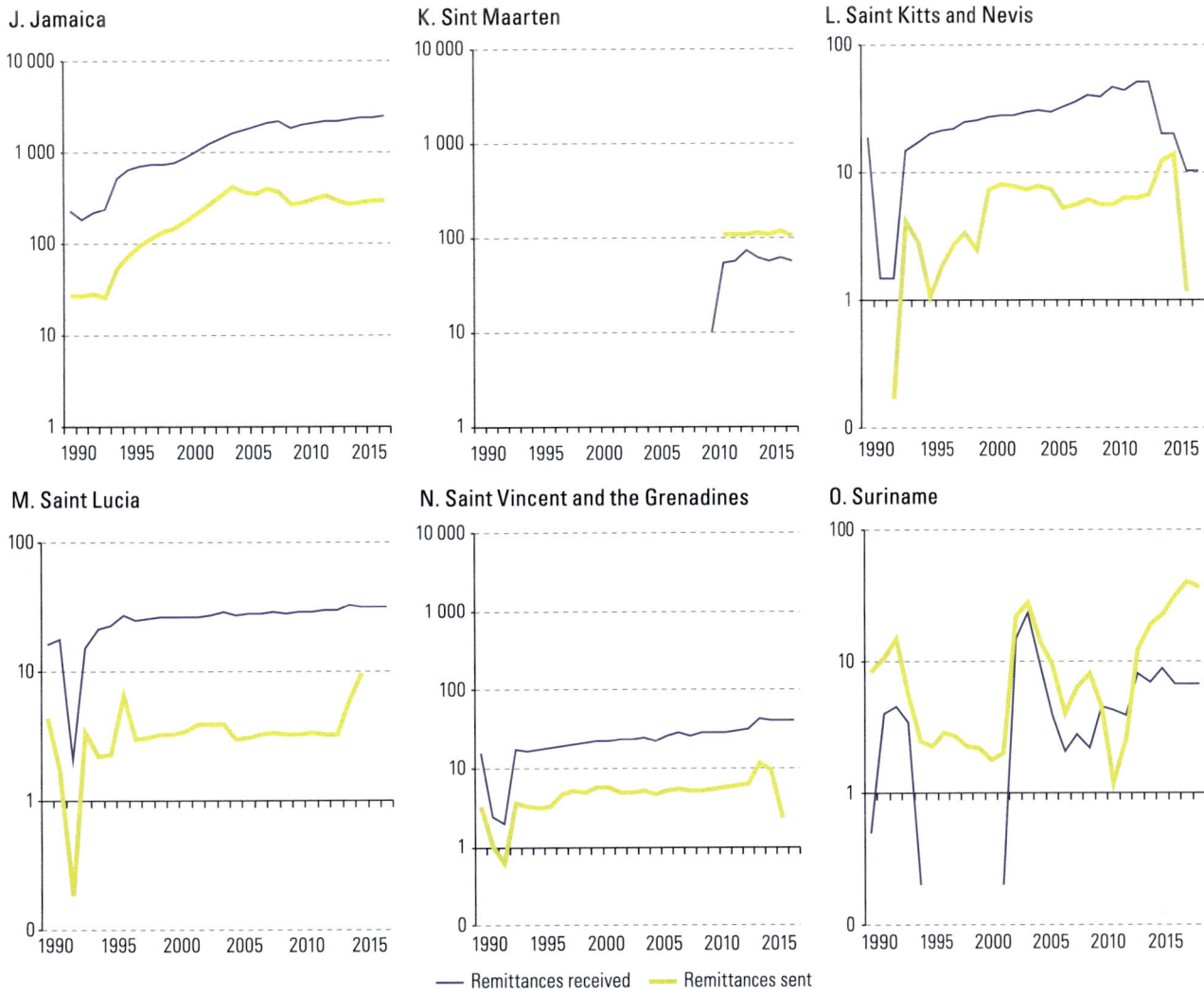

J. Jamaica

K. Sint Maarten

L. Saint Kitts and Nevis

M. Saint Lucia

N. Saint Vincent and the Grenadines

O. Suriname

— Remittances received   — Remittances sent

Source: Economic Commission for Latin America and the Caribbean (ECLAC), on the basis of World Bank, Data Bank [online] https://databank.worldbank.org.
[a] Calculated from the total remittances sent by workers abroad, employees' earnings and transfers from emigrants received by the country. Employees' earnings means the income of borderland, seasonal and other short-term workers employed in an economy where they are not residents and that of residents employed by non-resident entities. Calculations based on countries' balance of payments data from the International Monetary Fund (IMF) and on information provided by central banks and the national statistics offices.
[b] A logarithmic scale has been used because of the differences in remittance volumes between the countries.

(c) The importance of remittances in alleviating household poverty in Latin America

The limitations inherent to those instruments notwithstanding, household survey data allow an analysis of the extent to which income from overseas remittances helps improve the economic situation of the recipient households.[6]

According to the available information, the proportion of households reporting incoming remittances exceeds 15% in El Salvador and Honduras. The rate is close to 9% in Guatemala and the Dominican Republic, slightly above 6% in the Plurinational State of Bolivia and close to 5% in Mexico (see table V.5). In turn, the share of the population's total income for which remittances account reaches its maximum levels in Honduras (5.2%), El Salvador (4.9%) and the Dominican Republic (4.8%) (see table V.6).

Households that receive remittances are distributed across the five per capita income quintiles. In 7 of the 13 countries examined, the presence of households receiving remittances tends to be higher in the middle- and high-income groups. In Honduras, for example, the maximum share is found in the fourth quintile, where remittances accounted for 6% of total income in 2016.

The contributions that remittances make to poverty reduction can be analysed from two perspectives: first, with respect to the national population as a whole, and, second, with a focus on the subgroup of households that actually receive remittances from abroad. The information on table V.7 shows that, with respect to the first of those approaches, the aggregate contribution made by remittances to poverty reduction totalled two percentage points in El Salvador, Honduras and the Dominican Republic.

Table V.5
Latin America (13 countries): households receiving income from remittances, by per capita income quintiles, around 2017[a]
(Percentages)

	Quintile					Total
	I	II	III	IV	V	
Bolivia (Plurinational State of) (2017)	3.9	5.1	6.3	8.0	8.0	6.3
Chile (2017)	0.9	1.2	0.7	0.8	0.7	0.9
Colombia (2017)	1.2	1.6	2.1	2.1	2.5	1.9
Costa Rica (2017)	0.3	0.6	0.8	1.3	1.2	0.9
Dominican Republic (2017)	11.5	10.2	10.4	10.4	5.2	9.5
Ecuador (2017)	2.0	2.8	3.3	3.7	3.8	3.1
El Salvador (2017)	20.7	20.5	18.5	19.2	12.2	18.2
Guatemala (2014)	5.8	8.1	9.5	11.2	9.8	8.9
Honduras (2016)	9.1	16.1	16.9	22.3	24.9	17.8
Mexico (2016)	5.3	5.9	5.5	4.4	2.7	4.8
Paraguay (2017)	8.9	7.7	8.5	7.5	5.9	7.7
Peru (2017)	0.2	0.7	1.4	2.1	3.4	1.6
Uruguay (2017)	0.6	0.9	0.8	1.0	0.6	0.8

Source: Economic Commission for Latin America and the Caribbean (ECLAC), on the basis of Household Survey Data Bank (BADEHOG).
[a] Income from foreign-based pensions or retirement payments is not included in remittance income.

[6]   Note that the concept of overseas remittances includes not only funds transferred by workers abroad to the residents of a given economy, but also earnings paid for the work of individuals who are resident in one economy but who work, on a temporary basis, in another. Household survey data do not include the employees' earnings component, because it cannot be clearly distinguished. In addition, and in the interests of comparability, only remittances in cash are included.

Table V.6
Latin America (13 countries): share of remittances in income, by quintiles of per capita income, around 2017[a]
(Percentages)

	Quintile					Total
	I	II	III	IV	V	
Bolivia (Plurinational State of) (2017)	0.8	1.2	1.3	1.9	2.2	1.5
Chile (2017)	0.3	0.3	0.2	0.2	0.2	0.3
Colombia (2017)	0.3	0.3	0.4	0.4	0.4	0.4
Costa Rica (2017)	0.1	0.1	0.3	0.3	0.3	0.2
Dominican Republic (2017)	6.0	5.0	5.3	5.1	2.4	4.8
Ecuador (2017)	0.7	0.9	0.8	1.1	1.1	0.9
El Salvador (2017)	8.0	5.5	4.3	4.1	2.8	4.9
Guatemala (2014)	2.4	3.3	3.3	3.0	2.4	2.9
Honduras (2016)	3.6	5.6	5.7	6.0	5.2	5.2
Mexico (2016)	1.2	1.6	1.4	1.0	0.6	1.1
Paraguay (2017)	1.5	1.0	1.4	1.2	1.3	1.3
Peru (2017)	0.0	0.2	0.2	0.4	0.7	0.3
Uruguay (2017)	0.2	0.2	0.1	0.2	0.1	0.2

Source: Economic Commission for Latin America and the Caribbean (ECLAC), on the basis of Household Survey Data Bank (BADEHOG).
[a] Income from foreign-based pensions or retirement payments is not included in remittance income.

Table V.7
Latin America (13 countries): poverty rate with and without remittances, for the total population and for households receiving remittances, national totals, around 2017
(Percentages)

	Poverty rate for the total population			Poverty rate for households receiving remittances		
	Total	Without remittances	Difference	Total	Without remittances	Difference
Bolivia (Plurinational State of) (2017)	35.1	35.9	0.8	27.3	39.9	12.5
Chile (2017)	10.7	10.8	0.1	15.5	24.8	9.4
Colombia (2017)	29.8	30.0	0.2	21.1	31.2	10.1
Costa Rica (2017)	15.1	15.2	0.1	8.8	19.6	10.8
Dominican Republic (2017)	25.0	27.2	2.2	33.3	60.8	27.6
Ecuador (2017)	23.6	24.1	0.5	12.7	29.9	17.2
El Salvador (2017)	37.8	39.9	2.1	41.5	54.1	12.6
Guatemala (2014)	50.5	52.0	1.5	39.5	57.2	17.7
Honduras (2016)	53.1	55.5	2.4	39.5	53.3	13.8
Mexico (2016)	43.7	44.4	0.7	46.2	61.7	15.5
Paraguay (2017)	21.5	22.1	0.6	26.1	33.5	7.4
Peru (2017)	18.9	18.9	0.1	4.1	8.2	4.1
Uruguay (2017)	2.7	2.7	0.1	3.3	15.7	12.4

Source: Economic Commission for Latin America and the Caribbean (ECLAC), on the basis of Household Survey Data Bank (BADEHOG).

The biggest impact on poverty in the recipient households is found in the Dominican Republic, where the poverty rate within that group would almost double without incoming remittances, to reach 61%. A slightly lower effect can be seen in Guatemala and Ecuador, where the poverty rate among the same group would increase by 17 points. The remaining countries would also see major increases in poverty among recipient households, with the percentage of people considered poor rising by between 5 and 20 percentage points. Although remittances help improve the lot of the recipient households, the estimates indicate that they do not contribute to any substantial reductions in poverty in the general population. These results are similar to those of earlier studies conducted in the region (see, for example, Acosta, Fajnzylber and López, 2007) and they can be explained in part by the fact that a significant proportion of remittances go to the richest quintiles of the income distribution.

Nevertheless, these figures do not allow firm conclusions to be drawn about the impact of international remittances on poverty reduction. A rigorous assessment of the impact of remittances requires the development of strategies to control for a series of factors that affect the estimates of remittances' impact on well-being. Progress must be made with improving how remittances are quantified, in light of their importance for the economies of many of the region's countries and also because of the political relevance they have acquired in recent years. There are indications that household surveys have a limited ability to detect these revenue flows, and so an approach combining information from those surveys and other records (national accounts or other data sources) could offer better estimates of the contribution of remittances to household well-being (Brown and others, 2014).

B.   Migration and social and labour inclusion

Migrants report different levels of social and labour inclusion compared to the local population (born in the country), as measured in terms of their access to social services and employment, both of which are central elements for the well-being of people and their families.[7] The results of the analysis of selected countries' household surveys are outlined below. The limitations of household surveys notwithstanding (see box IV.1), they can represent a source of information with comparative advantages over censuses and administrative records, in that they provide a more detailed socioeconomic portrait of both the local and migrant populations. Taking into account the stylized facts on the evolution of migratory flows described in the previous chapter, a distinction can be drawn, where possible, between recent migrants and those of longer standing (less than and more than five years in the destination country, respectively) in order to highlight certain significant gaps in social and labour inclusion.

1.   Differences in the social and labour inclusion of the local population and of recent and long-term migrants

The sociodemographic characteristics of migrants, in terms of sex, age and education, differ from those of the local population. Figure V.4 shows that among long-standing migrants, women are overrepresented in Argentina, Chile, Costa Rica and Uruguay. In contrast, the opposite is the case in Brazil, the Dominican Republic and Mexico. As regards recent immigration, Brazil, the Dominican Republic and Mexico again report mostly male migrants among their recent arrivals, with Mexico's figures reporting 36% more men than women. In the remaining countries, recent immigration tends to be relatively balanced in its gender breakdown.

Figure V.5 shows the age-group breakdown into three cohorts: 0 to 14 years, 15 to 64 years and 65 years and over. First of all, it confirms the importance of labour migration among the migrant population of the destination countries (ILO, 2017, and ILO/ECLAC, 2017). Among recent migrants, it can be seen that people of working age account for a relatively higher proportion (by between 8 and 18 percentage points) than among the local-born population. This pattern remains in place among migrants of

---

[7]   This section builds on the findings of Carrasco and Suárez (2018). Since the information used is from household surveys conducted around 2015, it does not reflect the impact of recent intraregional migration flows, such as the Venezuelan and Haitian migrants now found in several of the region's countries.

longer standing, except in Argentina, Brazil and Uruguay. Second, with the exception of Chile, the proportion of children aged under 14 is higher in the local population than among migrants in all the destination countries. Nevertheless, that age group accounts for a significant proportion of recent migrants, with figures ranging from 12% to 23%. Third, long-term migrants report a higher proportion of people aged 65 and older, which points to a higher level of ageing than among the local population and recent migrants in Argentina, Brazil and Uruguay.

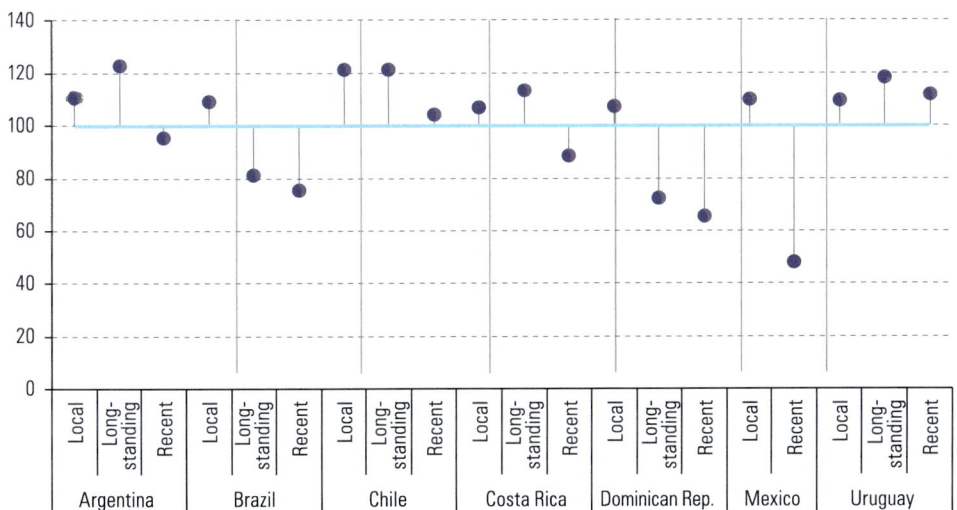

Figure V.4
Latin America
(7 countries): female
presence in the local
population and among
long-term and recent
migrants, people
aged 15 years and
over, around 2015
(Percentages)

Source: I. Carrasco and J. Suárez, "Migración internacional e inclusión en América Latina: análisis en los países de destino mediante encuestas de hogares", *Social Policy series*, No. 231 (LC/TS.2018/57), Santiago, Economic Commission for Latin America and the Caribbean (ECLAC), 2018.

Figure V.5
Latin America (7 countries): age structure, local population and recent and long-term migrants, both sexes, around 2015
(Percentages and years)

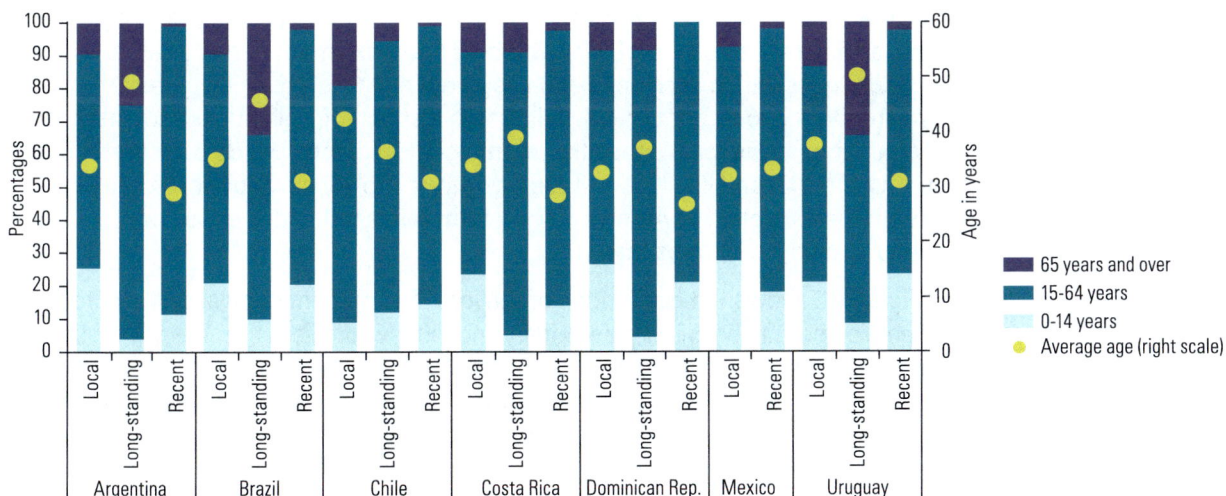

65 years and over
15-64 years
0-14 years
Average age (right scale)

Source: I. Carrasco and J. Suárez, "Migración internacional e inclusión en América Latina: análisis en los países de destino mediante encuestas de hogares", *Social Policy series*, No. 231 (LC/TS.2018/57), Santiago, Economic Commission for Latin America and the Caribbean (ECLAC), 2018.

The local and migrant populations also report different educational profiles: whereas migrants to Brazil, Chile and Uruguay are generally more qualified, the opposite is true in the Dominican Republic, particularly among recent migrants, while in Argentina, Costa Rica and Mexico the local and migrant populations report, on average, similar numbers of schooling years. In Argentina, however, there is a large proportion of recent migrants with higher educations (figure V.6).

Figure V.6
Latin America (7 countries): educational achievement (complete cycles) of the local population and recent and long-term migrants, population aged 18 and over, both sexes, around 2015
(Percentages and years)

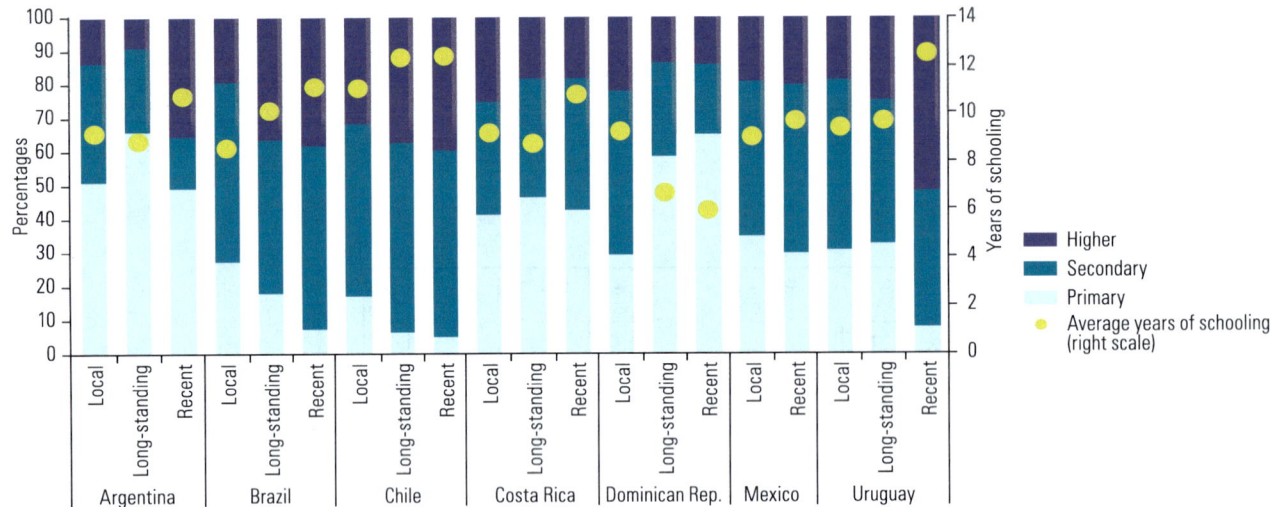

Source: I. Carrasco and J. Suárez, "Migración internacional e inclusión en América Latina: análisis en los países de destino mediante encuestas de hogares", *Social Policy series*, No. 231 (LC/TS.2018/57), Santiago, Economic Commission for Latin America and the Caribbean (ECLAC), 2018.

Unemployment levels among recent and long-term migrants and the sectors in which they find employment also vary from those of the local population, and there are sex-based differentials as well. Table V.8 shows unemployment rates by sex, along with the gender gaps within each population segment and those gaps by type of migration (compared to the local population). With the exception of Chile, unemployment rates are lower among the local population than recent migrants, which is consistent with ILO/ECLAC (2017) and ILO (2017). If the figures are broken down by sex, it can be seen that with the exception of Argentina (long-term migrants) and Mexico, women report higher unemployment rates than men.

Figure V.6 shows the distribution of the local and migrant populations according to their employment in the primary, secondary and tertiary sectors in the different destination countries, in addition to the percentages employed in low-productivity activities.[8] The situation here is far from uniform, with a greater presence of the migrant population in certain sectors: for example, long-term migrants in industry and construction in Brazil and Costa Rica and in agriculture in the Dominican Republic, and recent migrants in industry and construction in both Argentina and Brazil. In Uruguay, migrants report greater insertion in the commercial and services sectors, and in agriculture in Chile.

---

[8]   Low-productivity jobs among the employed urban population cover employers and employees (neither professional nor technical) working in companies with up to five employees (microenterprises), working in paid domestic employment and independent unqualified workers (own-account workers and unpaid family members without professional or technical qualifications).

Table V.8
Latin America (6 countries): unemployment rate of the local population and recent and long-term migrants, by sex, around 2015
(Percentages)

Country	Population	Total	Men	Women	Gap among long-term migrants	Gap among recent migrants	Gender gap
Argentina 2014	Local	7.0	6.2	8.1	-1.8	...	2
	Long-term	5.2	6.0	4.1			-2
	Recent	12.3	...	...			...
Brazil 2015	Local	9.6	7.9	11.7	-5.5	6.0	4
	Long-term	4.0	3.5	5.2			2
	Recent	15.6	8.1	..			...
Chile 2015	Local	7.1	6.2	8.1	-1.7	-0.1	2
	Long-term	5.4	4.8	6.0			1
	Recent	6.9	5.8	8.3			3
Costa Rica 2015	Local	8.5	7.2	10.4	-0.5	7.3	3
	Long-term	8.0	6.0	10.7			5
	Recent	15.7	13.1	...			...
Mexico 2014	Local	5.3	6.1	3.9		2.7	-2
	Recent	8.0	8.6	5.1			-4
Uruguay 2015	Local	7.5	6.3	8.9	-0.6	4.9	3
	Long-term	6.9	6.6	7.2			1
	Recent	12.4	11.7	13.2			2

Source: I. Carrasco and J. Suárez, "Migración internacional e inclusión en América Latina: análisis en los países de destino mediante encuestas de hogares", *Social Policy series*, No. 231 (LC/TS.2018/57), Santiago, Economic Commission for Latin America and the Caribbean (ECLAC), 2018.
Note: No data reported for categories with fewer than 40 members: Argentina (recent migration, men and women), Brazil and Costa Rica (recent migration, women).

A worthwhile question would be to ask whether those insertion characteristics arise from differences in the education profiles of the long-term and recent migrant population, or whether certain types of activity are more accessible during the first years after arrival. As regards employment by area of activity, ILO/ECLAC (2017) indicates that migrants with lower levels of formal schooling tend to concentrate in less qualified occupations. For 2010, three different insertion profiles can be identified: (i) insertion in less qualified jobs, in Argentina, Costa Rica and the Dominican Republic, where immigrants are more likely to find employment in paid domestic work, construction and farming, (ii) Mexico, where are there significant numbers of immigrants employed in jobs that require higher levels of education, and (iii) Chile, which presents a more diversified scenario among different kinds of employment.

Finally, an analysis of the population's concentration in low-productivity jobs —which are characterized by greater informality and precarity and lower wages and social protection— reveals a greater preponderance of such kinds of employment among the migrant population than their local counterparts, with the exceptions of Brazil and Uruguay (see figure V.7).

Two types of activity warrant particular attention because of their weight in the distribution of employment by sex, in line with gender stereotypes that also apply to local workers: construction among men,[9] and paid domestic work among women. Those biases are particularly heavy when the local population is compared with the intraregional migrant population, i.e. migrants from other Latin American and Caribbean countries. As shown in figure V.8, in the countries under analysis, with the exception of Brazil and Uruguay, migrant men are overrepresented in the construction sector compared to the local population. The widest gaps are found in the Dominican Republic and Argentina, with differences of 19 and 13 percentage points respectively. In the paid

---

[9]   Includes electricity, gas and water utilities.

domestic work sector, gender inequalities and society's undervaluation of care work combine with the inequalities generally faced by the migrant population. Figure V.9 shows that in all the countries, migrant women are overrepresented compared to the local population. In Argentina, 32.5% of migrants are employed in paid domestic work, compared to 11.6% of the local population. In Costa Rica, the high proportion of women migrants employed in paid domestic work is particularly notable, where they more than double the percentage corresponding to local women. At play here are gender inequalities and society's undervaluation of care work, intertwined with the inequalities faced by the migrant population in general. Unpaid work allows many women immigrants to enter the job market, but with scant possibilities of occupational mobility, and, in many cases, they also participate in global care chains.

Figure V.7
Latin America
(7 countries): proportion
of the employed
population working in
low-productivity sectors,
around 2015
(Percentages)

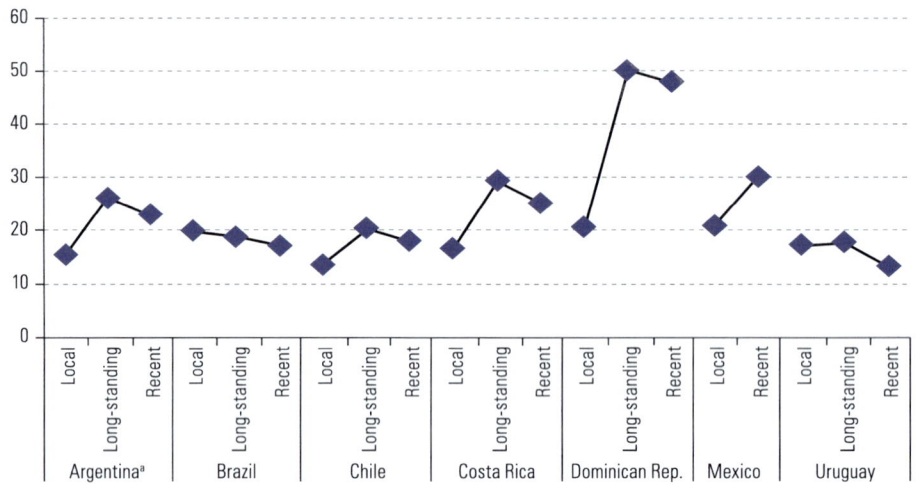

Source: I. Carrasco and J. Suárez, "Migración internacional e inclusión en América Latina: análisis en los países de destino mediante encuestas de hogares", *Social Policy series*, No. 231 (LC/TS.2018/57), Santiago, Economic Commission for Latin America and the Caribbean (ECLAC), 2018.
[a] Argentina only has information available for its urban areas.

Figure V.8
Latin America
(5 countries): proportion
employed in construction,
men aged 15 and over,
around 2015
(Percentages)

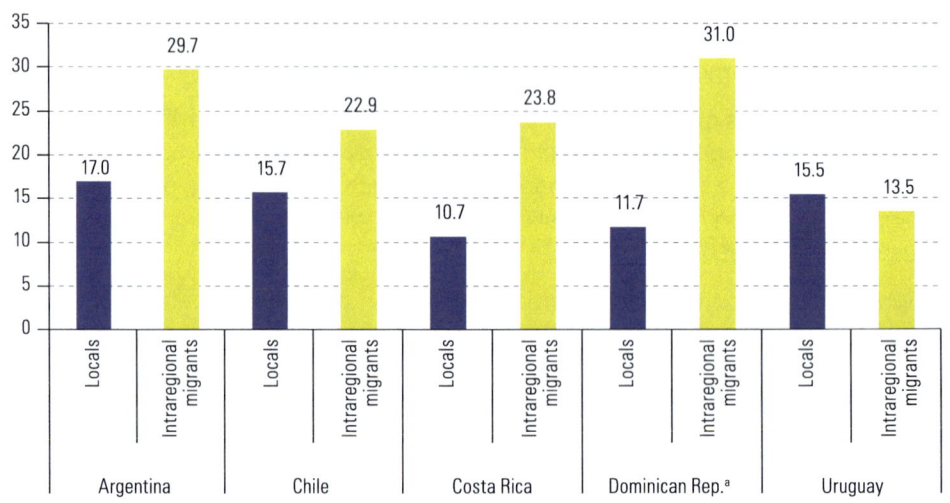

Source: I. Carrasco and J. Suárez, "Migración internacional e inclusión en América Latina: análisis en los países de destino mediante encuestas de hogares", *Social Policy series*, No. 231 (LC/TS.2018/57), Santiago, Economic Commission for Latin America and the Caribbean (ECLAC), 2018.
[a] Dominican Republic n < 40 cases.

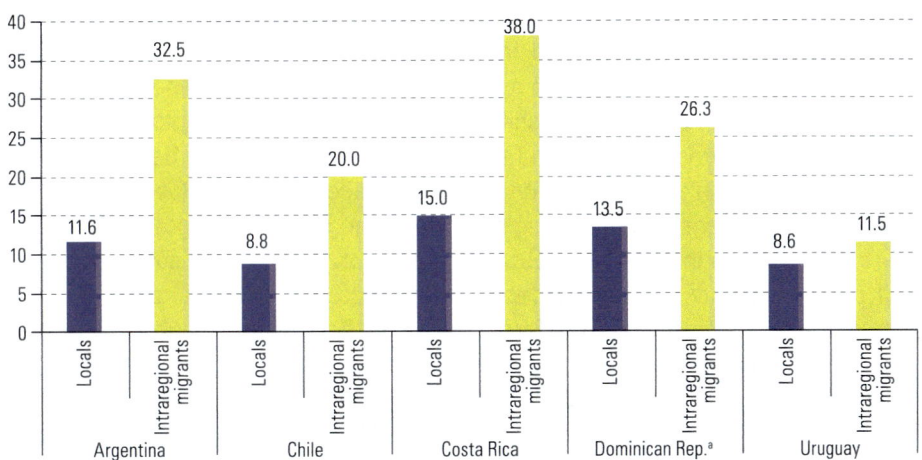

Figure V.9
Latin America
(5 countries): proportion
employed in paid
domestic work, women
aged 15 and over,
around 2015
(Percentages)

Source: I. Carrasco and J. Suárez, "Migración internacional e inclusión en América Latina: análisis en los países de destino mediante encuestas de hogares", *Social Policy series*, No. 231 (LC/TS.2018/57), Santiago, Economic Commission for Latin America and the Caribbean (ECLAC), 2018.
a Dominican Republic n < 40 cases.

The characteristics of migrants' labour insertion help understand the wider gaps in inclusion and access to social protection found in destination countries. Informal employment among migrant workers is common in the destination countries of Latin America (ILO, 2017), and it leads to a lack of social protection.

Figure V.10 showcases the gaps in occupational overqualification.[10] In most of the countries, overqualification is higher among the migrant population than among locals, and it is particularly pronounced in Costa Rica (10 points for men and 16 for women), Argentina (almost 14 percentage points for both sexes), among women in Chile (10 percentage points) and among men in Mexico. No gaps are seen in Uruguay, among men in Brazil and Chile or among women in Mexico, and there is only one case in which occupational overqualification is lower in the migrant population (among women in Brazil). That result indicates that, as a general rule, even migrants who have tertiary education have a higher probability than local workers of entering employment in low-productivity sectors.

Figure V.10
Latin America (6 countries): overqualification in migrant and local populations, employed persons over 14 years of age, by sex, around 2015
(Percentages)

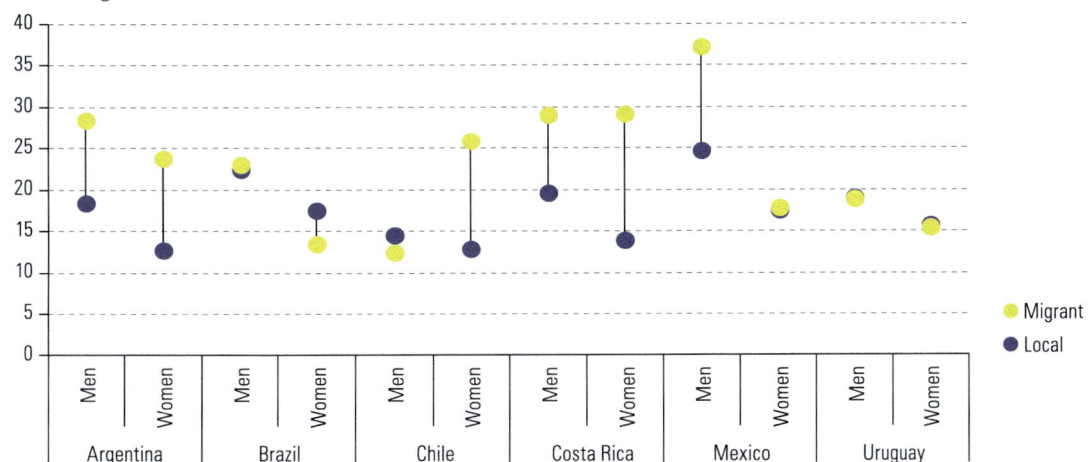

Source: I. Carrasco and J. Suárez, "Migración internacional e inclusión en América Latina: análisis en los países de destino mediante encuestas de hogares", *Social Policy series*, No. 231 (LC/TS.2018/57), Santiago, Economic Commission for Latin America and the Caribbean (ECLAC), 2018.

10 The percentage of workers with higher educations employed in the low-productivity sector is used as a proxy for occupational overqualification.

A set of six indicators are used to analyse the social and labour inclusion of the local population and of long-term and recent immigrants: overcrowding, access to basic services, enrolment in the health system, contributing to social security, school attendance among young people and children of school age, and employment rate.[11] In the countries under review, in general a higher rate of inclusion can be seen among the local population than among both long-term and recent migrants (see figure V.11). Nevertheless, the dimensions of the gaps between the groups vary greatly from one country to the next. On the one hand, Brazil and Uruguay's figures indicate reasonable levels of parity, with narrower gaps between the local population and immigrants. In contrast, there are pronounced differences in the Dominican Republic and Costa Rica, both between different groups of migrants and between migrants and the local population. Also, with the exception of Chile, employment rates are slightly lower among recent migrants compared to the local population and long-term migrants, which could be an indication of lower labour inclusion.

Figure V.11
Latin America (7 countries): social and labour inclusion indicators, local population and recent and long-term migrants, around 2015
(Percentages)

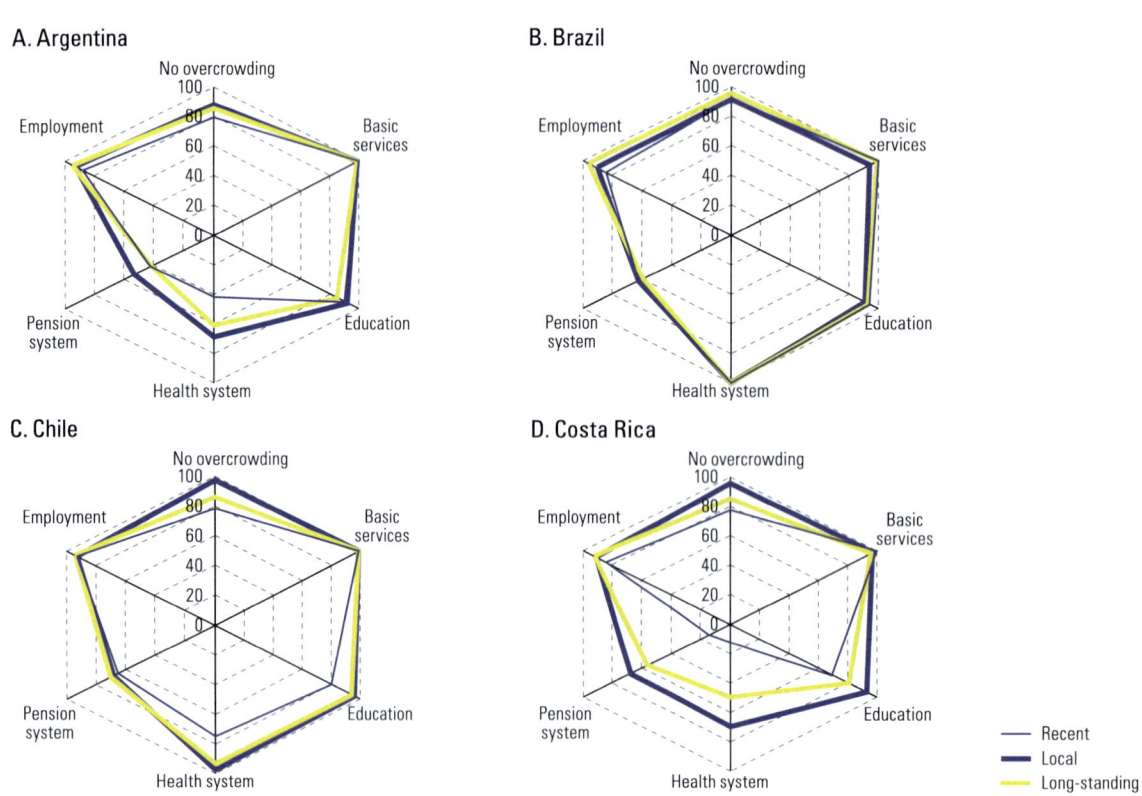

11   The first two indicators use the household as the unit of analysis, while the remainder focus on the individual, with the relevant filters for age and employment status. The indicators in the analysis are ordered positively, with which the data indicate the percentage of people not reporting the absence of the corresponding factor of inclusion: in other words, high results for "employment" and "overcrowding" indicate a high percentage of people in employment and living in conditions that are not overcrowded, respectively (Carrasco and Suárez, 2018).

Figure V.11 (concluded)

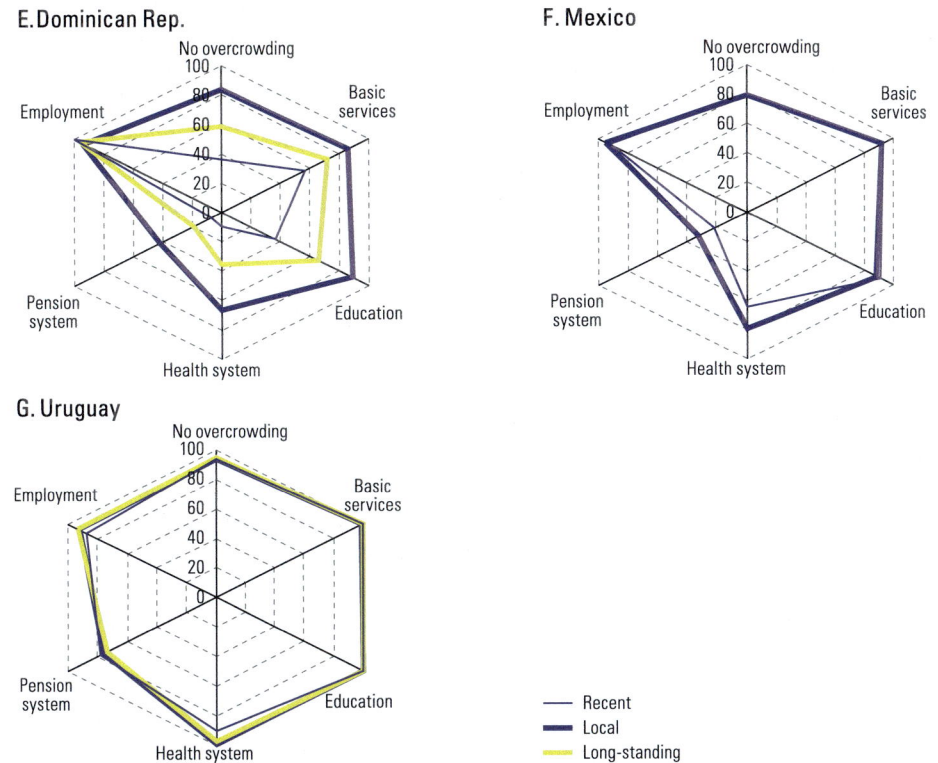

Source: I. Carrasco and J. Suárez, "Migración internacional e inclusión en América Latina: análisis en los países de destino mediante encuestas de hogares", *Social Policy series*, No. 231 (LC/TS.2018/57), Santiago, Economic Commission for Latin America and the Caribbean (ECLAC), 2018.

Note: The indicators used are: overcrowding: percentage of households in which the ratio of people to a room is 3:1 or higher; basic services: percentage of households with water available off the property, or without a toilet or latrine; employment rate: percentage of active persons aged 15 or over who are employed; access to education: percentage of children of school age (6–18 years) in formal education; access to health: percentage of employed aged 15 or over registered in the health system; access to the pension system: percentage of employed aged 15 or over registered in the contributory pension system.

C. Racism, discrimination and migration

Ethnic and racial origin and migrant status are component axes of the social inequality matrix in Latin America (ECLAC, 2016); racist and xenophobic practices contribute to —and can feed off each other in determining— the levels of inclusion or exclusion faced by migrants with respect to their rights, status and general well-being. Both within the region and in the rest of the world, racism and xenophobia towards migrant populations are frequently found in conjunction. The culture of privilege that has historically been present in Latin America and the Caribbean and that practices and institutions continue to perpetuate make for fertile ground for feeding those phenomena (ECLAC, 2018). In light of these challenges to migrants' social and labour inclusion, the following paragraphs re-examine certain key issues that affect how the topic of racism can be incorporated into analyses of migratory phenomena and, above all, into policy design, before exploring some of the factors behind aversion towards migrants.

Defining the concept of "race" is a complex task. Many authors hold that the idea of race arose in the eighteenth century, although others place it much earlier (Banton, 1977) and still others trace its emergence back to the colonization of the Americas as part of the process of European conquest and colonial domination (Quijano, 2005). Agreement exists, however, that the term "race" arose in several European languages to refer to the populations that the Europeans encountered and dominated (Wade, 2011) and that, in the course of the nineteenth century, it acquired the connotation of physical traits, whereby peoples and individuals were seen as biologically different and humankind was divided into races (Banton, 1977).

The sense of the concept evolved between the end of the nineteenth century and the first half of the twentieth, in particular following the atrocities committed during the Second World War. In broad terms, that evolution went from the establishment of a supposedly scientific racism, which used pseudoscientific tools and techniques to justify the existence of differences and physical, intellectual and moral hierarchies between purportedly distinct races of human beings, to the conclusion that, in biological (and subsequently genetic) terms, those races did not exist as such but were actually a social and historical —in other words, cultural— construct. As a result, talk of relative superiority between them was inadmissible and was replaced by a discourse involving diversity and, additionally, contradictions and conflicts between distinct cultures, associated in turn with specific population groups, each with their own identity and history (Lévi-Strauss, 1952). Based on that conclusion and the absolute supremacy of individual human rights, the conceptual apparatus of the United Nations adopted a series of treaties and international rules applicable to racism and discrimination.

But in Latin America and the Caribbean, the idea of race as a social and political marker of inequality, discrimination and differentiation has a historical specificity on account of its roots in colonialism and slavery. In fact, one of the elements that accompanied the emergence of the notion of race arose from the European domination and colonization of the Americas in the sixteenth century, when this hemisphere was integrated into the global economic system. That position enabled the Europeans not only to impose their idea of race, but also to create categories that would define new identities ("Indian", "black", "white", "mestizo"). The idea of race put in place by European colonialism served the interests of the colonial system, was in line with the global division of labour and justified the social stratification of colonial societies. The hierarchical system based on the idea of race in terms of skin colour and the physical traits of their colonized subjects invested the domination imposed by the conquest with legitimacy and was essential in the process whereby territories were conquered and entire peoples subjugated to benefit, first, the European colonial powers and, later, the nascent nation States of the nineteenth century.

After science had demonstrated that races did not exist in biological terms, the concept of ethnicity —while not a perfect synonym— began to be used more frequently because it was less value-laden; racial categories were not eliminated, however, and the term "racism" acquired eminently negative connotations (Wade, 2000). Nevertheless, even the term "ethnicity" has frequently contained connotations of exclusion, discrimination and inferiority, in that "ethnic groups" are invariably seen as "others" by the dominant groups imposing that classification. In addition, the term is used to classify groups that do not see themselves in that way or use that label, but that instead conceive of themselves as peoples with individual names and whose members feel bound to each other on account of their shared origin. Finally, like the notion of race, the concept of ethnicity has evolved over time and must be handled with the utmost care (Giménez, 2006).

In other words, deciding that races did not exist biologically and that they were *per se* social and historical constructs did not lessen the importance of the concept of race as a social marker or its presence in society's mind, both because racial status plays a major role in structuring social relations and determining gaps in access to rights and well-being (ECLAC, 2016) and because many people continue to discriminate against others because they consider them racially or ethnically different and/or inferior, on occasions using rationales based on purported genetic traits or characteristics (Wade, 2011). Neither has the reality of racial discrimination changed with the adoption of the concept of ethnicity, which is less related to physical traits. To summarize, beyond —and in spite of— the evolution and abandonment of the concept of race as a scientific category, racism on the grounds of skin colour and ethnicity are far from disappearing from global social structures and thinking and, in Latin America and the Caribbean, it is one of the components of what ECLAC has termed the culture of privilege in the region, marked by a cultural predisposition towards embracing, perpetuating and justifying inequalities and discrimination in Latin American societies.

Against that backdrop, increasing and diversifying intraregional migration flows have been accompanied by the racialization of migrants (see box V.1) —the classification of human groups in racial terms—[12] and heightened xenophobia: fear of what is foreign, of different ethnic or racial groups and of strangers. This purported fear of differences leads to acts of discrimination based on prejudices (historical, religious, cultural and national) and to the perpetrators' justification of segregation and discrimination. Thus, one of the commonest forms of rejection can connect xenophobia with racism towards migrants (or foreigners) and bring into play other grounds for discrimination, such as social status, gender, age or other factors (Kundnani, 2001). The racialization of migrants has been intimately associated with the process of globalization. The intersection of the "foreign" and "race" categories bolsters racism and xenophobia by enabling the construction of a "national we" and a group of "others" who, in addition to not being nationals, may have undesired racial origins (Castells, 2004).

Feelings of uncertainty and precarity generally hinder the construction of inclusive and less unequal societies and, at the same time, showcase the importance of expanding access to social protection and decent work for the population as a whole as a factor in building inclusion, social cohesion and development. Investing in social protection, which would provide the entire population with greater certainty and stability, could at the same time have a positive effect by helping instil a climate of greater acceptance towards immigration. The challenge is therefore to design social protection systems that include new migratory flows and that, at the same time, are defined in such a way that does not make the local population feel that they are facing competition from migrants.

In Latin America and the Caribbean, where indigenous (see box V.2) and Afro-descendent people have traditionally faced greater marginalization and exploitation, the exclusion of migrants —particularly those from within the region— interconnects with those processes of historic discrimination, in that the ethnic and racial discrimination present in social relations and relations of power in the countries of origin, transit and destination perpetuates the production, maintenance and reproduction of hierarchies, exclusions and privileges as well as the existing distribution of opportunities and social well-being.[13] This can be seen, notably, among those migrants engaged in paid domestic employment, a type of work that in Latin America was and remains racialized and has its origins in positions of servitude.

---

[12] Better known are the phenomena whereby poverty or justice are racialized, through which people of African origin are more likely to be poor or to be victims of the judicial system. However, the process whereby meaning is attached to race is not always one of domination: it can also be a consequence of resistance projects with the power to influence social agendas (Campos, 2012).

[13] One example of the persistence of a mindset shaped by racial inequality in many countries can be found in the vocabulary used in everyday life and by the media, whereby white migrants and those from developed countries are frequently labelled "expatriates", whereas the classification "migrants" refers to people from other countries in the region, from low social strata or with darker skin.

Box V.1
Racialization of migrants

In several of the region's countries, discrimination exists against indigenous and Afro-descendent migrants. In **Argentina**, since the 1990s, migrants from within the region (chiefly from the Plurinational State of Bolivia,[a] Paraguay and Peru) have been subjected to discriminatory treatment, as part of a process of ethnicization of social relations, particularly those involving regional migrants, whereby they are attributed characteristics that are seen negatively ("indigenous features", "rural origin" and "black skin")[b] and giving common currency to the idea that immigrants from elsewhere in the region are endangering the purported social harmony and first-world status towards which Argentina was aspiring. According to Halpern (2010), immigrants from the region were included, albeit precariously, in economic activities but were excluded from —or restricted in their access to— civil, political and social rights.

In the **Dominican Republic**, the ethnic and racial dimension is intertwined with issues of nationality and migration on account of the proximity of Haiti, a country with a predominantly Afro-descendent population that sends significant flows of migrants (both seasonal and permanent) into the Dominican Republic. However, the issue of ethnicity and race is rendered invisible, which hampers efforts against the discrimination faced not only by Haitians but also by darker-skinned Dominicans, who are often confused with Haitians and, on occasions, arrested on suspicion.[c] There is evidence of acts of racial discrimination in the country. As an example, the Constitutional Court's judgment No. 168 of 2013 ordered not only the expulsion of irregular Haitian immigrants, but also the cancellation of the rights of Dominican people born to parents who were not legally resident in the country at the time of their birth, thus triggering the possibility of Haitian migrants and their descendants being socially excluded on grounds of heredity, in a legal and bureaucratized way, and of the Dominican children of Haitian migrants being expelled from the country (Martínez and Wooding, 2017).

In the case of **Chile**, the arrival in recent years of people of African descent, Haitians in particular, has also served to reveal processes of racialization and racial discrimination.[d] Against the distant backdrop of nineteenth-century policies that encouraged European migration in order to (as in other countries of the region) "improve the race", the current migrant population —Peruvians, Colombians, Haitians, Dominicans, indigenous people and others— is redefining a cultural matrix defined by hierarchies and the subordination of given social groups on account of their skin colour and/or origins (indigenous and/or Afro-descendent) (Tijoux, 2011 and 2016; Tijoux and Palominos, 2015).

Source: G. Halpern, "Desigualdades y diferencias: inmigrantes regionales en la Argentina", *América Latina interrogada: mecanismos de la desigualdad y exclusión social*, Mexico City, Miguel Ángel Porrúa, 2010; S. Martínez and B. Wooding, "El antihaitianismo en la República Dominicana: ¿un giro biopolítico?", *Migración y Desarrollo*, vol. 15, No. 28, Zacatecas, International Network on Migration and Development, 2017; M. Tijoux, *Racismo en Chile: la piel como marca de la inmigración*, Santiago, Editorial Universitaria, 2016; "Negando al 'otro': el constante sufrimiento de los inmigrantes peruanos en Chile", *Mujeres inmigrantes en Chile: ¿mano de obra o trabajadoras con derechos?*, C. Stefoni (ed.), Santiago, Alberto Hurtado University, 2011; M. Tijoux and S. Palominos, "Aproximaciones teóricas para el estudio de procesos de racialización y sexualización en los fenómenos migratorios de Chile", *Polis: Revista Latinoamericana*, vol. 14, No. 42, Santiago, University of Los Lagos, 2015.

[a] For example, in 1992, the press began to "Bolivianize" and "indigenize" migration. Bolivian people were portrayed in the media as being synonymous with disease. It took almost one month for some of the papers to begin publishing stories blaming the Argentine State for an outbreak of cholera. The press "embraced the idea of 'mass immigration' (which was never substantiated by any official statistics) without a single figure to support that claim" (Halpern, 2009, p. 5).

[b] Numerous studies accuse Argentina of racist, xenophobic and discriminatory practices, including Belvedere and others (2007), Casaravilla (1999), Grimson (2006), Margulis and Belvedere (1998), Oteiza, Novick and Aruj (1997) and Pizarro (2009 and 2012).

[c] Neither country allows for ethnic or racial self-identification in their population censuses or household surveys. The majority of Dominicans use the categories "Afro-descendants" and "black" solely to refer to Haitians (Afro Alianza Dominicana, 2013).

[d] Chile's *Annual Report on the Human Rights Situation* for 2017 identified "the presence of prejudiced speech and manifestations of arbitrary discrimination on the grounds of national or ethnic origin, skin colour and other physical and cultural traits of 'non-Chilean' people" (INDH, 2017, p. 22). In addition, an opinion survey conducted by Cadem (2018) revealed that 38% of the respondents considered the arrival of immigrants to be something negative; 80% thought that the current number of immigrants was high and that more restrictive policies should be adopted; and 66% were in favour of the expulsion of those immigrants without legal permits. Irrespective of the foregoing, 84% of respondents were in favour of encouraging the arrival of foreigners and more than 60% said that immigrants offered an opportunity for development and contributed to the country's cultural enrichment (Cadem, 2018).

Box V.2
Indigenous peoples and migration

The territorial mobility of indigenous peoples is a process that predates the colonial conquest but today remains a part of the region's migration reality. A range of very different movements are involved: people seeking better standards of living, either individually or in groups, forced displacements (due to armed conflicts, violence, human rights violations or natural disasters) and relocations driven by political, economic or environmental factors. Regardless of the reasons behind these movements of people, the constant problems they face include maintaining ties with their communities of origin and the sociocultural continuation of their peoples in their final destinations, processes that are supported by family networks and by organizations that promote ethnic identity (Del Popolo, 2018).

As shown in the table, in those countries for which census information is available, around 2010 the region's international immigrants of indigenous origin totalled more than 83,000 and represented a very small proportion of the indigenous populations in their countries of destination (less than 3.3%); the one exception to that was Costa Rica, where 12.4% of the total indigenous population were born beyond the country's borders. In absolute terms, Mexico (47,979) and Costa Rica (12,962) reported the largest numbers of indigenous international immigrants, while the lowest figures were recorded in Uruguay (2,442) and Panama (1,807).

Latin America (9 countries): proportion of foreign-born indigenous people within the total indigenous population of each country, around 2010
(Percentages)

Country	Percentages
Costa Rica	12.4
Uruguay	3.2
Nicaragua	0.8
Brazil	0.6
Ecuador	0.4
Panama	0.4
Mexico	0.3
Colombia	0.2
Peru	0.1

Source: F. del Popolo (ed.), *Los pueblos indígenas en América (Abya Yala): desafíos para la igualdad en la diversidad* (LC/PUB.2017/26), Santiago, Economic Commission for Latin America and the Caribbean (ECLAC), 2018; on the basis of census microdata.

D. The institutional framework for migrants in the region

The institutional public policy framework plays an important role in determining how effective, efficient and successful policies in this area will be in promoting inclusion and upholding people's rights (ECLAC, 2018 and 2019a; Martínez, 2017). The following discussion will deal with the social institutions in the region that work with migrants and will explore how they have changed over the years. The objective of this analysis is to identify some of the institutional challenges faced by the countries of the region as they seek to safeguard the rights of all and to address problems faced by the population as a whole, including migrants. The focus will be on two of the four dimensions of the institutional structure: its juridical/normative dimension (the national and international laws and standards that make up the framework for State action and the commitments that it makes) and its organizational dimension (the structure, mandates and coordination mechanisms of the government apparatus in each policy sector).[14]

The aim is to contribute to the formation of broad-based intersectoral forums or mechanisms for responding to this group's many different needs and rights. To this end, an overview of the juridical/normative and organizational dimensions (the two aspects on which the most official information is available) of the institutional framework for migration issues will be presented here.[15]

1. The international and national juridical/normative dimension of migration-related issues

(a) The international normative framework

The various treaties on this subject, together with constitutional provisions, general laws and regulations, play a part in determining States' objectives and commitments regarding migrants, particularly with regard to the guarantees they provide for the exercise of certain rights. The general international human rights treaties and conventions and those that deal specifically with migrants' labour rights and the portablity of social security benefits are of particular interest in this respect. At the national level, laws that shape migration policies —and especially policies on migrants' labour rights and the regularization of their status— are of special significance, as are laws and policies on human trafficking, since migrants are exceedingly vulnerable to abuse at all the various points along the migration cycle.

International instruments and conventions focusing specifically on migrants include the International Labour Organization (ILO) Migration for Employment Convention, 1949 (No. 97), the ILO Migrant Workers (Supplementary Provisions) Convention, 1975 (No. 143) and the United Nations International Convention on the Protection of the Rights of All Migrant Workers and Members of Their Families (1990). The eight treaties known as the "fundamental conventions" of ILO are also of central importance.

---

[14] The other two dimensions are the technical/operational aspect (the management systems and tools in place for enforcing laws and implementing policies and programmes) and financial considerations (the available resources for funding public action in each sector or on each issue). These four dimensions are interdependent, so all of them will have to be developed and consolidated in order to strengthen policy impacts on each sector or issue.

[15] Sources include the official information published by the countries concerned and by various international agencies. Most of this information is available in the Institutional Framework Database for Social Policy in Latin America and the Caribbean (see [online] https://dds.ECLAC.org/bdips/), updated to July 2019) and, secondarily, from studies cited in the bibliography, notably Maldonado, Martínez and Martínez (2018b).

Figure V.12
Latin America and the Caribbean (33 countries): signature and ratification of or accession to covenants, conventions and treaties on the economic, social and cultural rights of migrants

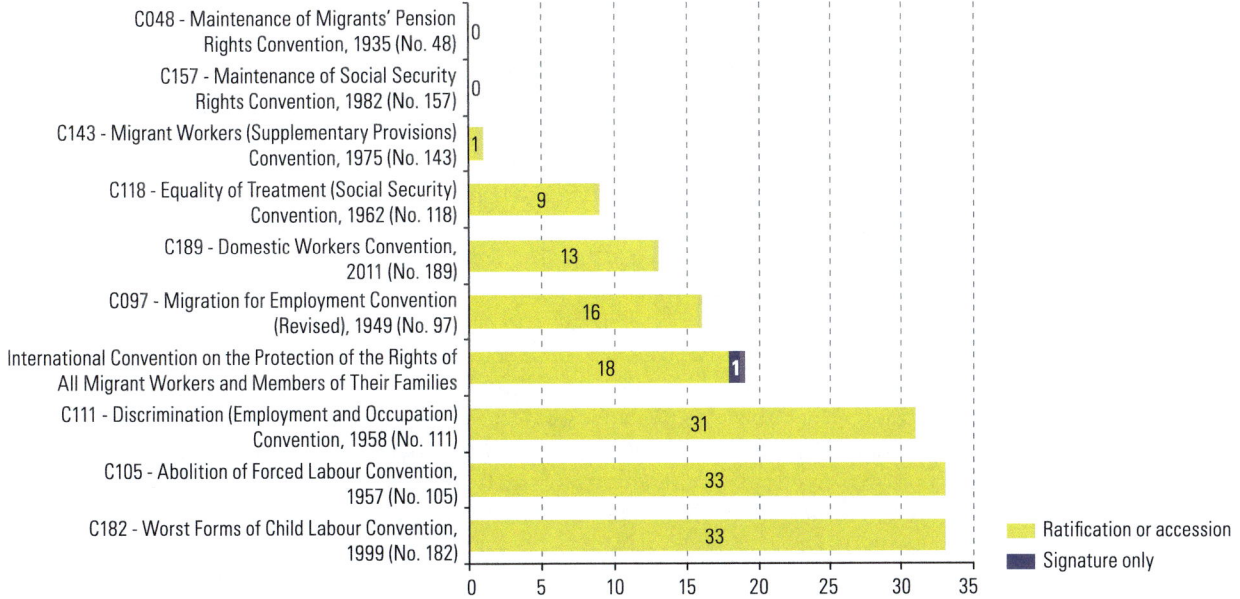

Source: Economic Commission for Latin America and the Caribbean (ECLAC), on the basis of C. Maldonado, J. Martínez and R. Martínez, "Protección social y migración: una mirada desde las vulnerabilidades a lo largo del ciclo de la migración y de la vida de las personas", *Project Documents* (LC/TS.2018/62), Santiago, Economic Commission for Latin America and the Caribbean (ECLAC), 2018; and oficial information of the respective countries.

As may be seen from figure V.12, most of the countries in the region have ratified general international conventions on the rights of the population as a whole, such as the ILO Worst Forms of Child Labour Convention, 1999 (No. 182) and the ILO Abolition of Forced Labour Convention, 1957 (No. 105), which have been ratified by 33 countries in the region, and the ILO Discrimination (Employment and Occupation) Convention, 1958 (No. 111), which has been ratified by 31 countries. The number of countries that have ratified conventions dealing with specific population groups is much lower, however, with the treaty of this type with the largest number of ratifications by countries in the region —18— being the International Convention on the Protection of the Rights of All Migrant Workers and Members of Their Families. It is followed by the ILO Migration for Employment Convention (Revised), 1949 (No. 97), with 16 ratifications, and the ILO Domestic Workers Convention, 2011 (No. 189), which has been ratified by fewer than half of the countries of Latin America and the Caribbean (13 countries). The ILO Equality of Treatment (Social Security) Convention, 1962 (No. 118) has been ratified by only nine countries. The only country in the region that has ratified the ILO Migrant Workers (Supplementary Provisions) Convention, 1975 (No. 143) is the Bolivarian Republic of Venezuela, while no country in the region at all has signed, much less ratified, either the ILO Maintenance of Social Security Rights Convention, 1982 (No. 157) or the ILO Maintenance of Migrants' Pension Rights Convention, 1935 (No. 48). This state of affairs points up the need to move forward with the signature and ratification of treaties protecting the rights of given segments of the population, including, in particular, migrant workers (see box V.3).

Box V.3
International Labour
Organization conventions
on migrant workers

The International Labour Organization (ILO) coordinates with the workers, employers and governments of its 187 member States to conclude standards, policies and programmes for promoting decent work for all. The mission of achieving decent work for all clearly includes migrant workers, whose rights ILO has been defending since the conclusion of the Treaty of Versailles in 1919. That treaty called for the creation of ILO and for the economic equality of all legal residents in any given country. The goal of labour equality is also reflected in the ILO charter, the 1944 Declaration of Philadelphia, which incorporates a rights-based perspective and places the utmost emphasis on the equality of treatment of migrant workers. ILO took up the issue of migrant workers once again in its Convention No. 97 of 1949 and later in its Convention No. 143 of 1975. Taken together, these instruments establish the normative foundation for migrant workers' rights. The first of these instruments guarantees equality of treatment for migrant workers having a regular migration status in the country where they are located and sets out a number of guarantees for labour rights, benefits and social protection, but it does not cover the cases of workers whose migration status is irregular. Accordingly, the ILO Convention on Migrations in Abusive Conditions and the Promotion of Equality of Opportunity and Treatment of Migrant Workers went a step further to include all migrants, regardless of their legal migration status, and addresses crucial issues such as abusive or forced labour, discrimination and a lack of opportunity. Other ILO conventions and recommendations also deal, implicitly and explicitly, with migrant workers, with examples being the Indigenous and Tribal Peoples Convention, 1989 (No. 169), the Equality of Treatment (Accident Compensation) Convention, 1925 (No. 19) and the Maintenance of Social Security Rights Convention, 1982 (No. 157). ILO has developed a body of standards that, in line with its basic principles, are designed to promote equal rights for all migrant workers and enjoins States parties to protect those rights. The case of irregular and clandestine migrants continues to be the area in which the greatest difficulty in achieving the full implementation of these standards is being encountered.

Source: Economic Commission for Latin America and the Caribbean (ECLAC), on the basis of E. López, "La protección de los trabajadores migrantes basada en derechos: la respuesta normativa de la OIT", *Temas Socio-Jurídicos*, vol. 38, No. 76, Bucaramanga, Autonomous University of Bucaramanga, 2019.

(b) National legislation on migration

Until recently, the needs of migrants had not been addressed by social development policy. But as migration issues have become increasingly important in the region, policy and regulatory frameworks have begun to be developed with a view to ensuring the social inclusion of migrants and their protection from abuses and rights violations. Some countries have framed legislation that covers the entire range of situations (those of emigrants, immigrants, migrants in transit, returning migrants), and some have developed instruments specifically for their emigrant population. Because migrants are so vulnerable to human traffickers, the various policy and regulatory frameworks dealing with trafficking are also an important factor.

The Constitutions of only 7 of the 33 countries for which information is available accord migrants or foreign nationals the same social rights as their nationals (Cuba, the Dominican Republic, Ecuador, Haiti, Mexico, Panama and the Plurinational State of Bolivia), and Ecuador is the only country whose Constitution makes explicit mention of the protection of the rights of migrants in various areas, regardless of their migration status. The Constitutions of Argentina, the Bolivarian Republic of Venezuela, Brazil,

Colombia, Costa Rica, El Salvador, Guatemala, Honduras, Nicaragua and Uruguay do, however, refer to the overall protection of both foreign nationals and their citizens and state that they enjoy equal rights and must not be discriminated against, although they do not mention social rights in that context as such. The age of some of the countries' Constitutions provides a partial explanation for this, as many of them were written at a time when migration, and especially immigration, had a different political or social significance, since a majority of immigrants came from outside the region, and when concerns about border controls and national security were very different from what they are today.

Changes in the national migration laws of the 31 countries for which information is available reflect a shift towards stronger safeguards for some types of rights. Figure V.13 and annex table V.A1.2 provide an overview of national migration laws in the region and the years in which they were passed. The migration laws of 10 of the countries (9 of which are in the Caribbean) are over 40 years old. These laws have been amended over the years with the introduction of a number of revised provisions and the repeal of other articles but, generally speaking, their main thrust is to safeguard national security and ensure border controls that will allow those governments to monitor the entry of members of certain groups. Yet even in more recent legislation and more recent amendments to earlier laws, little mention is made of the civil, political and social rights of migrants, as is shown in table V.9. Of the available migration laws that have been analysed, those of Antigua and Barbuda, the Bahamas, Chile, Cuba, El Salvador, Grenada, Guyana and Jamaica contain no explicit reference to any specific right for migrants.

Figure V.13
Latin America and the Caribbean (31 countries): year of promulgation of countries' principal migration laws

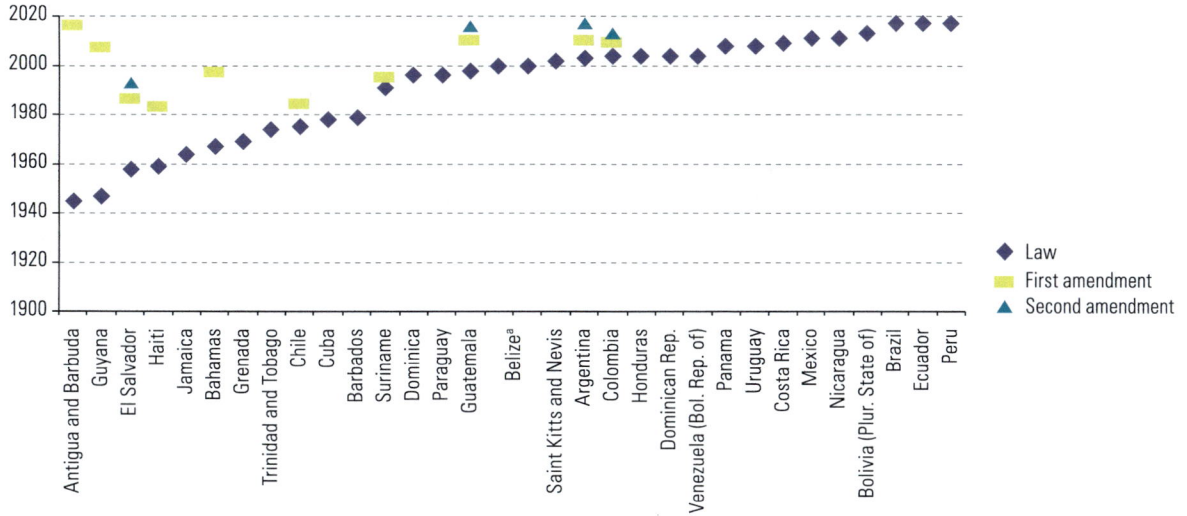

Source: Economic Commission for Latin America and the Caribbean (ECLAC), on the basis of C. Maldonado, J. Martínez and R. Martínez, "Protección social y migración: una mirada desde las vulnerabilidades a lo largo del ciclo de la migración y de la vida de las personas", *Project Documents* (LC/TS.2018/62), Santiago, Economic Commission for Latin America and the Caribbean (ECLAC), 2018; constitutional texts and main national legislations on social matters.
ᵃ The migration laws of Belize are the Immigration Act and the Foreign Nationals Act, both of which were passed in 2000 and remain in force.

Of the five national migration laws enacted between 1980 a 1999, only those of Paraguay and Guatemala state that migrants are rights holders, but even they do not specify which ones. In the case of Guatemala, however, the Migration Code of 2016 does specify the social rights to which migrants are entitled (the rights to social security and protection, education, health, work, access to justice and due process, housing and family reunification). These laws are thus at an intermediate stage in terms of the recognition of migrants' fundamental, economic and social rights.

The migration laws enacted since 2000 by 16 countries reflect a growing tendency to include and explicitly mention the social rights of migrants, but this is still done in only some of the countries' laws, such as those of Argentina, Brazil, Costa Rica, Ecuador, Guatemala, Mexico, Peru, the Plurinational State of Bolivia and Uruguay. The laws of the Dominican Republic, Honduras and Panama make only a general reference to the human rights of migrants, while those of Belize, Colombia, and Saint Kitts and Nevis do not specifically refer to rights and reflect an approach focusing on security rather than human rights. In the laws that do take a rights-based approach, the rights that are mentioned most often are those of access to justice and due process, followed by family reunification, health and education.

Nine countries also have laws that deal specifically with emigration. Most of these laws set out the rights or protective services to which emigrants are entitled and contain provisions designed to ensure the availability of effective consular assistance in the country of destination, especially in cases in which an emigrant's rights have been violated, as in cases where they fall victim to human traffickers, or in which they have an irregular migration status, have an accident or are involved in a disaster situation (see annex table V.A1.3). This group of nations is made up of two Caribbean countries from which a large number of people have emigrated and whose laws in this area pre-date their independence (Antigua and Barbuda and Trinidad and Tobago) and seven that have large emigrant populations and emigration laws enacted after the 2000s (Colombia, El Salvador, Guatemala, Honduras, Mexico, Paraguay and Peru).

As for the more recently established institutional structures in this area, the laws and amendments passed since the year 2000 also specify the functions of intersectoral coordination mechanisms and duties of the main agencies or offices responsible for migration-related matters, whereas the older laws make no mention of the accompanying institutional framework, which has instead been developed by means of regulations, decrees and various other types of rules or standards. The advantage of using lower-order instruments to establish the institutional structure in this area is that it can then be more easily adapted to new situations or challenges; the downside can be that, if changes are made too frequently when there is a change of government administration, the structure may suffer from a certain degree of discontinuity.

Table V.9
Latin America and the Caribbean (15 countries): specific rights of migrants identified in migration laws, by country

Country	Instrument	Law	Year	Where	Human rights	Health	Education	Work	Due process/ justice	Social protection/ social security	Sexual and reproductive rights	Vote	Housing	Family reunification	Rights of migrant children and adolescents
Argentina	Decree 70/2017	Amendments to Acts No. 25.871 and No. 346	2017		✓				✓					✓[a]	
	Decree No. 616	Implementing regulations for Migration Act No. 25.871 and its amendments	2010	Title I: Rights and obligations of foreign nationals	✓	✓	✓	✓	✓	✓		✓[b]		✓	
	Act No. 25.871	Migration Act	2003	Title I: Rights and obligations of foreign nationals	✓	✓	✓	✓	✓	✓				✓	
Bolivia (Plurinational State of)	Act No. 370	Migration Act	2013	Chapter I: Rights of foreign migrants	✓	✓	✓	✓	✓	✓	✓	✓	✓	✓	✓
Brazil	Act No. 13.445	Migration Act	2017		✓	✓	✓		✓					✓	✓
Costa Rica	Act No. 8764	General Act on Migration and Immigration	2009	Article 3	✓	✓			✓						✓
Dominican Republic	Act No. 285-04	General Migration Act	2004		✓										
Ecuador	Organization Act on Human Mobility	Organization Act on Human Mobility	2017	Chapter III: Foreign nationals in Ecuador. Section I. Definition, rights and obligation	✓	✓			✓	✓		✓[c]		✓[d]	
El Salvador	Decree-law No. 670	Amendment of the Migration Act	1993												
	Decree No. 299	Immigration Act	1986		✓										
	Decree No. 2772	Migration Act	1958												
Guatemala	Decree No. 44/2016	Migration Code	2016	Title 1: The right to migrate and the rights of migrants	✓	✓	✓	✓	✓	✓	✓		✓	✓	✓
	Decree No. 10	Amendment of the Migration Act	2010		✓										
	Decree No. 95-98	Migration Act	1998		✓										

Table V.9 (concluded)

Country		Law	Year	Where	Human rights	Health	Education	Work	Due process/justice	Social protection/social security	Sexual and reproductive rights	Vote	Housing	Family reunification	Rights of migrant children and adolescents
Honduras	Decree No. 208	Migration and Immigration Act	2004	Title III: On the rights and obligations of foreign nationals. Chapter I: Rights and obligations	✓										
Mexico	Decree-law	Migration Act	2011		✓	✓	✓		✓					✓	✓
Panama	Decree-law No. 3	National Migration Service and Officials Act (which also sets out other provisions as well)	2008		✓	✓									
Paraguay	Act No. 978	Migration Act	1996		✓	✓	✓		✓						
Peru	Legislative Decree No. 1350	Legislative Decree on Migration	2017	Article 9: Rights of foreign nationals	✓	✓	✓	✓	✓						✓
Uruguay	Act No. 18250	Migration Act	2008		✓	✓	✓	✓	✓	✓			✓	✓	
Venezuela (Bolivarian Republic of)	Act No. 37944	Immigration and Migration Act	2004	Title II: Rights and duties of foreign nationals	✓				✓						

Source: Economic Commission for Latin America and the Caribbean (ECLAC), on the basis of C. Maldonado, J. Martínez and R. Martínez, "Protección social y migración: una mirada desde las vulnerabilidades a lo largo del ciclo de la migración y de la vida de las personas", *Project Documents* (LC/TS.2018/62), Santiago, Economic Commission for Latin America and the Caribbean (ECLAC), 2018; and official information of the respective countries.

a When the right to family reunification is invoked under the terms of the preceding paragraph, the cohabitation of the family group must be established. This right shall not be afforded to a foreign national who has been shown to have become emotionally or economically distanced from the person whose family ties are invoked.

b The National Migration Directorate of the Ministry of Internal Affairs shall adopt the measures, as appropriate, to inform foreign nationals of the conditions and requirements pertaining to the right to vote.

c Foreign nationals residing in Ecuador shall have the right to vote and to be elected to public office provided that they have resided legally in the country for at least five years in accordance with the Constitution and the law.

d In accordance with the implementing regulations of this Act, evidence must be provided of the existence of a lawful livelihood sufficient to support the applicant and the family group with whom he or she lives.

As for the types and hierarchical status of the various legal instruments, migration laws predominate, with 15 of the countries regulating migration-related matters by means of general laws; 11 Caribbean countries (Antigua and Barbuda, Bahamas, Barbados, Belize, Dominica, Grenada, Guyana, Jamaica, Suriname, Trinidad and Tobago, and Saint Kitts and Nevis) have migration and immigration laws that, in the common law system, have a hierarchical rank similar to that of the migration laws of the 15 countries mentioned above. In the four remaining cases, regulations, decrees or other such instruments are used.

The increasing tendency to refer explicitly to rights in these laws and other instruments reflects a shift in the perception of migrants as they cease to be viewed solely as a person whose entry into the country must be controlled, regulated and registered and come to be seen as a person who is also a rights holder and, as such, is a person towards whom the State has certain duties. One cause of concern, however, is that many of the legislative provisions and legislated rights are contingent on the person's migration status, with mention being made of the rights of migrants whose migration status is irregular only in rare cases.

Another important consideration is the presence or mainstreaming of a gender perspective in migration laws, as the laws of only 12 countries systematically address the specific needs, rights and vulnerabilities of women migrants (see box V.4).

The challenge that is to be taken up, then, is for the countries of the region to incorporate a rights-based approach into their migration laws whereby recognition is accorded to migrants' fundamental civil rights and freedoms, such as the freedoms of movement, assembly, expression, thought and religion, the right to own property and the right to justice, and political rights such as the rights to criticize, evaluate and have political views and preferences. Economic, social and cultural rights —understood as the right to economic and social well-being— are also of importance in order for migrants to be included in the economy and society, to prevent their marginalization and to protect them from discrimination.

Because of the links between migration and human trafficking, many Latin American countries have developed an institutional structure for combating human trafficking and assisting the victims of traffickers. Human trafficking and migrant smuggling are international crimes involving very serious violations of migrants' human rights. The inclusion of laws on human trafficking in the countries' legislative frameworks is a relatively recent development, with the first countries to do so being the Dominican Republic and Paraguay, in 2003, and Uruguay being the country to have most recently followed in their footsteps (in 2018). The entry into force of the Protocol to Prevent, Suppress and Punish Trafficking in Persons, Especially Women and Children, supplementing the United Nations Convention against Transnational Organized Crime in 2003 has been an incentive for the adoption of specific national laws on trafficking, and 28 countries in the region now have special laws on this crime (see figure V.14).

Box V.4
Gender mainstreaming in institutional and regulatory frameworks for the protection of the rights of women migrants: evidence from the repository of regulations on international migration of the Gender Equality Observatory for Latin America and the Caribbean of ECLAC

Women have been present in all the migration flows that have ever taken place, but they have not always been taken into consideration in analyses or the discourse around migration issues (Fries, 2019, p. 9). What is more, until a few decades ago, theoretical approaches to migration issues entirely overlooked the part played by women or, if they dealt with the subject at all, did so in inappropriate ways when viewed from a gender perspective (ECLAC/CELADE, 2006, p. 240). This has inevitably changed, however, as the presence of women migrants has grown in recent decades. At the global level, women have come to play an important part in international migration, as their numbers have been growing steadily since 1960, although they are still in the minority. However, they have indeed been in the majority, strictly speaking, in the main destination areas for immigrants since 1990 (ECLAC/CELADE/UNFPA, 2003, p. 19 in Friés Monleon, 2019).

The parallel development of international and national laws on the protection of migrants and women's rights has contributed to a progressively greater mainstreaming of the gender perspective in the identification of the needs of the female migrant population. At the same time, quantitative and qualitative changes in women's participation in migration have led to their explicit inclusion in international, regional and subregional conferences and consultative mechanisms dealing with women's issues and with migration.

The repository of regulations on international migration of the ECLAC Gender Equality Observatory for Latin America and the Caribbean contains a total of 95 laws from 21 countries in Latin America and the Caribbean. Of that total, the main focus of 31 of those instruments (including a number of Constitutions) is migration, its regulation and the protection of migrant populations; 19 refer to the prevention of human trafficking, the punishment of human traffickers and assistance for victims of trafficking and people smuggling; and the remaining 45 deal with a variety of related matters (Fries, 2019).

By cross-referencing the hierarchical rank of the legal instruments contained in the repository, by country, with the areas that they govern, it can be seen that 12 countries have laws on migration that refer to women migrants. This is of interest because these instruments are framework laws and, as such, govern entries and departures, the bodies responsible for migration issues, and migrants' rights and protection. In effect, the higher the position in the legal hierarchy of a law or regulatory instrument that refers either explicitly or tacitly to women migrants, the greater the degree of protection that is afforded to them. One of the reasons why this is true is because the higher-ranking laws determine the content of lower-ranking ones. In addition to those 12 countries, Brazil, Chile, Colombia, the Dominican Republic and Peru also include references to women migrants but do so in lower-ranking migration laws and regulations. Cuba, Haiti, Paraguay and Puerto Rico refer to women migrants only in statutes concerning related matters (Fries, 2019).

Latin America (12 countries): countries with migration laws that contain provisions on migrant women

Country	Law
Argentina	Migration Act No. 25.871 (2004)
Bolivia (Plurinational State of)	Migration Act No. 370 (2013)
Costa Rica	General Act on Migration and Immigration No. 8.764 (2009)
Ecuador	Organization Act on Human Mobility (2017)
El Salvador	Decree No. 655: Special Act for the Protection and Development of Salvadoran Migrants and their Families (2011)
Guatemala	Decree 44/2016: Migration Code (2016)
Honduras	Decree 106/2013: Act for the Protection of Honduran Migrants and their Families (2013)
Mexico	Migration Act (2011)
Nicaragua	General Migration and Immigration Act (2011)
Panama	Decree-law No. 3: National Migration Service and Officials Act (which also sets out other provisions as well) (2008)
Uruguay	Migration Act No. 18.250 (2008)
Venezuela (Bolivarian Republic of)	Immigration and Migration Act No. 37.944 (2004)

Source: L. Fries, "Las mujeres migrantes en las legislaciones de América Latina: análisis del repositorio de normativas sobre migración internacional del Observatorio de Igualdad de Género de Latin America and the Caribbean", *Gender Affairs series*, No. 157 (LC/TS.2019/40), Santiago, Economic Commission for Latin America and the Caribbean (ECLAC), 2019.

Figure V.14
Latin America and the Caribbean (28 countries): year of the enactment of the main national laws
on human trafficking

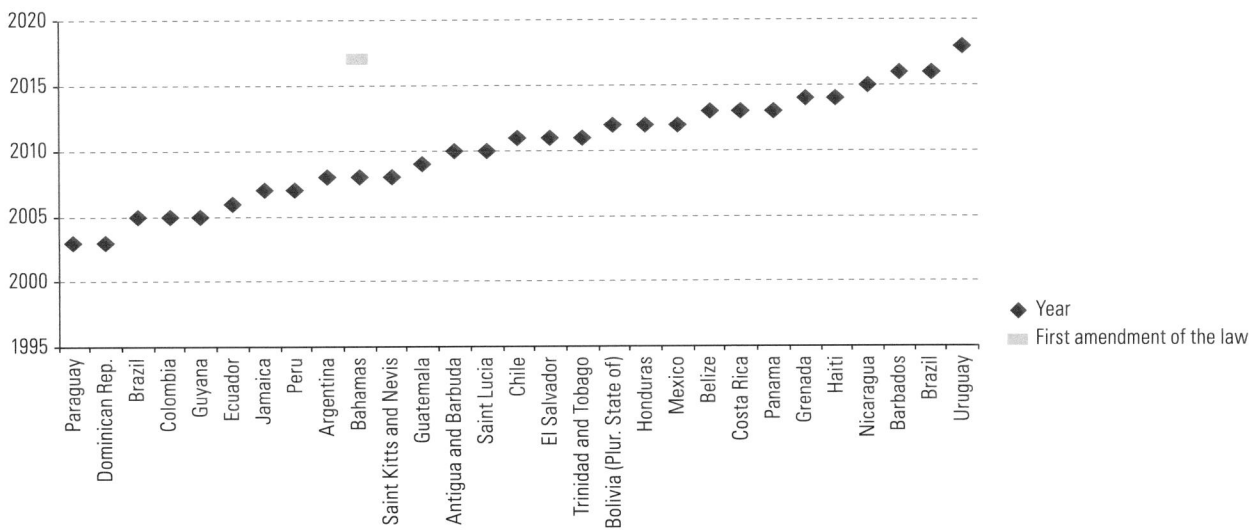

Source: Economic Commission for Latin America and the Caribbean (ECLAC), on the basis of C. Maldonado, J. Martínez and R. Martínez, "Protección social y migración: una mirada desde las vulnerabilidades a lo largo del ciclo de la migración y de la vida de las personas", *Project Documents* (LC/TS.2018/62), Santiago, Economic Commission for Latin America and the Caribbean (ECLAC), 2018; constitutional texts and main national laws on trafficking in persons.

While the countries have developed bilateral mechanisms for coordinating efforts with other countries' embassies and consulates to identify and assist trafficking victims, there is as yet no regional forum or agency for multilateral discussions and coordination in this area. Meeting this challenge is a matter of urgency, given that the United Nations Office on Drugs and Crime (UNODC) has estimated that 93 of every 100 trafficking victims in Latin America and the Caribbean are still located somewhere in the region itself. The development of regional coordination mechanisms and plans of action would make it possible to combat this kind of crime more effectively and to get help to trafficking victims more swiftly.

Given the serious human rights violations associated with the smuggling and trafficking of girls, adolescents and women, 14 countries have adopted legal instruments for the protection of women migrants; in 12 of those cases, these instruments take the form of actual laws, while, in the other 2, they are regulations governing some operational aspect of other legislation (see table V.10). Most of them are special-purpose laws, although others are embedded in framework laws on migration, as in the case of the Bolivarian Republic of Venezuela and Ecuador. The soundness and alignment of the laws on this subject reflect the efforts made by governments around the world to combat human trafficking since 2003, which was the year of the entry into force of the Protocol to Prevent, Suppress and Punish Trafficking in Persons, Especially Women and Children, supplementing the United Nations Convention against Transnational Organized Crime. This is why all the laws and lower-ranking legal instruments on the prevention of trafficking, the punishment of traffickers and victim assistance make specific reference to women. The fact that most of the victims of this crime are women has also certainly contributed to the inclusion of targeted measures for helping and protecting women on a non-discriminatory basis (Fries, 2019).

Table V.10
Latin America (14 countries): instruments on human trafficking and migrant smuggling and their ranking in the legal hierarchy, by country

Country	Instruments on human trafficking and migrant smuggling and their ranking in the legal hierarchy
Bolivia (Plurinational State of)	Act No. 263 on Human Trafficking and People Smuggling (2012)
Brazil	Act No. 13.344, on the prevention and suppression of domestic and international trafficking in persons and on victim assistance (2016)
Colombia	Decree No. 1.069 of the Ministry of Internal Affairs, which sets out regulations for the application of some of the provisions of Act No. 985 of 2005 on human trafficking and victim protection (2014)
Costa Rica	Human Trafficking Act No. 9.095, which provides for the establishment of the National Coalition against Migrant Smuggling and Human Trafficking
	Executive Directive No. 057, which provides for assistance to persons in transit who have an irregular migration status, migrants who have been smuggled and trafficking victims in mixed migration flows (2012)
	Executive Decree No. 39.325, which sets out the regulations needed to implement the Human Trafficking Act and authorizes the establishment of the National Coalition against Migrant Smuggling and Human Trafficking (CONNATT), (2015)
Dominican Republic	Migrant Smuggling and Human Trafficking Act No. 137/2003 (2003)
	Decree No. 97/1999, which authorizes the creation of the Inter-Agency Committee for the Protection of Migrant Women (CIPROM) (1999)
Ecuador	Organization Act on Human Mobility, which covers both human trafficking and people smuggling (2017)
Honduras	Decree No. 59/2012, Human Trafficking Prevention Act (2012)
	Executive Order No. 36 of the Secretariat for Human Rights, Justice, Governance and Decentralization, whereby it approved the implementing regulations for the Human Trafficking Prevention Act (2015)
Haiti	Act on the Prevention of Human Trafficking (2014)
Mexico	General Act for the Prevention, Punishment and Eradication of Human Trafficking and for Victim Protection and Assistance (2014)
Nicaragua	Anti-Trafficking in Persons Act No. 896 (2015)
Panama	Trafficking in Persons and Related Activities Act No. 79 (2011)
	Migrant Smuggling and Related Activities Act No. 36 (2013)
	Executive Decree No. 303-2016, which sets out the implementing regulations for Trafficking in Persons and Related Activities Act No. 79 (2016)
	Executive Decree No. 464, which approves the National Plan to Combat Human Trafficking (2012)
Peru	Supreme Decree No. 001/2016, which approves the implementing regulations for the Prevention of Migrant Smuggling Act No. 28.950 and authorizes the establishment of the Multisectoral Commission to Combat Human Trafficking and Migrant Smuggling (2016)
Uruguay	Migration Act No. 18.250 (2008)
Venezuela (Bolivarian Republic of)	Immigration and Migration Act No. 37.944, which also deals with human trafficking (2004)

Source: Economic Commission for Latin America and the Caribbean (ECLAC), on the basis of Gender Equality Observatory for Latin America and the Caribbean, "Regulations on international migration", Santiago [online] https://oig.cepal.org/en/laws/6.

2.   The institutional and organizational dimension of migration and human trafficking issues

The organizational dimension of these issues encompasses the governmental structure, mandates and coordination mechanisms of the various agencies concerned. It involves the distribution of tasks and the formation of a hierarchical structure, along with, in certain cases, the designation of an overarching social policy authority or a sectoral social policy authority to deal with specific issues or segments of the population. The agencies officially in charge of assisting migrants are backed up by inter-agency coordination mechanisms that seek to serve this group.

The organizational dimension of the institutional framework for combating human trafficking encompasses, first of all, the regional and subregional intergovernmental offices or forums that define the shared priorities and challenges faced by the countries as they work to combat this crime. This section will also look at the main institutions that make up the countries' organizational frameworks for migration policy and will outline the workings and composition of the inter-agency coordination mechanisms whose job it is to define and coordinate policies dealing with migrants and trafficking victims.

(a) International and regional forums and bodies dealing with international migration and human trafficking in Latin America and the Caribbean

Various regional and subregional forums, councils, conferences and other bodies and assemblies have been established in Latin America and the Caribbean as migration issues have taken their place on the regional agenda. Their decisions are not binding, but they do provide a way of sharing experiences and information concerning the various aspects of migration that then inform new standards, agreements and principles, most of which are declarative in nature. These forums may also develop shared agendas concerning such social issues as the situation of women, child and adolescent migrants, for example, and sectoral issues relating to health, education and food security, or the impact of climate change and natural disasters on migration, among many others.

These forums fall into one of two main categories: there are 7 main forums that deal exclusively with migration issues, and 10 intergovernmental forums in which migration is one of the main focuses.[16] Within the United Nations system, an important role is played by the Montevideo Consensus on Population and Development issued by the Regional Conference on Population and Development in Latin America and the Caribbean, which is a subsidiary body of ECLAC (see box V.5).

---

[16] Four of the forums in the first category are linked to the International Organization for Migration (IOM): the South American Conference on Migration, the Regional Conference on Migration, the Central American Commission for Migration (OCAM) and the Ibero-American Network of Migration Authorities (RIAM). The International Conference on Hunger, Poverty, and Migration in the Countries of the Central American Integration System (SICA) is sponsored by the World Food Programme (WFP), while the other two forums are associated with the Ibero-American General Secretariat (SEGIB) and the Community of Latin American and Caribbean States (CELAC). In the second category, three of the forums —the Annual Meeting of Vice-Ministers of the Regional Conference on Migration (also known as the Puebla Process), the South American Conference on Migration and the Regional Conference on Population and Development of Latin America and the Caribbean— have links to two United Nations bodies: IOM and the Economic Commission for Latin America and the Caribbean (ECLAC). Another six have ties to regional and subregional agencies, such as the Southern Common Market (MERCOSUR), Community of Latin American and Caribbean States (CELAC), the Organization of American States (OAS), SEGIB, the Secretariat of the African, Caribbean and Pacific Group of States and the European Commission. There is also the Ibero-American Forum on Migration and Development of SEGIB and the CELAC high-level meeting on migration. These forums all work along much the same lines as those set out in the Global Compact for Safe, Orderly and Regular Migration.

Box V.5
The 2013 Montevideo
Consensus: international
migration and protection
of the human rights
of all migrants

One of the main focuses of the Montevideo Consensus is the human rights of migrants, and one of its central tenets is that migrants' full exercise of their human rights and their access to basic public services, in particular education and health, including sexual health and reproductive health, should not depend on their migration status. It recognizes the substantial contributions that migrants make to their home and host countries and calls attention to concerns regarding their living conditions, their integration and the increasing complexity of migrants' journeys when they are in transit, crossing national borders and returning to their home countries. It also voices the countries' concern in the face of the evident and systematic human rights violations suffered by migrants as a result of racism, xenophobia and homophobia, as well as the lack of due process guarantees and the specific problems of different groups, especially women, children and adolescents, that are targets of discrimination, abuse, human trafficking, exploitation and violence. In the light of these concerns, the countries agreed to do the following:

66. Ensure that international migration issues, including migration regularization policies are fully incorporated into global, regional and national post-2015 development agendas and strategies;

67. Provide assistance and protection to migrants regardless of their migration status, especially vulnerable groups, with full respect for their rights and in accordance with the provisions of the International Convention on the Rights of All Migrant Workers and Members of their Families and those of the Vienna Convention on Consular Relations, highlighting the need to afford them comprehensive attention in countries of transit and destination;

68. Prepare comprehensive global and regional strategies to prevent infringement of the human rights of migrants, as well as to take advantage of the benefits and face the challenges arising from migration, including those relating to remittances and skilled migration in high-demand sectors, as well as the differential participation of men and women and the transnationalization of care;

69. Promote the signing of bilateral and multilateral social security conventions to enable migrant workers to accumulate years of service;

70. Incorporate principles of consistency and reciprocity in dealing with the various situations faced by emigrants from the countries in the region, at all stages of the migration process, whether at the intraregional level or outside the region;

71. Achieve concrete results through dialogue and international cooperation relating to migration, human rights and development in regional forums as well as in forums linked to other regions of the world, in particular North America and the European Union, with a view to reducing existing asymmetries in this area and asserting the interests of Latin American and Caribbean countries;

72. Protect decisively the human rights of all migrants, avoiding any form of criminalization of migration, and guarantee migrants access to basic social services in education and health, including sexual health and reproductive health, where appropriate, regardless of their migration status, with special attention to highly vulnerable groups, including unaccompanied minors, displaced persons in an irregular situation, women who are victims of violence, victims of trafficking, returnees and forcibly displaced asylum-seekers;

73. Give priority, in each country, to strengthening coordination channels between sectors and between countries, to reinforcing intergovernmental cooperation mechanisms in order to guarantee the exercise of the human rights of all migrants, regardless of their migration status, from a gender-based perspective;

74. Strengthen cooperation between countries of origin, transit and destination to address the causes and challenges of irregular migration, so as to generate safe, orderly, humane migration conditions through bilateral arrangements for labour force mobility and ensure protection of the human rights of migrants;

Source: Economic Commission for Latin America and the Caribbean (ECLAC), *Montevideo Consensus on Population and Development* (LC/L.3697), Santiago, 2013.

(b) National bodies and offices that deal with migrants and human trafficking, andrelated inter-agency coordination

Almost all the Latin American and Caribbean countries have some institution or department in charge of migration-related matters, although the type of organization varies considerably. Historically, the main area of emphasis has been internal governance and security, and, in fact, in 20 of the 29 countries, the institution in charge of migration-related matters is either the Ministry of Internal Affairs (17 countries) or the Ministry of Public Security (3 countries) (see figure V.15). It should be pointed out, however, that there is no direct correlation between the nature of the institution concerned and whether the country's migration laws are based on a human rights approach or not or what that approach will look like when it is translated into actual practice.

In five cases, the institution in charge of migration is also the one responsible for conducting the country's foreign affairs. In other cases, the lead agency varies, with examples being the Office of the Prime Minister of Barbados, the Ministry of the Presidency in Guyana and the Ministry of Legal Affairs in Grenada. Belize has a dedicated institution, the Department of Immigration and Nationality Services, to serve its large immigrant population, which represents around 16% of the total population —one of the highest percentages in all of Latin America and the Caribbean.

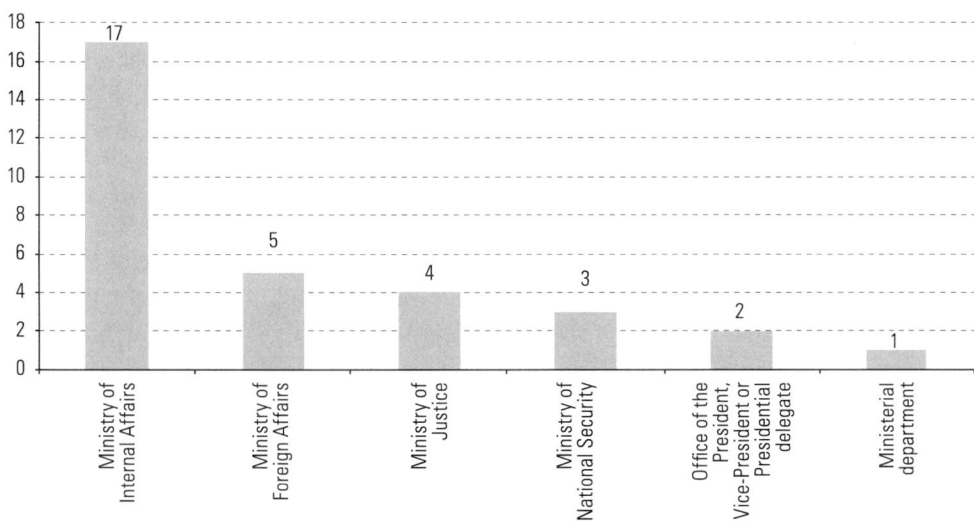

Figure V.15
Latin America and the Caribbean (32 countries): lead official government agency responsible for coordinating public action for migrants
(Number of agencies)

Source: Economic Commission for Latin America and the Caribbean (ECLAC), on the basis of C. Maldonado, J. Martínez and R. Martínez, "Protección social y migración: una mirada desde las vulnerabilidades a lo largo del ciclo de la migración y de la vida de las personas", *Project Documents* (LC/TS.2018/62), Santiago, Economic Commission for Latin America and the Caribbean (ECLAC), 2018; and official data from the respective bodies.
[a] The countries are: Antigua and Barbuda, Argentina, Bahamas, Barbados, Belize, Bolivarian Republic of Venezuela, Brazil, Chile, Colombia, Costa Rica, Cuba, Dominica, Dominican Republic, Ecuador, El Salvador, Grenada, Guatemala, Guyana, Haiti, Honduras, Jamaica, Mexico, Nicaragua, Panama, Paraguay, Peru, Plurinational State of Bolivia, Saint Kitts and Nevis, Saint Lucia, Suriname, Trinidad and Tobago, and Uruguay.

In addition to the lead government agency serving the migrant population, many of the countries of the region have set up inter-agency coordination mechanisms mainly since 2000, as in the 17 countries shown in figure V.16. This reflects a shift towards a more integrated and inclusive legislative approach whereby the lead agency works with other ministries and offices responsible for other sectors that make up part of the social agenda. This paves the way for closer coordination among the various stakeholders and the development of shared inter-ministerial standards and parameters.

Figure V.16
Latin America and the
Caribbean (17 countries):
year of founding of
the main intersectoral
coordinating offices for
migrant protection and
policies, 1900–2020

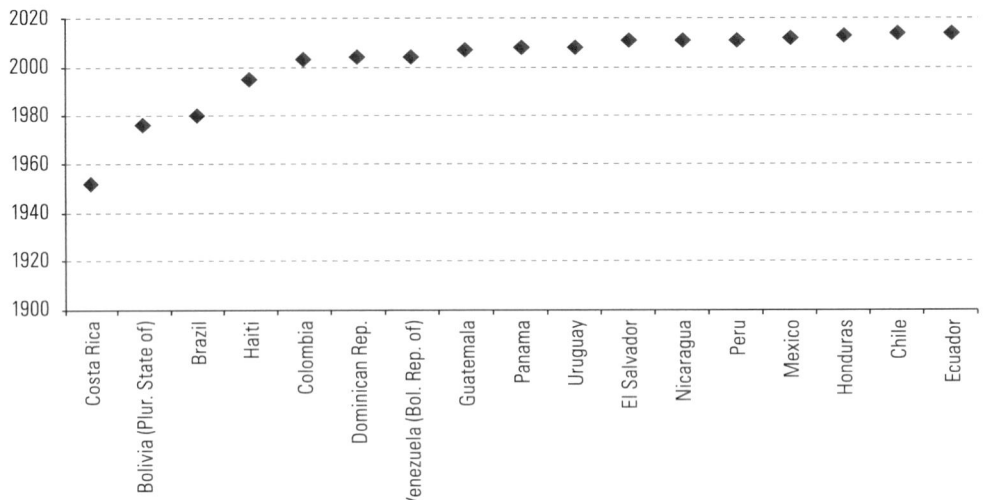

Source: Economic Commission for Latin America and the Caribbean (ECLAC), on the basis of C. Maldonado, J. Martínez and R. Martínez, "Protección social y migración: una mirada desde las vulnerabilidades a lo largo del ciclo de la migración y de la vida de las personas", Project Documents (LC/TS.2018/62), Santiago, Economic Commission for Latin America and the Caribbean (ECLAC), 2018; and official data from the respective bodies.

The ministry that is most often in charge of intersectoral coordination is the Ministry of Foreign Affairs or its equivalent (six countries) (see annex table V.A1.6). In the rest of the countries, the nature of the coordinating office varies a great deal, with this function being performed by the Ministry of Labour in some countries and the Ministry of Justice or the Ministry of Internal Affairs in others. The ministries or agencies that make use of these coordination services also vary a great deal. Nonetheless, they include the Ministry of Foreign Affairs in 15 cases, the Ministry of Labour or its equivalent in 13 countries and the Ministry of Internal Affairs or its equivalent in 8. Other ministries in the social sector that make use of these intersectoral coordination services in fewer than half the countries include the Ministry of Social Development (6), Ministry of Health (5), Ministry of Education (5) and Ministry of Justice (2).

This is a significant development, given the challenges that migrants face in terms of social inclusion. In addition to putting inter-agency coordination mechanisms in place, the move towards working in tandem with social agencies in the areas of health, education, housing, discrimination and gender equality is surely a step in the right direction. It would also be a positive step for these intersectoral mechanisms to involve civil society, since, in many cases, civil society organizations play an important role in helping to meet the needs of the most vulnerable migrants and to address the difficulties that they face, as well as raising awareness of those needs and difficulties. As yet this has been done in only four countries, however. Another crucial factor is coordination between different levels of the government apparatus, especially given the pivotal role that local governments can play in assisting migrants. Box V.6 describes what is being done in the City of São Paulo, where a succession of local government administrations have been working to coordinate and consolidate a multisectoral, rights-based and gender- and lifecycle-sensitive migration policy framework at the municipal level.

Intersectoral mechanisms for combating human trafficking have also been established on the basis of special-purpose legislation in this area in 16 countries of the region, although this has taken longer to occur than in the case of migration policy. The first such mechanism was created in 2005 in Brazil and the most recent was established in 2017 in Peru (see figure V.17).

Box V.6
Building an institutional framework for the City of São Paulo's municipal policy for the immigrant population

The Constitution of Brazil states that only the federal government may pass legislation on matters relating to emigration and immigration. The operationalization of the nation's migration policy has, however, led to the duplication of measures at the different levels of government and the fragmentation of government responses to the needs that arise. It has also resulted in an almost total lack of government support for some of the civil society organizations that serve the migrant population. Against this backdrop, the City of São Paulo, which has a long-standing tradition of hosting migrant populations, has taken on a leading role in constructing a policy designed for, and together with, immigrants and refugees.

The Coordinating Office for Migration Policy was founded by local government and civil society representatives in 2013. The values and guiding principles of the Office are based on the mainstreaming of rights, intersectorality and participation. One of the Office's first participatory initiatives was the creation of a seat for a special immigrant representative on the Participatory Municipal Council (Decree No. 54.645/2013), where civil society oversees municipal planning activities, government action and government expenditures and makes suggestions concerning public actions and policies. The representation of immigrants was later expanded to take in all of the city's 32 subprefectures, with the number of seats varying on the basis of migrant population density. In all cases, at least 50% of these seats are held by women. The Participatory Municipal Planning and Budget Council has also had the assistance of an immigrant representative in developing and implementing its planning cycle. The Coordinating Office for Migration Policy has held conferences on municipal policies for immigrants, conducted awareness-raising and anti-xenophobia campaigns and provided support for cultural fairs and events, as well as offering ongoing training and Portuguese-language courses for immigrants.

The Coordinating Office partners with the municipal government to implement the Municipal Policy for the Immigrant Population, which was launched in 2016 (Municipal Act No. 16.478/16). The framework for this policy is provided by international human rights instruments, the Federal Constitution and the Foreign Nationals Statute. The policy's priority areas include guaranteed right of access to social assistance, health care and education; the promotion of the right to decent work; recognition of the value of cultural diversity; promotion of the right to decent housing; and promotion of access to sports and recreation. One of the major developments in this policy has been the inclusion of targets and goals for specific groups (older adults, the homeless, marginalized youth), although more disaggregated data are needed in order to fine-tune various aspects of the policy. Some of the more recent policy actions have focused on promoting the regularization of people's migration status, decent work and access to financial and banking services; raising awareness about the value of immigrants' cultures; and the establishment of the Immigrant Referral and Welcome Centre. Initially, the Coordinating Office had no permanent staff, a situation which demanded extraordinary efforts in order to carry out the proposed actions.

It is difficult to determine the size of the Office's budget, but it is clear that it is no more than a fraction of the budget of its parent organization, the Municipal Human Rights and Citizenship Department (2.6% in 2018), and an even smaller portion of the budget of the Municipality of São Paulo as a whole (0.005% in 2018). Strengthening this social institutional structure would increase the likelihood that the Municipal Policy for the Immigrant Population will prove to be an effective, efficient, sustainable and transparent instrument.

The Municipal Policy has been consolidated and its continuity has been assured thanks to the work of successive municipal government administrations, even though the arrival of an unexpectedly large and growing number of immigrants has posed a challenge, as well as opening up an opportunity to strengthen this pioneering policy. This policy has succeeded in opening the way for a horizontal, cross-cutting intersectoral dialogue within and outside the government and in gaining the trust and fostering the engagement of all the various individuals and groups concerned. The Municipal Policy for the Immigrant Population has thus become a model for other local governments in Brazil and around the world, thanks to the approaches that it promotes, the results it has achieved and the central role it assigns to local government in an area of policy (migration) that has traditionally been the purview of national governments. The challenge now is to continue to work to develop quality social policies and to consolidate them in a way that makes any future policy discontinuity unlikely by virtue of an awareness and appreciation of the valuable contributions to the social fabric that migrants make.

Source: C. Sampaio and C. Baraldi, "Políticas migratórias em nível local: análise sobre a institucionalização da política municipal para a população imigrante de São Paulo", *Project Documents* (LC/TS.2019/16), Santiago, Economic Commission for Latin America and the Caribbean (ECLAC), 2019.

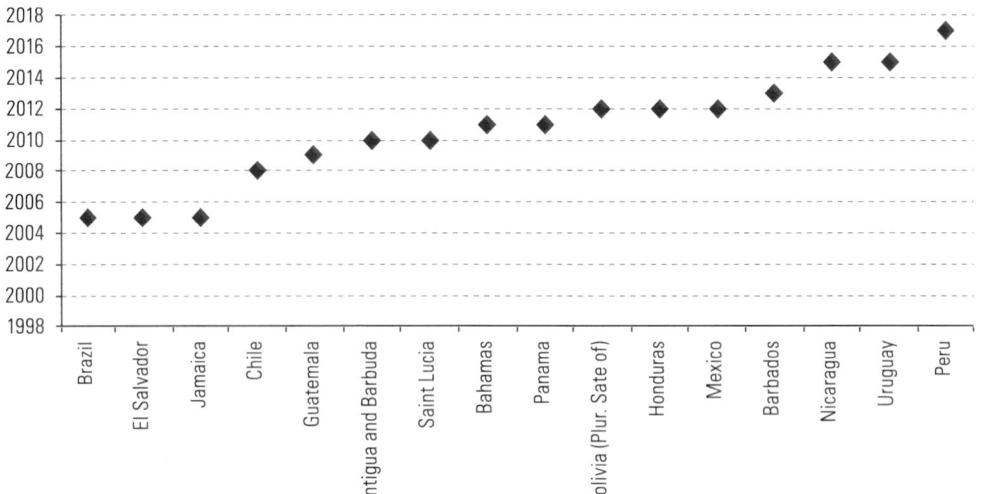

Source: Economic Commission for Latin America and the Caribbean (ECLAC), on the basis of C. Maldonado, J. Martínez and R. Martínez, "Protección social y migración: una mirada desde las vulnerabilidades a lo largo del ciclo de la migración y de la vida de las personas", *Project Documents* (LC/TS.2018/62), Santiago, Economic Commission for Latin America and the Caribbean (ECLAC), 2018; and official data from the respective bodies.

The ministries that preside over these intersectoral boards or councils vary across countries, but the Ministry of Internal Affairs heads them up in seven of the countries and the Ministry of Justice and Public Security does so in five others (see figure V.18 and annex table V.A1.5). Civil society plays a part in these mechanisms in 12 of the countries (Antigua and Barbuda, Barbados, Brazil, Chile, Honduras, Mexico, Nicaragua, Panama, Peru, the Plurinational State of Bolivia, Saint Lucia and Uruguay). The position of civil society organizations within these mechanisms differs from country to country, however. In some cases, they have a consultative role; in others, they are included at the behest of one authority or another; and in still others, they participate on an equal footing with the ministerial bodies concerned.

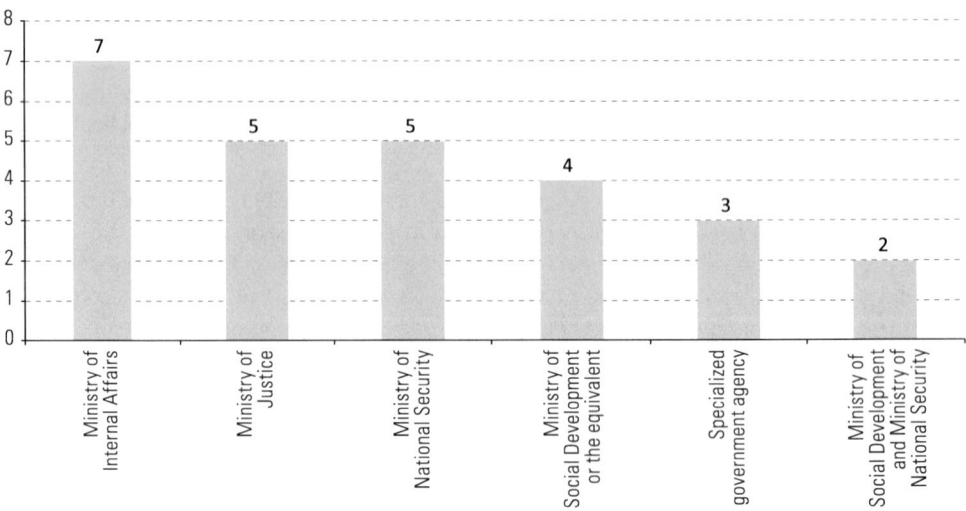

Source: Economic Commission for Latin America and the Caribbean (ECLAC), on the basis of C. Maldonado, J. Martínez and R. Martínez, "Protección social y migración: una mirada desde las vulnerabilidades a lo largo del ciclo de la migración y de la vida de las personas", *Project Documents* (LC/TS.2018/62), Santiago, Economic Commission for Latin America and the Caribbean (ECLAC), 2018; and official data from the respective bodies.
[a] The countries are: Antigua and Barbuda, Argentina, Bahamas, Barbados, Belize, Brazil, Chile, Colombia, Costa Rica, Dominican Republic, Ecuador, El Salvador, Grenada, Guatemala, Guyana, Haiti, Honduras, Jamaica, Mexico, Nicaragua, Panama, Paraguay, Peru, Plurinational State of Bolivia, Saint Lucia and Uruguay.

The ministries and other agencies that make use of these coordination mechanisms vary from country to country (see annex table V.A.1.5), but the Ministry of Foreign Affairs or its equivalent is invariably one of them. The national police force or its equivalent is an independent participant in eight countries, which is to be expected, since human trafficking is such a serious crime. The Ministry of Social Development is involved in these mechanisms in nine of the countries of the region, along with other social ministries such as the Ministry of Labour (13 countries), the Ministry of Education (11) and the Ministry of Health (10). The Ministry of Women's Affairs or its equivalent is involved in these mechanisms in 11 of the countries, which points up the degree to which human trafficking is associated with human rights violations and gender-based discrimination in the countries of the region. A greater number of ministries, other bodies and civil society organizations and stakeholders are involved in the intersectoral coordination mechanisms for government efforts to combat human trafficking than is the case in the corresponding mechanisms for migrant services.

E.   Migration cycle and challenges for inclusion and social protection: some priority policy areas

Public policies and institutions are faced not only with the urgent need to provide protection to the many recent forced migrants in the region, but also long-term responses to international migration, within and towards Latin America and the Caribbean.

The great challenge regarding the social protection of migrants is dealing with mobile populations, whose needs extend beyond nation-State borders because they maintain responsibilities on both sides of these borders (Serra and Mazzucato, 2017), whereas most institutions are national in nature and designed to cater to sedentary populations. However, in the absence of national policies and strategies to address this challenge, civil society organizations and some local governments fill the policy gap by providing legal, social and even medical attention to foreign residents who need it (de las Heras, 2016, p. 11). There follows a description of some social protection instruments that are particularly important for migrants.

1.   Social protection instruments in the migration cycle

Historically speaking, social protection systems have not been designed with the migrant population in mind, be it regular or irregular, much less those forced to migrate by disasters or economic or political crises. As a result, fully integrating this ever-growing group into social protection poses major institutional and coverage challenges today. Given these developments, ECLAC (2017b) has proposed advancing towards universal social protection systems, seeking to integrate the contributory and non-contributory components, along with labour market regulation and the establishment of care systems, as the necessary bases for achieving greater social inclusion, reducing inequality and providing stronger guarantees of exercise of rights.

For this, both the overarching institutional framework and social protection frameworks in particular must recognize migrants as bearers of the same human and civil rights as the national population, at least as regards access to essential services, with a view to ensuring their economic, social and cultural rights. Achieving such progress is a highly complex proposition, given that in most of the countries in the region social protection coverage is not universal even for non-migrant citizens and humanitarian crises put pressure on already scarce resources. Strategies to broaden coverage thus need to consider a heterogeneous population. The case of irregular migrants presents particular difficulty: should systems aim to ensure universal coverage open to all regardless of migratory status, or should steps first be taken to regularize and formalize irregular migrants to provide them with a basic legal identity in the country? Much depends on the specific components of social protection in discussion: for example, the importance of ensuring universal access to basic education and health care for the whole child population and other groups vulnerable to poverty is obvious. A number of priority areas of action in this regard are described later in this section. Be this as it may, given the panorama of the institutional framework in relation to migration, it is essential to build and deepen intersectoral spaces in which the complex issues facing migrants can be addressed.

Following Sabates-Wheeler and Koettl (2010) and Sabates-Wheeler and Waite (2003), several types of specific social protection instruments for migrants may be identified. First are promotion measures aimed at improving people's income and capacities in destination countries. These include labour market policies, for example, which are aimed at ensuring decent work for the population in general, including migrants, regulating access to employment, job quality and working conditions and combating discrimination. In relation to the points above, these instruments safeguard egalitarian access to social services such as education and health, while also promoting initiatives in areas where migrants need specific support, such as access to housing and help for transport. In this regard, measures to provide support for transport feature throughout the migration cycle.

Second are instruments to protect migrants' rights and safeguard against discrimination and abuse. Here, the countries' legal and normative frameworks and the effective application of these are especially important; hence the importance of international conventions on the protection of migrants being in force and of awareness-raising of the rights and contributions associated with migration in the destination country. Third are preventive instruments which help to avoid the disadvantages and deprivations associated with different risks and vulnerabilities. These include different modalities of insurance, public and private. Lastly, there are instruments for alleviating deprivations after they have already arisen. An example is housing subsidy for migrants, so that they can turn to this additional support to realize that right. Information campaigns and legal (especially consular) advice are also widely used at different stages of the migration cycle and help to foster informed, safe, orderly and regular migration. Some instruments are important at all stages of the cycle, such as labour market policies to promote decent work and the adaptation of national normative frameworks to international standards to ensure the human rights of migrants, as discussed in chapter IV.

2.   Areas of priority attention to protect migrants and foster their social and labour inclusion

This section identifies some priority areas for government action to promote the inclusion and social protection of migrants. These areas are largely associated with social protection and have to do with aspects that have an impact on migrants' well-being and their power vis-à-vis acts of discrimination and breaches of their rights. These are particularly important in the current complex conditions in relation to migration in northern Central America, and in the cases of Venezuelans, Haitians and other nationalities.

(a) Access to legal identity

Identity is a human right enshrined in a number of international instruments, including the Universal Declaration of Human Rights (1948), the International Covenant on Civil and Political Rights (1966), the American Convention on Human Rights (1969) and the Convention on the Rights of the Child (1989). The 2030 Agenda for Sustainable Development captures this priority in target 16.9 of the Sustainable Development Goals (SDGs), "By 2030, provide legal identity for all, including birth registration". Registration of the birth of a child is an official record of his or her existence and recognition by the law. Non-registration of the birth of a child is a violation that child's rights, because it leads to statelessness and prevents social participation, later inclusion in economic life and access to education, health, social protection and care, among other basic satisfiers.

Access to identity is closely bound up with social inclusion policies for combating discrimination and enabling people to enjoy their social, economic, civil and cultural rights. However, Latin America and the Caribbean still suffers from a high level of birth underregistration.

Importantly, registration procedures need to be free of charge, to contribute to universality and opportunity and, precisely, to remove entry barriers for those without resources. Children must be registered immediately after birth, or within the period established by the law. However, the risk of non-registration is very high among some population groups, one of these being the children of regular and —especially— irregular migrants. Parents with irregular status often leave their children unregistered, despite their right to be registered and to take the nationality of the place of destination, mainly because of fear of identification and punishment by the authorities (AECID/UNICEF, 2012).

Non-registration and, thus, lack of documentation leads to a series of disadvantages, such as deportation or being statelessness, that is, having no nationality. Above all, however, lacking a birth certificate or documentation, irregular migrants are barred from enjoyment of their human rights, which jeopardizes their future development. Indeed, a birth certificate is still a requirement for access to a range of social entitlements, such as registering for school and for health services. It is a matter of concern that, because it is treated as a requirement, it becomes a factor of exclusion. Some countries that take a universalist stance on education may allow the children of irregular migrants to enrol in school; however, these children may be at risk of not receiving a certificate of primary school completion at the end of this stage, which prevents their progress to secondary school. With regard to health access, unregistered persons can often aspire only to emergency care. Lack of identification is also a barrier to owning property and exercising the civic right to vote in elections, among other disadvantages and flagrant rights violations.

SDG 16 thus recognizes that official identity has a dual benefit: on the one hand, it allows people to interact with the authorities, and on the other, it enables the authorities to plan and budget for basic services more effectively. Broadening and facilitating routes towards regularization and adapting these to the profile of migrants is crucial to expand the battery of policies, especially social protection policies, without the need for special arrangements or exceptions with respect to the rest of the population.

(b) Access to decent work

Work is a core axis in the link between migration and social protection. First, because one of the main reasons why people migrate is precisely in search of better employment opportunities. Even where work is not the main driver of the decision to migrate, it is the principal vehicle by which migrants acquire social rights and access to multiple services in their destination country. Work and employment quality determine, to a great extent, migrants' integration into the country they arrive in: people who are integrated into the formal job market are able to earn wages, pay into the social security system, take out medical insurance and obtain coverage to protect their dependants. Formal work brings entitlements and offers a quick route to social inclusion.

Access to work is related to local regulations regarding entry and permitted length of stay. In some of the region's countries, a contract of employment is a necessary condition to remain there legally, unless the purpose of entry is other than work, i.e. as a partner, student or other non-labour-related status.

However, most of the Latin American and Caribbean labour markets are characterized by high levels of informality. An unavoidable challenge is to improve legislation in order to broaden coverage and bring informal migrant workers into social protection systems, as well as sensitizing employers to these workers' rights (ILO, 2015). In this regard, it is necessary to place the employment conditions of migrants on the agendas of trade union organizations with a view to integrating the immigrant population. A more active role in this area on the part of labour inspection bodies is also needed, and abuse by employers must be reduced. In order to plan these policies, the specific features of sectors where migrants tend to work need to be taken into account.

If migrant women enter paid domestic work, it must be borne in mind that unionization in this sector tends to be limited and policies should engage employer families. Paid domestic employment is one of the occupations involving greater risks of violence and harassment at work, owing to a number of factors, including the following: it is performed in a private sphere, i.e. the employers' household; it takes place in the framework of asymmetric power relations, i.e. labour relations marked by extreme inequality and verticality; it is isolated work, insofar as there are no other workers present; it is undervalued and little recognized; and, despite legal advances, there is still too little effective legal protection.

Patriarchal cultural patterns have naturalized the idea that women have innate aptitudes for domestic and care work; this prevents this work from being socially valued and the household being recognized as a place of work. The failure to recognize that paid domestic work should —like any other work— be protected by employment law, leaves paid domestic workers more exposed to violence and harassment (ECLAC, 2019a).

Stronger channels of communication are needed between countries to coordinate social security systems to achieve genuine portability of rights for migrants. Labour inspection to ensure decent employment conditions also contributes to changing employers' practices, because discrimination against migrants —by disregarding social and labour rights— also makes migrants cheaper to employ, at the expense of local workers (Sabates-Wheeler and Koettl, 2010, p. 153). This is a key factor contributing to sentiments of rejection or even xenophobia towards the migrant population.

(c) Access to health in general and sexual and reproductive health, in particular

Health care is a basic human right which should be guaranteed for migrants in all circumstances. However, it is an unfulfilled right at all stages of the migration cycle, especially for women and children. Migrants are particularly vulnerable in terms of health, owing, among other things, to the emotional turmoil of leaving one's place of origin, changes in diet or difficulties in eating properly, uncertainty during the journey and threats against physical integrity along the route, especially in the case of journeys undertaken in inhumane conditions under difficult climate conditions or through hostile territory.

Some groups of migrants warrant priority treatment in the health system of countries of transit, destination or return; for example, unaccompanied children seeking to join family or other adults, who are exposed to abuse and the health effects of undernourishment, which is especially worrying given that are still developing physically. Sexual and reproductive health is also a necessity for many children and adolescents who suffer sexual abuse and must receive preventive care in order to avoid unwanted early pregnancies and ensure respect for bodily and sexual rights.

(d) Access to education

SDG target 4.1 —"By 2030, ensure that all girls and boys complete free, equitable and quality primary and secondary education leading to relevant and effective learning outcomes"— offers the guidance, in relation to the case of migrants, that education must be guaranteed for all children (ECLAC, 2017a). However, continuity of education tends to be compromised in the case of children and adolescents of school age who have undergone irregular migration experiences, whether they have migrated alone or with family or other adults. Universal access for all children and adolescents to education systems should be a less controversial topic, owing to the benefits that fulfilling the right to education brings in terms of inclusion and social adaptation to the destination country, and in terms of future productivity.

What is more, migrant workers should not have limitations placed on their possibilities of training in order to facilitate their entry to decent work. This also applies to migrants who, having trained in their country of origin, need to validate their studies to improve their work prospects. Recognition of studies often encounters barriers and institutional failings (slow and complicated processes). Multilateral agreements on education matters facilitate this process, which can be crucial for the well-being of individuals and their dependants. This is particularly important in the case of return migrants, especially children and young people, who often have to re-enter the school system in their return country and therefore need to validate the studies completed in their previous country of residence and ensure they are recognized.

(e) Access to housing

Access to decent housing is one of migrants' main needs and is closely related to the well-being, health and safety of their dependants, both short term and over the longer run. With a sound dwelling, understood in terms of the quality of materials, space and location, comes access to basic services, such as drinking water, electricity and removal of waste, among others, in both rural and urban areas.

However, overcrowding and lack of access to housing and basic services are areas where migrants tend to be worse affected, even when they have networks of family and friends who provide them with accommodation.

People arriving in a new country do not usually invest in property right away, but seek out rental accommodation in line with their needs and financial resources. Migrants come up against a whole range of difficulties and abuses in this process, from discrimination and overpricing to overcrowding and lack of services in the dwelling. In practice, they are often forced to resort to strategies involving severe overcrowding and sublets in poor conditions.

The route to ensuring the right to housing includes standards on housing quality and their enforcement by the authorities, proper regulation of the housing market to avoid abuses and access to residential property subsidies or mortgage loans that enable immigrants to start out on the road towards owning their own home.

(f) Access to care services

Care is an essential service for human reproduction. Its importance is recognized in the 2030 Agenda for Sustainable Development in SDG target 5.4, "Recognize and value unpaid care and domestic work through the provision of public services, infrastructure and social protection policies and the promotion of shared responsibility within the household and the family as nationally appropriate".

Care-related needs are closed tied to higher-dependency stages of the life cycle, especially childhood, older persons, and those of advanced age. There are also several factors that make care one of the social, family and individual needs that is growing fastest in importance. From the perspective of social protection, care has ceased to be seen as a private matter with which policy should not interfere, given that it is something that family members (especially women) perform on an unpaid basis, sometimes at the expense of their own well-being, autonomy and enjoyment of rights.

In Latin America, work in the domestic sector and care represented 27.2% of employment for women and 5.6% for men around 2017. Of these figures, 11.2% and 3.2%, respectively, consisted of direct provision of care services (ECLAC, 2019a). The female migrant labour force plays a large role in this sector, since many migrant women have specialized in this work, often in precarious and informal conditions. The global care chains formed by migrant women transfer care tasks from households in countries of origin to households in the host country, leading to the formation of transnational families in which motherhood is exercised remotely. It also means that in countries of origin where care systems are absent, unmet care needs must be satisfied in other ways, either through family and community networks or by purchasing care services in the local market, again increasingly being provided by women in precarious and poorly paid conditions.

(g) Financial inclusion

The financial system and bankarization form part of the process of productive inclusion. However, not only migrants, but some of the native population as well, find it difficult to access this system. The structural barrier this represents is not insignificant. Here, the region also suffers from large access gaps between individuals and between large and small firms, as well as from phenomena such as informality, where access barriers in the formal financial system lead people to seek often costly and precarious informal alternatives (Pérez and Titelman, 2018). The fact that migrants cannot access credit, save and then send remittances to meet needs at home at a low cost is an additional disadvantage. Generally speaking, the first requirement to enter the banking system is to have a valid legal identity, so migrants who remain in irregular conditions cannot access the financial system. This also affects their chances of starting up an enterprise or saving resources to generate a wealth stock that could serve as a source of income and assets for the family in the medium and long terms.

Many migrants have the ability to make real contributions to the production process by performing an economic activity, creating sources of employment and paying taxes. However, this is hard to materialize if they face barriers to entering the financial system. Hence the importance of creating routes into this system and considering the potential of migrants to contribute to the economy of their host country.

3.   Institutional challenges in relation to migrants and social protection

(a) Bilateral and multilateral coordination

Because migrants are often employed in the informal economy, they tend to face lower levels of social protection than the average (ECLAC/ILO, 2017). To address this situation, the governments of destination countries may adjust their legislations to regulate and broaden the benefits to which migrants are entitled. Governments can also sign bilateral and multilateral agreements to ensure continuity of the coverage that migrants have in their respective country of origin. This does not mean exchanging money between countries, but rather recognizing periods of affiliation or contribution that enable migrants to meet entitlement requirements (Arellano, 2013, p.120). Bilateral social security agreements pursue two aims: (i) to help ensure continuity of coverage for those whose working life has spanned two countries, so that they can access benefits in either country, and (ii) to eliminate the double contribution to social security that can arise when a worker from one country works in another. In this respect, active and effective implementation of the Ibero-American Multilateral Agreement on Social Security of the Ibero-American Social Security Organization (OISS) is extremely important within the Ibero-American sphere.

At the same time, social protection for international migrant workers has four areas that must be considered: (i) access to contributory social security in countries of origin and destination; (ii) subrogation of acquired social security entitlements between countries of origin and destination; (iii) decent work conditions for migrants in host countries and proper recruitment processes for migrants in their countries of origin; and (iv) access to formal and informal support networks for migrants and their families.

(b) Portability of migrant workers' social protection rights

The discussions surrounding migration have still touched little upon the topic of rights portability. However, as well as migrants and remittances, in the future, entitlements, benefits and rights of access to services acquired in countries of origin or destination should be brought within formal and predictable channels. Portability concerns the situation in which many migrant workers find themselves: after paying into the social security system in their host country they find upon return to their country of origin that the entitlements they have built up are not recognized. In this scenario, the fact of migration leaves migrants and their families unprotected, and entails a loss for those who otherwise have a legitimate right to return to their country of origin. Portability of rights is no small challenge for countries with large flows of migrants, since they must not only adjust legal frameworks but also create the institutional structure to make them operational.

Bilateral or multilateral agreements between countries and their effective implementation through active strategies are the route towards recouping these rights. The Ibero-American Multilateral Agreement on Social Security is an instrument established for this purpose, which includes the countries of Latin America, as well as Spain and Portugal. It thus offers a long-term solution for migrants in the Ibero-American sphere, insofar as it addresses the needs of a highly dynamic intra- and interregional migration flow which, in the first case, is increasing rapidly.

The main virtue of this Convention is that it seeks to coordinate national legislations in relation to pensions, without altering them, as a way of ensuring economic security in old age between States with very different social security models. Thus far, it has been ratified by 12 countries: Argentina, Bolivarian Republic of Venezuela, Brazil, Chile, Ecuador, El Salvador, Paraguay, Peru, Portugal, Plurinational State of Bolivia, Spain and Uruguay. Of these countries, all but one has also signed the respective Agreement for Application.

At the regional level, the Montevideo Consensus on Population and Development, which was adopted in 2013 by the Regional Conference on Population and Development in Latin America and the Caribbean, proposed under its priority measure number 69 to "Promote the signing of bilateral and multilateral social security conventions to enable migrant workers to accumulate years of service" (ECLAC, 2013, p. 27). The step from formal portability to subrogation or enforceability requires active strategies and policies to materialize access to the benefits, entitlements, services and, in general, the rights acquired by migrants.

F.   Concluding remarks

Migration —which is increasingly forced in several corridors of the region— will remain a core trend within and between our societies, owing to persistently disparate levels of development, enjoyment of rights, well-being, economic and political stability, the state of processes of demographic change in different locations, greater relative ease of movement and communication across borders and, more generally, a multitude of motivations and driving factors. Although in the medium to long term, migration flows generally contribute positively to the economy, increase diversity and enrich culture, in the near term they pose numerous policy challenges at the local, national and regional levels.

In this context, the 2030 Agenda and Global Compact for Safe, Orderly and Regular Migration adopted by States represent a commitment to safeguard the rights and well-being of migrants (Guterres, 2018). All public policies, and particularly social policies, must "facilitate orderly, safe, regular and responsible migration and mobility of people" (target 10.7 of the Sustainable Development Goals). Guaranteeing the human rights of migrants at all stages of the migration cycle is closely linked to addressing the multiple vulnerabilities at each point in the cycle.

Significant changes are occurring in the three foremost patterns of international migration in the Latin America and the Caribbean, which have been apparent since the second half of the twentieth century: emigration outside the region, historical immigration from overseas and intraregional flows. A fourth, often less prominent pattern is planned or forced repatriation (Martínez, Cano and Soffia, 2014). In the case of emigration outside the region, there appear to be recent indications of an unstable trend in flows to the main extraregional destinations, especially from Mexico to the United States, which seems to have slowed, but not from Central America. The relative importance of immigration of people from other regions has declined, but this remains part of the migratory reality of the region.

Flows within the region have intensified the most, since the bulk of the current immigrant population originated from other countries in the region. However, in recent years the number of countries of origin has increased and new destination countries have emerged, examples being the wave of Venezuelan emigration and the presence of Venezuelan migrants in a number of countries in the region, including Colombia, Peru, Chile and some Caribbean countries. The negative net migration in the region, that is to say a predominance of emigration, remains a defining feature of movements. Current estimates put the ratio at six emigrants for every two immigrants.

One of the great difficulties the region faces in addressing all of the complexities of these migration trends is the lack of reliable, timely and suitable information. The intervals between population censuses —the most comprehensive sources of data— are very long, hindering their use in analysis of prevailing conditions, and other valuable sources of information, such as household surveys, still only allow for limited use. Nonetheless, this report has attempted to draw on these elements. Other national instruments (such as national registers or national surveys focusing on migration) are very useful, but they are difficult to compare between countries. In short, migration is a topic that merits generation of better statistical information, given its complexity and the number of related social and economic issues.

Faced with this great diversity of situations and scenarios, this section has underscored the great importance of adopting a perspective that takes into account the different vulnerabilities of migrants in the different stages of the migration cycle, and of guaranteeing an approach that is sensitive to gender and peoples' life cycles. In the current situation, this is a particularly pressing issue in the migration corridors of people originating from Central America and the Bolivarian Republic of Venezuela. Migration poses a challenge with regard to social inclusion, and there are signs of numerous gaps in access to basic services, decent work and social protection mechanisms in countries of destination, while in countries of origin or return there are multiple unmet needs; in turn, in transit scenarios, addressing the needs of migrants pose challenges of their own. Moreover, there are countries that are simultaneously countries of origin, transit, destination and return, with very diverse needs that must be met.

In addition to the issues related to social inclusion, migration poses challenges regarding the fight against discrimination, whether against foreigners per se of on ethnic and racial grounds, as in the case of migrants who are Afrodescendants or indigenous persons. With respect to this, there are indications that the greater precariousness people are perceiving in their environment (precarious income or job uncertainty, for example) can feed feelings of rejection of migrants. For all these reasons, progress towards higher levels of well-being, enjoyment of rights and access to social protection for the population as a whole is another front in the battle against discrimination of migrants.

Although there is a heterogeneous relationship between poverty and migration (migrants are not necessarily poorer, in the different countries that have information available), remittances play an important role in alleviating the poverty of many families in several countries in the region. In some cases, remittances are important in macroeconomic terms (as a percentage of GDP or of exports and imports), particularly in Central America and several Caribbean countries. This underscores the need to facilitate access to remittances and lower their cost, as stated in SDG target 10.c: "By 2030, reduce to less than 3 per cent the transaction costs of migrant remittances and eliminate remittance corridors with costs higher than 5 per cent" (ECLAC, 2016).

The response to these challenges of inclusion and guaranteeing rights requires a national institutional framework with mechanisms for social and labour inclusion (especially access to social protection and decent work) and international cooperation (regional and subregional) to guarantee the rights and well-being of migrants —particularly the most vulnerable— during transit and return, if these journeys are not made by choice but by force. With respect to social and labour inclusion, some priority areas for action have been proposed in which access mechanisms must be built or strengthened, such as: legal identity, decent work and portability of social security rights, health and sexual and reproductive health, education, housing (especially overcrowding and access to housing services), care services and financial inclusion (especially to facilitate access to remittances).

Advances in this area should begin by adapting national regulatory frameworks to international standards and implementing such standards effectively, as well as achieving effective intersectoral coordination at the central level, resulting in national and systemic strategies for social and labour inclusion of migrants and the protection of their rights (Maldonado, Martínez and Martínez, 2018; Martínez, 2017). As previously mentioned, the most recent migration legislation shows significant progress, in terms of adopting a rights-based approach rather than an approach centred solely on national security or control. In particular, the principles of this legislation need to be put into practice, avoiding at all costs discretionary measures resulting from administrative decisions. In addition to coordination at the central level, another important dimension is territorial coordination between levels of government. The emergence in recent years of multisectoral coordination bodies, for example in the form of National Migration Councils, is an important step forward.

With regard to the effective incorporation of a gender perspective, progress has been made, as reflected by the repository of regulations on international migration of the Gender Equality Observatory for Latin America and the Caribbean of ECLAC, which contains 95 laws from 21 countries in Latin America and the Caribbean. Of this total, 31 legal systems (including constitutions) refer centrally to migration, its regulation and the protection of migrant populations; 19 refer to matters relating to prevention of trafficking and smuggling of persons, punishment of such acts and assistance for victims; 45 refer to miscellaneous related issues. Also, given the role played by civil society organizations in the very different migration scenarios, the space for collaboration and complementarity between authorities and civil society must be defined, without this resulting in policies that fail to fulfil national and international commitments in relation to migrants.

Lastly, one area where more work is needed in the medium term is the portability of contributory social protection rights. As migration flows have become more complex and a person's working life is likely to include fluctuations between episodes of formality and informality, possibly in two or more countries, it is crucial to build access channels and guarantee pension benefits.

Bibliography

Acosta, P., P. Fajnzylber and H. López (2007), "The impact of remittances on poverty and human capital: evidence from Latin American household surveys", *Policy Research Working Paper*, No. 4247, Washington, D.C., World Bank.

AECID/UNICEF (Spanish Agency for International Development Cooperation/United Nations Children's Fund) (2012), *Sistematización de buenas prácticas desarrolladas para la promoción de estilos de vida saludables y la atención de la salud materno-infantil en la población indígena Ngöbe: Área de Salud de Coto Brus*, San José.

Afro Alianza Dominicana (2013), *Informe Alternativo en relación a la Convención Internacional sobre la Eliminación de Todas las Formas de Discriminación Racial*, Santo Domingo [online] http://www2. ohchr.org/English/bodies/cerd/docs/ngos/AfroAlianzaDominicana_DominicRepublic_CERD82.pdf.

Arellano, P. (2013), "Propiedad sobre los fondos de pensiones y continuidad de las prestaciones para los trabajadores técnicos extranjeros", *Ius et Praxis*, vol. 19, No. 2, Talca, University of Talca.

Banton, M. (1977), *A idéia de raça*, Lisboa, Edições 70.

Belvedere, C. and others (2007), "Racismo y discurso: una semblanza de la situación argentina", *Racismo y discurso en América Latina*, T. van Dijk (coord.), Barcelona, Gedisa.

Brown, R. and others (2014), "Measuring remittances through surveys: methodological and conceptual issues for survey designers and data analysts", *Demographic Research*, vol. 31, Rostock, Max Planck Institute for Demographic Research.

Cadem (2018), "Encuesta N° 215, 26 de febrero de 2018", Santiago [online] https://www.cadem. cl/encuestas/encuesta-no215-26-de-febrero-de-2018/.

Campos, A. (2012), "Racialización, racialismo y racismo: un discernimiento necesario", *Revista de la Universidad de La Habana*, No. 273, Havana, University of Havana.

Carrasco, I. and J. Suárez (2018), "Migración internacional e inclusión en América Latina: análisis en los países de destino mediante encuestas de hogares", *Social Policy series*, No. 231 (LC/TS.2018/57), Santiago, Economic Commission for Latin America and the Caribbean (ECLAC), August.

Casaravilla, D. (1999), *Los laberintos de la exclusión: relatos de inmigrantes ilegales en Argentina*, Buenos Aires, Lumen Humanitas.

Castells, M. (2004), "Immigrant workers and class struggles in advanced capitalism: the Western European experience", *Migration, Globalization and Ethnic Relations: An Interdisciplinary Approach*, M. Mobasher and M. Sadri (eds.), New Jersey, Pearson Prentice Hall.

Cena, R. (2014), "Fronteras complejas: protección social e inmigración. Asignación universal por hijo para protección social e inmigración en Argentina", *Polis: Revista Latinoamericana*, vol. 13, No. 38, Santiago, University of Los Lagos.

Del Popolo, F. (ed.) (2018), *Los pueblos indígenas en América (Abya Yala): desafíos para la igualdad en la diversidad* (LC/PUB.2017/26), Santiago, Economic Commission for Latin America and the Caribbean (ECLAC).

De las Heras, M. (2016), "Los migrantes como sujetos del sistema de protección social en Chile", *Temas de la Agenda Pública*, vol. 11, No. 91, Santiago, Pontifical Catholic University of Chile, November.

ECLAC (Economic Commission for Latin America and the Caribbean) (2019a), *Women's autonomy in changing economic scenarios* (LC/CRM.14/3), Santiago, forthcoming.

____(2019b), *Critical obstacles to inclusive social development in Latin America and the Caribbean: background for a regional agenda* (LC/CDS.3/3), Santiago.

____(2018), *Towards a regional agenda for inclusive social development: bases and initial proposal* (LC/MDS.2/2), Santiago, September.

____(2017a), *Linkages between the social and production spheres: gaps, pillars and challenges* (LC/CDS.2/3), Santiago.

____(2017b), "Situacíón de las personas afrodescendientes en América Latina y desafíos de políticas para la garantía de sus derechos", *Project Documents* (LC/TS.2017/121), Santiago.

____(2016), *The social inequality matrix in Latin America* (LC/G.2690(MDS.1/2)), Santiago.

____(2013), *Montevideo Consensus on Population and Development* (LC/L.3697), Santiago, September.

Fries, L. (2019), "Las mujeres migrantes en las legislaciones de América Latina: análisis del repositorio de normativas sobre migración internacional del Observatorio de Igualdad de Género de América Latina y el Caribe", *Gender Affairs series*, No. 157 (LC/TS.2019/40), Santiago, Economic Commission for Latin America and the Caribbean (ECLAC).

Gatica, G. (2013), "Perspectivas socioeconómicas de la población migrante en Costa Rica", *XIX Informe Estado de la Nación*, San José, Programa Estado de la Nación.

Giménez, G. (2006), "El debate contemporáneo en torno al concepto de etnicidad", *Revista Cultura y Representaciones Sociales*, vol. 1, No. 1, Mexico City, National Autonomous University of Mexico.

Grimson, A. (2006), "Nuevas xenofobias, nuevas políticas étnicas en la Argentina", *Migraciones regionales hacia la Argentina: diferencia, desigualdad y derechos*, A. Grimson and E. Jelin (comps.), Buenos Aires, Prometeo.

Guterres, A. (2018), "Towards a new global compact migration", New York, United Nations, January.

Halpern, G. (2010), "Desigualdades y diferencias: inmigrantes regionales en la Argentina", *América Latina interrogada: mecanismos de la desigualdad y exclusión social*, Mexico City, Miguel Ángel Porrúa.

ILO (International Labour Organization) (2017), "Panamá: mercado laboral y condiciones laborales" [online] http://libguides.ilo.org/migracionlaboralALCpaises/Panama-mercadolaboral.

____(2015), *World of Work 2014: Developing with Jobs*, Geneva.

ILO/ECLAC (International Labour Organization/Economic Commission for Latin America and the Caribbean) (2017), "Labour immigration in Latin America", *Employment Situation in Latin America and the Caribbean* (LC/TS.2017/30), Santiago.

INDH (National Human Rights Institute) (2017), *Informe Anual 2017: Situación de los Derechos Humanos en Chile*, Santiago.

Kundnani, A. (2001), "From Oldham to Bradford: the violence of the violated", *Race and Class*, vol. 43, No. 2, Thousand Oaks, SAGE Publications.

Lévi-Strauss, C. (1952), *Race et histoire*, Paris, United Nations Educational, Scientific and Cultural Organization (UNESCO).

López, E. (2019), "La protección de los trabajadores migrantes basada en derechos: la respuesta normativa de la OIT", *Temas Socio-Jurídicos*, vol. 38, No. 76, Bucaramanga, Autonomous University of Bucaramanga, June.

Maldonado, C., J. Martínez and R. Martínez (2018), "Protección social y migración: una mirada desde las vulnerabilidades a lo largo del ciclo de la migración y de la vida de las personas", *Project Documents* (LC/TS.2018/62), Santiago, Economic Commission for Latin America and the Caribbean (ECLAC), September.

Margulis, M. and C. Belvedere (1998), "La 'racialización' de las relaciones de clase en Buenos Aires: genealogía de la discriminación", *La segregación negada: cultura y discriminación social*, M. Margulis and others, Buenos Aires, Biblos.

Martínez, R. (ed.) (2017), *Institutional frameworks for social policy in Latin America and the Caribbean*, ECLAC Books, No. 146 (LC/PUB.2017/14-P), Santiago, Economic Commission for Latin America and the Caribbean (ECLAC).

Martínez, J., M. Cano and M. Soffia (2014), "Tendencias y patrones de la migración latinoamericana y caribeña hacia 2010 y desafíos para una agenda regional", *Population and Development series*, No. 109 (LC/L.3914), Santiago, Economic Commission for Latin America and the Caribbean (ECLAC).

Martínez, S. and B. Wooding (2017), "El antihaitianismo en la República Dominicana: ¿un giro biopolítico?", *Migración y Desarrollo*, vol. 15, No. 28, Zacatecas, International Network on Migration and Development.

MIDES (Ministry of Social Development) (2017), *Caracterización de las nuevas corrientes migratorias en Uruguay: nuevos orígenes latinoamericanos: estudio de caso de las personas peruanas y dominicanas. Informe final*, Montevideo.

Morales, A., G. Acuña and K. Li Wing-Ching (2010), "Migración y salud en zonas fronterizas: Nicaragua y Costa Rica", *Population and Development series*, No. 94 (LC/L.3249-P), Santiago, Economic Commission for Latin America and the Caribbean (ECLAC).

Morales, A., D. Lobo and J. Jiménez (2014), "La travesía laboral de la población Ngäbe y Buglé de Costa Rica a Panamá: características y desafíos", San José, Latin American Faculty of Social Sciences (FLACSO).

Oteiza, E., S. Novick and R. Aruj (1997), *Inmigración y discriminación: políticas y discursos*, Buenos Aires, Grupo Editor Universitario.

Pérez, E. and D. Titelman (eds.) (2018), *La inclusión financiera para la inserción productiva y el papel de la banca de desarrollo*, ECLAC Books, No. 153 (LC/PUB.2018/18-P), Santiago, Economic Commission for Latin America and the Caribbean (ECLAC).

Pizarro, C. (2012), "El racismo en los discursos de los patrones argentinos sobre inmigrantes laborales bolivianos: estudio de caso en un lugar de trabajo en Córdoba, Argentina", *Convergencia*, vol. 19, No. 60, Toluca, Autonomous University of the State of Mexico.

___(2009), "XOlor a negroX: discurso, discriminación y segmentación étnica en el lugar de trabajo", document presented at the IV Symposium of Researchers in Discourse Studies, Córdoba, National University of Córdoba [online] http://aledar.fl.unc.edu.ar/files/PizarroCynthia.pdf.

Quijano, A. (2005), "Colonialidade do poder, eurocentrismo e América Latina", *A colonialidade do saber: eurocentrismo e ciências sociais: perspectivas latinoamericanas*, Buenos Aires, Latin American Social Sciences Council (CLACSO).

Sabates-Wheeler, R. and J. Koettl (2010), "Protección social para los migrantes: los desafíos de la prestación en el contexto del cambio en los flujos migratorios", *Revista Internacional de Seguridad Social*, vol. 63, No. 3-4, Hoboken, Wiley.

Sabates-Wheeler, R. and M. Waite (2003), "Migration and social protection: a concept paper", *Working Paper*, No. T2, Sussex, University of Sussex.

Sampaio, C. and C. Baraldi (2019), "Políticas migratórias em nível local: análise sobre a institucionalização da política municipal para a população imigrante de São Paulo", *Project Documents* (LC/TS.2019/16), Santiago, Economic Commission for Latin America and the Caribbean (ECLAC).

Segura, G. (2015), "Informe final: acceso a la regularización migratoria e integración social de las personas migrantes en Costa Rica", *Vigésimo Segundo Informe Estado de la Nación en Desarrollo Humano Sostenible*, San José, Programa Estado de la Nación.

Serra, E. and V. Mazzucato (2017), "Mobile populations in immobile welfare systems: a typology of institutions providing social welfare and protection within a mobility framework", *The European Journal of Development Research*, vol. 29, No. 4, Berlin, Springer.

Teixidó, E. and G. Baer (2003), "La migración laboral en Argentina", *Migraciones laborales en Sudamérica: el Mercosur ampliado*, Estudios sobre Migraciones Internacionales, No. 63, E. Teixidó and others, Geneva, International Labour Organization (ILO).

Tijoux, M. (2016), *Racismo en Chile: la piel como marca de la inmigración*, Santiago, Editorial Universitaria.

___(2011), "Negando al 'otro': el constante sufrimiento de los inmigrantes peruanos en Chile", *Mujeres inmigrantes en Chile: ¿mano de obra o trabajadoras con derechos?*, C. Stefoni (ed.), Santiago, Alberto Hurtado University.

Tijoux, M. and S. Palominos (2015), "Aproximaciones teóricas para el estudio de procesos de racialización y sexualización en los fenómenos migratorios de Chile", *Polis: Revista Latinoamericana*, vol. 14, No. 42, Santiago, University of Los Lagos.

United Nations (2001), "Protocol to Prevent, Suppress and Punish Trafficking in Persons, Especially Womenand Children, supplementing the United Nations Convention against Transnational Organized Crime", *United Nations Convention against Transnational Organized Crime* (A/RES/55/25), New York, January.

UNODC (United Nations Office on Drugs and Crime) (2018), *Global Report on Trafficking in Persons 2018*, New York.

Wade, P. (2011), "Raza y naturaleza humana", *Tabula Rasa*, N° 14, Bogotá, Colombian Cultural Journals Association.

___(2000), *Raza y etnicidad en Latinoamérica*, Quito, Ediciones Abya-Yala.

Annex V.A1

Table V.A1.1
Quality indicators of the probit regression model adjusted to explain the poverty situation
based on a set of determinants, 2014–2017

Country	Area under the receiver operating characteristic (ROC) curve	Sensitivity (percentages)	Specificity (percentages)	Cases correctly classified (percentages)	Pseudo R2
Argentina (2017)	0.8343	31.76	96.10	84.02	0.2485
Bolivia (Plurinational State of) (2017)[a]	0.8114	50.00	88.75	75.85	0.2304
Brazil (2015)	0.8348	34.06	96.28	84.06	0.2576
Chile (2017)	0.8209	14.07	98.75	82.29	0.2089
Colombia (2017)	0.8289	46.99	92.08	79.54	0.2571
Costa Rica (2017)	0.8416	30.77	97.28	86.64	0.2658
Dominican Republic (2016)	0.7999	47.85	88.65	74.81	0.2138
Ecuador (2017)	0.8175	40.25	93.98	80.38	0.2413
Guatemala (2014)	0.8166	75.50	71.59	73.65	0.2482
Honduras (2016)[a]	0.8027	77.24	68.44	73.19	0.2244
Nicaragua (2014)[a]	0.8082	62.07	81.95	73.99	0.2278
Panama (2017)	0.8749	48.59	94.72	85.35	0.3343
Paraguay (2017)[a]	0.8531	50.63	92.33	82.35	0.2934
Peru (2017)[a]	0.8564	45.79	93.96	83.18	0.2996
Uruguay (2017)[a]	0.9241	12.02	99.83	97.65	0.3502

Source: Economic Commission for Latin America and the Caribbean (ECLAC), on the basis of Household Survey Data Bank (BADEHOG).
Note: The model adjusts the probability of being poor for a set of determinants that includes migrant status, age, gender, education, employment status, area of residence, age and sex of the head of household, type of household and a set of deprivations related to basic services and housing structure, employment status and social protection in the household. Sensitivity measures the percentage of poor people that the model predicts correctly. Specificity measures the percentage of non-poor people correctly predicted by the model. The area under the ROC curve allows for evaluation of the predictive power of the model through a balance between sensitivity and specificity. Values close to 1 indicate an almost perfect forecast from the model; values close to 0.5 indicate that the model has no predictive power.
[a] Countries in which the required level of precision is not reached in estimates of the poverty of the migrant subpopulation.

Table V.A1.2
Latin America and the Caribbean (31 countries): main instruments regulating migration, by country, August 2019[a]

Country	Year	Law	Area	Purpose
Antigua and Barbuda	2016	Act	Immigration and Passport Amendment Act	Amending the Immigration and Passport Act No. 6 of 2014, and related and secondary purposes.
	1945	Act	Immigration and Passport Act	No official information available.
Argentina	2017	Decree no. 70/2017	Amendment of Acts No. 25.871 and No. 346	Amending the name of Chapter I of Title II of Act No. 25.871 to: "categories, requirements and deadlines for admission". Amendment of Acts No. 25.871 and No. 346.
	2010	Decree No. 616	Regulation of Migration Act No. 25.871 and its amending instruments	Regulating fundamental political lines and strategic bases to facilitate the procedures that foreigners must complete.
	2003	Act No. 25.871	Migration Act	Establishing fundamental policy lines and strategic bases in the area of migration.
Bahamas	1997	Act No. 4 of 1997	Immigration (Amendment) Act, 1997	Amending the Immigration Act by granting residence permits without restrictions on work to persons born outside the Bahamas whose mother is a Bahamian citizen, and to persons married to Bahamian citizens.
	1967	Act	Immigration Act	No official information available.
Barbados	1979	Act	Immigration Act (Cap. 190)	No official information available.
Belize	2000	Act	Immigration Act (Cap. 156)	No official information available.
	2000	Act	Aliens Act (Cap. 159)	No official information available.
Bolivia (Plurinational State of)	2013	Act No. 370	Migration Act	Regulating the entry, transit, stay and departure of persons in the territory of the Plurinational State of Bolivia, and establishing institutional coordination spaces that guarantee the rights of Bolivian and foreign migrants.
Brazil	2017	Act No. 13.445	Migration Act	Regulating the rights and duties of migrants and visitors, regulating their entry and stay in the country and establishing principles and guidelines for public policies concerning emigrants.
Chile	1984	Decree No. 597	New Regulation on Foreign Nationals (1984)	Issuing a new Regulation on Foreign Nationals, which is necessary in view of the decentralization of functions, the incorporation of computational tools into the functions relating to foreign nationals and amendments to Decree Law No 1.094 of 1975.
	1975	Decree Law No. 1094	Rules on foreigners in Chile	Regulating the entry, residence, permanent residence, exit, re-entry, expulsion and control of foreign nationals.
Colombia	2009	Decree No. 2622	Amendments to Decree No. 4000 of 2004	Amending Decree No. 4000 of 2004 and issuing general provisions applicable to migration.
	2004	Decree No. 4000	Migration provisions (amended by Decree No. 2622 of 2009)	Establishing provisions on issuance of visas, control of foreign nationals and other migration matters.
	2013	Decree No. 834	Decree of provisions relating to migration	Establishing provisions on migration for the Republic of Colombia.
Costa Rica	2009	Act No. 8764	General Act on Migration and Foreign Nationals	Regulating the entry of Costa Ricans and foreign nationals into the territory of the Republic of Costa Rica, and their exit from said territory and regulating stays by foreign nationals in the country.
Cuba	1978	Act No. 1312	Migration Act	Regulating provisions on migration in a single legal instrument, to facilitate their application and interpretation.
Dominica	1996	Act	Immigration and Passport Act, Chapter 18:01	No information available.
Dominican Republic	2004	Act 285 of 2004	General Migration Act	Ordering and regulating migratory flows in the national territory, both in terms of entry, stay and exit, as well as immigration, migration and the return of Dominican nationals.
Ecuador	2017	Organic Law on Human Mobility	Organic Law on Human Mobility	Regulating the exercise of rights, obligations, institutions and mechanisms relating to persons in the area of human mobility, including emigrants, immigrants, persons in transit, Ecuadorian returnees, persons in need of international protection, victims of the crimes of trafficking in persons and smuggling of migrants, and members of their families.
El Salvador	1993	Legislative Decree No. 670	Migration Act Reform	Reforming the Migration Act
	1986	Decree No. 299	Act on Foreign Nationals	No official information available.
	1958	Legislative Decree No. 2772	Migration Act	Organizing and coordinating services related to Salvadorans and foreign nationals entering and exiting the territory of the Republic of El Salvador, through examination and classification of their documents; studying the problems caused by such movements, and monitoring compliance with legal provisions regarding stays and activities of foreign nationals in the country.
Grenada	1969	Act	Act No. 26 of 1969, Chapter 145	No official information available.
Guatemala	2016	Decree No. 44 of 2016	Migration Code	Maintaining the unity of the legal framework that regulates migration, in order to guarantee legal certainty for individuals and to enable full access to knowledge of the country's current provisions, as well as incorporating international standards on protection and assistance for migrants and their families in transit, at destination and upon return.
	2010	Decree No. 10	Migration Act Reform	Reforming the Migration Act
	1998	Decree No. 95-98	Migration Act	Guaranteeing an effective regulation of migration, regulating Guatemalans and foreign nationals entering and exiting the national territory, and regulating stays by foreign nationals in national territory.

Table V.A.2 (concluded)

Country	Year	Law	Area	Purpose
Guyana	1947	Act	Immigration Act (Cap. 14:02) (No. 42 of 1947)	No official information available.
	2007	Act	Immigration (Amendment) Act	Amending the Immigration Act of 1947.
Honduras	2004	Decree No. 208	Act on Migration and Foreign Nationals	Regulating Honduras' migration policy, the entry or exit of Hondurans and foreign nationals, stays by foreign nationals in Honduran territory and issuance of migration documents.
Haiti	1984	Decree	Decree updating the Labour Code of 12 September 1961, Chapter VI - Foreign Labour	Establishing that no foreign nationals may exercise a trade or profession of any kind for profit, either as self-employed workers or as employees, unless they have work permits issued by the labour directorate, pursuant to the Decree.
	1984	Decree	Decree on permanent residence	Creating a suitable structure to regulate the permanent residence of all those who meet the conditions established in the Decree.
	1959	Decree	Immigration and Emigration Decree	Enacting a decree on immigration and emigration on the basis of the reports of the Secretaries of State for the Interior and National Defence, Foreign Affairs, Finance, Trade and Industry, and by virtue of the following considerations: that special care should be taken in the ports and airports of the Republic of Haiti to provide more facilities to travellers and visitors to the country; that, in order to achieve this, it is important to obtain the necessary funds, and that, with the current state of finances, such funds cannot be provided in the Budget of the Republic of Haiti without a combination of certain immigration and emigration taxes.
	1978	Law	Organic Law on the Immigration and Emigration Service	Not available
Jamaica	1964	Act 48 of 1964	Foreign Nationals and Commonwealth Citizens (Employment) Act	The Act provides that in order for foreign nationals (or Commonwealth citizen) to obtain gainful employment they must have work permits, which they must be presentable upon request. Offences against the Act are punishable as crimes. An application for a work permit may be granted at the absolute discretion of the minister. Work permits are granted in writing and may be changed or cancelled at any time. The minister may also grant general or group exemptions from application of the Act.
Mexico	2011	Decree Law	Migration Act	Regulating Mexicans and foreign nationals entering and exiting the territory of the United Mexican States, as well as the transit and stay of foreign nationals in said territory, within a framework of respect, protection and safeguarding of human rights, contribution to national development, and preservation of national sovereignty and security.
Nicaragua	2011	Act No. 761	General Act on Migration and Foreign Nationals	Regulating the entry of Nicaraguans and foreign nationals into the territory of the Republic of Nicaragua, and their return to said territory, as well as stays by foreign nationals in the country, without prejudice to the provisions of the Political Constitution of the Republic of Nicaragua, duly ratified international treaties and conventions and duly approved regional integration agreements.
Panama	2008	Decree Law No. 3	Decree Law No. 3 creating the National Migration Service, the Migration Corps and establishing other provisions	Regulating migratory movements by Panamanians and foreign nationals entering and exiting the country, and regulating stays by foreign nationals in national territory, establishing the requirements and procedures for acquiring Panamanian nationality by naturalization, and creating the National Immigration Service and the Migration Corps.
Paraguay	1996	Act No. 978	Migration Act	Regulating the migration of foreign nationals and the emigration and repatriation of Paraguayans, in order to promote the population and workforce flows that the country requires, establishing the organization responsible for implementing national migration policy and implementing the provisions of the Act.
Peru	2017	Legislative Decree No. 1350	Legislative Decree on Migration	Regulating entry, stay and departure of foreign nationals, issuance of travel documents for Peruvians and foreign nationals, and contributing to the integration of migrants and guaranteeing their rights.
Saint Kitts and Nevis	2002	Act No. 10 of 2002	Immigration Act (Cap. 6.02)	No official information available.
Suriname	1995	State Decree No. 85	Aliens Decree	No official information available.
	1991	Act	Aliens Act 1991	Regulating the admission and expulsion of foreign nationals.
Trinidad and Tobago	1974	Act	Immigration Act, 1969 (Cap. 18:01)	No official information available.
Uruguay	2008	Act No. 18.250	Migration Act	Recognizing the inalienable right of migrants and members of their families —without prejudice to their migration status— to migration, family reunification, due process and access to justice, as well as to equality of rights with nationals, without distinction of any kind on the basis of gender, race, colour, language, religion or belief, political views or other opinions.
Venezuela (Bolivarian Republic of)	2004	Act No. 37.944	Act on Foreign Nationals and Migration	Regulating all matters related to admission, entry, stay, registration, control and information, departure and re-entry of foreign nationals, as well as their rights and obligations.

Source: Economic Commission for Latin America and the Caribbean (ECLAC), on the basis of C. Maldonado, J. Martínez and R. Martínez, "Protección social y migración: una mirada desde las vulnerabilidades a lo largo del ciclo de la migración y de la vida de las personas", *Project Documents* (LC/TS.2018/62), Santiago, Economic Commission for Latin America and the Caribbean (ECLAC), 2018; and official information updated to August 2019 from the respective countries.

a The legal instruments mentioned in the table are those identified through available official information. In each country there are various decrees and other types of secondary regulations that have not been included, given the scope and extent of the study. Those decrees or regulations complement and develop some sectoral aspects in areas such as health, education, work, social security and housing.

Table V.A1.3
Latin America and the Caribbean (9 countries): main instruments regulating emigration, by country, August 2019[a]

Country	Year	Law	Area	Purpose
Antigua and Barbuda	1929	Act	Emigrants Protection Act, Cap. 150	Establishing that workers wishing to migrate from the country must first obtain a permit from the competent authority. Regulating recruiting agents and establishing penalties for offences against the Act. Establishing a fund for distressed emigrants for repatriation of emigrant workers.
Colombia	2011	Act No. 1465	Act on Nationals Living Abroad	Creating the National Migration System as a harmonious set of institutions, civil society organizations, rules, processes, plans and programmes, to contribute to the design, implementation, monitoring and evaluation of migration policy.
	2011	Resolution No. 5813	"Colombia Nos Une" Programme	Creating the Internal Working Group of the "Colombia Nos Une" programme of the Office of Migratory, Consular and Citizen Service Affairs. Supporting the Office and, through it, the General Secretariat and the Minister responsible for the comprehensive migration policy of the Colombian State. Supporting the design of public policies, strategies and programmes of regional governments that benefit the Colombian population living abroad and their families at origin.
El Salvador	2011	Decree No. 655	Special Law for the Protection and Development of Salvadoran Migrants and their Families	Creating the guiding constitutional principles that guarantee the rights of Salvadoran migrants and their families by designing, formulating, evaluating and monitoring comprehensive public protection and development policies, through inter-institutional and intersectoral coordination between the State and civil society, in national development processes. Defining the Strategic Plan for the Protection and Development of Salvadoran Migrants and their Families.
Guatemala	2008	Decree No. 46-2007	Act on the National Migrant Assistance Council of Guatemala	Creating the National Migrant Assistance Council of Guatemala, which may be referred to as CONAMIGUA and is the governmental entity that coordinates, defines, supervises and oversees the actions and activities of State bodies and entities to protect, serve, assist and aid Guatemalan migrants and their families in Guatemala, as well as migrants in the national territory.
Honduras	2013	Decree No. 106	Act on Protection of Honduran Migrants and their Families	Establishing the rules and conditions to enable Hondurans abroad to exercise their constitutional rights and duties. Establishing the legal framework within which the State of Honduras must exercise its protective action with respect to the dignity, human rights and other constitutional guarantees and rights of Hondurans abroad.
Mexico	2003	Decree	Decree establishing the Institute for Mexicans Living Abroad	The purpose of the Institute for Mexicans Living Abroad is to promote strategies, integrate programmes, collect proposals and recommendations from communities, their members, their organizations and consultative bodies, all aimed at raising the standard of living of Mexican communities abroad, as well as implementing the guidelines issued by the National Council for Mexican Communities Abroad.
Paraguay	2009	Act No. 3958	Act amending and expanding Act No. 227/93 creating the Secretariat of Development for National Repatriates and Refugees and amending Act No. 978/96 on Migration	Amending and expanding Act No. 227/93 creating the Secretariat of Development for National Repatriates and Refugees and amending Act No. 978/96 on Migration.
Peru	2005	Act No. 28182	Migration Incentives Act	Promoting the return of Peruvians from abroad to engage in professional or business activities. Establishing incentives and actions that encourage their return to contribute to generating productive employment and greater tax collection.
	2010	Act No. 29.495	Act on Consultative Councils of Peruvian Communities Abroad	Forming a space for dialogue and cooperation with the consular office of their jurisdiction, to support the tasks of protection of Peruvian nationals and to ensure better linkage of nationals with Peru's specific problems.
Trinidad and Tobago	1918	Act 2 of 1918	Emigration (Children) Act (Cap. 18:02).	Regulating emigration of children from Trinidad and Tobago. Establishing that no child shall be allowed to leave Trinidad and Tobago for the purpose of proceeding to any country to which the Act applies unless the child is accompanied by a parent or legal guardian, or unless his parent, legal guardian, or the person who has for the time being the charge of or control over the child has obtained the written permission of the Minister.

Source: Economic Commission for Latin America and the Caribbean (ECLAC), on the basis of C. Maldonado, J. Martínez and R. Martínez, "Protección social y migración: una mirada desde las vulnerabilidades a lo largo del ciclo de la migración y de la vida de las personas", *Project Documents* (LC/TS.2018/62), Santiago, Economic Commission for Latin America and the Caribbean (ECLAC), 2018; and official information updated to August 2019 from the respective countries.

[a] The legal instruments mentioned in the table are those identified through available official information.

Table V.A1.4
Latin America and the Caribbean (32 countries): structure and oversight of agencies responsible for migrants, August 2019

Country	Body specialized in migration	Lead or coordinating authority
Antigua and Barbuda	Department of Immigration	Ministry of Foreign Affairs, International Trade and Immigration
Argentina	National Bureau of Migration	Ministry of the Interior, Public Works and Housing
Bahamas	Department of Immigration	Ministry of Foreign Affairs and Department of Immigration
Barbados	Barbados Immigration Department	Prime Minister's Office
Belize	Department of Immigration and Nationality Services	Department of Immigration
Bolivia (Plurinational State of)	Directorate-General for Migration	Ministry of the Interior
Brazil[a]	Migration Department	Ministry of Justice and Public Security
Chile	Department for Foreign Nationals and Migration	Ministry of the Interior and Public Security
Colombia	Migración Colombia	Ministry of Foreign Affairs
Costa Rica	Directorate-General for Migration and Foreign Nationals	Ministry of the Interior and Policing
Cuba	Office for Identification, Immigration and Foreign Nationals	Ministry of the Interior
Dominica	Immigration Division	Ministry of Justice, Immigration and National Security
Dominican Republic	Directorate-General for Migration	Ministry of the Interior and Policing
Ecuador	Police General Headquarters/National Migration Office	Ministry of the Interior
El Salvador	Directorate-General for Migration and Foreign Nationals	Ministry of Justice and Public Security
Grenada	Ministry of Legal Affairs	Ministry of Legal Affairs
Guatemala	Directorate-General for Migration	Ministry of the Interior
Guyana	Department of Citizenship and Immigration Support Services	Ministry of the Presidency
Haiti	Office for Immigration and Emigration	Ministry of the Interior and of Territorial Authorities, Ministry of National Defence
Honduras	Directorate-General for Migration and Foreign Nationals	Secretariat for Governance, Justice and Decentralization
Jamaica	Passport, Immigration and Citizenship Agency (PICA)	Ministry of National Security
Mexico	National Institute of Migration	Secretariat of the Interior
Nicaragua	Directorate-General for Migration and Foreign Nationals	Ministry of the Interior
Panama	National Immigration Service for Panama	Ministry of Interior and Justice
Paraguay	Directorate-General for Migration	Ministry of the Interior
Peru	National Superintendency of Migration	Ministry of the Interior
Saint Kitts and Nevis	Immigration Department	Ministry of National Security
Saint Lucia	Immigration Department	Ministry of Home Affairs, Justice and National Security
Suriname	Ministry of Foreign Affairs	Ministry of Foreign Affairs
Trinidad and Tobago	Immigration Division	Ministry of National Security
Uruguay	National Directorate for Migration	Ministry of the Interior
Venezuela (Bolivarian Republic of)	National Migration Commission	Ministry of People's Power for Foreign Affairs

Source: Economic Commission for Latin America and the Caribbean (ECLAC), on the basis of C. Maldonado, J. Martínez and R. Martínez, "Protección social y migración: una mirada desde las vulnerabilidades a lo largo del ciclo de la migración y de la vida de las personas", *Project Documents* (LC/TS.2018/62), Santiago, Economic Commission for Latin America and the Caribbean (ECLAC), 2018; and official data from the respective bodies.
[a] In the case of Brazil, migration is also partly managed by the labour portfolio, which was the Ministry of Labour and Employment until January 2019, when it was brought within the Ministry of the Economy.

Table V.A1.5
Latin America and the Caribbean (16 countries): ministerial portfolios that include the intersectoral coordination bodies responsible for matters relating to victims of trafficking in persons, August 2019

Country	Collegial mechanism of intersectoral social policy coordination	Mechanism chaired by	Ministry of foreign affairs or equivalent	Ministry of social development or equivalent	Ministry of the interior or equivalent	Policing or equivalent	Ministry of justice	Ministry of health	Ministry of defence	Ministry of education	Ministry of labour	Ministry for women's affairs	Ministry of human rights	Ministry for foreign nationals or similar	Social protection	Civil society
Antigua and Barbuda	Trafficking in Persons Prevention Committee	Ministry of Legal Affairs, Public Safety and Labour	✓		✓	✓					✓	✓		✓		✓
Bolivia (Plurinational State of)	Plurinational Council for the Prevention of Trafficking and Smuggling of Persons	Ministry of Justice	✓		✓	✓	✓			✓	✓				✓	✓
Bahamas	Inter-Ministry Committee on Trafficking in Persons	Minister of National Security	✓	✓	✓											
Barbados	National Task Force on Human Trafficking	Attorney General	✓	✓	✓	✓								✓		✓
Brazil	Advisory Group for the National Plan to Combat Trafficking in Persons (PNETP)	Ministry of Justice	✓	✓			✓	✓		✓	✓	✓	✓			✓
Chile	Intersectoral Committee on Trafficking in Persons	Undersecretary of the Interior, Ministry of the Interior	✓		✓	✓	✓				✓	✓		✓		✓
El Salvador	National Council for the Prevention of Trafficking of Persons	Ministry of Justice and Public Security	✓	✓	✓	✓	✓	✓		✓	✓	✓				
Guatemala	Inter-institutional Commission on the Prevention of Trafficking in Persons	Office of the Vice-President	✓	✓	✓			✓		✓	✓	✓				
Jamaica	National Taskforce Against Trafficking in Persons (NATFATIP)	Ministry of Justice	✓	✓		✓	✓		✓	✓		✓		✓		
Honduras	Inter-institutional Commission against Commercial Sexual Exploitation and Trafficking in Persons	Board of Directors (elected by majority, comprising seven members sitting for two years)	✓	✓			✓	✓		✓		✓				✓
Mexico	Inter-Secretariat Commission to Prevent, Combat and Punish Offences Related to Trafficking in Persons	Secretariat of the Interior	✓	✓	✓		✓	✓		✓	✓	✓	✓	✓	✓	✓
Nicaragua	National Coalition for the Prevention of Trafficking of Persons	Ministry of the Interior	✓		✓	✓		✓		✓	✓	✓	✓	✓	✓	✓
Panama	National Commission for the Prevention of Trafficking of Persons	Ministry of Public Security	✓	✓	✓			✓		✓	✓	✓	✓			✓

Table V.A1.5 (concluded)

Country	Collegial mechanism of intersectoral social policy coordination	Mechanism chaired by	Ministry of foreign affairs or equivalent	Ministry of social development or equivalent	Ministry of the interior or equivalent	Policing or equivalent	Ministry of justice	Ministry of health	Ministry of defence	Ministry of education	Ministry of labour	Ministry for women's affairs	Ministry of human rights	Ministry for foreign nationals or similar	Social protection	Civil society
Peru	Multisectoral Standing Commission on the Prevention of Trafficking in Persons and Smuggling of Migrants	Ministry of the Interior	✓		✓		✓	✓		✓	✓	✓				✓
Saint Lucia	Anti-trafficking Task Force	Ministry of Home Affairs, Justice and National Security	✓		✓					✓	✓				✓	✓
Trinidad and Tobago	National Task Force Against Trafficking in Persons															
Uruguay	Inter-institutional Committee to Prevent and Combat Trafficking in Persons	Ministry of Social Development	✓	✓	✓			✓		✓	✓					✓

Source: Economic Commission for Latin America and the Caribbean (ECLAC), on the basis of official data from the respective countries.

Table V.A1.6
Latin America and the Caribbean (17 countries): ministerial portfolios that include the intersectoral coordination mechanisms for protecting and assisting migrants, August 2019

Country	Collegial mechanism of intersectoral social policy coordination	Mechanism chaired by	Ministry of foreign affairs or equivalent	Ministry of social development or equivalent	Ministry of the interior or equivalent	Ministry of justice	Ministry of health	Ministry of defence	Ministry of education	Ministry of labour	Ministry for women's affairs[a]	Ministry of human rights	Ministry for foreign nationals or similar[b]	Social protection[b]
Bolivia (Plurinational State of)	National Migration Council[a]	No official information available.												
Brazil	National Immigration Council	Ministry of Justice[c]										✓		✓
Chile	National Migration Policy Council	Ministry of the Interior and Public Security	✓	✓	✓	✓	✓		✓	✓	✓			✓
Costa Rica	National Migration Council	Directorate-General for Migration and Foreign Nationals	✓		✓		✓	✓	✓	✓			✓	✓
Colombia	National Intersectoral Migration Commission	Ministry of Foreign Affairs	✓	✓	✓					✓				✓
Dominican Republic	National Migration Council	Ministry of the Interior and Policing	✓		✓		✓			✓				
Ecuador	National Council for Equality in Human Mobility	Ministry of Foreign Affairs and Human Mobility	✓											

Table V.A1.6 (concluded)

Country	Collegial mechanism of intersectoral social policy coordination	Mechanism chaired by	Ministry of foreign affairs or equivalent	Ministry of social development or equivalent	Ministry of the interior or equivalent	Ministry of justice	Ministry of health	Ministry of defence	Ministry of education	Ministry of labour	Ministry for women's affairs[a]	Ministry of human rights	Ministry for foreign nationals or similar[b]	Social protection[b]
El Salvador	National Council for the Protection and Development of Migrants and their Families	Vice-Ministry for Salvadorans Living Abroad	✓		✓		✓		✓	✓				
Guatemala	National Migrant Assistance Council of Guatemala	National Migrant Assistance Council of Guatemala								✓		✓		
Honduras	National Council for the Protection of Honduran Migrants	Secretariat of Foreign Affairs and International Cooperation	✓							✓		✓		
Haiti	National Migration Office	Ministry of Social Affairs and Labour	✓	✓	✓					✓				
Mexico	Migration Policy Advisory Council	Secretariat of the Interior	✓							✓		✓		
Nicaragua	National Council on Migration and Foreign Nationals	Ministry of the Interior	✓	✓						✓		✓		
Panama	Advisory Council on Migration	Ministry of Interior and Justice	✓					✓		✓			✓	
Peru	Standing Multisectoral Commission "Intersectoral Working Group for Migration Management"	Ministry of Foreign Affairs	✓	✓	✓	✓	✓		✓	✓			✓	✓
Uruguay	National Migration Board	Ministry of Foreign Affairs	✓	✓	✓					✓			✓	
Venezuela (Bolivarian Republic of)	National Refugee Commission	Minister responsible for foreign affairs and migration	✓					✓	✓	✓				

Source: Economic Commission for Latin America and the Caribbean (ECLAC), on the basis of C. Maldonado, J. Martínez and R. Martínez, "Protección social y migración: una mirada desde las vulnerabilidades a lo largo del ciclo de la migración y de la vida de las personas", *Project Documents* (LC/TS.2018/62), Santiago, Economic Commission for Latin America and the Caribbean (ECLAC), 2018; and official information updated to August 2019 from the respective countries.

a Included only when participating as an independent party.

b Included only when its functions are independent of the Ministry of Social Development or equivalent body.

c The legislation originally identified the Ministry of Labour, which in January 2019 was brought within the Ministry of the Economy.

Publicaciones recientes de la CEPAL
ECLAC recent publications

www.cepal.org/publicaciones

Informes Anuales/*Annual Reports*
También disponibles para años anteriores/*Issues for previous years also available*

Estudio Económico de América Latina y el Caribe 2019
Economic Survey of Latin America and the Caribbean 2019

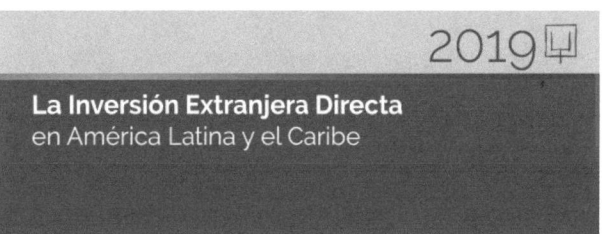

La Inversión Extranjera Directa en América Latina
y el Caribe 2019
*Foreign Direct Investment in Latin America and the
Caribbean 2019*

Balance Preliminar de las Economías de América Latina
y el Caribe 2018
*Preliminary Overview of the Economies of Latin America
and the Caribbean 2018*

Anuario Estadístico de América Latina y el Caribe 2018
*Statistical Yearbook for Latin America
and the Caribbean 2018*

Panorama Social de América Latina 2018
Social Panorama of Latin America 2018

Perspectivas del Comercio Internacional
de América Latina y el Caribe 2018
*International Trade Outlook for Latin America and the
Caribbean 2018*

El Pensamiento de la CEPAL/*ECLAC Thinking*

Desarrollo e igualdad: el pensamiento de la CEPAL en su séptimo decenio.
Textos seleccionados del período 2008-2018

La ineficiencia de la desigualdad
The Inefficiency of Inequality

Horizontes 2030: la igualdad en el centro del desarrollo sostenible
Horizons 2030: Equality at the centre of sustainable development
Horizontes 2030: a igualdade no centro do desenvolvimento sustentável

 Libros y Documentos Institucionales/*Institutional Books and Documents*

Informe de avance cuatrienal sobre el progreso y los desafíos regionales de la Agenda
2030 para el Desarrollo Sostenible en América Latina y el Caribe
Quadrennial report on regional progress and challenges in relation to the 2030 Agenda
for Sustainable Development in Latin America and the Caribbean

Hacia una agenda regional de desarrollo social inclusivo: bases y propuesta inicial
Towards a regional agenda for inclusive social development: bases and initial proposal

 Libros de la CEPAL/*ECLAC Books*

Recursos naturales, medio ambiente y sostenibilidad. 70 años de pensamiento
de la CEPAL

La bonanza de los recursos naturales para el desarrollo: dilemas de gobernanza

Logros y desafíos de la integración centroamericana: aportes de la CEPAL

 Páginas Selectas de la CEPAL/*ECLAC Select Pages*

Los cuidados en América Latina y el Caribe. Textos seleccionados 2007-2018

Empleo en América Latina y el Caribe. Textos seleccionados 2006-2017

Desarrollo inclusivo en América Latina. Textos seleccionados 2009-2016

Revista CEPAL/*CEPAL Review*

Series de la CEPAL/*ECLAC Series*

Notas de Población

Observatorio Demográfico
Demographic Observatory

Documentos de Proyectos
Project Documents

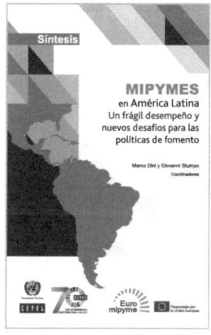

Metodologías de la CEPAL

Coediciones/*Co-editions*

Copublicaciones/*Co-publications*

Suscríbase y reciba información oportuna sobre las publicaciones de la CEPAL

Subscribe to receive up-to-the-minute information on ECLAC publications

www.cepal.org/es/suscripciones   www.cepal.org/en/suscripciones

NACIONES UNIDAS
UNITED NATIONS

CEPAL
ECLAC

CEPAL
ECLAC

POR UN DESARROLLO
SOSTENIBLE CON IGUALDAD
FOR SUSTAINABLE
DEVELOPMENT WITH EQUALITY

www.cepal.org/publicaciones

 facebook.com/publicacionesdelacepal

Las publicaciones de la CEPAL también se pueden adquirir a través de:
ECLAC publications also available at:

shop.un.org

United Nations Publications
PO Box 960
Herndon, VA 20172
USA

Tel. (1-888)254-4286
Fax (1-800)338-4550
Contacto/Contact: publications@un.org
Pedidos/Orders: order@un.org